A RECIPE FOR GENTRIFICATION

A Recipe for Gentrification

Food, Power, and Resistance in the City

Edited by
Alison Hope Alkon, Yuki Kato, and Joshua Sbicca

NEW YORK UNIVERSITY PRESS
New York

NEW YORK UNIVERSITY PRESS
New York
www.nyupress.org

© 2020 by New York University
All rights reserved

References to Internet websites (URLs) were accurate at the time of writing. Neither the author nor New York University Press is responsible for URLs that may have expired or changed since the manuscript was prepared.

Library of Congress Cataloging-in-Publication Data
Names: Alkon, Alison Hope, editor. | Kato, Yuki, editor. | Sbicca, Joshua, 1982– editor.
Title: A recipe for gentrification : food, power, and resistance in the city / edited by Alison Hope Alkon, Yuki Kato, and Joshua Sbicca.
Description: New York : New York University Press, 2020. |
Includes bibliographical references and index.
Identifiers: LCCN 2019033831 | ISBN 9781479834433 (cloth) | ISBN 9781479811373 (paperback) | ISBN 9781479809042 (ebook) | ISBN 9781479878239 (ebook)
Subjects: LCSH: Gentrification—United States. | Food—Political aspects. | Food consumption—United States. | Minorities—Nutrition—United States. | Discrimination—United States.
Classification: LCC HT175 .R427 2020 | DDC 307.76—dc23
LC record available at https://lccn.loc.gov/2019033831

New York University Press books are printed on acid-free paper, and their binding materials are chosen for strength and durability. We strive to use environmentally responsible suppliers and materials to the greatest extent possible in publishing our books.

Manufactured in the United States of America

10 9 8 7 6 5 4 3 2 1

Also available as an ebook

CONTENTS

Introduction: Development, Displacement, and Dining   1
Alison Hope Alkon, Yuki Kato, and Joshua Sbicca

PART I: DINING DOWNTOWN: FOOD RETAIL AND
URBAN DEVELOPMENT

1. The Taste of Gentrification: Difference and Exclusion on
San Diego's Urban Food Frontier   31
Pascale Joassart-Marcelli and Fernando J. Bosco

2. Savior Entrepreneurs and Demon Developers:
The Role of Gourmet Restaurants and Bars
in the Redevelopment of Durham   54
Nina Martin

3. Making Sense of "Local Food," Urban Revitalization,
and Gentrification in Oklahoma City   71
Eric Sarmiento

PART II: RIPE FOR GROWTH: ALTERNATIVE FOOD SYSTEMS

4. The Urban Agriculture Fix: Navigating Development
and Displacement in Denver   93
Joshua Sbicca

5. From the Holy Trinity to Microgreens: Gentrification
Redefining Local Foodways in Post-Katrina New Orleans   111
Pamela Arnette Broom and Yuki Kato

6. The Cost of Low-Hanging Fruit? An Orchard, a Nonprofit,
and Changing Community in Portland   132
Emily Becker and Nathan McClintock

7. Gardens in the Growth Machine: Seattle's P-Patch Program
and the Pursuit of Permanent Community Gardens   154
Charlotte Glennie

PART III: UNEVEN ALLIANCES: CONTESTING GENTRIFICATION FROM WITHIN AND WITHOUT

8. Diverse Politics, Difficult Contradictions: Gentrification and the San Francisco Urban Agriculture Alliance — 179
   Michelle Glowa and Antonio Roman-Alcalá

9. "Ethical" Gentrification as a Preemptive Strategy: Social Enterprise, Restaurants, and Resistance in Vancouver's Downtown Eastside — 202
   Zachary Hyde

10. "You Can't Evict Community Power": Food Justice and Eviction Defense in Oakland — 223
    Alison Hope Alkon, Yahya Josh Cadji, and Frances Moore

PART IV: GROWING RESISTANCE: COMMUNITY-BASED STRATEGIES

11. Community Gardens and Gentrification in New York City: The Uneven Politics of Facilitation, Accommodation, and Resistance — 245
    Justin Sean Myers, Prita Lal, and Sofya Aptekar

12. *No Se Vende*: Resisting Gentrification on Chicago's *Paseo Boricua* through Food — 266
    Brooke Havlik

13. Black Urban Growers and the Land Question in Cleveland: Externalities of Gentrification — 284
    Justine Lindemann

14. Citified Sovereignty: Cultivating Autonomy in South Los Angeles — 305
    Analena Hope Hassberg

    A Conflicted Conclusion: Seeing and Contesting Gentrification through Food — 325
    Alison Hope Alkon, Yuki Kato, and Joshua Sbicca

    Acknowledgments — 345
    About the Editors — 349
    About the Contributors — 351
    Index — 355

Introduction

Development, Displacement, and Dining

ALISON HOPE ALKON, YUKI KATO, AND JOSHUA SBICCA

The sign was intended to be ironic, a joke even, but the community was not laughing. On one side, it read "ink! Coffee. Happily gentrifying the neighborhood since 2014." The other proclaimed "Nothing says gentrification like being able to order a cortado."

The neighborhood is Denver's Five Points, long home, not always by choice, to nearly all of the city's Black residents. In a history common to many Black communities across the United States, residents were prevented from living in other parts of the city through segregation, redlining, and racial covenants. The neighborhood became a vibrant cultural center, colloquially known as the "Harlem of the West," where more than fifty jazz clubs hosted many of the early twentieth century's most well-known performers (Dowlen n.d.). But Five Points is no longer a predominantly Black neighborhood, as gentrification has brought an influx of younger, whiter, and wealthier residents. Indeed, realtors and developers no longer refer to the area as Five Points at all, but as the River North Arts District or RiNo. These new residents patronize the area's many new galleries, restaurants, breweries, and cafes like ink! Coffee.

The sign became a flash point for political organizing. Community members understood, sometimes viscerally, that gentrification doesn't just mean cleaning up the neighborhood. It also means, in the words of community organizer Lisa Calderon, "pushing us out of our community." Although most activists did not engage in property damage, someone spray painted "white coffee" across the building, unsubtly gesturing at the racialized nature of food's place in urban "revitalization." The coffee shop's window was broken, and an unnamed skateboarder stole the offensive sign. These incidents, along with the ongoing protest, forced the business to close for several days. They did reopen, and maintain their storefront to this day, but the controversy cost them a valuable contract with University of Colorado Denver. Perhaps more important, it sparked broader organizing against gentrification, including one lifelong resident and activist's successful campaign to replace the current city council member in 2019.

* * *

"New Orleans is not cosmopolitan. There's no kale here." With these words, reported in the *New York Times* in 2014, Dutch actress Tara Elders set off the social media controversy that became known as "kalegate" (Goodman 2014). The quote appeared in an article that followed some of the city's new bohemian residents as they engaged with the city's varied cultural scenes. A barrage of think pieces, tweets, and hashtags followed. *Times-Picayune* reporter Jarvis DeBerry opened his scathing response with a description of the iconic restaurant Dooky Chase's Gumbo Z'herbs, traditionally served on Holy Thursday and consisting of no less than nine greens, kale included. He called for New Orleanians to email or tweet photos of the many places kale was available within the city, and hundreds responded. Johanna Gilligan, the director of Grow Dat Youth Farm, observed that "people are buying kale at [their farmers'] market with a new sense of pride." The annual Big Easy Theater Awards were hosted by "Citizen Kale," a local actor in a homemade kale suit. Local restaurants and farmers' markets offered kalegate specials, and *Eater*, an online food magazine with a site for most major cities, constructed an interactive map showcasing restaurants where the green was available. In the words of *Grist* writer Heather Hansman (2014), "You can insult New Orleans . . . but if you talk bad about its greens, the locals get up in arms."

Kalegate angered so many New Orleanians because it represented a pervasive sense that the power to define and represent the city lies not with its long-term residents, but with the newcomers. These newcomers, like many before them, romanticize a view of the city that celebrates a sense of magic and mysticism while eliding the legacies of colonialism, slavery and struggle, and of deluge and drowning, that continue to shape residents' everyday lives (Cannon 2014). The exceptionalist narrative casts New Orleanians as wild spirits, too busy costuming and drinking to address social ills, leaving the city to sink, perhaps literally, into a sort of languid decline. Countering this romanticized view, local writers used kalegate to offer a glimpse into New Orleans' complex histories and cultures, including struggles for civil rights, workers' rights, and food justice, and to proclaim their own sense of place in a city they are struggling to define.

* * *

The table runs an entire West Oakland city block, and seats 500. This diverse group of diners has been brought together by the People's Kitchen Collective (PKC), a trio of activist-artist-storyteller-chefs who create "accessible, healthy and loving food spaces . . . not only to fill our stomachs, but also nourish our souls, feed our minds, and fuel a movement" (People's Kitchen Collective n.d.). The meal was the final installment of a four-part series: From the FARM to the KITCHEN to the TABLE to the STREETS! A critique of the farm-to-table movement which, according to PKC, too often ignores the contributions of people of color, these meals centered on the recipes and stories of diverse communities. STREETS was a public meal and protest piece designed to celebrate shared resilience in the face of rapid gentrification and displacement. According to the Collective:

> This is a reclaiming of the commons, of the streets that are rapidly being disconnected from their history through gentrification. Here, we will eat publicly at the intersection of food, art, and justice. We also meet at the intersection of Yuri Kochiyama and Malcolm X's birthdays, and at 28th St. and Magnolia St., the site of [Black Panther] Lil Bobby Hutton's murder by the Police 50 years ago . . . We deliberately create and take up space, while focusing on building health and connection. In the face of a gentrifying Oakland, this is how we feed a revolution.

The community began the meal with locally gathered yerba buena and rosehip tea offered by Café Ohlone, which features and promotes local indigenous foodways. The Collective then offered Japanese pickles to represent the community uprooted from the neighborhood during World War II. The main course of pulled chicken, beans, corn bread, and collard greens paid homage to both the Black Panther Party's Free

Figure I.1. *STREETS!* was a free community meal for 500 people provided by the People's Kitchen Collective in celebration of resilience amidst gentrification in West Oakland. Photo by Sana Javeri Kadri.

Breakfast for School Children program, which began in this neighborhood and which the PKC often cites as an inspiration, as well as to the neighborhood's Black history more generally. The day was warm and so was the atmosphere, filled with hugs and handshakes in a sort of extended family reunion. During the meal, diners shared music, poetry, and conversation centered around the question "what does your neighborhood need?" Collective co-founder Sita Kuratomi Bhaumik read a letter written on behalf of Donald Foster, a longtime journalist and community activist who is being evicted from the street where the event took place, and urged attendees to support him.

Jocelyn Jackson, another co-founder, describes West Oakland as "the perfect place to speak to gentrification. On the blocks we're setting tables, people are being displaced. Even if transition is happening, it's important to claim the space as home."

* * *

Taken together, these stories reveal the complex entanglements between food and gentrification that this volume seeks to unpack. The furor over ink! Coffee speaks to the role of food retail in upscaling communities. The trendy coffee shop, restaurant, or grocery store in the long divested neighborhood is often viewed as a harbinger of things to come. In the words of spoken word poet Bobby LeFebre, who read his powerful poem "Denver, Where Have You Gone" at ink! Coffee, protests:

> Remember that food desert, Denver?/
> The one on the block overrun with liquor stores/
> There's a Whole Foods there now/
> Remember that affordable rent, Denver?/
> The one that comfortably accommodated a family of five/
> There's a $500,000 loft there now, Denver/

By juxtaposing changes in the food landscape with increasing housing prices, LeFebre suggests a link between dining and dispossession. Our goal in this volume is to unpack this link, illuminating the variety of ways that food businesses and food activists can drive, augment, and contest gentrification.

In today's food-focused popular culture, cafes like ink! Coffee and upscale grocery stores like Whole Foods, are essential to how neighborhoods brand themselves as hip, creative places. To investors, these businesses indicate that an area is ripe for redevelopment. According to Stan Humphries, chief economist for the real estate online marketplace Zillow, "The entry of a coffee shop into a location provides a signaling

Figure I.2. ink! Coffee in Five Points tagged after community outrage over gentrification sign. Photo by Lindsey Bartlett.

function to other types of investors . . . that this neighborhood has now arrived and is open for business in a way that it was not before" (quoted in Kohli 2015). In this sense, food retail serves to shape the larger built environment; hip coffee shops are imbued with a cultural capital that translates into economic capital in the form of rising land values. Perhaps the problem with ink! Coffee's sign was not only that it was obnoxious, but that it was true in a way that reaches beyond the shop owners' presumed intentions. Coffee shops really can gentrify a neighborhood, or at least they can play a material and symbolic role. The first half of this volume examines the role of food spaces—restaurants, grocery stores, and alternative food initiatives like urban farms and gardens—in drawing new investors and residents into a neighborhood.

Kalegate represents the processes through which changing foodscapes and foodways have become symbols of gentrification. The *New York Times* coverage was not really about food; the sole comment about kale is buried several paragraphs in. And yet it was kale that became a flash point for debates about gentrification, and who gets to speak, publicly and privately, for and about a city. Kale has become symbolic of gentrification, of the foodways of new residents, and in this case, of their unwillingness to recognize and engage with anything but a superficial version of their city's long-standing, vibrant culture. Deriding the perceived absence of kale casts the city as removed from mainstream dining trends, and more broadly, from the everyday concerns of those who occupy privileged social locations. In response, New Orleanians mocked the cultural cluelessness of many recent transplants and asserted their own longstanding senses of place. Food is implicated not only in controversies about who gets to (or has to) live where, but about how and by whom a city is defined. The changing foodways that push and accompany gentrification are a theme that runs throughout many of the chapters in this volume, from the high-end taco shops in San Diego's Barrio Logan (chapter 1) to the "reinvention" of working-class cuisine in Vancouver's long-impoverished Downtown Eastside (chapter 9). Black feminist writer Mikki Kendall (2014) calls this "food gentrification," and worries that this will put "traditional meals out of reach of those who created the recipes" (see also Ho 2014). But our concerns in this volume go beyond food access. Here we link the symbolic gentrification of foods to increased property values, rising rents, and dispossession and displacement.

Because food has become such a strong symbol of gentrification, as well as a marker of a neighborhood's "readiness" for redevelopment, food justice activists like the People's Kitchen Collective deploy food as a lens through which to resist the dispossession of their communities (Crouch 2012; Markham 2014; Massey 2017). Sometimes, activists' goals are limited to maintaining access to their own urban gardens (Glowa 2017). Other times, they seek to safeguard the ability of long-term inhabitants to claim their right to the city, whether for growing food, eating, or just gathering. The chapters in the second half of this volume tell of the struggles of long-term residents and newcomers, sometimes in conflict with one another and other times working together, who attempt to influence cities that increasingly orient themselves toward developers, wealthy industries, and foreign investment. Some, like the immigrant gardeners in Brooklyn's Bedford Stuyvesant and East New York neighborhoods (chapter 11) and Cleveland's Black urban gardeners (chapter 13), draw on longstanding and deeply held practices of food production and community organizing. Or, in the case of Chicago's Puerto Rican diaspora, culturally significant commercial food zones like East Humboldt Park's *Paseo Boricua* become frontline struggles for food sovereignty and to stop gentrification (chapter 12). Others, such as Oakland's Phat Beets Produce (chapter 10), use food as a sort of gastrodiplomacy (Chapple-Sokol 2013) intended to foster positive interactions between new and long-term residents. Sometimes, a long-term community-based organization, such as Los Angeles' Community Services Unlimited, can organize the resources necessary to buy land, ensuring their constituents' abilities to continue to grow and distribute food in their gentrifying neighborhood, but remain concerned about the signals their new food retail can send (chapter 14). None of these efforts have yet succeeded in stemming the tides of revitalization and displacement, but they have developed creative ways to incorporate food into this struggle.

The central claim of this volume is that food is an important lens through which to understand the process of gentrification. Exploring food offers a visceral opportunity to move beyond the scholarly focus on residential growth and displacement to understand how urban development affects the economic, cultural, and ecological dimensions of place. This book also extends conversations about urban agriculture, race, and food justice by examining them in the context of urban development, which has often been an underlying but unacknowledged theme in critical food studies. Last, this volume brings together theories of the production of urban space, which view gentrification as a structural process fostered by urban growth machines comprised of developers and city officials, together with those that analyze culture and consumption through taste, foodways, and cultural capital. These perspectives are often in tension with one another, but the diverse array of theoretical and methodological approaches present in this volume allow us to better understand how social structure orients but does not determine lived experiences on the ground.

In a practical sense, this book takes a broad approach to a complex topic. The forthcoming chapters examine a wide range of food enterprises, including grocery stores, restaurants, community gardens, farmers' markets, and non-profit organizations, as well as developers and city officials. Working from these multiple and situated perspectives allows us to highlight the myriad and sometimes contradictory ways that food and gentrification intersect. This volume also attends to both cities that have become synonymous with gentrification and smaller cities that are usually left out of the conversation but are nonetheless experiencing these dynamics. Relatedly, we feature a diverse set of contributors, including graduate students, professors, and community activists, who share deep and embedded knowledges of the changing places we call home.

What Does Food Bring to Gentrification Scholarship?

Gentrification is commonly understood and studied as an economic and residential phenomenon, with a focus on the displacement of long-term residents as a neighborhood experiences demographic, housing, and commercial transitions. Prominent urban theorists argue that gentrification must be understood fundamentally as a structural process of capitalist urbanization (Harvey 2000; Heynen et al. 2007; Smith 2008 [1982]), in which capital expands through the (re)production of urban space, as guided by city and regional policy (Hackworth and Smith 2001; Smith 2008 [1982]). Gentrification is also a racialized process, predicated on the previous divestment from the urban core that characterized segregation and redlining (Lees, Slater, and Wyly 2008; Shaw 2007).

Gentrification transforms a neighborhood in many ways. Crime rates decrease, real estate markets expand, infrastructure improves, and new businesses and amenities become available. While some long-term residents can benefit from these changes, displacement limits the extent to which they can take advantage of these positive outcomes. Displacement follows the racialized contours of development as low-income communities of color are increasingly subject to police scrutiny at the behest of new residents (Ospina 2015; Shaw 2015) and are pushed out of their homes, at best resettling in less expensive areas and at worst becoming homeless (Applied Survey Research 2015; Slater 2006). But to focus strictly on the residential and commercial realities of this process would be to miss the significant social and cultural dimensions of displacement (Hyra 2008; Ocejo 2011; Zukin 1987, 2009).

In the public eye, the most notable signs of gentrification are changes in amenities and infrastructure, including artisanal coffee shops, brunch-serving cafes, and farm-to-table restaurants. As the vignettes that begin this chapter indicate, food retail and foodways have become flash points signifying whose food matters. For long-term residents, these changes are not simply economic transitions; they signify the loss of their way of life and sense of local ownership. Because food is such a mundane yet vitally multifaceted part of our everyday lives, it can bring together structural and cultural approaches to the processes, consequences, and trajectories of gentrification that are intimately linked in the popular imagination.

Gentrification manifests differently in each urban context, with varying outcomes on its scale, pace, and process (Billingham 2015; Brown-Saracino 2009; Hyra 2008). So, our research uses a comparative approach (Brown-Saracino 2016), employing what Lees (2000) calls the "geography of gentrification" to illuminate differences and similarities across place. As the public awareness of gentrification grows, community activists described in parts III and IV of this volume have begun to engage in organizing efforts to push back against forces that exacerbate historical ethnoracial and class inequalities. In this context, examining how place-specific foodways are valorized, transformed, or lost in the process of promoting and resisting gentrification critically engages with the cultural geography of locality: What is local, who are the locals, and who gets to define these terms? All of which is to say that food offers a means to freshly explore the inherent heterogeneity of gentrification.

Gentrification is now spreading well beyond the major urban centers in North America, occurring in former industrial and mid-size cities. Chapters in this edited volume present cases from many regions of the United States and Canada, including cities typically ignored by gentrification studies such as Durham, Oklahoma City, and Cleveland. Some cities in this volume are post-disaster cities (natural or economic), such as New Orleans and Denver, experiencing gentrification in the context of neoliberal rebuilding and restructuring. That said, by one estimate four of our case cities (Chicago, Los Angeles, New York, and San Diego) are among the top seven cities that account for half of all gentrification nationally (Richardson, Mitchell, and Franco 2019). Comparing this range of cases reveals local differences, especially when it comes to gentrification's effect on food security and food sovereignty, while also underscoring similarities in terms of power and resource disparities. Taken together, these chapters exhibit how the politics of place, as well as existing sociocultural institutions, shape the ability to promote and fight gentrification.

Gentrification occurs as a dynamic process rather than as a singular event. The classic "rent gap" model points to the economic rationale that promotes investment to maximize the profit potential of undervalued land (Smith 1979). Policymaking and private investment trends among growth coalitions in the city encourage and justify reinvestment (Logan and Molotch 1987), providing the "institutional scaffolding" for gentrification (Zukin 2016). In contrast to structural explanations, cultural approaches to gentrification examine how the tastes of newcomers encourage and shape investment into formerly underserved neighborhoods. Early gentrifiers are attracted to low-rent areas not only for economic reasons, but also for what they collectively perceive as the authentic cultural significance of these places (Hyra 2017; Ley 2003; Mele 1996). While authenticity is, of course, socially constructed and socially differentiated, new residents tend to attach its heightened significance to dive bars, ethnic markets, or corner stores, regarding them as gritty places with a history (Brown-Saracino 2010; Lloyd 2005).

But newcomers do not just assimilate to the existing community. Some consumption spaces may present themselves as being *too authentic* and not safe for the newcomers (Grazian 2003), prompting them to develop or redefine the spaces that suit their taste and sensibilities. Boutiquing gentrifiers can displace locally owned businesses that low-income residents have relied on (Zukin 2009), creating what Lloyd (2005) calls a "neo-bohemia" that selectively celebrates the memory of the place. Because food is so intimately connected to culture and place (Hondagneu-Sotelo 2014; DeSoucey 2016; Winsome 1993), many food businesses, such as bars, butcher shops, or distilleries, drive the rearticulation of a community's identity (Ocejo 2017). For example, the San Diego restaurant Barrio Dogg profiled in chapter 1 draws on the neighborhood's Latinx history by featuring gourmet, all-beef, "Tijuana-style" hot dogs at a counter built from a low-rider Chevy. But as is common to businesses that attempt to reconstruct authentic visions of a food or place in upscale settings, this restaurant is often perceived by long-term residents as catering to new ones and even tourists, simultaneously gentrifying the neighborhood and the food itself (Gotham 2015; Helm 2017; Ho 2014). Chapters 2 and 9 also speak to these dynamics in Durham, North Carolina and Vancouver, Canada. In each case, restaurateurs brand their businesses as "of the community" through their menus and public relations work, but these efforts replicate structural inequalities as newcomers with resources and privileges end up dominating local social change efforts. That said, there are activists in other places that resist newcomers' vision of the long-term community's cultural foodscape by actively asserting a collective identity and ownership of their foodways and businesses, as we see in New Orleans and Chicago in chapters 5 and 12.

These food-focused developments shed light on one of the unifying theoretical threads that run through this book: Structural investment in new food spaces and individual consumers' tastes *interact* to intensify the social, economic, and cultural transformation of gentrifying neighborhoods. Food retail and food activism serve as ideal, tangible focal points for examining how this process unfolds. For example, a healthy supermarket's establishment in a neighborhood that previously lacked access to fresh food could be an initiator of gentrification rather than an attempt to expand neighborhood food security (Anguelovski 2016; Figueora and Alkon 2017). Chapters in this volume investigate when and how new food retail enters a neighborhood; how long-term and new residents respond to new food retail; and how and under what circumstances local activists use food as a tool to embrace or organize against gentrification.

Another important contribution of this volume is the inclusion of multiple studies that examine urban agriculture in the context of gentrification. Urban gardens and farms are sites of food production and social gathering but are distinct urban spaces from conventional food retail venues. Urban gardens have historically served as a place for low-income people of color in the city to grow food that supplements their pantry, reminds them of home, and provides a place for ethnic or neighborhood solidarity (Hondagneu-Sotelo 2014; Saldivar-Tanaka 2004). In recent years, however, urban agriculture has gained broader popularity in cities across North America, often embraced as a part of the "green city" ethic that urban officials and planners use to promote environmental sustainability (Campbell 2017). But recent scholarship has warned, and indeed found, that urban gardens, like farmers' markets and farm-to-table restaurants, can contribute to green or ecological gentrification (Alkon and Cadji 2018; Brasswell 2018), the process through which the elimination of hazardous conditions or the development of green spaces is mobilized as a strategy to draw in affluent new residents and capital projects (Bryson 2013; Checker 2011; Dooling 2009; Gould and Lewis 2016; Quastel 2009).

For the most part, green gentrification is conceptualized as a top-down process led by cities and is sometimes even described as a "planning effort" (Dooling and Simon 2002, 104). With regard to urban agriculture, Nathan McClintock (2018) argues that "household-scale UA [urban agriculture]—a socially reproductive practice—becomes cultural capital that a sustainable city's growth coalition in turn valorizes as symbolic sustainability capital used to extract rent and burnish the city's brand" (579). While we highlight examples of green gentrification initiated by cities' growth coalitions, most notably chapter 4's S*Park, which offers a commercial urban farm as an amenity for a new, upscale housing complex, chapters 5 and 10 examine the everyday practices of gardeners and food activists in New Orleans and Oakland who see their own work appropriated by urban boosters. In contrast, chapter 7 describes how Seattle's predominantly affluent community gardeners successfully preserved their gardens by hitching them to urban growth coalition values. These cases broaden our understanding of how green gentrification can operate as a multidimensional process, pushing us to attend to powerful actors, such as developers and city officials, as well as the everyday practices of communities.

Public sentiments toward gentrification have shifted over the last decade, with an increasing number of "social preservationists" expressing appreciation for and a desire to safeguard local culture and traditions (Brown-Saracino 2009; Hyra 2017). Regardless of their motives, many educated, liberal newcomers feel conflicted about their role in changing neighborhoods (Donnelly 2018; Schlichtman, Patch, and Hill 2017). This conundrum complicates newcomers' everyday consumption decisions. Where do they shop to satisfy their ideological sensibilities toward social equity *and* their desire for cultural experiences? Food becomes a particularly pronounced point of contention for these decisions, as food purchases and consumption occur daily and yet represent a public performance of social differentiation. Thus, food has the potential to serve as a point of connection between new and long-standing residents while also becoming a form of green distinction (Horton 2003), or what Elizabeth Currid-Halkett (2017) calls "inconspicuous consumption," in which elites and those aspiring to elite status elevate the importance of intangible experiences over the accumulation of flashy things.

Can these conflicted gentrifiers help strengthen local activism against gentrification, or are food purchasing decisions simply a symbolic gesture that resolves "white guilt" with few real outcomes—or worse yet, becomes another form of displacement by dominating anti-gentrification efforts? In what ways could or should grassroots activism engage with well-intended newcomers with privileges and resources in resisting and calling out negative impacts of gentrification? The chapters in the final sections of this volume explore these questions and offer candid and humble examinations of the parameters of challenging gentrification with food. Chapters in parts III and IV present varying degrees of success in raising awareness, framing food injustices, and building solidarity. This volume does not offer any definitive methods for preventing gentrification. We instead highlight how people use food and foodways to reclaim their communities. Growing, preparing, and eating food mobilize the public around issues of social justice in ways that are distinct from housing, the criminal justice system, or employment.

What Does Gentrification Bring to Food Scholarship?

Just as food has much to offer to scholars and activists interested in unpacking gentrification, studying gentrification brings valuable insights to the study of food. To date, interdisciplinary approaches to food have explored a variety of questions: what and with whom we eat, how food is produced and processed, and how food fits into various aspects of contemporary social life (Belasco 2008; Carolan 2016; DeSoucey 2017). The field, though, has begun to move away from a food systems focus on the material and social processes that are involved in the cultivation, processing, distribution, and consumption of food (Allen 2008; Kloppenberg et al. 2000; Hinrichs and Lyson 2008; McMichael 1994) and toward what we call a "food intersections" approach, which examines the ways food is shaped by, and has consequences for, various aspects of social, political, and ecological life. Not only does food commonly become a target for social movements, markets, and states—what Michaela DeSoucey (2016) calls "gastropolitics"—but, when viewed through the lens of food intersections, it becomes enmeshed in struggles over land, resources, identity, and culture that reach far beyond food itself.

An important example of this approach, and one that is relevant to each of the chapters in this volume, concerns food justice, which can be defined as "the struggle against racism, exploitation, and oppression taking place within the food system that addresses inequalities' root causes both within and beyond the food chain" (Hislop 2014). Food justice scholarship initially began to cohere around the question of access to healthy food, and the observation that this access was severely limited in many low-income communities and communities of color (Beulac et al. 2009; Cummins and Macintyre 2002; Walker et al. 2010). Scholars examining this disparity as a part of the food system looked at the presence or absence of grocery stores and alternative sites of food distribution, such as farmers' markets or community gardens. The food intersections approach, on the other hand, requires us to look beyond the food itself. Monica White's *Freedom Farmers* (2018), for example, examines the roles that Black farmers have historically played in establishing and supporting Black freedom struggles, while Joshua Sbicca's *Food Justice Now!* (2018) emphasizes the existing and potential alliances between activists focused on food and those working for immigrant rights, improved labor conditions, and prison abolition.

This volume lends support to this emerging focus on food intersections by drawing connections between food and the processes of racialized under-development that first devalued urban neighborhoods and later incentivized the return of (often white) capital to these places (Ramírez 2015; Reese 2019). We demonstrate that food influences the urbanization of neoliberalism, the process through which cities become increasingly central to elite accumulation of capital (Pinson and Morel Journel 2016), and the racialization of everyday life for new and long-term urban residents (Alkon and Cadji 2018; Egerer and Fairbain 2018; McClintock 2018; Sbicca and Myers 2017). Several of the chapters in this volume (4, 5, 8, 13, 14) highlight that underdevelopment has created opportunities for communities to reclaim space through urban agriculture, who then struggle to maintain these spaces as land values escalate. Other chapters (2, 3, 9) describe how cities encourage and celebrate local food and new food retail as evidence of their revitalization, which often brings devastating consequences for historically rooted communities of color. Each of these analyses examines the ways that food impacts and is impacted by the racialized processes of development and neglect.

A second way that gentrification contributes to food scholarship is by bridging debates between Marxist-inspired scholars that focus on the political economy of food production (Friedland 1984; Friedman 1982; McMichael 2009) and post-structural scholars that emphasize the cultural politics of food consumption (Coveney 2006; DeVault 1994; Murcott 1983; Warde 1997). The first group seeks to explain how capitalism's growth logic compels agricultural practices that harm people and the planet, often suggesting that overthrowing capitalism is necessary for a sustainable and just food system (Magdoff, Foster, and Buttel 2000; Guthman 2014). On the other hand, scholars focused on culture attend to shifts in consumption, believing that they may nudge the food system, even if it is still capitalist, in greater alignment with environmental and human needs (Johnston and Baumann 2010; Lyson 2004), an approach that draws on and contributes much to JK Gibson-Graham's (2006) influential work on alternative economies. This conflict between structure and culture is not unique to the study of food and indeed is an overarching commonality between research on food and gentrification.

Examining gentrification's food intersections helps to highlight the relationships between political economy/ecology and culture as they play out in particular places. Gentrification carries with it a set of distinctions, clearly embodying Bourdieu's (1984) notion of taste as culturally produced and inseparable from social positioning and power. With regard to food, these tastes include a "desire for alternative foods, both gourmet and organic" (Zukin 2008) and gentrification has long been associated with the emergence of alternative food spaces such as farmers' markets, community gardens, and health food stores (chapters 6, 7 and 8 in this volume, and Anguelovski 2015; McClintock 2018; Zukin 2009). Cities use their regional culinary traditions, particularly the upscaling of working-class regional dishes, such as tacos in San Diego (chapter 1) or refined Cajun and Creole dishes in New Orleans (chapter 5), to produce socially constructed "authentic" cultural identities (Gaytan 2008) that can appeal to the so-called creative class (Florida 2003). This is also a racialized process, as the foodways of communities of color are repackaged, often by white chefs, for primarily white audiences (Passidomo 2017; Twitty 2016). Food is clearly tied to the aesthetic dimension of gentrification, but the production of these tastes is a method through which capital becomes reproduced and further concentrated. If political economy is the primary driver of gentrification (Quastel 2009; Smith 2008 [1982]), then culture is the terrain on which it is driven, and a means by which capitalists compete with one another to accumulate profits. Because food retail is so essential to the development of gentrifying places and the aesthetics of gentrification preference local, organic, and elevated working-class foodways, examining the intersection of food and gentrification provides new insights on how food production works in tandem with the cultural politics of consumption.

One topic that has been the subject of tremendous interest in recent years includes examinations of alternative food systems and food movements, particularly with regard to how activists address, or fail to address, issues of social, racial, and environmental justice (Alkon and Agyeman 2011; Gottlieb and Joshi 2010; Sbicca 2018). Social scientists have been critical of these alternatives, which tend to be dominated by white, wealthy, and formally educated individuals, for their lack of ethnoracial and economic inclusiveness, and for failing to seek out, understand, and promote initiatives already present in marginalized communities (Guthman 2008; Kato 2013; Reynolds and Cohen 2016; Slocum 2007). Moreover, food movements tend to focus on the creation of alternative food systems that stress organic production and local distribution rather than making strategic interventions through policy or collective action that can transform the food system and the systems of oppression and exploitation with which it interacts, though to some degree, this is beginning to change (Alkon and Guthman 2017; Holt-Giménez and Shattuck 2011; Roman-Alcalá 2018; Sbicca 2018).

In a context of unabashed popular media praise for these alternatives, paying attention to gentrification offers a sobering corrective. Initiatives like farmers' markets and urban agriculture have spread rapidly over the last 20 years, providing new economic opportunity to local and regional farmers (Low et al. 2015). But several of the chapters in this volume reveal how urban boosters highlight these spaces to appeal to newcomers (chapters 4, 7, 8), a process that can directly oppose the food justice goals that sometimes motivated their initiation (chapter 10). In contrast, chapter 3 argues convincingly that local food retailers in Oklahoma City consciously chose to market their products to the city's newer and upscale residents, and in doing so, abandoned the progressive political potential of their initiative. Our focus on food and gentrification adds to scholarly critiques about the sometimes unintended consequences of alternative food systems; not only are they often associated with privileged people and places, but they can help to create new exclusionary places by contributing to the ethnoracial and economic shifts wrought by gentrification.

Another common focus in food studies is urban agriculture, and here, gentrification plays out through conflicts over land. Urban agriculture must compete with other land uses, especially development pressure that seeks out the "highest and best use" of land. In short, what land use will produce the most profit? Urban agriculture produces little economic value compared to housing and retail development. For-profit urban farmers are struggling to stay afloat given the tight profit margins of growing food in cities (Oberholtzer, Dimitri, and Pressman 2014; Reynolds and Cohen 2016). Instead, urban agriculture produces many useful values like community, a local food supply, a space to interact with plants and animals, and a learning environment. Urban agriculture can be, as Justine Lindemann describes it with regard to Black urban farmers in Cleveland, an "integral part of the path to social, economic, political, and spiritual liberation" (chapter 13, "Black Urban Growers in Cleveland"). However, like farmers' markets, urban agriculture can attract people to a gentrifying neighborhood, especially when it signals a shift from abandoned or vacant land to a popular land use. As an amenity, realtors and developers can use it to "sell" a neighborhood (Alkon and Cadji 2018; McClintock 2018; chapters 4, 7, and 8) in a way that provides the urban, northern counterpart to the history of corporate land grabs across the global South (Williams and Holt-Giménez 2017). There is also localized resistance to these pressures. Long-term residents under threat of displacement, such as those profiled in chapters 10, 11, and 13, are often very attached to their gardens and are willing to fight for their right to the city. We have grouped these stories at the end of the book, as they inspire us to think through how food activism can lead to new ways to oppose displacement.

Just as these stories connect food activism to struggles for housing, a final important reason for discussing gentrification and food together is to link the essential human needs for shelter and sustenance. This can nuance the study of food in new ways. While what we eat reflects political economy, culture, and taste, so too does housing (Lees et al. 2008), and both are fundamentally rooted in access to land and place (Williams and

Holt-Giménez 2017). Current patterns of returning to the city provide an opportunity to interrogate how people experience changing economic, political, and social conditions. For example, looking at gentrification through the lens of food identifies pressing biopolitical connections between bodies, health, and the built environment. The slow violence (Nixon 2011) of living in a place with little food access only to be uprooted through the violence of gentrification connects directly to inequalities in race and income that privilege white and rich bodies who can actualize their tastes beyond bodily need (Guthman 2011; Hatch 2016).

In sum, studying the intersections between food and gentrification has much to offer. In contrast to a food systems perspective, this volume calls for examining food vis-à-vis wider social processes, particularly ethnoracial and economic inequalities. Second, because food businesses are material evidence of gentrification, while particular foods have become symbolic of this form of urban development, gentrification provides a means to integrate political economy and cultural approaches to the study of food. More practically, attention to gentrification shows the limitations of contemporary food politics. As urban boosters and food entrepreneurs orient their projects toward new residents of gentrifying cities, proponents of alternative food systems are at best unwittingly implicated in the displacement of long-term communities. This becomes particularly ironic when projects were designed for or even by long-term community members in order to augment their access to fresh food. Last, interrogating the relationship between food and gentrification provides an opportunity to better link struggles for food justice to other movements for social justice. This is happening with regard to indigenous food sovereignties, prison abolition, water rights, the Movement for Black Lives, workers' rights, and immigrant rights (Alkon and Guthman 2017; Daigle 2019; Minkoff-Zern 2019; Myers forthcoming; Movement for Black Lives n.d.; Reese 2019; Reynolds and Cohen 2016; Sbicca 2018; White 2018). In our conclusion, we highlight some ways that food movements are joining the struggles for tenants' rights and against displacement.

The Landscape to Come

Taken together, the chapters in this volume argue that food and gentrification are deeply entangled, and that examining food retail and food practices is critical to understanding urban development. In part I, "Dining Downtown," three chapters investigate the roles of food businesses in upscaling cities and attracting wealthy residents. First, Pascale Joassart-Marcelli and Fernando J. Bosco examine how changing dining options add value to two San Diego neighborhoods in different stages of gentrification, highlighting the cultural politics of taste in what is often theorized as an economic process. Similarly, Nina Martin's chapter draws on examples from Durham, North Carolina to illustrate the role of "savior entrepreneurs," restaurateurs who act as small-scale developers, in buying and refurbishing downtown buildings and helping to rebrand this post-industrial city as hip and creative. In the final chapter in this section, Eric Sarmiento dissects the emerging local food movement in Oklahoma City, arguing that in orienting their work toward the city's growing "creative class," they redefined local food as a luxury good rather than a product that could embody environmental sustainability and social justice.

Part II, "Ripe for Growth," examines urban agriculture's role in both signaling and responding to a city's readiness for development. In chapters 4 and 5, Joshua Sbicca, Pamela Arnette Broom, and Yuki Kato describe how community-based urban agriculture projects that emerged from economic and ecological crises have weathered the ensuing land booms. First, Sbicca investigates how the city of Denver's official support for urban agriculture in the wake of the Great Recession, in tandem with urban farmers growing food in up-and-coming neighborhoods, became an "urban agriculture fix" fostering increased land values and green gentrification. Following, the authors draw on Broom's experience as a leader in New Orleans' urban agriculture movement to show how gardens drew in new residents, creating both alliances and tensions with long-term residents and gardeners. In the subsequent chapter, Emily Becker and Nathan McClintock investigate how gentrification affects the meaning of community in a community orchard in Portland with an intent to serve long-term residents. In contrast, Charlotte Glennie's chapter demonstrates the power of racially and class privileged community gardeners in Seattle to solidify their own land tenure by convincing urban boosters that their gardens are an important amenity for new residents.

Parts III and IV delve into various community responses to gentrification. Part III describes what we call "Uneven Alliances" between middle-class food activists and long-term community members. First, Michelle Glowa and Antonio Roman-Alcalá investigate how the organizations that comprise the San Francisco Urban Agriculture Alliance negotiate ethnoracial and economic differences in the context of gentrification. Next, Zachary Hyde critically analyzes the role of community-minded social entrepreneurs who develop "ethical" restaurants in Vancouver's Downtown Eastside, arguing that while they may intend to act as social preservationists, they co-opt community-based dissent and resistance to gentrification. In contrast, Alison Hope Alkon, Yahya Josh Cadji, and "Aunti" Frances Moore describe the formation of an alliance between long-term resident Aunti Frances's Self-Help Hunger Program and relative newcomer Phat Beets Produce. This alliance has used food to create strong relationships and to engage in campaigns against gentrification in their North Oakland neighborhood. In the last chapter in this section, Justin Myers, Prita Lal, and Sofya Aptekar discuss community gardens to show how the impacts of gentrification vary within New York City; while new residents have come to dominate a garden in rapidly gentrifying Astoria (Queens), long-term gardeners in Bedford-Stuyvesant and East New York (Brooklyn) use their urban food cultivation practices to resist gentrification and maintain their right to the city.

Part IV, "Growing Resistance," highlights the work of long-term residents and non-profit organizations that have long served their communities. Brooke Havlik explains how Puerto Ricans in Chicago see food as an important lever for asserting self-sufficiency and cultural autonomy in the face of gentrification. Next, Justine Lindemann documents the work of Cleveland's African American urban agriculture community, who are navigating the gentrification occurring adjacent to their long divested neighborhood. Last, Analena Hope Hassberg documents the inspiring work of Community Services Unlimited to create "citified sovereignty," an urbanized form of food sovereignty that positions community control of local foodways as a counter to the potential negative impacts of redevelopment and revitalization.

As a whole, chapters in this volume demonstrate that you cannot talk about gentrification without considering food. Changing food offerings are often the first ingredient of a neighborhood's redevelopment, and upscale coffee shops, gourmet interpretations of working-class cuisines, and community gardens can symbolize an area's ripeness for increased investment. Many city governments have officially supported the development of urban agriculture, but farmers and gardeners have seen urban boosters appropriate their spaces as lures for new residents, and often struggle to maintain access to land as property values increase. And yet, a variety of actors are using food to resist development and displacement, or at least to diminish its harshest effects. From urban gardeners to established non-profits to restaurateurs, individuals and communities are working to provide food and claim space in the gentrifying city. Our conclusion builds on the various chapters in these sections to ask how additional forms of policy and practice might support these efforts.

REFERENCES

Alkon, Alison and Julian Agyeman. 2011. *Cultivating Food Justice*. Cambridge, MA: MIT Press.

Alkon, Alison Hope. 2012. *Black, White, and Green: Farmers Markets, Race, and the Green Economy*. Athens: University of Georgia Press.

Alkon, Alison Hope and Julie Guthman. 2017. *The New Food Activism: Opposition, Cooperation, and Collective Action*. Berkeley: University of California Press.

Alkon, Alison Hope and Yahya Josh Cadji. 2018. "Sowing Seeds of Displacement: Gentrification and Food Justice in Oakland, CA." *International Journal of Urban and Regional Research*. DOI:10.111/1468–2427.12684.

Allen, Patricia. 2008. "Mining for Justice in the Food System." *Agriculture and Human Values* 25(2): 157–161.

Allen, Patricia. 2010. "Realizing Justice in Local Food Systems." *Cambridge Journal of Regions, Economy and Society* 3: 295–308.

Allen, Patricia and Julie Guthman. 2006. "From 'Old School' to 'Farm-to-School': Neoliberalization from the Ground Up." *Agriculture and Human Values* 23(4): 401–415.

Anguelovski, Isabelle. 2015. "Healthy Food Stores, Greenlining and Food Gentrification: Contesting New Forms of Privilege, Displacement and Locally Unwanted Land Uses in Racially Mixed Neighborhoods." *International Journal of Urban and Regional Research* 39(6): 1209–1230.

Anguelovski, Isabelle. 2016. "From Toxic Sites to Parks as (Green) LULUs." *Journal of Planning Literature* 31(1): 23–36.

Applied Survey Research. 2015. "San Francisco Homeless Point in Time Count and Survey." www.appliedsurveyresearch.org/.

Belasco, Warren. 2008. *Food: The Key Concepts*. Oxford, UK: Berg.

Beulac, J. E. Kristjansson and S. Cummins. 2009. "A Systemantic Review of Food Deserts 1966–2007." *Preventing Chronic Disease* 6(3): 1–10.

Billingham, Chase M. 2015. "The Broadening Conception of Gentrification: Recent Developments and Avenues for Future Inquiry in the Sociological Study of Urban Change." *Michigan Sociological Review* 29: 75–102.

Bourdieu, Pierre. 1984. *Distinction*. Cambridge, MA: Harvard University Press.
Braswell, Taylor Harris. 2018. "Fresh Food, New Faces: Community Gardening as Ecological Gentrification in St. Louis, Missouri." *Agriculture and Human Values* 35(4): 809–822.
Brown-Saracino, Japonica. 2009. *A Neighborhood That Never Changes: Gentrification, Social Preservation and the Search for Authenticity*. Chicago: University of Chicago Press.
Brown-Saracino, Japonica. 2016. "An Agenda for the Next Decade of Gentrification Scholarship." *City & Community* 15(3): 220–225.
Bryson Jeremy, 2013. "The Nature of Gentrification." *Geography Compass* 7(8): 578–587.
Campbell, Lindsay K. 2017. *City of Forests, City of Farms: Sustainability Planning for New York City's Nature*. Ithaca, NY: Cornell University Press.
Cannon, C. W. 2014. "A Kale of Two Cities." *The Lens*. https://thelensnola.org/.
Carolan, Michael. 2016. *The Sociology of Food and Agriculture*. New York: Routledge.
Chapple-Sokol, Sam. 2013. "Culinary Diplomacy: Breaking Bread to Win Hearts and Minds." *Hague Journal of Diplomacy* 8: 161–183.
Checker, Melissa. 2011. "Wiped Out by the 'Greenwave': Environmental Gentrification and the Paradoxical Politics of Urban Sustainability." *City & Society* 23(2): 210–229.
Coveney, John. 2006. *Food, Morals, and Meaning: The Pleasure and Anxiety of Eating*. 2d ed. London: Routledge.
Crouch, Patrick. 2012. "Evolution or Gentrification: Do Urban Farms Lead to Higher Rents?" *Grist*. http://grist.org/.
Cummins, Steven and Sally Macintire. 2002. "Food Deserts—Evidence and Assumption in Health Policy Making." *British Medical Journal* 325(7361): 436–438.
Currid-Halkett, Elizabeth. 2017. *The Sum of Small Things*. Princeton, NJ: Princeton University Press.
Daigle, Michelle. 2019. "Tracing the Terrain of Indigenous Food Sovereignties." *Journal of Peasant Studies* 46(2): 297–315.
DeSoucey, Michaela. 2016. *Contested Tastes*. Princeton, NJ: Princeton University Press.
DeSoucey, Michaela. 2017. "Food." *Oxford Bibliographies*. www.oxfordbibliographies.com.
DeVault, M. L. 1994. *Feeding the Family: The Social Organization of Caring as Gendered Work*. Chicago: University of Chicago Press.
Donnelly, Kathleen. 2018. "The Gentrifier's Dilemma: Narrative Strategies and Self-Justifications of Incoming Residents in Bedford-Stuyvesant, Brooklyn." *City & Community* 17(2): 372–393.
Dooling, Sarah. 2009. "Ecological Gentrification: Research Agenda Exploring Justice in the City." *International Journal of Urban and Regional Research* 33(3): 621–639.
Dooling, Sarah and Gregory Simon. 2012. *Cities, Nature and Development: The Politics and Production of Urban Vulnerabilities*. Farnham, UK: Ashgate.
Dowlen, Linda. n.d. "The History of Five Points." www.fivepointsbid.com/history---culture.

Egerer, Monika and Madeleine Fairbain. 2018. "Gated Gardens: Effects of Urbanization on Community Formation and Commons Management in Community Gardens." *Geoforum* 96: 61–69.

Figueora, Meleiza and Alison Hope Alkon. 2017. "Cooperative Social Practices, Self Determination and the Struggle for Food Justice in Oakland and Chicago." In *The New Food Activism*, edited by Alison Alkon and Julie Guthman, 206–231. Berkeley: University of California Press.

Fitzgerald, Deborah Kay. 2003. *Every Farm a Factory: The Industrial Ideal in American Agriculture*. New Haven, CT: Yale University Press.

Florida, Richard. 2003. "Cities and the Creative Class." *City & Community* 2(1): 3–19.

Friedland, William H. 1984. "Commodity Systems Analysis: An Approach to the Sociology of Agriculture." *Research in Rural Sociology and Agriculture* 1: 221–236.

Friedmann, H. 1982. "The Political Economy of Food: The Rise and Fall of the Postwar International Food Order." *American Journal of Sociology* 88S: 248–286.

Gaytán, Marie Sarita. 2008. "From Sombreros to Sincronizadas: Authenticity, Ethnicity, and the Mexican Restaurant Industry." *Journal of Contemporary Ethnography* 37(3): 314–341.

Gibson-Graham, J. K. 2006. *A Postcapitalist Politics*. Minneapolis: University of Minnesota Press.

Glowa, K. Michelle. 2017. "Urban Agriculture, Food Justice and Neoliberal Urbanization: Rebuilding the Institution of Property." In *The New Food Activism*, edited by Alison Alkon and Julie Guthman, 232–256. Berkeley: University of California Press.

Goodman, David and E. Melanie DuPuis. 2002. "Knowing Food and Growing Food: Beyond the Production-Consumption Debate in the Sociology of Agriculture." *Sociologia Ruralis* 42(1): 5–22.

Goodman, Lizzy. 2014. "Experiencing New Orleans through Fresh Eyes and Ears." *New York Times*. www.nytimes.com/.

Gotham, Kevin Fox. 2015. "Racialization and Rescaling: Post-Katrina Rebuilding and the Louisiana Road Home Program." International Journal of Urban and Regional Research. 38(3): 773–790.

Gottlieb, Robert and Anupama Joshi. 2010. *Food Justice*. Cambridge, MA: MIT Press.

Gould, Kenneth A. and Tammy Lewis. 2016. *Green Gentrification: Urban Sustainability and the Struggle for Environmental Justice*. New York: Routledge.

Grazian, David. 2003. *Blue Chicago: The Search for Authenticity in Chicago Blues Clubs*. Chicago: University of Chicago Press.

Guthman, Julie. 2003. "Fast Food/Organic Food: Reflexive Tastes and The Making of 'Yuppie Chow.'" *Social & Cultural Geography* 4(1): 45–58.

Guthman, Julie. 2008. "If They Only Knew: Color Blindness and Universalism in California Alternative Food Institutions." *Professional Geographer* 60(3): 387–397.

Guthman, Julie. 2011. *Weighing In: Obesity, Food Justice, and the Limits of Capitalism*. Berkeley: University of California Press.

Guthman, Julie. 2014. *Agrarian Dreams: The Paradox of Organic Farming in California*. Berkeley: University of California Press.
Hackworth, J. and Neil Smith. 2001. "The Changing State of Gentrification." *Journal of Economic and Social Geography* 92(4): 464–477.
Hansman, Heather. 2014. "What Kalegate Taught Us About New Orleans and Food." *Grist*. https://grist.org/.
Harvey, David. 2000. *Spaces of Hope*. Berkeley: University of California Press.
Hatch, Anthony Ryan. 2016. *Blood Sugar: Racial Pharmacology and Food Justice in Black America*. Minneapolis: University of Minnesota Press.
Helm, Angela. 2017. "On Whole Foods, Gentrification and the Erasure of Black Harlem." *The Root*. www.theroot.com/.
Heynen, Nik, A. Perkins. and Parama Roy. 2007. "The Political Ecology of Uneven Urban Green Spare: The Impact of Political Economy on Race/Ethnicity in Producing Environmental Inequality in Milwaukee. *Urban Affairs Review* 42(1): 3–25.
Hinrichs, C. Clare. 2003. "The Practice and Politics of Food System Localization." *Journal of Rural Studies* 19: 33–45.
Hinrichs, C. Clare and Patricia Allen. 2008. "Selective Patronage and Social Justice: Local Food Consumer Campaigns in Historical Context." *Journal of Agricultural and Environmental Ethics* 21(4): 329–352.
Hinrichs, Clare and Thomas Lyson. 2008. *Remaking the North American Food System*. Lincoln: University of Nebraska Press.
Hislop, Rasheed. 2014. "Reaping Equity across the USA: FJ Organizations Observed at the National Scale." Master's thesis, University of California–Davis.
Ho, Soleil. 2014. "#Foodgentrification and the Culinary Rebranding of Traditional Foods." www.bitchmedia.org.
Holt Giménez, Eric and Annie Shattuck. 2011. "Food Crises, Food Regimes and Food Movements: Rumblings of Reform or Tides of Transformation?" *Journal of Peasant Studies* 38(1): 109–144.
Hondagneu-Sotelo, Pierrette. 2014. *Paradise Transplanted: Migration and the Making of California Gardens*: Berkeley: University of California Press.
Horton, Dave. 2003, "Green Distinctions: The Performance of Identity Among Environmental Activists." In *Nature Performed: Environment, Culture and Performance*, edited by Bronislaw Szerszynski, Wallace Heim, and Claire Waterton, 63–77. Oxford: Blackwell.
Hyra, Derek S. 2008. *The New Urban Renewal: The Economic Transformation of Harlem and Bronzeville*. Chicago: University of Chicago Press.
Hyra, Derek S. 2017. *Race, Class, and Politics in the Cappuccino City*. Chicago: University of Chicago Press.
Johnston, Josée and Shyon Baumann. 2010. *Foodies: Democracy and Distinction in the Gourmet Foodscape*. New York: Routledge.
Kato, Yuki. 2013. "Not Just the Price of Food: Challenges of an Urban Agriculture Organization in Engaging Local Residents." *Sociological Inquiry* 83(3): 369–391.

Kendall, Mikki. 2014. "#Breaking Black: 1 in 5 Children Face Food Insecurity." *theGrio*. https://thegrio.com.
Kohli, Sonali. 2015. "Developers have Found the Secret Sauce for Gentrifying." *Quartz*. https://qz.com.
Lees, Loretta. 2000. "A Reappraisal of Gentrification: Towards a 'Geography of Gentrification.'" *Progress in Human Geography* 24(3): 389–408.
Lees, Loretta, Tom Slater, and Elvin Wyly. 2008. *Gentrification*. New York: Routledge.
Levkoe, Charles. 2011. "Towards a Transformative Food Politics." *Local Environment* 16(7): 687–705.
Ley, David. 2003. "Artists, Aestheticization and the Field of Gentrification." *Urban Studies* 40(12): 2527–2544.
Lloyd, Richard D. 2005. *Neo-Bohemia: Art and Commerce in the Post-Industrial City*. New York: Routledge.
Logan, John and Harvey Molotch. 1987. *Urban Fortunes: The Political Economy of Place*. Berkeley: University of California Press.
Low, Sarah A., Aaron Adalja, Elizabeth Beaulieu, Nigel Key, Steve Martinez, Alex Melton, Agnes Perez, Katherine Ralston, Hayden Stewart, Shellye Suttles, Stephen Vogel, and Becca B. R. Jablonski. 2015. *Trends in U.S. Local and Regional Food Systems*. AP-068. Washington, DC: US Department of Agriculture.
Lyson, Thomas. 2004. *Civic Agriculture: Reconnecting Farm, Food and Community*. Boston: Tufts University Press.
Magdoff, Fred, John Bellamy Foster, and Frederick H. Buttel. 2000. *Hungry for Profit: The Agribusiness Threat to Farmers, Food, and the Environment*. New York: Monthly Review Press.
Markham, Lauren. 2014. "Gentrification and the Urban Garden." *New Yorker*. http://www.newyorker.com.
Massey, Brian. 2017. "DC's Urban Farms Wrestle with Gentrification and Displacement." *Civil Eats*. http://civileats.com.
McClintock, Nathan. 2018. "Cultivating (a) Sustainability Capital: Urban Agriculture, Ecogentrification, and the Uneven Valorization of Social Reproduction." *Annals of the American Association of Geographers* 108(2): 579–590.
McMichael, Phillip. 2009. "A Food Regime Genealogy." *Journal of Peasant Studies* 36(1): 139–169.
McMichael, Phillip. 1994. *The Global Restructuring of the Agri-Food System*. Ithaca, NY: Cornell University Press.
Mele, Christopher. 1996. "Globalization, Culture, and Neighborhood Change: Reinventing the Lower East Side of New York." *Urban Affairs Review* 32(1): 3–22.
Minkoff-Zern, Laura-Anne. 2019. *The New American Farmer: Immigration, Race, and the Struggle for Sustainability*. Cambridge, MA: MIT Press.
Movement for Black Lives. n.d. "A Vision for Black Lives: Policy Demands for Black Power Freedom & Justice." https://policy.m4bl.org.

Murcott, Anne, ed. 1983. *The Sociology of Food and Eating: Essays on the Sociological Significance of Food*. Gower International Library of Research and Practice. Aldershot, UK: Gower.

Myers, Justin Sean. Forthcoming. *Growing Gardens: Food Justice and Urban Agriculture in Brooklyn*. New Brunswick, NJ: Rutgers University Press.

Nixon, Rob. 2011. *Slow Violence and the Environmentalism of the Poor*. Cambridge, MA: Harvard University Press.

Oberholtzer, Lydia, Carolyn Dimitri, and Andrew Pressman. 2014. "Urban Agriculture in the United States: Characteristics, Challenges, and Technical Assistance Needs." *Journal of Extension* 52(6): 6FEA1.

Ocejo, Richard E. 2011. "The Early Gentrifier: Weaving a Nostalgia Narrative on the Lower East Side." *City & Community* 10(3): 285–310.

Ocejo, Richard E. 2017. *Masters of Craft: Old Jobs in the New Urban Economy*. Princeton, NJ: Princeton University Press.

Ospina, Tulio. 2015. "Racially Profiled, Drummers Make Noise about Gentrification in Oakland." http://blog.oaklandxings.com/.

People's Kitchen Collective. n.d. "Beginnings." http://peopleskitchencollective.com.

Pinson, Gilles and Christelle Morel Journel. 2016. "The Neoliberal City—Theory, Evidence, Debates." *Territory, Politics, Governance* 4(2): 137–153.

Pulido, Laura. 2000. "Rethinking Environmental Racism: White Privilege and Urban Development in Southern California." *Annals of the Association of American Geographers* 90(1): 12–40.

Quastel, Noah. 2009. "Political Ecologies of Gentrification." *Urban Geography* 30(7): 694–725.

Ramírez, Margaret Marietta. 2015. "The Elusive Inclusive: Black Food Geographies and Racialized Food Spaces." *Antipode* 47(3): 748–769.

Reese, Ashanté M. 2019. *Black Food Geographies: Race, Self-Reliance, and Food Access in Washington*. Chapel Hill: University of North Carolina Press.

Reynolds, Kristin and Nevin Cohen. 2016. *Beyond the Kale: Urban Agriculture and Social Justice Activism in New York City*. Athens: University of Georgia Press.

Richardson, Jason, Bruce Mitchell, and Juan Franco. 2019. *Shifting Neighborhoods: Gentrification and Cultural Displacement in American Cities*. Washington, DC: National Community Reinvestment Coalition.

Roman-Alcalá, Antonio. 2018. "(Relative) Autonomism, Policy Currents and the Politics of Mobilisation for Food Sovereignty in the United States: The Case of Occupy the Farm." *Local Environment* 23(6): 619–634.

Saldivar-Tanaka, Laura and Marianne E. Kransy. 2004. "Culturing Community Development, Neighborhood Open Space, and Civic Agriculture: The Case of Latino Community Gardens in New York City." *Agriculture and Human Values* 21(4): 399–412.

Sbicca, Joshua. 2018. *Food Justice Now!: Deepening the Roots of Social Struggle*. Minneapolis: University of Minnesota Press.

Sbicca, Joshua and Justin Sean Myers. 2017. "Food Justice Racial Projects: Fighting Racial Neoliberalism from the Bay to the Big Apple." *Environmental Sociology* 3(1): 30–41.

Schlichtman, John Joe, Jason Patch, and Marc Lamont Hill. 2017. *Gentrifier*. Toronto: University of Toronto Press.

Shaw, A. R. 2015. "Whites Who Gentrified Oakland Are Calling the Police on Innocent Black Residents." *Rolling Out*. http://rollingout.com.

Shaw, Wendy S. 2007. *Cities of Whiteness*. Malden, MA: Blackwell.

Shiva, Vandana. 1993. *Monocultures of the Mind: Perspectives on Biodiversity and Biotechnology*. New York: Zed Books.

Slater, Tom. 2006. "The Eviction of Critical Perspectives from Gentrification Research." *International Journal of Urban and Regional Research* 30(4): 737–757.

Slocum, Rachel. 2007. "Whiteness, Space and Alternative Food Practice." *Geoforum* 38(3): 520–533.

Smith, Neil. 1979. "Toward a Theory of Gentrification: A Back to the City Movement by Capital, Not People." *Journal of the American Planning Association* 45(4): 538–547.

Smith, N. [1982] 2008. *Uneven Development: Nature, Capital and the Production of Space*. Athens: University of Georgia Press.

Twitty, Michael. 2016. "Dear Sean, We Need to Talk." *Afroculinaria*. https://afroculinaria.com.

Walker, Renee E., Christopher R. Keane, and Jessica G. Burke. 2010. "Disparities and Access to Healthy Food in the United States. A Review of Food Deserts Literature." *Health and Place* 16(5): 879–884.

Warde, Alan. 1997. *Consumption, Food, and Taste: Culinary Antinomies and Commodity Culture*. London: SAGE.

Wey, Tunde. 2017. "Locol Is a Righteous Answer to the Wrong Question." *San Francisco Chronicle*. http://www.sfchronicle.com.

White, Monica. 2018. *Freedom Farmers: Agricultural Resistance and the Black Freedom Movement*. Chapel Hill: University of North Carolina Press.

Williams, Justine M. and Eric Holt-Giménez, eds. 2017. *Land Justice: Re-Imagining Land, Food, and the Commons*. Oakland, CA: Food First Books.

Winsome, Anthony. 1993. *The Intimate Commodity*. Toronto: University of Toronto Press.

Zukin, Sharon. 1987. "Gentrification: Culture and Capital in the Urban Core." *Annual Review of Sociology* 13: 129–147.

Zukin, Sharon. 2008. "Consuming Authenticity: From Outposts of Difference to Means of Exclusion." *Cultural Studies* 22(5): 724–748.

Zukin, Sharon. 2009. *Naked City: The Death and Life of Authentic Urban Places*. New York: Oxford University Press.

Zukin, Sharon. 2016. "Gentrification in Three Paradoxes." *City & Community* 15(3): 202–207.

PART I

Dining Downtown

Food Retail and Urban Development

1

The Taste of Gentrification

Difference and Exclusion on San Diego's Urban Food Frontier

PASCALE JOASSART-MARCELLI AND FERNANDO J. BOSCO

The crowd, hipster. The decor, artsy. The peeps, gangsta. The food, legit. I dig this place.

The food is good but the experience is ridiculous! These are tacos for goodness sake [. . .] This place is a joke. [. . .] I wish I could turn back time and drive down to Ed Fernandez or Gordo's or any other taco shop in the county for that matter.
—*Yelp* reviews of *¡Salud!* in Barrio Logan, San Diego[1]

In a context where culture has become a key determinant of the economic success of cities, food and taste have emerged as symbols of neighborhood transformation and powerful tools of urban renewal. According to Bourdieu (1984), *taste* reflects identities, reveals differences, and reinforces class positions. Similarly, food distinguishes places, giving some neighborhoods character and value, while stigmatizing others as *food deserts* or *food swamps*, characterized respectively by the absence of healthy food or the abundance of so-called junk food (Joassart-Marcelli and Bosco 2018a). In contested places, debates about food and taste—including those taking place online on social media platforms like *Yelp*—reflect changing cultural aesthetics and social dynamics and illustrate ongoing processes of spatial exclusion.

In gentrifying neighborhoods, farmers' markets, community gardens, cosmopolitan restaurants, microbreweries, and *authentic* eateries have gained popularity and often play an important role in branding locales and attracting people from other places (Joassart-Marcelli and Bosco 2018b). Unlike upscale restaurants and high-end stores, these contemporary food projects appear to embrace a multicultural and democratic ethos that seemingly values diversity and community. Social media posts about those spaces, including *Yelp* reviews, both reflect and reinforce these ideas, with terms such as "authentic," "legit," and "the real thing" used liberally to describe the food and dining experience. Urban elites, including developers, local politicians, and financiers, encourage and capitalize on these cultural narratives and symbolic assets in order to promote specific neighborhoods.

At the same time, however, food insecurity remains a significant concern especially among lower-income residents, who have lived in these neighborhoods and patronized local food stores and restaurants for a long time. Although these residents may welcome some changes in their foodscape, particularly those that improve access to affordable, healthy, and culturally appropriate food, evidence suggests that they feel excluded from the new developments and experience them with ambivalence, if not resentment (Joassart-Marcelli and Bosco 2020). Their apprehension over current changes in their neighborhood's food scene is also reflected on social media where fears of gentrification and lost sense of place are commonly expressed. Persistent economic hardships and social tensions put into question the democratic and cosmopolitan posture that the majority of new businesses adopt.

Taste then becomes a way for newcomers and longer-term residents to relate to each other and to place. As discussed in chapters 2, 3, and 5 of this volume, these encounters may forge connections, but they may also exacerbate difference rooted in broader socio-spatial processes associated with class, race, and ethnicity that shape cultural understandings of "good food." New food businesses take a particularly active part in both reflecting and molding taste and shaping the social and cultural character of place. The type of food they sell, the way they present themselves, the values they seem to support, and the aesthetics they embrace are all central in producing a foodscape that is more or less inclusionary.

In this chapter, we intersect literature on gentrification with research on taste and food to investigate how taste and place relate to each other in ways that reproduce social distinctions based on class, race, and other factors. In particular, we explore how new food spaces and practices are represented and promoted in Barrio Logan and North Park—two urban neighborhoods of San Diego that are characterized by different stages of gentrification. Our goal is to highlight the role of taste, as a social, cultural, and emotional construct, in contributing to gentrification and displacement—what we call the *taste of gentrification*.

We begin with a review of theoretical research on the social construction of taste, including Bourdieu's work, and argue for the benefit of inflecting this scholarship with a place perspective. Next, we turn to debates within the gentrification literature and discuss the significance of food and taste in reconciling theoretical differences between political-economic and cultural approaches. Using mixed methods, we then combine mapping with analysis of qualitative data from various media sources, including social media and local food publications and news outlets, to explore the key elements of the taste of gentrification, as well as how and where it is produced.

Place and the Social Production of Taste

Although taste has long been understood as a social construct, its relationship to place remains poorly theorized. Sociologist Pierre Bourdieu (1984) provides us with a solid theoretical foundation to study the social construction of taste. According to him, taste serves as a way for the upper class to distinguish itself from lower social groups. Even though *good taste* appears to come naturally to social elites, it is developed through socialization and cultivated by a rigid set of norms. This notion of taste is particularly applicable to the realm of food, which is so rich in symbolism. In contrast to the working class who by necessity favor heavy and filling food, those with higher socioeconomic status are free from the worldly concerns of biological sustenance and have the leisure to enjoy food aesthetically. The settings, ingredients, presentations, table manners, and timing of meals all contribute to creating a sense of sophistication denied to the lower classes.

Bourdieu's work has been criticized for privileging class over other forms of social difference (Sloan 2004). In a postmodern context where individual identities are seemingly less constrained by socioeconomic attributes and more fluid than in the past, many scholars have argued that class has become less relevant in understanding taste and culture (Ollivier 2008). Today, people use lifestyles, including food, fashion, décor, travel, and music, to define their identities and reveal their good taste in new ways (Binkley 2007). Lifestyle practitioners embrace unique diets and exotic ingredients that relate to their ethnicity, gender, sexuality, and other aspects of identity. For example, the recent popularity of turmeric, which was named "spice of the summer," "ingredient of the year," and "the world's healthiest food" in 2016, illustrates the way food defines identities in fluid ways. Typically associated with immigrants from southeast Asia who use it for cooking and medicine, turmeric has now become popular among cultural elites and health-conscious urbanites who enjoy it in "gold lattes" and "anti-inflammatory stir-fries," revealing very different identities or values. The ostensible cultural openness to a much greater variety of food has been described as "omnivorousness" and "cosmopolitanism" (Johnston and Baumann 2010). The idea of omnivorousness has been applied to cultural studies of music, art, and food and refers to the rejection of overt snobbery and the espousal of eclecticism as signals of social status (Peterson and Kern 1996). Similarly, cosmopolitanism emphasizes a preference for ethnic and international cultures (Beck 2006). Both have been facilitated by globalization, immigration, and a new kind of cultural politics that has made identities less rigid and more malleable through individual lifestyles and experiences. In that context, food is providing individuals, especially those with economic means, with more freedom to express various aspects of their identities.

Bourdieu's work has also—perhaps unfairly—been criticized for its emphasis on the representational aspect of taste over its more active role in shaping class relations (Sloan 2004). As Bourdieu noted, taste is not static but negotiated. For example, when luxury or exotic food commodities become more affordable, the upper class must redefine taste to maintain its distance from the vulgarity and tastelessness of the lower classes. Taste itself becomes contested, appropriated, manipulated, and guarded in ways that are constitutive of class relations. In that context, practices often become more important than objects of consumption. Although cosmopolitanism and omnivorousness threaten the exclusiveness of upper-class behavior, distinction is reproduced through consumption of food described as "authentic," "communal," "locally produced," and "ethically sourced." Cultural elites are therefore not literally omnivorous, but instead pick and choose food carefully to navigate the fine line between the authentic and the vulgar and maintain their social position.

In the large body of research influenced by Bourdieu's work on taste, little attention is given to the role of place (Cheyne and Binder 2010). We argue that a place perspective may be useful in generating a broader understanding of how taste is produced—one that acknowledges social difference beyond class and the active role of taste in (re)producing these differences. By "placing" taste within the material settings and geographic imaginaries where it is formed, acquired, and enacted, we aim to draw attention to the intricate and co-constitutive connections between taste and place. In particular, we highlight how food and understandings of good taste have an impact on place, while at the same time, place contributes social and cultural meanings to particular foods and influences the formation of taste. As Urry (1995) argues, the significance of place is heightened in a postmodern context where aesthetics and sensory experiences are an important aspect of consumer cultures. An aesthetically stimulating restaurant, for instance, is a place that broadens the role of food in the pursuit of postmodern lifestyles and the expression of cosmopolitan tastes. In other words, there is an increasingly important dynamic relationship between taste and place in ways that tend to reproduce social difference.

Within that place-based framework, it is also useful to think about taste as an embodied experience (Holt 1997). Cresswell (2002) suggests that Bourdieu's work on the body might be his most influential contribution to critical human geography and an important step toward conceptualizing place. According to Bourdieu (1984: 190), "the body is the most indisputable materialization of class taste." It is in the body that social distinctions are activated through practices like standing, walking, speaking, eating, and feeling. These practices are part of the "habitus" of social groups—the "embodied dispositions that reproduce social difference." Time and place are critical in imbuing such practices with social significance. For instance, the concert hall, the museum, the travel destination, or the restaurant are social spaces that shape bodily functions in ways that permit the upper class to express their superiority while exposing the lower class's social inadequacies and lack of cultural capital. In a cosmopolitan environment where consumers venture into increasingly more diverse cultural worlds, places that are perceived as authentic have more symbolic value (Zukin 2008; Johnston and Baumann 2010). Yet, some people are better positioned than others to explore the outer reaches of their taste by accessing and controlling space that is culturally exciting and valuable, hinting at a colonial mind-set.

Thus, although scholars have acknowledged the role of place in shaping taste, it is primarily as a setting or backdrop to social interactions that play a more important role in defining social superiority (Cheyne and Binder 2010). In this chapter, we want to go beyond this perspective to consider how taste and place work jointly and dynamically to reproduce social inequality.

The Taste of Gentrification

The way taste and place influence each other is uniquely visible in gentrifying neighborhoods, where rapid demographic change and associated social tensions can be witnessed in the foodscape. In these previously neglected urban areas, the transformation of the material and discursive food environment creates what we call a "taste of gentrification" which in turn exacerbates the process of cultural and spatial displacement (see also chapters 2, 3, and 5).

Recent research, including work published in this volume, has highlighted the role of food in promoting gentrification. Studies have focused primarily on two elements of urban foodscapes, including so-called alternative food spaces such as community gardens and farmers' markets (Joassart-Marcelli and Bosco 2018b; Paddock 2015), and new retailers like upscale supermarkets (Anguelovski 2015), craft breweries (Matthews and Picton 2014), coffee shops, and artisanal food boutiques (Zukin et al. 2009). Many of these spaces display an urban aesthetic of simplicity and authenticity, while seemingly embracing ideals of community, sustainability, and food justice (Bosco and Joassart-Marcelli 2017; Joassart-Marcelli and Bosco 2018b). However, they tend to attract primarily affluent and white people and exclude longtime residents who do not have the time, financial resources, and/or cultural capital to enjoy them (Slocum 2007; Guthman 2008). As more people are drawn to these new food spaces and the bohemian character of the neighborhood, lower-income households are eventually displaced financially and physically by rising rents and ensuing evictions, as well as culturally and emotionally through a lost sense of place and belonging (Zukin 2008;

Kern 2015). This seriously challenges the legitimacy of the moral claims that are explicitly or implicitly made through various representations of the changing foodscape.

Together these studies point to changing urban dynamics that are partly reflected in current debates within the literature on gentrification regarding the relative role of political-economic and cultural forces. Early studies of gentrification emphasized the process of capital accumulation that led investors to allocate financial resources to neighborhoods they had previously abandoned (see Lees, Slater, and Wyly 2008). The return to inner-city neighborhoods was motivated by a rent gap that promised significant economic returns and was facilitated by a political elite eager to capitalize from redevelopment (Smith 1996). In recent years, however, scholars have drawn attention to the cultural aspects of gentrification, including the appeal of urban consumption lifestyles associated with creativity, bohemia, and authenticity (Zukin 2008). This newer research tends to attribute gentrification to changing individual preferences for urban living rather than to a political-economic structure that encourages an inflow of capital in particular areas (see Lees et al. 2008). In this framework, consumption is prioritized over production as an explanation for the changing character of urban neighborhoods. This perspective has been criticized for minimizing the negative effects of gentrification and "gut[ting] the concept of its inherent class character" (Slater 2008: 216).

Understandings of gentrification do not need to be so dichotomous, as Hammett (1991) suggested long ago. Building on this recognition, we argue that the place-based conceptualization of taste outlined above might be helpful in bridging cultural explanations of gentrification that emphasize lifestyles with political-economic theory highlighting the role of class and capital. In many gentrifying urban neighborhoods, the interaction of taste and place produces a certain urban imaginary that facilitates capital accumulation. Urban elites, including developers, public officials, leaders of cultural economies, and the media, work hand-in-hand to create cultural representations of urban places and lifestyles that reward investors and favor affluent residents (Hollows et al. 2014; Vanalo 2008). Restaurants, public markets, gardens, food festivals, and breweries are increasingly important parts of efforts deployed to maximize symbolic value and minimize the risk of investing in neglected neighborhoods (Joassart-Marcelli and Bosco 2018a). In immigrant neighborhoods, the idea of authenticity has been particularly important in adding value to the food landscape. New and revamped restaurants attracting urban elites and educated tourists are frequently described as serving "authentic" food created by an "innovative chef" and served by "a very attractive girl with great vintage tattoos." In contrast, older establishments that primarily serve a local, immigrant, and low-income clientele are perceived as "cheap joints" where "cooks" who "barely speak English" and have "dirty nails" prepare "cheap," "fast," and "filling" food. This contrast points to a contradiction in the concept of authenticity, which relies on outsiders to define what is presumably original and local. Indeed, newcomers' understanding of what is authentic does not resonate with long-term residents, whose more proximate claim of authenticity is being dismissed by racist and classist biases.

The food spaces that are viewed as authentic by food experts and affluent consumers are instrumental in permitting new residents to exhibit the sort of omnivorousness and cosmopolitanism that is currently considered in good taste (Johnston and Baumann 2010). Through these spaces, new residents simultaneously make spatial claims on gentrifying neighborhoods and create symbolic boundaries between themselves and longtime residents. The taste of gentrification becomes a strategy for urban redevelopment; it is not merely an expression of consumer preference, but a social distinction that is carefully produced by developers and foodies based on a set of consumption objects, activities, and places that encourage capital accumulation. Although it wants to be authentic, omnivorous, and cosmopolitan, the taste of gentrification perpetuates inequality through social exclusion and physical displacement.

In this chapter, we are interested in understanding how taste facilitates gentrification by creating symbolic boundaries and social distinction through unique urban imaginaries. Elsewhere we have published research documenting the food practices of urban residents and their experiences with neighborhood change. Here, we seek to analyze representations of food spaces and focus primarily on media content, including online local food publications (e.g., restaurant reviews and neighborhood guides) and social media. We identify and map key themes from these various media sources in order to document recent changes in the layout and representations of gentrifying foodscapes. Interpretation of these data will be facilitated by our intimate knowledge of these neighborhoods, where we have conducted extensive fieldwork including audits, interviews, surveys and participant observation, for over a decade.

Urban Geographies of Food Gentrification

We chose to focus on the neighborhoods of Barrio Logan and North Park in San Diego, California because they both face high gentrification pressure but differ in their appeal to elite urban consumers. There has been significant demographic change in both neighborhoods (see table 1.1), including a rise in median property values, household incomes, and rents, especially during the first decade of this century. North Park's gentrification began in the late 1990s, spreading north from the most affluent section of the neighborhood. Its proximity to downtown and Balboa Park, its old-fashioned main streets lined with broad sidewalks

TABLE 1.1. Neighborhood Change in Barrio Logan and North Park

	Barrio Logan				North Park			
	Value	Change			Value	Change		
	2016	1990–2000	2000–2010	2010–2016	2016	1990–2000	2000–2010	2010–2016
Median property value	$225,000	67.9%	195.6%	−51.1%	$407,841	18.5%	125.8%	−1.9%
Median rent	$877	28.1%	55.7%	14.5%	$1,113	24.1%	63.3%	14.0%
Percentage renters	92.1%	2.90%	3.80%	1.40%	75.1%	0.8%	−2.5%	−0.2%
Median household income	$22,440	68.5%	−15.7%	3.8%	$57,143	33.6%	40.2%	22.2%
Poverty rate	44.0%	−9.4%	3.4%	3.5%	12.8%	4.8%	0.7%	−4.6%
Percentage with college degree or more	6.0%	0.0%	2.9%	0.0%	50.3%	4.6%	10.0%	12.7%
Percentage non-Latino white	9.9%	−2.0%	0.9%	2.2%	54.7%	−11.4%	1.1%	1.3%

Data source: Authors' computation using data from the US Census (1990, 2000, 2010, and 2016).

and storefronts, and the quaint architecture and relative affordability of its craftsmen- and Spanish-style cottages attracted college-educated people in search of urban lifestyles.

Change in Barrio Logan is less noticeable because the neighborhood remains home to a large low-income and mostly Latinx population, despite the rapid increase in property values and rents. For these reasons, its census tract is considered as "eligible for gentrification," but is not yet categorized as gentrified. In fact, the transformation of Barrio Logan is still in its early stage and appears to be in part motivated by a selective attraction to the Latinx culture, including its presumed authenticity and sense of community (Dávila 2004). In contrast to North Park, where community organizations appear mostly supportive of ongoing trends, Barrio Logan's residents have actively mobilized against budding gentrification pressures, continuing a long tradition of activism linked to the Chicano movement (Le Texier 2007).

In both places, there has been a proliferation of new restaurants, craft breweries, cafés, and alternative food spaces that are attracting growing numbers of non-residents to the area and receiving considerable media attention, giving us ample data to analyze. To map the changing geographies of food, we turned to two types of data: social media (*Yelp*), which reflects the opinions of relatively young and affluent consumers, and professional reviews (*Eater, Thrillist, Zagat,* and local magazines), which represent the perspectives of food experts—although this line between consumer and expert is becoming increasingly blurred.[2] Affluent urbanites, foodies, and tourists frequently rely on these sources to identify "places not to miss," "hottest new restaurants," and "cheapeats" that make San Diego's food landscape increasingly resemble New York's or San Francisco's. Of course, these reviews are biased and represent the perspectives of certain types of consumers, but it is this very bias that makes them useful to explore gentrification trends.

Figure 1.1 reveals clusters of "good taste" in San Diego, based on the density of positive restaurant reviews in the local media. Note that very popular restaurants that are reviewed on multiple platforms may appear more than once to reflect popularity. The core of downtown, which has historically received most of the city planners' and developers' attention and caters primarily to tourists and suburbanites, has the

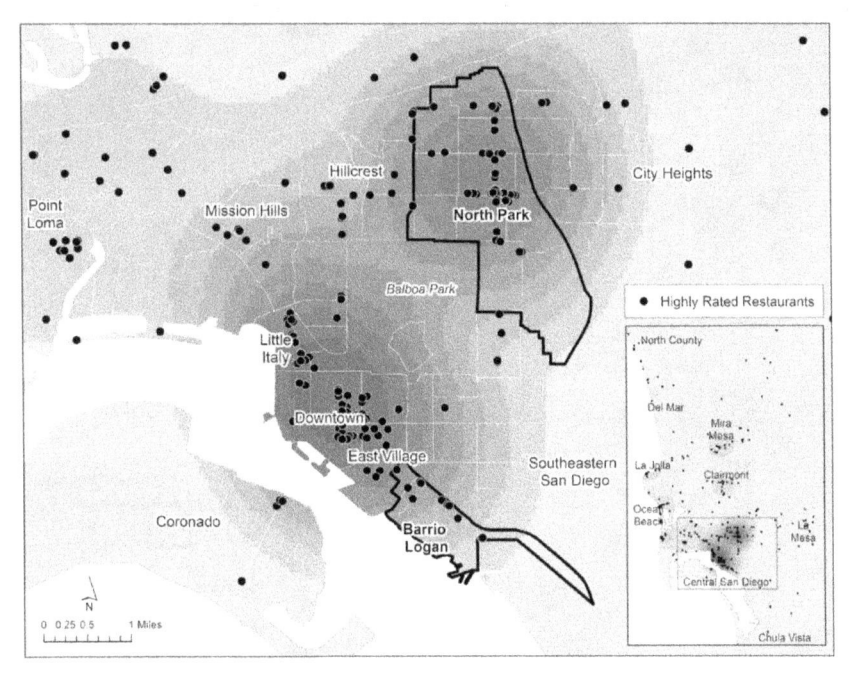

Figure 1.1. Kernel Density of Highly Rated Restaurants in Central San Diego and San Diego County (2016–2017). Map created by author using 2016–2018 data from *Yelp*, *Eater*, *Thrillist*, *Zagat*, *San Diego Magazine*, and *San Diego Brewers' Guild*.

highest density of positive reviews. This cluster spreads north toward Little Italy and south toward the East Village and Barrio Logan. Although Barrio Logan includes fewer restaurants on the regional recommendation lists, a small cluster of trendy restaurants is emerging along Logan Avenue and Main Street and drawing attention among food critics and consumers alike. The attraction to "locals"—or wannabe locals—increases as one moves away from downtown and enters more residential neighborhoods. North Park is the second major foodie destination in the region, with more than seventy-three positive restaurant, bakery, or brewery reviews in the past 2 years. Here too, the historical and mixed-use character of the neighborhood is attractive to both locals and visitors.

The density of positive restaurant reviews in North Park and Barrio Logan is geographically tied to gentrification. As figure 1.2 illustrates,

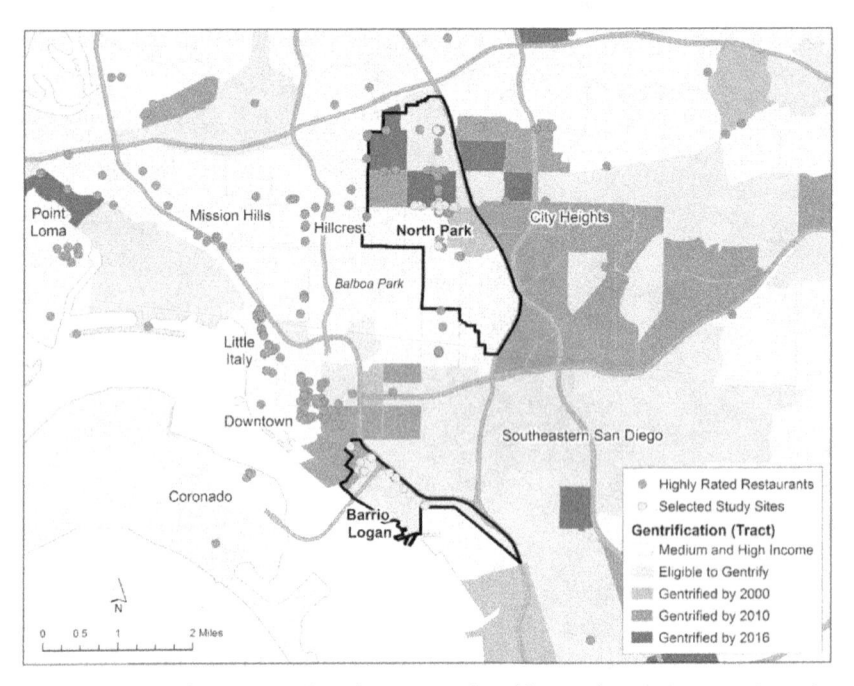

Figure 1.2. Gentrification Trends and Location of Highly Rated Restaurants in Central San Diego, including Barrio Logan and North Park (2016–2017). Map created by author using data from the US Census of Population and Housing 1990–2010 and the American Community Survey 5-year Estimates (2016).

several of the noteworthy restaurants are located in census tracts that are considered "eligible to gentrify" and are adjacent to previously gentrified tracts and already established entertainment zones.[3]

Areas that were recently gentrified or are on the cusp of gentrification appear to draw much attention from the food media. In contrast, those that show few signs of change, such as southeastern San Diego, rarely have a restaurant reviewed. Similarly, more established areas, that are either affluent (e.g., Mission Hills) or were gentrified decades ago (e.g., Hillcrest), lose their appeal to consumers in search of trendier places and food adventures. These patterns reflect the ebb and flows of capital that underlie uneven urban development (Smith 1996), suggesting an intimate relationship between production/economy and consumption/culture in the process of gentrification, as we noted earlier in the theoretical section of this chapter.

Authenticity, Democracy, and Community

What type of restaurants locate in gentrifying neighborhoods and what does it say about their potential role in this process of neighborhood transformation? To answer this question, we turned our attention to the content of restaurant reviews and created word clouds—a visualization tool increasingly used by geographers in exploratory qualitative data analysis to identify frequently used terms (Cidell 2010).[4] Figure 1.3 reveals the one hundred most common terms used by consumers and professionals in their online reviews, with font sizes proportional to word frequencies.

Several key themes stand out, as previously identified in the literature on contemporary urban foodscapes (Joassart-Marcelli and Bosco 2018a; Johnston and Baumann 2010; Zukin et al. 2009). First, authenticity and cosmopolitanism appear to be of great importance to many consumers, who value food and dining experiences reflecting their appreciation of ethnic diversity and knowledge of exotic cuisine. For many, this is associated with a sense of discovery and a willingness to trade certain amenities like safety, speed, décor, and even cleanliness for "authentic" food. This is especially true in Barrio Logan, which is often described in the media as a "rough" neighborhood with a rich Chicano culture. For example, *Las Cuatro Milpas* is one of the most frequently reviewed restaurants:

> Mexican food doesn't get more authentic on this side of the border than at Las Cuatro Milpas. Don't be deterred by the line. You just have to accept the fact that there is always a line, so stand in it like everyone else has been doing for the last 82 years. (Jackson and Norris 2016)

> I can't believe such delicious food could come out of a hole in a wall. I thought this place might be one of those secret joints that only locals know about, but apparently yelpers are in the know! The diners are mostly locals and most of the workers don't speak a lot of English. It can be a little intimidating when ordering since the lines are long and there's really not much of a menu. We basically got almost one of everything. It feels truly authentic and their food reflects that. The decor is bare and nothing fancy. Just some old tables and chairs with tablecloths over them in an open room with brown tiled floors. EVERYTHING is ridiculously delicious and tastes like it's been made by a Mexican grandmother. (*Yelp* 2018)

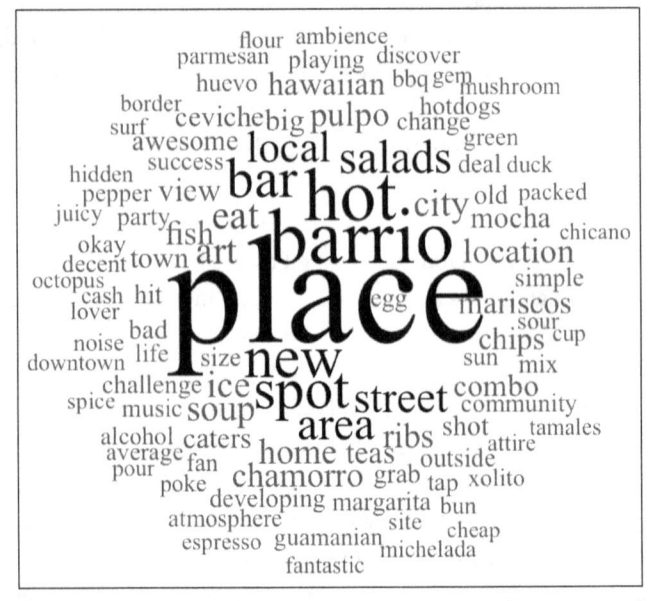

Figure 1.3a–b. Word Clouds of Common Terms Used in Reviews of Ten Most Popular Restaurants in North Park and Barrio Logan. Author's computation based on *Yelp*, *Eater*, *Zagat*, and *Thrillist* top reviews of ten most popular restaurants (2018).

The ability to identify authentic food is an important aspect of cosmopolitan taste, which distinguishes foodies from other consumers who presumably do not have the knowledge or interest to venture out of their comfort zone to try new foods. Yet, as Heldke (2003) and others have noted, claims of authenticity are usually made by outsiders and therefore reflect a position of power and appropriation. Indeed, reviews suggest that authenticity is a contested and evolving idea, with outsiders' understanding of authenticity clashing with that of long-term residents. For instance, out-of-town visitors "really felt like [they] were living an authentic Chicano cultural experience" or had "somehow crossed the border" at ¡Salud!. However, a long-term Barrio Logan resident disagreed:

> All these people writing these great reviews saying how great their tacos are don't know what good tacos are or haven't had any great tacos in their life. I'm just being honest with everyone. I ordered three tacos de carne asada which almost have identical taste as those from [a less hyped local taco shop]. The Birria was decent but lacks a bit of flavor. My neighbor across the street knows how to make Birria and let me tell you right now he makes better Birria than them. And that's a Fact!

Unfortunately, claims of authenticity also represent a way of determining what elements of the food landscape are worth keeping, forcing restaurant owners to adapt in order to remain in place (Gaytán 2008). While newly discovered "hidden gems" that appeal to new residents may stay and even flourish, "dumps" will likely disappear because they symbolize a past that no longer fits with the new identity of the neighborhood.

Second, the appeal of casual and simple food is also striking, indicating a democratization of food. Reviewers in both neighborhoods invoke simplicity as an important criterion for assessing the value of food. The word clouds in figure 1.3 include terms such as simple, basic, and home. Tacos, hot dogs, donuts, and BBQ are among the most highly praised foods in both communities. Similarly, beer has replaced wine as the beverage of choice, signaling an appreciation for simple products historically associated with the working class. Indeed, as we write this chapter, a brand-new restaurant named *Working Class* just opened in North Park, reinforcing the legitimacy of seemingly simple food and drinks as new markers of good taste.

As Johnston and Bauman (2010) argue, the democratization of dining, which appears to be taking place in many cities, may reflect a false egalitarianism that masks a persistent desire for social distinction, particularly "in a cultural context that endorses democratic ideals and rejects overt snobbery" (p. 2). Other food characteristics, such as local, organic, vegan, authentic, homemade, and artisanal, become signifiers of distinction. Although foodies may be willing to eat hot dogs, not every hot dog is equally appealing. In that sense, simplicity overlaps with authenticity and other values in reinforcing social differences between eaters. For instance, in Barrio Logan, a new hot dog stand has received significant attention as a "casual counter-service spot with inventive hot dogs." One review's author claims that although "tacos will always be San Diego's one true love, [. . .] this ultra-casual counter service outfit in the Barrio makes a strong argument for specialty hot dogs suited up with inspired toppings like pickled jicama and wasabi sesame seeds" (Jackson 2017). In many cases, classic food is "reinvented" and "updated" with an exaggerated sense of nostalgia that, like authenticity, tends to appeal to outsiders who experience the food and the setting with greater attention to details, particularly those worth posting on social media.

It is perhaps not surprising that in both neighborhoods the words place, spot, city, street, and area appear quite frequently in the reviews, underscoring the importance of place in distinguishing restaurants. While these may not be used in the way that geographers conceptualize place as a set of social relations, they nevertheless reflect the importance of context, which was often described in detail in the reviews. It is also worth noting that *Yelp* reviewers often refer to Barrio Logan as "the barrio," with an odd mixture of admiration and aversion. The terms discover and developer/ing also suggest that these places are in flux and not yet fully established. In fact, the neighborhoods themselves contribute to the attractiveness and authenticity of many food establishments that would not be valued equally in a different setting. For instance, a *Yelp* reviewer writes about her experience discovering *Rolando's Taco Shop* in Barrio Logan:

> I am scared! Scared of a lot of things about this place. Going there by myself. Sitting at a table. Touching anything. But I am not scared of the food. And that is why, I am giving this place in Barrio Logan 4 stars

despite the . . . ummm . . . unsavoriness of the surroundings [. . .] A little sketchy but the food is GREAT! [. . .] Better than great. Hands down the best Carnitas and best Tortillas I have EVER had. [. . .] We all left with full bellies and happy smiles. But we rushed to our car . . . didn't want to be caught hanging around.

The urban aesthetic of the food establishments features prominently in the reviews and is often associated with values such as historic preservation, sustainability, and sociability—revealing a form of ethical consumerism whereby consumers seek to support causes or assert their moral values through consumption choices. Interest in sociability can be observed in the popularity of communal tables where strangers eat side by side and of open kitchens where diners can interact with bartenders, servers, and chefs. The expectation of social interaction is also an important aspect in gastropubs and breweries, which are very common in both neighborhoods. Outdoor eating areas also tend to be more casual and often include a small edible garden, which appeals to many educated and environmentally conscious consumers.

The desire to preserve—or more accurately recreate—historic character can be observed in figure 1.4, which illustrates the material foodscape of City Heights and Barrio Logan. Many of the new restaurants embrace an industrial and urban architectural style that capitalizes on the existing hardscape of the neighborhood, but also seeks to reframe or elevate it by exaggerating certain details and appropriating elements from the past or other cultures. Vintage signs, colorful murals, rusted steel, wall gardens, and reclaimed wood are all very popular. The emerging landscape resembles what Jameson (1991) calls a "postmodern pastiche"—an imitation or cannibalization of the past that reflects our consumer culture and the commodification of style. This is especially noticeable in Barrio Logan, where elements of Chicano culture are used by many new businesses. For instance, *Barrio Dogg*'s counter is built out of a 1964 lowrider Chevy Impala; *Por Vida*'s signage resembles murals found in nearby Chicano Park—a key site of the Chicano movement which represents Mexican Americans' struggles for social and environmental justice and was recently added to the National Register of Historic Places; and *¡Salud!*'s interior décor includes both of these elements. These cultural symbols, however, appeal mostly to outsiders who interpret them as

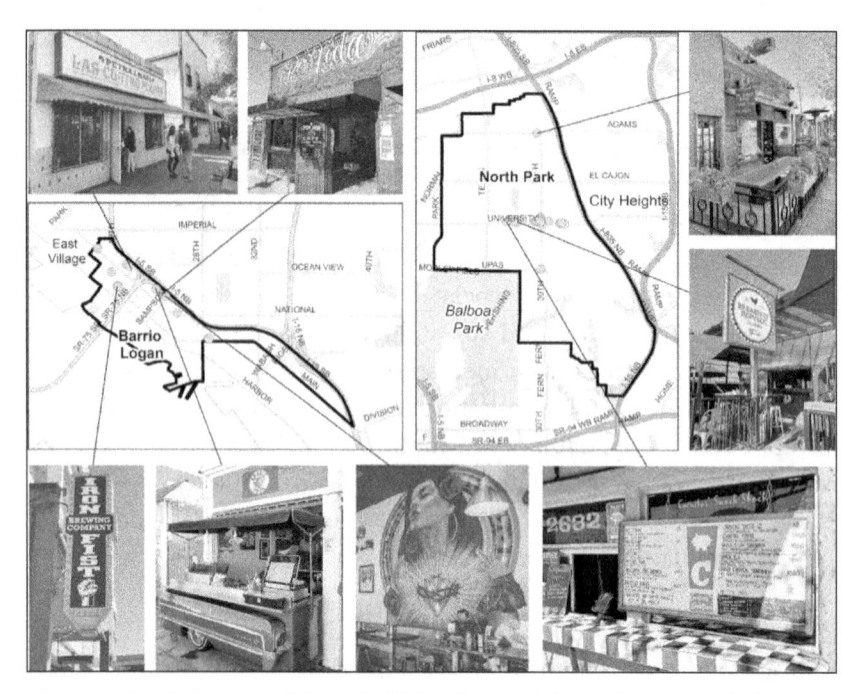

Figure 1.4. Barrio Logan and North Park's Foodscapes. Maps and photographs by author.

signs of authenticity and cosmopolitanism, while longtime residents for whom these symbols carry a different meaning tend to resent their commodification and decontextualization from the historic struggles they symbolize (Joassart-Marcelli and Bosco 2019).

Conclusion

Food has become a central element of the transformation of urban areas in San Diego and elsewhere, simultaneously reflecting and promoting gentrification. The examples of North Park and Barrio Logan illustrate that gentrification has a unique taste: a combination of cosmopolitanism, authenticity, democracy, and ethical consumerism that builds on existing assets for the benefits of new residents who use these attributes to set themselves apart from previous dwellers. These contemporary narratives of "good taste" are associated with particular food practices that are inherently connected to places but at the same time deny parts of their social histories. The ethnic and urban aesthetic of popular restaurants is an essential element of the geographic imaginary surrounding good taste and a key mechanism for pushing the gentrification frontier and assigning value to previously neglected urban areas. As older food outlets are replaced by expensive new eateries, the resulting discursive foodscape no longer reflects the lifestyle of longtime residents who feel increasingly excluded by the symbolic boundaries it creates (Joassart-Marcelli and Bosco 2020). In addition to the rising cost of purchasing food, residents feel out of place in many of the new shops and restaurants where the food, music, drinks, décor, and customers' behavior reflect whiteness and class privilege. The displacement of classed and racialized residents in places that claim to be multicultural and authentic is poignantly illustrated in this *Yelp* post about a new Barrio Logan eatery:

> The last time I came to this place I was extremely disappointed with the service I received [. . .] I don't know what's worse: getting treated like shit by sorry to say it but white people who see nothing but a dark colored man in construction clothes or getting treated like shit in your own neighborhood by your own people who see nothing but a dark guy in construction clothes. The whole experience made me really upset and sad.

The "good taste" narratives that reify ethnic and working-class foods and commodify the neighborhoods where such foods have been historically prepared and consumed—albeit in different ways—are not produced in a vacuum. Neither are they simply the reflection of changing consumer preferences. As Zukin et al. (2009) argue, gentrification is a cultural process that is shaped by powerful actors. In our study neighborhoods, these actors include the restaurant industry, developers, neighborhood organizations, and local governments, who benefit from creating foodscapes that are perceived as authentic and cosmopolitan. For instance, in our two study areas, events such as the *Taste of North Park*, *Ray at Night*, or the *Barrio Art Crawl* are organized by neighborhood business associations to encourage visitors to come and explore art and food. The City of San Diego is also actively using food as a way to draw people to these neighborhoods through various sponsored events and publications praising Barrio Logan's "authentic culinary delights" (San Diego Tourism Authority 2018) and describing North Park as a "true food lover's sanctuary, for every craving and every taste bud" (Explore North Park 2018). *San Diego Magazine*, which publishes extensive restaurant reviews and annual "best of" lists, is primarily funded by advertising from local businesses, including restaurants as well as real estate and construction companies that may have common interests in the gentrification of neighborhoods around downtown San Diego.

To resist food gentrification, therefore, we must contend with these popular narratives that mask social exclusion under the guise of authenticity, cosmopolitanism, and democratic values. In doing so, we must consider the various actors involved in producing the taste of gentrification and the motives behind their efforts. More research on the urban politics of food retail will help bridge the gap between cultural and political-economic explanations of gentrification and identify avenues for resisting social exclusion and spatial displacement.

NOTES

1 To preserve the anonymity of *Yelp* reviewers, who made their comments public but did not explicitly agree to participate in this study, we do not provide identifying reference to any posts quoted in this chapter, except for the name of the restaurant reviewed.

2 To obtain consumer data, we used *Yelp*—the most widely used social media platform where individuals post comments about restaurants. For each of our two study neighborhoods, we downloaded the fifty most recent *Yelp* reviews for the ten most reviewed restaurants (as of January 25, 2018). Following Zukin et al. (2009), we assume that the most reviewed restaurants are those attracting large numbers of relatively young and affluent consumers. To obtain data from food experts, we downloaded restaurant reviews from a number of popular websites, including the San Diego editions of *Eater*, *Thrillist*, and *Zagat*. These sites are all supported by national media companies that offer similar publications in large cities across the United States and tend to highlight the same type of restaurants. In addition, we gathered data from *San Diego Magazine*—a lifestyle publication that features the "Best of San Diego"—and the *San Diego Brewers' Guild*, which has been actively involved in promoting craft brewing in the region and supporting the "gastropub" and "bar dining" trend. We collected a total of 589 reviews published during a two-year period (2016 and 2017), with a number of popular restaurants reviewed across multiple platforms.

3 The categorization of tracts into eligible to gentrify, gentrified, and affluent groups is based on computations using data on median income, property

values, proportion of college educated residents, race, and changes in these variables (see Joassart-Marcelli and Bosco 2018b for details). Under this definition, a census tract is considered gentrified if its median income was in the bottom third at the beginning of the period and it experienced a rapid increase in property value, percentage of college educated, and percentage of white residents.

4 Using the NVivo qualitative analysis software, we conducted a word frequency analysis of online reviews of the ten most popular restaurants in each neighborhood, relying on *Yelp, Eater, Thrillist, Zagat,* and *San Diego Magazine*. Our frequency analysis accounted for words describing the food, eating establishments, and neighborhood environment as well as reviewers' attitudes toward each of these three. Aided by the software, we filtered our results, excluding proper names and other non-necessary and redundant words, to create word clouds.

REFERENCES

Anguelovski, Isabelle. 2015. "Healthy Food Stores, Greenlining and Food Gentrification:
Contesting New Forms of Privilege, Displacement and Locally Unwanted Land Uses in Racially Mixed Neighborhoods." *International Journal of Urban and Regional Research* 39(6): 1209–1230.

Beck, Ulrich. 2006. *The Cosmopolitan Vision*. Malden, MA: Polity Press.

Binkley, Sam. 2007. "Governmentality and Lifestyle Studies." *Sociology Compass* 1(1): 111–126.

Bosco, Fernando J. and Pascale Joassart-Marcelli. 2017. "Gardens in the City: Community, Politics and Place." In *Global Urban Agriculture: Convergence of Theory and Practice between North and South*, edited by Antoinette WinklerPrins, 50–65. Boston: CABI International.

Bourdieu, Pierre. 1984. *Distinction: A Social Critique of the Judgment of Taste*. Cambridge, MA: Harvard University Press.

Bridge, Gary and Robyn Dowling. 2001. "Microgeographies of Retailing and Gentrification." *Australian Geographer* 32(1): 93–107.

Cheyne, Andrew and Amy Binder. 2010. "Cosmopolitan Preferences: The Constitutive Role of Place in American Elite Taste for Hip-Hop Music 1991–2005." *Poetics* 38(3): 336–364.

Cidell, Julie. 2010. "Content Clouds as Exploratory Qualitative Data Analysis." *Area* 42(4): 514–523.

Cresswell, Tim. 2002. "Bourdieu's Geographies: In Memorium. Guest Editorial." *Environment and Planning D: Society and Space* 20: 379–382.

Dávila, Arlene. 2004. *Barrio Dreams: Puerto Ricans, Latinos, and the Neoliberal City*. Berkeley: University of California Press.

Deener, Andrew. 2007. "Commerce as the Structure and Symbol of Neighborhood Life." *City & Community* 6(4): 291–314.

Eater. 2018. *San Diego Eater*. Various dates 2018, https://sandiego.eater.com.

Explore North Park. 2018. "Restaurants and Dining." January 18, at www.explorenorthpark.com.

Gaytán, Marie Sarita. 2008. "From Sombreros to *Sincronizadas*: Authenticity, Ethnicity, and the Mexican Restaurant Industry." *Journal of Contemporary Ethnography* 37(3): 314–341.

Guthman, Julie. 2008. "'If They Only Knew': Color Blindness and Universalism in California Alternative Food Institutions." *Professional Geographer* 60(3): 387–397.

Hamnett, Chris. 1991. "The Blind Men and the Elephant: The Explanation of Gentrification." *Transactions of the Institute of British Geographers* 16(2): 173–189.

Heldke, Lisa. 2003. *Exotic Appetites: Ruminations of a Food Adventurer*. New York: Routledge.

Hollows, Joanne, Steve Jones, Ben Taylor, and Kimberley Dowthwaite. 2014. "Making Sense of Urban Food Festivals: Cultural Regeneration, Disorder and Hospitable Cities." *Journal of Policy Research in Tourism, Leisure and Events* 6(1): 1–14.

Holt, Douglas B. 1997. "Distinction in America? Recovering Bourdieu's Theory of Tastes from Its Critics." *Poetics* 25(2–3): 93–120.

Jackson, Erin. 2017. "San Diego's Best New Restaurants of 2017." *Thrillist*, January 22, 2018, www.thrillist.com.

Jackson, Erin and Sara Norris. 2016. "50 Things You Need to Eat in San Diego Before You Die." *Thrillist*, January 22, 2018, www.thrillist.com.

Jameson, Fredric. 1991. *Postmodernism, or, the Cultural Logic of Late Capitalism*. Durham, NC: Duke University Press.

Joassart-Marcelli, Pascale and Fernando J. Bosco. 2018a. "Food and Gentrification: How Foodies Are Transforming Urban Neighborhoods." In *Food and Place: A Critical Exploration*, edited by Pascale Joassart-Marcelli and Fernando J. Bosco, 129–146. Lanham, MD: Rowman & Littlefield.

Joassart-Marcelli, Pascale and Fernando J. Bosco. 2018b. "Alternative Food and Gentrification: Farmers' Markets, Community Gardens and the Transformation of Urban Neighborhoods." In *Just Green Enough: Urban Development and Environmental Gentrification*, edited by Winifred Curran and Trina Hamilton, 92–106. New York: Routledge.

Joassart-Marcelli, Pascale and Fernando J. Bosco. 2020. "The Contested Ethnic Urban Foodscape: Immigration, Race, Class, and Displacement." In *The Immigrant-Food Nexus*, edited by Julian Agyeman and Sydney Giacalone, 59–80. Cambridge, MA: MIT Press.

Johnston, Josée and Shyon Baumann. 2010. *Foodies: Democracy and Distinction in the Gourmet Foodscape*. New York: Routledge.

Kern, Leslie. 2015. "Rhythms of Gentrification: Eventfulness and Slow Violence in a Happening Neighbourhood." *Cultural Geographies* 23(3): 441–457.

Le Texier, Emmanuelle. 2007. "The Struggle against Gentrification in Barrio Logan." In *Chicano San Diego: Cultural Space and the Struggle for Justice*, edited by Richard Griswold del Castillo, 202–221. Tucson: University of Arizona Press.

Lees, Loretta, Tom Slater, and Elvin Wyly. 2008. *Gentrification*. New York: Routledge.

Mathews, Vanessa and Roger M. Picton. 2014. "Intoxifying Gentrification: Brew Pubs and the Geography of Post-Industrial Heritage." *Urban Geography* 35(3): 337–356.

Ollivier, Michèle. 2008. "Revisiting Distinction: Bourdieu Without Class?" *Journal of Cultural Economy* 1(3): 263–279.

Paddock, Jessica. 2015. "Invoking Simplicity: 'Alternative' Food and the Reinvention of Distinction." *Sociologia Ruralis* 55(1): 22–40.

Peterson, Richard and R. Kern. 1996. "Changing Highbrow Taste: From Snob to Omnivore." *American Sociological Review* 61: 900–907.

San Diego Brewers' Guild. 2018. Gastro Pubs. Various dates in 2018, https://www.sdbeer.com.

San Diego Tourism Authority. 2018. "Barrio Logan: A Hidden Hub for Art. *Explore San Diego*." February 5, 2018, https://www.sandiego.org.

Slater, Tom. 2008. "'A Literal Necessity to Be Re-Placed': A Rejoinder to the Gentrification Debate." *International Journal of Urban and Regional Research* 32(1): 212–223.

Sloan, Donald, ed. 2004. *Culinary Taste: Consumer Behavior in the International Restaurant Sector*. London: Routledge.

Slocum, Rachel. 2007. "Whiteness, Space and Alternative Food Practice." *Geoforum* 38(3): 520–533.

Smith, Neil. 1996. *The New Urban Frontier: Gentrification and the Revanchist City*. New York: Routledge.

Thrillist. 2018. *San Diego*. Various dates in 2018, www.thrillist.com.

Urry, John. 1995. *Consuming Places*. London: Routledge.

US Census. 1990, 2000, 2010. *Census of Population of Housing*. Washington, DC: Department of Commerce.

US Census. 2016. *American Community Survey 5-year Estimates* (2012–2016). Washington, DC: Department of Commerce.

Vanolo, Alberto. 2008. "The Image of the Creative City: Some Reflections on Urban Branding in Turin." *Cities* 25(6): 370–382.

Yelp. 2018. *Best Restaurants in San Diego*. Various dates in 2018, www.yelp.com.

Zagat. 2018. San Diego Restaurant Reviews. Various dates in 2018, www.zagat.com.

Zukin, Sharon. 2008. "Consuming Authenticity." *Cultural Studies* 22(5): 724–748.

Zukin, Sharon, Valerie Trujillo, Peter Frase, Danielle Jackson, Tim Recuber, and Abraham Walker. 2009. "New Retail Capital and Neighborhood Change: Boutiques and Gentrification in New York City." *City & Community* 8(1): 47–64.

2

Savior Entrepreneurs and Demon Developers

The Role of Gourmet Restaurants and Bars in the Redevelopment of Durham

NINA MARTIN

In 2013, *Southern Living Magazine* chose an unlikely candidate as its "tastiest town" in the South: Durham, North Carolina. Known for its depiction in the film, *Bull Durham* (1988), where minor league baseball players fight for their future in the gritty tobacco town, Durham beat out New Orleans, Charleston, Atlanta, and other well-known "foodie" cities. The city's culinary offerings have been widely celebrated in such publications as *Vogue* (2017), *Bon Appétit* (2016), and the *New York Times* (2013, 2017), which notes that Durham's emergence as a food city paralleled the regeneration of its downtown area. Indeed, until 15 years ago Durham's deindustrialized city center had many empty storefronts, abandoned tobacco warehouses, and depopulated streets. But visit Durham today and you can experience the following itinerary: Begin your day at an independent coffee shop by enjoying drinks made with single-origin beans, then walk over to the farmers' market where you will find locally grown organic produce, snag lunch at a food truck that specializes in culturally hybrid street foods from around the world, shop at boutiques and art galleries with curated collections, have dinner at a farm-to-table restaurant, wrap up the night at a craft brewery specializing in old-world beers, and return to your boutique hotel where you can indulge in a craft cocktail in the lobby bar. Eating and drinking define the downtown Durham experience.

In the current phase of urbanism, gourmet restaurants and bars are not just about feeding people, creating jobs, or earning money for their owners and investors. Restaurants have symbolic value in shaping a city's image and signaling the kind of people who live there and the values they hold. Restaurants may be the contemporary version of the museums and concert halls built by American captains of industry in the nineteenth century: They demonstrate the cultural aspirations of residents and their purported global connectivity. Gourmet restaurants then hold an exalted place in the retail ecology of urban areas competing for a foothold in the service-sector economy. The values of city residents can be symbolized by the food they eat: A plethora of restaurants serving fair, local, and organic foods, for example, can be inferred to mean that this community is progressive, open-minded, and ethical.[1] Namely, the characteristics that cities must possess to attract *creative class* workers and employers.

Cities have long been in fierce competition to attract footloose capital to create jobs, build infrastructure, and invest in arts and culture. City and state relocation assistance in the form of tax breaks, free or low-cost land, and workforce development are still commonly used to attract business. While this approach to economic development continues apace, cities increasingly compete to attract a creative class workforce with particular lifestyle needs (Florida 2002). Amazon's search for a site for its second headquarters exemplified this. In addition to government incentives, Amazon wanted a location that would provide its educated and affluent workforce with certain amenities summarized in the *New York Times* as "restaurants, outdoor recreation, cultural attractions and general cool of Amazon's first home, Seattle" (Badger, Bui, and Miller 2017). These demands are now part of the competitive plane on which cities must compete for their economic future.[2]

Within this context, restaurant development in Durham is central to the city's transition from a post-industrial economy to one based around knowledge economy jobs. Durham has gone through two phases of restaurant and bar-driven redevelopment. In the first phase, individual entrepreneurs opened food establishments in buildings that needed full renovations and had been sitting empty for some time. In undertaking this work, they also became small-scale developers and contributed to the radical changes in the downtown and adjacent neighborhoods. I call these developers the "savior entrepreneur," because they are represented as being key to pulling the city back from the brink and into its creative class status. This savior narrative also claims that they are cutting-edge creatives, even though many of them are following trends set in other cities. In the second phase, "demon developers" enter the landscape, seeing the potential to profit from the newly hip city. Many residents who like the gritty aspects of Durham feared that developers with a corporate ethos and aesthetic would kill the city's quirky vibe. In contrast to these expectations, some of these developers are in fact providing spaces for local food businesses to expand without having to undertake major building remodels and assuming the risk that comes with that.

I illustrate the phases of development using the Central Park neighborhood and the Liberty Warehouse complex. This contentious residential and retail development project brought "demon developers" into conflict with "savior entrepreneurs" over the future of the neighborhood and its "soul." I seek to complicate the simple categories of saviors and demons, by showing the complex roles each plays in the development process and any ensuing gentrification. The savior narrative often underplays the role of this group in sparking displacement while overstating the corporatization impact of the developers. I conclude the chapter by exploring the professional and personal tensions faced by the savior group, who daily confront the dissonance of their high social status and democratic values.[3]

Durham, North Carolina

Located in central North Carolina, Durham County had an estimated population of 311,000 people in 2017, having grown by 15 percent since 2010 (US Census Bureau 2017). The city has gone through several periods of explosive growth and precipitous decline. Industrialization of the "bull city" was driven by the tobacco and textile industries in the nineteenth and early twentieth centuries, drawing workers from all over the South to jobs in factories and warehouses (Anderson 2011; Brown 2008). But Durham's undiversified economy left it vulnerable, and starting in the 1970s, these industries lost out to changing tastes and global competition. Factories were abandoned, shops closed, and a significant percentage of the population dispersed to the suburbs or further afield.

Despite the loss of industrial employment, regional economic growth was strong in industries such as education, health care, and technology. A large office park, the Research Triangle Park, was established in the 1950s and is home to companies such as IBM, GlaxoSmithKline, and

Lenovo. Duke and its vast medical facilities are also large drivers of jobs in the knowledge economy. Since the late 1990s, downtown redevelopment has been driven by a growth coalition composed of Duke University, Mayor Bill Bell (who retired in 2017 and was replaced by Council Member Steve Schewel) and the City Council, the County of Durham, banks, real estate developers, foundations, nonprofit organizations, and entrepreneurs. Redevelopment happened in fits and started during the 1990s and the first decade of the 2000s. Anchor projects like a new baseball stadium for the Durham Bulls minor league team and the adjacent mixed-use American Tobacco Campus were risky projects that brought together partners from the private and public sectors. While successful in attracting visitors, they had minimal spread effect through the city center. It wasn't until the latter part of the 2000s that the economic wealth in the area started to translate into downtown development. A creative class of residents and entrepreneurs has since been attracted to the city by a palpable sense of pride in the city's gritty character, renovated industrial architecture, and its "DIY" spirit. Along with inexpensive real estate, minimal business competition, a cooperative business environment, and help from the city and county, upscale businesses have blossomed. Historic industrial buildings that once housed thousands of middle-income jobs in tobacco are now loft condominiums, retail, and commercial space. Buildings that were either abandoned or occupied by retail focused on low-income patrons (for example, a discount furniture store and bail bonds) have evolved into the latest trendy restaurants.

The city is shedding its image among regional residents as dangerous and deserted. This characterization of the city was coded language that signified a large African American and low-income population in the central city. Durham is 47.9 percent white alone, 40.0 percent Black or African American alone, 5.1 percent Asian alone, and 13.9 percent Hispanic or Latinx in 2017 (US Census Bureau 2017). By contrast, the influx of new residents and the businesses that cater to them are mostly upper-income and white. Durham now sells itself as a hip city where restaurants and bars dominate the commercial streets, and affluent, predominantly white consumers feel welcome. As in other cities (see Hyra 2017; Zukin 1995, 2010), Durham's post-industrial decline is a point of pride among many of the city's residents and business owners. Urban grit is a marker of authenticity, in particular in contrast to the adjacent cities of Raleigh (seen as too corporate) and Chapel Hill (too college oriented). This ethos is exemplified in some of the slogans commonly seen on t-shirts and bumper stickers around town. For example, "Keep it dirty, Durham," which encourages city residents to respect and celebrate the gritty character of the city. And, "Durham: it's not for everyone," which signals that the city is not intended to appeal to corporate, suburban, and/or unimaginative people. In an ironic twist, this slogan can be reinterpreted to mean that Durham is not a comfortable or affordable space for people who do not fit into some of these same categories.

The transformation of downtown Durham has created and exacerbated a number of social problems, such as housing affordability, economic inequality, and loss of cultural "soul." Once known as the "capital of the Black middle class" (Frazier 1925:333), African American and Latinx communities have struggled to find a place in the new Durham. Displacement of existing businesses and the surge of new retail have changed the character of the city. Businesses that catered to lower-income people and people of color have mostly been priced out, replaced by stores and restaurants focusing exclusively on wealthy patrons. Additionally, median home prices in key neighborhoods have risen by 100 to 400 percent since 2005, causing gentrification and displacement of people of color and low-income populations (Norton 2015).

Durham's Food Scene

The Five Points Intersection is the nexus of the redeveloped downtown area and the heart of Durham's foodie culture. A short walk around this area will take you past some of these businesses and development projects: two tapas restaurants, three buildings under renovation, a newly completed 27-story office and condominium building, three boutique hotels, an expensive clothing store specializing in small-batch production labels, several bars, a pet boutique, a deli, an Italian restaurant, a sandwich shop specializing in Italian-influenced sandwiches, two upscale pizza places, two stores selling African clothing and objects, a vinyl record store, several culturally hybrid restaurants, a café that often offers jazz acts, a cocktail bar, an architect's office, a book store, and several other establishments. Each of these specializes in high-quality products, aimed at discerning consumers who are willing to pay high prices. By my estimate, all these businesses, with the exception of two or three, have opened since 2008.

The growth of restaurants in the central city (the so-called loop) has been exponential. There are twenty-six restaurants and the average year of opening is 2011, with a continued year-over-year increase in openings since then (City and County of Durham 2017). Restaurants were the first places of consumption that sprouted up in the downtown area. Durham's redevelopment has been driven by its wealthy residents' appetites, and the price points are well out of reach of lower-income Durhamites.

Durham's food scene follows along the gourmet characteristics outlined by Johnston and Baumann (2015): It aims to be authentic and exotic, blending "low-brow" and "high-brow" foods (Peterson and Kern 1996). Foods that were long held in contempt—such as hamburgers, macaroni and cheese, fried chicken, and other staples of American mass cooking—are slowly being embraced in fancier restaurants. Low-brow foods in gourmet restaurants might represent an ethos of tolerance and inclusion, as cultural elites celebrate the contributions of lower-status social groups. The description of the food at the high-priced restaurants in boutique Durham Hotel, operated by a James Beard Award–winning chef, captures this: "The fried chicken is less North Carolina than chic North Carolina hotel. Three iPhone-size pieces of boneless, dark, tender meat come with a beautifully bumpy, shattering crust, more like airy tempura than the standard sturdy coating.... It's not the Southern fried chicken an out-of-towner might expect" (Laperruque 2015). Indeed, the stereotypically greasy, heavy fried chicken is not to be found. Rather, it is updated with finer cooking techniques and locally sourced ingredients. Such adoption of low-brow foods into high-brow eateries involves the redefinition and reinterpretation of these foods, however, which undermines the idea that there is now a democratic celebration of different cooking traditions. Another observer explicitly states that food itself can be gentrified: "The Durham local food movement is a gentrified version of what used to be Southern food. And that culture is now lost. It's why we [Black communities] are not involved" (quoted in Bouloubasis 2016).

The process rids the food of its connection to the people and history. Yet, those who produce and consume this gentrified food still make a claim to the cachet of local history and authenticity. The food itself then parallels the redevelopment of the city, as the uses and meanings of old buildings and neighborhoods are being repurposed for new patterns of consumption.

Savior Entrepreneurs and Demon Developers

Upscale restaurants were the first to venture into the untested retail waters of Durham's city center, and food businesses are still opening regularly. In telling the origin stories of their businesses, the early wave of restaurateurs and bar owners consistently emphasize the high vacancy rate of downtown and the risk that meant for them: "Downtown was basically abandoned . . . no one hung around after 5pm" and put most simply: "There was just nothing here." These entrepreneurs had to renovate buildings, as nothing was available to rent that met the specific needs of gourmet kitchens. Their narratives, and those in the popular press, emphasize their plucky and entrepreneurial spirit, as they took major personal risks to bring fancy foods to Durham. I term them "savior entrepreneurs" because of their self-representation as saviors of a city that was in precipitous decline, their integral role in its rescue, and the risk they assumed by taking on this role. Food entrepreneurs, then, are not just in the business of food, they are in the business of being urban developers.

These entrepreneurs have a cosmopolitan life history, having lived in, trained in, or extensively traveled to other metropolitan areas (e.g., New York City, Boston, Washington, DC) from where they draw inspiration. They draw on their *cultural capital* to know what is popular and will generate interest in a city such as Durham that includes many people with a similar cultural background. Rather than creating new trends, they followed what they saw in other cities, in particular Brooklyn, New York, and Portland, Oregon, are often evoked. They took a risk in locating downtown but, having seen the success of their business models in other cities, they had some assurance that there was market demand. As one bar owner noted: "I wrote my business plan while sitting in a brewery in Portland. I already had the idea for the kind of brewery I wanted to open. But being in that neighborhood and seeing what they did . . ."

In this sense, Durham's food industry is not especially cutting edge. A bartender captured this when comparing the city to Brooklyn: "Durham is not Brooklyn *yet*. But we are going that way. Nothing in Durham is new. All of these things were happening 15 years ago in New York."

Restaurateurs and bar owners are keenly aware of the city's standing compared to other places. There is also anxiety about the need to catch up and keep up with other cities, as stated by a bar owner: "Portland is obviously further ahead [than Durham] in funkiness. We're a little behind. But, in five years we could be like them. We're a similar kind of city. We have the neighborhoods, for example."

The potential of Durham to move along a similar trajectory to places like Portland, Oregon, given its similar characteristics, was viewed as a cause for optimism and tempers the risk narrative. In addition, given the national trend of gentrification and the local growth coalition's push to revitalize downtown, it seems that their efforts had a good chance of showing a quick return. City government agencies have assisted them with various programs, such as grants and low-interest loans, help finding an appropriate space, permitting, licensing, tax reductions on historic properties, and streetscaping (sidewalks, street lighting, etc.), thereby mitigating the risk of locating in the downtown core.

Of all of Durham's neighborhoods undergoing redevelopment, Central Park is the most illustrative of the power of eateries and bars to generate new development and neighborhood transformation. It is just a 10-minute walk to downtown and prior to Durham's regeneration it was a lower-middle income neighborhood with many immigrant families from Latin America. It gained its moniker of "DIY" due to the influx of new homeowners and entrepreneurs who flooded the area after about 2008. These DIY-ers purchased inexpensive homes and fixed them up, using personal savings, loans, and sweat equity. One by one, restaurants, breweries, bars, fitness studios, a theater, an event space, and other businesses catering to affluent consumers popped up in the area. When the *New York Times* featured Durham in its "36 Hours" series, the restaurants and bars in this area figured prominently because they offered evidence of the city's "youth-driven renaissance" (Williams 2013). As many business owners purchased their buildings, they are not threatened by rising rents. Instead, they marvel, bemoan, and perhaps secretly congratulate themselves on the price increases. These homeowners and business owners are strongly wedded to the savior narrative, as they describe the run-down character of the neighborhood before their interventions, often claiming that there was "nothing there."

However, the "nothing there" narrative ignores the immigrants, people of color, and low-income residents who populated the neighborhood before the DIY trend. "Nothing there" really means that there was nothing there of interest to affluent, hip, and/or white consumers. Rather, retail in the area was sparse but included a well-trafficked Hispanic grocery store, a corner store, an immigrant-rights nonprofit organization, and several mechanics (the grocery store, nonprofit, and some of the mechanics have been displaced because of rising rents). The reality of residential and business displacement due to the influence of these saviors on rising rents, home values, and property taxes is routinely ignored in this narrative.

The success of the neighborhood in attracting a youthful crowd with disposable income soon appeared on the radar of real estate developers. The savior narrative of the local residents and entrepreneurs was quickly replaced by a narrative of "demon developers," whose capitalist intentions to make a profit on the neighborhood's hip reputation would quash the same quirky small businesses that made the area popular among white and affluent residents. The awareness among this group that they themselves had a gentrifying effect on the neighborhood is superseded by their self-valorization compared to the demon developers. Against this backdrop, Durham's most controversial re-development project, Liberty Warehouse, sits in one corner of the neighborhood. To Durhamites committed to the idea of Durham as a gritty and affordable counterculture city that honors its architectural history, Liberty Warehouse is a nightmare come true in concrete, steel, and glass.

Built in 1940, Liberty Warehouse was the central tobacco auction house, where each season farmers brought their tobacco crop hoping to reap the best price from buyers representing the major cigarette brands. The area had many warehouses and was also surrounded by banks, car dealerships, and retail outlets where farmers could both save and spend their earnings while visiting the city. Liberty Warehouse was a victim of the changing dynamics of the tobacco industry and auctions ended here in 1984. Starting in the 2000s, several artists and businesses rented space in the building, and the affordable and central location led to its rebirth as a hub of arts activity (Thomson 2017).

In 2006, the owner sold the warehouse to Greenfire Development, a local real estate development company that was actively renovating buildings for sale and rent throughout the central city. Greenfire, however, failed to maintain the structure and in 2011, the roof collapsed during a rainstorm, forcing the relocation of the artists and other tenants. For the next three years Greenfire left the building to rot. The building had historic preservation status, which caused considerable issues for the developer. They petitioned the city to get the designation removed so that they could sell the building to another developer, East-West Partners. East-West was a regional development company known for building mixed-use condominium buildings, and they wished to mostly demolish the structure to make way for such a project. It quickly became apparent that the pro-development city council was going to vote to remove the listing. The mayor said: "We've waited for three years and nothing has happened. My rationale before and my rationale now is to get something done" (quoted in Mihaylova 2013). Preservation Durham, the local historic preservation group, supported the change and entered into a Memorandum of Understanding with the developers that allowed them to have input in the design process.

Many neighborhood residents attended city council meetings in protest, as they felt the project would be a threat to the neighborhood's character. One resident said: "I moved here because I didn't want to live in a place like Woodcroft.[4] I love the Liberty Warehouse. I would probably give a finger to save it" (quoted in Ball 2014). Ball (2014) also cites the concerns of another resident, saying, "the developer's proposed Rigsbee Street façade looks more like Raleigh's ultra-commercial Glenwood South area than downtown Durham's gritty northside."[5] These preservationists were defending a particular notion of the neighborhood. In their view, the neighborhood they were protecting was the gritty one they had helped to create by renovating homes and starting businesses for mostly white and affluent customers. They were not making reference to the community that preceded their entry. The preservationists never give a nod to their privilege to choose to live in a gritty neighborhood or the power they possess (in terms of economic and cultural capital) to transform a neighborhood into their visions.

The developer attempted to assuage fears that the development would be an architecturally stale luxury complex, saying: "It will not be luxury

Figure 2.1. The new Liberty Warehouse with the "Drive-In" sign, which is the only remaining feature of the original structure. Photo by author.

housing but workforce housing for people working in and around downtown. Rent won't be extraordinarily high because the units will be small, local businesses would be tenants in the ground floor retail, and as much of the original structure as possible would be saved" (Ball 2014). Like many such developments, however, the resulting development deviated from the developer's promises. It opened in phases in 2016 and 2017 and took precisely the form that many of its opponents feared. Very little of the original building was preserved (one brick façade wall and some signage) and it does look much like the glass and concrete condominium buildings that were denigrated by residents. The 246-unit apartment building, with 24,000 square feet of retail space and a 391-space parking deck at its center, rents (in 2018) from about $1300 for a 600-square foot studio apartment to $3125 for a 2-bedroom 2-bath apartment (Liberty Warehouse n.d.).[6]

Much like Zukin's study of New York City, many residents have framed Liberty Warehouse as a question of the city's "soul." A comprehensive documentary film tracing the history of the development, *The Rise and Fall of Liberty*, summarizes this view: "When developers in Durham, North Carolina, demolish an iconic tobacco auction house in the name of revitalization, they not only displace a community of artists, they also threaten the soul of the community" (Thomson 2017). The developers of Liberty Warehouse, however, represent themselves as embodying that same soul:

> Liberty Warehouse is where Durham's soulful history and cultural future converge. From the many craft breweries, farm-to-table eateries and a vibrant nightlife anchored by the electric art community, this is the place to feel engaged and connected with friends, both new and old. Liberty is situated in a prime location in downtown Durham. You'll find restaurants, local shops, and even Dame's Chicken & Waffles and your very own Coffee House right below your new home. Explore the area and see why so many are calling Liberty Warehouse their new home! (www.liberty-warehouse.com)

Retail developments have been slow to move in, perhaps stemming from the stigma of the building. But, as the above quote says, the development features three local food businesses, a coffee shop, a restaurant, and a food hall with stalls from various chefs, giving it the feel of a gourmet market. Food halls are now a common part of many creative class cities (Arreortura and Gómez del Campo 2018). The expressed fears of corporate developers quashing local businesses then seems overblown. Rather, a new source of retail space is leading more local restaurants to expand. This may be a real advantage for food entrepreneurs: They can be in the business of serving food rather than being urban saviors. Further, a growing customer base of people living in the neighborhood could be a boon, as one local retailer noted: "These changes are happening, and we want to be here. It will infuse a whole new life here. More people isn't going to affect us in a negative way. We just have to make the moves so we can afford higher rent" (quoted in Sorg 2015). And, as the quote highlights, affordability then becomes the key issue for businesses (always a contentious problem), rather than the concern around "soul."

The initial wave of savior residential and commercial gentrification led to the displacement of lower-income people of color, though this

Figure 2.2. Local vendors will be featured at the new Durham Food Hall in Liberty Warehouse, though vacant retail space remains. Photo by author.

displacement is rarely recognized. An article from *Indy Week* described it this way: "For newcomers who see the vibrant neighborhood's array of nightclubs, restaurants and distilleries, it may seem unthinkable, but not long ago, this neighborhood was a derelict, forgotten corner of downtown" (Sorg 2015). Forgotten by whom? The answer seems to be, the affluent of the city who now frequent it as part of their leisure consumption. Surely, it was not forgotten by the immigrants, people of color, and low-income populations who lived and worked there. The vocal defenders of Liberty Warehouse were extrapolating to a larger defense of Durham as "dirty," artistic, and community-oriented. They were defending a community they had created whereby the "authentic" and gritty character of the neighborhood was what made it special. The real threat of Liberty Warehouse and similar developments, according to this group, lies in its threat to the ability of this community to continue to build Durham in its own image rather than the image of the developers.

Conclusion

Many savior entrepreneurs view their hard work as serving to rescue areas from neglect and create an affluent clientele that appreciate the creative and quirky nature of local businesses, though this paves the way for demon developers to profit. The savior entrepreneurs and preservationists in Central Park and similar neighborhoods are also profit-motivated, but their relationship to profit is more complicated. They have clearly benefited from the restaurant-oriented redevelopment of the city, but they espouse a community ethic that they present as oppositional to the profit motive. My findings are similar to Brown-Saracino's (2009), who points out the different subjectivities of gentrifiers, in particular the "social preservationists" and "homesteaders" who recognize (to varying degrees) the downsides of gentrification. They see themselves as defenders of the values that make Durham special, and they see themselves as under threat from the development process they partially set in motion, yet they also recognize the negative effects of housing and retail gentrification on more marginalized populations. Nevertheless, because they "saved" the neighborhood from neglect, they rarely take personal responsibility for their role in gentrification. Rather, they attribute this negative role to demon developers. This energy was directed politically in the 2017 mayoral and city council elections. The six council seats and mayor are now held by people who all identify as "progressive" and motivated by social justice, and five are people of color.

The savior entrepreneur has a global awareness of social and political issues and highly values inclusion, tolerance, and diversity. It is a socio-spatial community of consumers and producers who have a self-perception of being creative and non-conformist. Their values are informed by global trends that exist alongside consumption that is driven by local loyalty and pride. In the case of Durham, they are conflicted because they share anxiety about the loss of the gritty and alternative identity of the city that gave it its "soul." In the face of gentrification, urban redevelopment, and the reality of segregated neighborhoods, they find it difficult to live their values of diversity and inclusion. They have a high level of anxiety that businesses are not diverse enough and that "diverse people" (read people of color) people are not participating in the businesses and communities where they live and work.

In gourmet restaurants this comes through most obviously in menus that feature fair, local, and organic foods. But it also comes through in the ways that food writers, chefs, and patrons discuss the role of restaurants and food in the development of the city. One food writer explicitly makes the connections between the urban social problems of the city and the fancy food served in the restaurants of the boutique hotel, The Durham:

> If a hotel is a transitory space where people never stay too long, the true challenge of its restaurant is not winning over guests but locals. Against a veil of socioeconomic concerns about gentrification and strata of race, class and privilege in the city, The Durham's restaurants are at least standing on their own merits, attempting to welcome locals with food that doesn't clash so much with its surroundings.

The author raises a central problem: They wish to continue to produce and consume this high-status food, but how can they feel okay about that when they are surrounded by a city that is plagued by inequalities? Despite the awareness of social problems, savior entrepreneurs give limited voice to how their own actions cause retail or residential gentrification. When asked if the bars and restaurants in Durham were becoming pretentious, one business owner said: "I can see how someone might say that but they kind of just don't get it. I know that sounds bad! But, we're trying to be creative and put our spin on things." While the awareness and anxiety about residential and retail gentrification is forefront in many minds, understanding how the spread of gourmet restaurants and bars is contributing to the problem of racial and income exclusion is rarely discussed. And, as much as concern is expressed, gourmet restaurants with $25 entrees continue to populate Durham.

NOTES

1 Food can be understood as a social construct, whereby it is used to express identities such as class, nationality, ethnicity, and gender. Food behavior, such as what people eat, who prepares it, when and where it is eaten, and the reason for its consumption, are all expressions of shared cultural values.
2 Raleigh (a 20-minute drive from Durham) was on Amazon's short list of candidate cities.
3 The data for this research are drawn from a series of twenty-six interviews with restaurant and bar owners, staff at these establishments, elected officials on the

Durham city council, and leaders of nonprofit organizations, conducted during the spring and summer of 2017. These semi-structured interviews covered a wide range of topics and here I draw on information that focuses on the nexus of food-based entrepreneurship and Durham's "revitalization" (here defined as the transition from a deindustrialized city to a "creative city"). I also draw on newspaper articles and websites that focus on the food culture of Durham. Data on food establishments, locations, and dates of opening were gathered from a City and County database. I also collected information from the menus of a random selection of restaurants located within the city center in order to determine prices and food offerings. Admittedly, these research methods were paired with my own extensive patronage of restaurants and bars.

4 A large suburban neighborhood known for its sprawling and homogenous built environment.
5 Durhamites often belittle Raleigh as being "corporate" and "conservative" and having a skyline dominated by glass and steel high-rise buildings.
6 In May 2017: East-West Partners sold Liberty Warehouse to an affiliate of Duck Pond Realty, located in Melville, New York. They own several other high-end apartment communities in the Triangle. At that time, the building was estimated to have 60 percent residential occupancy. The sale represents the increasing interest in Durham by developers located outside the region.

REFERENCES

Anderson, Jean Bradley. 2011. *Durham County: A History of Durham County, North Carolina* (2nd ed.). Durham, NC: Duke University Press.

Arreortura, Luis Alberto Salinas, and Luz de Lourdes Cordero Gómez del Campo. 2018. "Gourmet Markets as a Commercial Gentrification Model: The Cases of Mexico City and Madrid." In Sara González, ed., *Contested Markets, Contested Cities*. London: Routledge.

Badger, Emily, Quoctrung Bui, and Claire Cain Miller. 2017. "Dear Amazon, We Picked Your New Headquarters for You." *New York Times*, September 9. www.nytimes.com.

Ball, Bill. 2014. "Historic Liberty Warehouse to Be Demolished; Condos and Store to Replace It." *IndyWeek*, January 29.

Bouloubasis, Victoria. 2016. "Famed Nigerian Chef Tunde Wey Stirs Up a Conversation about Race and Food That Was Already Simmering in Durham." *IndyWeek*, December 21.

Brown, Leslie. 2008. *Upbuilding Black Durham: Gender, Class, and Black Community Development in the Jim Crow South*. Chapel Hill: University of North Carolina Press.

Brown-Saracino, Japonica. 2009. *A Neighborhood that Never Changes: Gentrification, Social Preservation, and the Search for Authenticity*. Chicago: University of Chicago Press.

City and County of Durham. 2017. "Restaurant and Services." https://live-durhamnc.

Florida, Richard. 2002. *The Rise of the Creative Class: And How It's Transforming Work, Leisure, Community, and Everyday Life*. New York: Basic Books.

Frazier, Franklin E. 2015 (reprint 1925). "Durham: Capital of the Black Middle-Class." In Alain Locke, ed., *The New Negro: An Interpretation*. Eastford, CT: Martino Fine Books.

Hyra, Derek. 2017. *Race, Class, and Politics in the Cappuccino City*. Chicago: University of Chicago Press.

Johnston, Josée, and Shyon Baumann. 2015. *Foodies: Democracy and Distinction in the Gourmet Foodscape* (2nd ed.). New York: Routledge.

Laperruque, Emma. 2015. "The Durham Hotel May Raise Uncomfortable Questions, but the Food Sure Feels Good." *IndyWeek*, November 25.

Liberty Warehouse. n.d. https://livelibertywarehouse.com.

Mihaylova, Raia. 2013. "Liberty Warehouse's Historic Landmark Designation Removed; Building to Be Sold and Redeveloped." *IndyWeek*, May 22.

Norton, Melissa. 2015. Data Cited in Lisa Sorg, "Take 5: Durham's Gentrification Challenge." *The News & Observer*, November 3, www.newsobserver.com.

Peterson, Richard A., and Roger M. Kern. 1996. "Changing Highbrow Taste: From Snob to Omnivore." *American Sociological Review* 61: 900–907.

Sorg, Lisa. 2015. "Old Durham Meets New Durham." *IndyWeek*, July 29, www.indyweek.com.

Thomson, Carol. 2017. *The Rise and Fall of Liberty* [Film]. United States: FireStream Media, LLC. www.libertywarehousefilm.com.

US Census Bureau. 2017. "QuickFacts: Durham City, North Carolina, Durham County, North Carolina." www.census.gov.

Williams, Ingrid K. 2013. "36 hours in Durham, N.C." *New York Times*, January 17, www.nytimes.com.

Zukin, Sharon. 1995. *The Culture of Cities*. Cambridge: Blackwell.

Zukin, Sharon. 2010. *Naked City: The Death and Life of Authentic Urban Spaces*. Oxford: Oxford University Press.

3

Making Sense of "Local Food," Urban Revitalization, and Gentrification in Oklahoma City

Eric Sarmiento

Critical scholars in urban geography and related fields have long studied the roles played in gentrification by cultural actors such as artists and art galleries, boutique shops, and restaurants and cafes (Deutsch and Ryan 1984; Ley 1980; Zukin 1981). Little of this work, however, examines the implications for food systems of the relationship between gentrification and alternative food networks (AFNs). Two notable exceptions to this are Julie Guthman's (2003) study of the restructuring of the organic salad mix industry in conjunction with gentrifying real estate markets in northern California, and Lucy Jarosz's (2008) work on urbanization and rural restructuring. These studies reveal that the AFN-gentrification interface may benefit some producers, but these benefits are tenuous due to two factors: the broader structure of agribusiness-dominated conventional food systems, and the larger political economic shifts within which gentrification has occurred, specifically the transition to post-Fordism, in which the food-conscious consumers colonizing gentrifying areas represent only a small, privileged fraction of the population. These studies, viewed alongside extensive research on gentrification and work that demonstrates the exclusive, classed, and racialized tendencies of AFNs (e.g., Alkon 2008; Guthman 2008; Slocum 2007; Watts, Ilbery, and Maye 2005), suggest the need for further study of the social and political implications of the AFN-gentrification interface, and call into question whether or not this interface could serve as a mechanism by which socially and ecologically oriented food initiatives might grow.

In this chapter, I contribute to these discussions in the form of a case study of the linkages between the local food movement in the state of Oklahoma and a period of urban revitalization in Oklahoma City. I argue that these two processes began largely independently of one another but became increasingly linked over time. I focus on the impacts of these linkages on the local food movement, ultimately concluding that while some well-situated local food producers benefited from their engagement with revitalization, the movement overall has been negatively affected by this relationship for several reasons. First, in concentrating on the expanding "creative class" of Oklahoma City, the movement has drifted away—*partly* as an intentional survival strategy—from the thicker engagements with social justice, economic development, and transforming food systems and food subjectivities that characterized the movement in its early years. Moreover, I argue that this drift has entailed a concomitant change in the meaning of *local food* itself, from a mechanism for political ecological change to a mostly fetishized, "feel-good" specialty product in a niche market for well-heeled consumers. Sapped of much of their early social and political ecological significance, the local food products offered by the movement have become less distinguishable from corporate mobilizations of fetishized local foods, which has made the movement more vulnerable to cooptation. At the same time, the local food movement has played an instrumental role in re-signifying spaces of the city targeted by revitalization efforts, some of which have undergone or are undergoing gentrification and displacement of lower-income residents and residents of color.

This account is drawn from ten months of fieldwork in Oklahoma, in addition to a number of preliminary and follow-up visits, examining the development of the local food movement, focusing in particular on the movement's links to urban revitalization.[1] To understand what has occurred in Oklahoma City, I draw on a theoretical approach known as assemblage thinking. In particular, I mobilize the Deleuzo-Guattarian notion of *territorialization*. Briefly stated, territorialization is the process through which a given arrangement of power relations—an *assemblage*—takes shape, empowering some suites of actors and enabling their control of space at the expense of others (Deleuze and Guattari 1987). This is a processual, practice-oriented approach to understanding the social production of space, centered around the idea that successfully constructing a durable territory requires conjoining the materials that constitute space and specific meanings or values. This in turn requires the enrollment of a range of actors in support of particular framings of or meanings accorded to space. In the case study below, for example, I demonstrate how the growing territory of urban revitalization depended in part on enrolling the local food movement in resignifying certain urban spaces, which in turn both required and facilitated a transformation in the meaning or value of the object *local food*.[2]

Before Revitalization and Local Food in Oklahoma City

Following an oil bust and a major banking collapse in the early 1980s, Oklahoma City experienced economic stagnation and scant investment in the built environment of the central city throughout the 1980s and into the 1990s. An economic impact assessment of revitalization commissioned by the city in 2003 described the inner city during the 1990s as constituted by four "quasi-separate economies," one based on oil and gas, legal services, and government employment, one based on healthcare, one based on entertainment and leisure, and one that the report called the "Low Socioeconomic Status Economy (SES)" (Warner 2003). The report notes that, with the exception of several long-standing wealthy communities north of the central business district (CBD), "the residents of the study area generally have relatively low incomes, low levels of educational attainment, and live in low-value housing units. Particularly in the southwestern part of the study is a concentration of homeless individuals at virtually the lowest level of SES" (Warner 2003:7). The prevalence of socioeconomically marginalized residents in the inner city resulted from decades of "white flight," the concentration of capital investment in the expanding suburbs, and urban renewal initiatives that razed many inner-city areas (Sarmiento 2015). While manufacturing was never a major part of the city's economic base, industrial activity had also declined by the 1990s, leaving a number of vacant manufacturing facilities and warehouses throughout the central city, especially in the area south of the CBD identified by the economic impact assessment as home to a concentration of homeless residents. This was the context in which the 1993 bombing of the Murrah Federal Building occurred, leaving a substantial gash in the urban fabric of the CBD. That December, voters approved the Metropolitan Area Projects Plan (MAPs), the first of a series of ambitious revitalization initiatives led by city government in conjunction with private sector actors. This plan in many respects follows a now-standard approach to redevelopment aimed at luring a more educated workforce to the city, which city officials viewed as essential to attracting and retaining the big businesses understood as fundamental to economic development. Members of "the creative class" would be drawn to the city by "quality of life" improvements (Florida 2014), particularly in the city's core.

In the early 2000s, as revitalization was gathering steam in Oklahoma City, *local food* scarcely existed in the state of Oklahoma. To be sure, an abundance of commodity crops was produced each year in the state, but the vast majority of this production departed the state and entered national and international networks of processing, marketing, and consumption. Alongside these crops foods continued to be consumed within a short radius of their production, from the backyard gardens that remain common to small farms selling their products at roadside stands and in farmers' markets. But these foods, prized as they may have been by gardeners and patrons of farmers' markets, did not tend to generate widespread enthusiasm, incite visions of fundamentally transforming food systems, or command premium prices under the name *local food*. This would change in the early years of the new millennium.

The Oklahoma Food Cooperative and the Emergence of *Local Food*

In 2003, just as interest in locally grown food was rising across the United States and abroad, a resident of Oklahoma City named Bob Waldrop gathered together a handful of producers and several dozen customers and formed the Oklahoma Food Cooperative (OFC), an enterprise that would sell only food items produced within the state's boundaries.[3] This enterprise expanded rapidly, and by 2013 the cooperative had nearly 5,000 members and handled approximately $750,000 annually.

Through the efforts of the OFC, local food began to be understood by a growing number of Oklahomans as distinct from and preferable to other foods for several broad reasons. Being produced and/or processed within the state's boundaries, local food entailed fewer *food miles* in its travels from producers to consumers; it was fresher and therefore considered tastier and more nutritious; and it kept money circulating within the state, rather than going to distant industrial growers and corporate processors. Beyond these basic attributes, however, the

OFC also initially framed local food around the group's "core values"—environmental stewardship, social justice, and economic sustainability—and insisted that these three values must be balanced in order to create a just and sustainable relocalized food system (see Sarmiento 2015 for further discussion).

I'll highlight two important points about how OFC members practiced and understood these values. First, members typically acknowledged that social justice was the core value least clearly understood in the group, that generated the most disagreements, and was least successfully put into practice. This distinction would become more pronounced over time. But despite divergent understandings of social justice, leadership tended to emphasize a producer-centered notion of justice, foregrounding that the cooperative provided an avenue through which small, environmentally oriented producers might be able to survive in a political economic context that is stacked against them.[4] Questions of consumer access and inclusivity were more contentious in the group, however, a point that I return to below.

Second, while there was considerable variation and interpretation among members of the precise meaning of each core value and how it should be practiced, such diversity in perspectives was explicitly held by some of the founders as a resource in the group's collective development, rather than an obstacle. Members who had been involved with the OFC from early on often used the term "evolution" as they talked about how membership influenced their opinions, shopping habits, and production practices. This evolutionary approach was built into the enterprise in that both food producers and consumers could be owner-members, an extremely unusual ownership structure. In spite of advice to the contrary, Waldrop and other founding members rejected assumptions that producers and consumers hold opposing interests. Rather, they adopted a discourse based on "mutual benefit," part of which involved personal and collective development through the ongoing negotiation of divergent political and social beliefs. Examples of this ranged from changing food consumption habits to becoming more tolerant of and in some cases supportive of different religious beliefs, sexualities, and personal lifestyle choices. In Waldrop's words (interview, 2009), "the conservative fundamentalist Baptist would actually be willing to shake hands with the lesbian Wiccan, as long as it was over a bag of locally grown carrots."

Following that logic, the OFC maintained an atmosphere in the early years in which the group's three core values were often invoked and deployed as devices to shape debates among members on a range of topics. Leadership held frequent discussions, for example, about what exactly made a product *local* and therefore admissible for sale through the cooperative, and these discussions often revolved around the meaning and practice of environmental stewardship and economic sustainability.

In sum, the OFC in its initial years of operation attempted to balance environmental, economic, and social justice concerns, and it relied on the diversity of political and social beliefs and positionalities of members to serve as an engine for personal and collective transformation. Given the cooperative's strong influence on the early development of what would eventually be called the local food movement in Oklahoma, these characteristics were key elements of what defined local food as it emerged into broader public awareness beyond the cooperative's membership. As the OFC expanded and a broader local food movement took shape, however, the OFC's framing of local food would be drawn into a different set of rationales and values, those associated with revitalization in Oklahoma City.

Catering to the "Creative Class" in Revitalizing Oklahoma City

In the years following the OFC's founding, several enterprises related to local food opened, particularly in Oklahoma City and Tulsa. These included small retail shops, farm-to-fork restaurants, community-supported agriculture operations, food processing firms, a restaurant distributor, and a local food and small farm lobbying group. Many of these emerged from the OFC, and members generally regarded the expansion of the local food movement as desirable and something the OFC should support. Earth Elements Bakery and Kitchen, for example, sold their local food-based processed products through the OFC for years, and eventually partnered with local food distributor Urban Agrarian to open a separate business called Earth to Urban, which combined food processing, retail, and a commercial kitchen. Moreover, the Department of Agriculture, Food, and Forestry was actively promoting its "Buy Fresh, Buy Local" campaign, and the number of farmers' markets operating in state had expanded considerably. Together, the growing array of local food enterprises began to build the infrastructural network required to make a relocalized food system a logistical possibility, from production to processing to distribution to retail (Beckie, Kennedy, and Wittman 2012; Bloom and Hinrichs 2011). While still a small fraction of food markets in the state, some variant of local foods now represented a large enough market to meaningfully impact the livelihoods of dozens of producers. USDA data show that, following a relatively stable period between 1982 and 2002, direct sales in Oklahoma rose markedly from 2002 to 2007, jumping from about $2 million to $11.5 million (National Agricultural Statistics Service 2014). This growth can be attributed to a number of factors: Local food enterprises gradually cultivated collaborative relationships with state agencies, interest in local food was rising nationally, and many of the small farmers and owner-operators of local food enterprises and their employees simply labored hard for years to build a market for local foods (Sarmiento 2015). But in addition to these factors, the relationship between local food and revitalization in Oklahoma City proved to be particularly important in shaping the movement.

By the late 2000s, when the local food movement was at its peak, the third MAPs initiative had been approved by voters, and much of the central city had been transformed by massive reinvestments, both public and private. Buildings were renovated, long-neglected infrastructure was upgraded, and a flurry of new construction brought high-end mixed-use developments and sports and entertainment venues, a downtown canal, an expansive city park, a trolley system, and so on. This strategy has benefited the city by transforming swathes of the built environment, retaining and attracting more educated workers with higher earning power, and creating a sense of pride in place for some city residents (Sarmiento 2015, 2018).

Several aspects of revitalization have also come under critique, a point I return to below, but for the moment I'll note that as part of their efforts to attract the creative class, proponents of revitalization, including a number of large fossil fuel companies headquartered in the city, mobilized specialty foods to resignify certain urban spaces (see figure 3.1). The most obvious example of this is the central role played by natural gas giant Chesapeake Energy in bringing Whole Foods Market to the city (Bustillo 2012), providing them with a favorable offer on rental property

Figure 3.1. A Central Oklahoma City restaurant featuring locally raised beef. Photo by author.

directly across the street from Chesapeake's headquarters on the north side of the metro area. Chesapeake's CEO asserted that Whole Foods' arrival "validates the revitalization we have experienced in Oklahoma City in the past 10 years" (Bustillo 2012), and "signifies a major step forward in our vision to create the most vibrant and dynamic urban environment for our employees and neighbors to live, work and play in Oklahoma" (Lackmeyer 2010). Chesapeake also built an "Employee Garden" on its corporate campus, where staff could spend a few hours each week during the workday gardening, using organic methods, and earning credits toward an employee wellness program. Devon Energy, another top five natural gas producer in the United States, included a gourmet restaurant featuring some local offerings near the top of its recently built office tower. One journalist dubbed the expansion of the city's foodscapes "the Whole Foods effect," noting, "local, organic and high-quality foods never had it so good in these parts" (Cathey 2011).

Several enterprises linked to the local food movement were instrumental in the makeover of the city's foodscapes. Native Roots Market, for example, was highly sought after by the new urbanist developers, who felt that this retail outlet would help to anchor new upscale housing (cf. Lackmeyer 2011). An initiative called Better Block OKC, which installs and performs a temporary redeveloped vision of a disinvested city block each year, chose sites in 2012 and 2013 that were centered around local food businesses. One of these sites was a building called the Farmers Public Market, a historic structure in and around which a few local food enterprises relocated in 2012–14. These firms included Earth to Urban, the local food lobbying firm the Oklahoma Food and Farm Alliance, and the OFC's distribution center, among others. In Deleuzo-Guattarian terms, such enrollments of specialty foods in reframing the inner city as a place in which the creative class would desire to "live, work, and play"—to use a phrase often deployed in Florida-inspired approaches to revitalization—were crucial to the expansion and stabilization of the growing territory of revitalization. But what did this mean for the local food movement?

There were elements of the relationship between revitalization and the local food movement that might be viewed as symbiotic. While city boosters and revitalization proponents deployed local food and other specialty foods in their quest to attract the creative class, several enterprises linked to the local food movement also clearly saw the expansion of the city's educated and relatively affluent population as an opportunity. Most OFC sales and growth in membership occurred in Oklahoma City and Tulsa, and most of the businesses specializing in Oklahoma-grown food more broadly are located in these cities' wealthier areas.

Furthermore, most producers who focused on local markets developed low-volume production approaches that sought to maximize prices, so targeting these more affluent customers made sense with their business models. The OFC itself gradually came to focus on the creative class, a strategy expressed in a range of contexts, from board meetings to several of my interviews with members. As one example, a general manager of the OFC described the dynamic in the following terms: "We've had to appeal to like, 'this is a specialty grocery' kind of thing and get those customers that can spend a lot of money to get us going." Similarly, Waldrop stated in a 2014 email to the Board of Directors: "I think we should concentrate on the 'educated, high discretionary income, environmentally aware' market segment."[5] This was partly a reflection of the long-standing emphasis on small producers in the OFC's understanding of social justice; from this perspective, focusing on the creative class in search of premium prices seemed to be more pressing than questions of accessibility, particularly given the negative impacts on the local food movement as the object *local food* was drawn into the assemblage of revitalization, to which I now turn.

Stasis: Cooptation and Fetishization

While there is no doubt that the market for some variant of local food expanded in Oklahoma City, producers were also keenly aware that only a few, particularly well-positioned local food producers were benefiting substantially from this expansion. The case of Whole Foods Market is instructive here: My discussions with several different types of local producers about their relations with Whole Foods suggest that a range of outcomes are possible, but in order for producers to reap a profit, their business model must be based on, or at least capable of, generating volumes of product sufficient to produce profits from a small margin. This is not the type of model that many local food businesses have developed, which tends to be based more on fetching premium prices for specialty products. As such, these enterprises generally must restructure their business or be excluded from volume-oriented larger markets, which include specialty supermarkets like Whole Foods as well as the conventional supermarkets that command the lion's share of the retail market. Returning to USDA data, it's worth noting that while direct sales increased markedly in Oklahoma between 2002 and 2007, they declined in the 2007–2012 period, dropping back down to $7.6 million. This observed trend correlates with the perspectives of many of the individual producers with whom I interacted, who frequently noted the increasingly challenging nature—for small producers—of the market for local foods. While my research did not specifically explore the issue, it is possible that the decline in direct sales represents the shift toward a larger portion of locally produced food items passing through supermarkets and other retail outlets, rather than through farmers' markets and other direct sale avenues. In any case, in the eyes of some smaller producers, this shift was associated with the entry of large corporate actors into the market for local foods.

Moreover, the expansion of the market for local foods also entailed major shifts in the meanings associated with the object *local food*. Whole Foods stocks its stores with only a handful of locally sourced products, a marginal percentage of its overall offerings.[6] But the company commissioned a 10-acre corn maze on a farm just outside Oklahoma City that read "Whole Foods Know Your Farmer, Know Your Food," attempting to latch on to growing enthusiasm for local food. Even McDonald's rolled out a marketing campaign implying that their products were in some way local, with the tagline, "Oklahoma bred, Oklahoma fed." This "Oklahoma bred" food turned out to be sausage biscuits that were indeed produced in an industrial processing facility located in eastern Oklahoma, but that also provided sausage biscuits for McDonald's outlets across the Southeastern region. Foods such as these being marketed as *local* shared a fetishized approach to localness, reducing its definition to being produced in some measure in the state, thereby eliding any meaningful engagement with the social justice and economic elements of these foods' provenance (Gunderson 2014).

That such foods were presenting themselves as *local* was profoundly worrying and frustrating to many who had worked for a decade to build very different visions of the local food movement, particularly within the OFC. One OFC member for example, referring to the Sunflower Farmers Market, a national supermarket chain that in 2011 opened a store in Oklahoma City, said in an interview, "if a business [. . .] is able to call itself a 'farmers' market' and is not in any way a farmers' market [. . .] that's a big threat to a real farmers' market. [. . .] I think that's really wrong. It's beyond false advertising, it's like straight-up lying." Many of my interviewees mentioned competition with such corporate retailers as a significant threat to the local food movement. "They have really wrecked my business a whole bunch," according to one small farmer who focused on selling locally. This farmer then went on to echo a common concern voiced by my participants, the sense that most Oklahomans do not understand the significant differences, in terms of farmer livelihoods and environmental impacts, between the products offered at an ostensibly *green* supermarket and those sold directly from farmers or through enterprises selling only Oklahoma-grown food: "The problem with Sunflower Market, I can swear to you that 80 percent of the people who walk into that store think they're helping Oklahoma's agriculture and they're helping farmers. They're doing everything but that." This purported lack of understanding on the part of consumers, in conjunction with efforts at cooptation by and competition from corporate retailers, were frequently invoked by my participants as some of the central challenges facing the movement. By 2014, when Waldrop suggested that the OFC focus on the creative class, the cooperative was no longer expanding and was in financial trouble. In that context, Waldrop's recommendation was more of a stopgap measure than a long-term vision. And this period of crisis was not limited to the OFC; Earth to Urban was struggling to stay afloat, the local food lobbying firm had scaled back its efforts, and the state's food policy council had fizzled out.

But this was not solely a matter of being outcompeted by corporate cooptation. The values associated with *local food* had also changed since the OFC's initial framing in 2003. Consider that all of the small, locally owned enterprises that splintered off from the OFC abandoned cooperative ownership in favor of capitalist ownership structures, i.e., owner-operator businesses with hourly employees. It's important to note that several of the business owners I interviewed decided to eschew a cooperative structure after laboring for years in the OFC, often in leadership roles, and feeling burned out and frustrated by their inability to direct the enterprise. In other words, the democratic governance structure of the OFC was, for these members, a wearying downside of the cooperative, and ultimately limited its potential. Even founder Bob Waldrop told me in 2011 that the cooperative, riven with internal power struggles and divergent views on a range of subjects, had reached the limits of the positive transformative power of difference. Nevertheless, by abandoning democratic governance structures and collective ownership, the businesses that splintered off from the OFC contributed to the shift toward a fetishized notion of local food, i.e., one in which social values were reduced to invocations of "community" and "supporting local farmers."

Even *within* the OFC, there was a notable drift away from social justice and deeper economic development concerns, alongside a gradual erosion of member participation in the firm's governance. This drift was expressed in numerous ways, and was partly an intentional, explicit decision, as noted earlier in reference to focusing on the "creative class" (see Sarmiento 2015, ch. 3). This partly reflected the OFC's long-standing emphasis on producers in their approach to social justice. However, this also involved shelving a long-standing debate in the cooperative about accepting EBT and other public assistance programs, one of the ways the OFC had long sought to make their food more accessible to lower-income Oklahomans.[7] This came at the end of a lengthy discussion among board members surrounding the best usage of a marketing grant that the OFC applied for, in which some members favored closing delivery sites around the state to focus primarily on the Oklahoma City and Tulsa sites, as these accounted for the vast majority of sales, while Waldrop and others wanted to use part of the grant money to pay for the costs associated with becoming certified to accept food stamps. The grant application was denied, and the board was left to deliberate about the best way to move forward in a situation of declining revenue. As one producer put it during this discussion:

> Speaking for myself, I am not willing to raise my prices on the off chance that an EBT recipient may buy a dozen eggs from me when I know that they can get a dozen eggs at CVS for 99 cents. If we are currently losing some of the membership due to high prices, why do we think EBT recipients are eager to shop with us? [. . .] People with a limited food budget are going to look for the best deals they can get and make their food dollars stretch as far as possible. The Coop is not a cheap place to shop nor is it a viable alternative with Wal-Mart.[8]

Questions of access and affordability—an issue for AFNs in general—loom particularly large in Oklahoma, which has the highest rate of hunger in the United States, and where the occurrence of diet-related illnesses and the rates of poverty and household food insecurity are significantly higher than the national averages (McDermott 2006). A number of members have recognized that social justice must also include access and inclusivity; in this sense, abandoning the effort to be able to accept public assistance vouchers represented an impoverishment of the cooperative's commitment to justice. And this decision was part of a broader shift away from social justice concerns in the OFC that was perhaps less intentional, but nevertheless pervasive. For example, the introductory orientation and training required of new customer- and producer-members have increasingly de-emphasized the meaning and practice of core values and cooperative principles. This is evidenced in the training materials themselves, including several documents distributed to new members and, in more recent years, videos posted on YouTube, which do not emphasize the core values or mention the importance of democratic participation in cooperative governance. I conducted a focus group in 2012 with several OFC members and personnel from Whole Foods, in which it became apparent that some of the Whole Foods employees held a more informed, nuanced understanding of cooperative ownership and governance than some of the OFC members present. By 2016, one OFC board member noted the shift away from social justice in plain terms in an email to the board, lamenting the cooperative's lost "social justice perspective, which," she wrote, "I don't think we mention anymore."[9]

Furthermore, the local food movement's instrumental role in revitalization—and especially the complicity of some enterprises with gentrification—further contributed to the changing significance of local food. The benefits of revitalization discussed above are highly uneven in their spatial and social distribution, with large sections of the city receiving little to no direct investment, notably the east side of the city, which is predominantly African American, and south side, where a concentration of Latinx residents live. Sections of the inner city have also been impacted by gentrification and displacement (Sarmiento 2015; Tierney and Petty 2015). A report commissioned by the city government makes no secret of this, noting "the natural tendency [is for low-income residents] to be crowded out of the area as new or remodeled housing is substituted for low-value units. This process of gentrification may only displace a problem population to other neighborhoods within the city" (Warner 2003). One gentrified neighborhood, Deep Deuce, even celebrates its history as a formerly African American neighborhood with plaques placed around the now relatively wealthy and predominantly white new urbanist development. Anita Arnold (2010:125), a popular historian of this neighborhood, describes the outcome of neighborhood change:

> The change was complete for Deep Deuce [in 2003 . . .]. People drove through Second Street to see the remake of the historic street, occasionally dropping in to look at the hanging pictures of jazz legends at the welcome center. Someone else's dream was taking place, and the realization of that sank deeply into the hearts and minds of those who remembered a different Second Street.

Given that local food enterprises have played a role in resignifying several inner-city spaces, including Deep Deuce, complicity with gentrification and displacement is arguably another way in which the local food movement's early engagements with social justice have diminished.

So, what were the characteristics of the object *local food* once it was drawn into the assemblage of revitalization? The object that emerged from this transformative process was defined primarily by its production within the state's boundaries, the significance of which was framed in terms of reduced food miles, individual health benefits, taste and freshness, and helping local, small farmers. But there is no linear sequence of cause and effect in the relationship between local food and revitalization. Instead, this *feel-good* framing of local food was driven in part by the corporate food actors that entered the market and the deployment of specialty foods by proponents of revitalization, in part by the enterprises that followed in the wake of the OFC, and in part by the OFC itself as leadership changed alongside the market conditions within which the enterprise operated. In my view, cooptation and market pressure by promoters of fetishized *local foods* fed into the OFC's producer-centered notion of social justice, even as the OFC and other enterprises struggling to survive in a market stacked against them were lured by premium prices to concentrate on the creative class. Mostly eclipsed along the way, however, were engagements with social justice, economic development, democratic participation, and individual/collective transformation that characterized the early OFC's framing of local food.

Conclusion: Following Lines of Flight toward Alternate Futures

In this chapter, I have demonstrated that, while urban revitalization in Oklahoma City helped to expand the market for local foods, the object *local food* was itself transformed in the process. Initially linked to goals of fundamentally transforming food systems to make them more just, environmentally friendly engines of local economic development and vehicles for individual and collective becoming, *local foods* in the territory of revitalization came to signify healthy living, taste and freshness, environmental concerns decoupled from questions of economic relationships, and helping small farmers with little explicit consideration for the political economic realities structuring food markets or access to healthy food. In this sense, the case of the local food movement's partnership with revitalization in Oklahoma City speaks to similar dynamics characterizing the AFN-gentrification interface in a number of cities, demonstrating that, even as a calculated strategy, catering to the creative class can lead AFNs away from the very things that potentially differentiate them from conventional food system actors: ongoing struggle to balance social, economic, and environmental questions, facilitated through agonistic democratic participation and deliberation.

While the OFC's membership was never unified in terms of the precise meaning and practice of their core values, their initial engagements with those values delved more deeply into the social and economic elements of food production, and were further set apart from fetishized versions of local food by the cooperative's efforts to produce a functional model that incorporated an atmosphere conducive to and mechanisms to facilitate active debate about the meanings of local food between differently situated actors in the food systems (Mount 2012). As such, the early OFC still stands as a highly innovative and relevant experiment in fundamentally transforming food systems. While the cooperative ceased operations in 2018, this enterprise may continue to exert influence as a model and inspiration—and a cautionary tale—for those seeking to address ongoing social and ecological problems associated with conventional food systems.

Following this point, it is important to emphasize that the relationship between local food and revitalization, far from being complete or settled, contains within it significant tensions and opportunities to forge alternate paths forward. Viewing the AFN-gentrification interface as an *assemblage*, these ongoing tensions must be understood as *lines of flight*, passageways leading to other means of configuring food systems and urban revitalization. While the need for critical scrutiny of the negative impacts of and on AFNs in the gentrifying city remains urgent, future research must also be oriented toward actively exploring these lines of flight and enhancing the potential for AFNs to be aligned with efforts to create more just and inclusive modes of redevelopment. In Oklahoma City, for example, there remains unexplored potential for a nascent local food hub to partner with food banks, homeless advocacy groups, and community organizations in making healthy foods and revitalizing spaces more inclusive, accessible, and affordable. Some of these collaborations were being discussed in Oklahoma but ultimately got sidelined due to market pressures and the strategy of focusing on the creative class. Flipping the script from being tragic "pioneers" of gentrification (Smith 1986) to advocates of a notion of social justice that is broad enough to encompass not just the right to healthy food but the right to the city will be challenging, but efforts like this are currently under way in a number of cities (e.g., Block, Chávez, Allen, and Ramirez 2012). Participatory action research approaches will be key moving forward, as will methodologies such as competency groups (Whatmore and Landstrom 2011) that are designed to situate knowledge production and knowledge producers within the politically charged assemblages we scrutinize and allow urban dwellers to shape research at fundamental levels.

NOTES

1 I conducted semi-structured interviews with proponents of the local food movement, public officials, developers, and residents of Oklahoma City; participant observation at a number of events; and visual and textual discourse analysis.
2 For a more detailed discussion of how I've deployed the concept of territorialization in this case study, see Sarmiento 2018.
3 The precise definition of what qualified as "local" and therefore could be sold through the OFC was a matter of debate for the cooperative's members, but broadly the OFC only sells items that are grown/raised in Oklahoma, or use primarily Oklahoma-made or -grown ingredients and are processed in the state.

Waldrop is a charismatic figure who embodied many of the characteristics and social/political dynamics of the early OFC. A white male, perhaps in his late sixties, he was raised in a farming community in southwestern Oklahoma and strongly identifies with rural Oklahomans but has lived in Oklahoma City for decades. He is a practicing Catholic and relates easily with the strong religious currents in the state. As the choir director of his church and a homeowner, he enjoys a degree of economic stability. He is also an openly gay man, ascribes to the liberation theology tradition in Catholicism, is a staunch advocate of social justice, and works with several organizations that serve the needs of low-income Oklahoma Citians.

4   This emphasis should be understood in the context of the realities of farming in Oklahoma. Poverty rates in rural counties suggest that the current structure of agriculture is not a viable basis for rural economies: in 2010, while the state's average poverty rate was 17 percent (compared to 15.1 percent nationally), rates were much higher in rural areas, exceeding 23 percent in eleven rural counties (Wertz 2011). This is a top-heavy agricultural economy: while sales in 2012 for the state's largest 3,500 farms—about 4.4 percent of the total number of Oklahoma farms—averaged more than $800,000, roughly 46,000 farms, or about 57 percent, generated less than $10,000 in sales that year (National Agricultural Statistics Service 2014). Ninety-seven farms generated $5 million or more in sales, together representing at least 66 percent of all agricultural sales in 2012. These issues help explain the OFC's framing of local food and social justice primarily around producers.

5   Email message, Robert Waldrop to [okfcgovern] listserv, April 26, 2014.

6   The company's definition of "local" varies somewhat at each store, but in general the company has shifted toward state boundaries as the point of demarcation.

7   This was partly a matter of the difficulty of being certified by the requisite public agencies to accept food stamps, which was greatly complicated by the unique structure of the enterprise. But there were also deep divisions among members, some of whom were against food stamps as a matter of principle, stating that the cooperative should not be in the business of "giving handouts," for example.

8   Email message, OFC producer to [okfcgovern] listserv, March 19, 2014.

9   Email message, OFC producer to [okfcgovern] listserv, May 27, 2016.

REFERENCES

Alkon, Alison. 2008. "From value to values: sustainable consumption at farmers markets." *Agriculture and Human Values* 25 (4): 487–498.

Arnold, Anita. 2010. *Oklahoma City Music: Deep Deuce and Beyond*. Charleston, SC: Arcadia Publishing.

Beckie, Mary, Emily Kennedy, and Hannah Wittman. 2012. "Scaling up alternative food networks: farmers' markets and the role of clustering in western Canada." *Agriculture and Human Values* 29 (3): 333–345.

Block, Daniel, Noel Chávez, Erika Allen, and Dinah Ramirez. 2012. "Food sovereignty, urban food access, and food activism: contemplating the connections through examples from Chicago." *Agriculture and Human Values* 29 (2): 203–215.

Bloom, J. Dara, and C. Clare Hinrichs. 2011. "Moving local food through conventional food system infrastructure: Value chain framework comparisons and insights." *Renewable Agriculture and Food Systems* 26 (1): 13–23.

Bustillo, Miguel. 2012. "Chesapeake's hometown woes: Oklahoma City benefitted from Aubrey McClendon's boosterism and largess, which now is at risk." *Wall Street Journal*, May 29.

Cathey, Dave. 2011. "Ten things that changed our dining habits in 2011." *The Oklahoman*, December 29.

Deleuze, Gilles, and Félix Guattari. 1987. *A Thousand Plateaus: Capitalism and Schizophrenia*. Minneapolis: University of Minnesota Press.

Deutsch, Rosalyn, and Cara Gendel Ryan. 1984. "The Fine Art of Gentrification." *October* 31 (Winter): 91–111.

Florida, Richard. 2014. *The Rise of the Creative Class—Revisited*. New York: Basic Books. Original work published 2002.

Gunderson, Ryan. 2014. "Problems with the defetishization thesis: ethical consumerism, alternative food systems, and commodity fetishism." *Agriculture and Human Values* 31 (1): 109–117.

Guthman, Julie. 2003. "Fast food/organic food: reflexive tastes and the making of 'yuppie chow.'" *Social and Cultural Geography* 4 (1): 45–58.

Guthman, Julie. 2008. "Bringing good food to others: investigating the subjects of alternative food practices." *Cultural Geographies* 15: 431–447.

Jarosz, Lucy. 2008. "The city in the country: Growing alternative food networks in Metropolitan areas." *Journal of Rural Studies* 24: 231–244.

Lackmeyer, Steve. 2010. "Market is due to open in 2011, company officials say: Whole Foods sets sight on Classen Curve site." *The Oklahoman*, May 13.

Lackmeyer, Steve. 2011. "Native Roots Market to open in Oklahoma City's Deep Deuce." *The Oklahoman*, June 30.

Ley, David. 1980. "Liberal ideology and post-industrial city." *Annals of the Association of American Geographers* 70: 238–258.

Malewitz, Jim. 2013. "Red River showdown: Texas-Oklahoma water war could reverberate across US" [Blog post]. *Stateline, The Pew Charitable Trusts*, April 24.

McDermott, Maura, ed. 2006. *Closer to Home: Healthier Food, Farms and Families in Oklahoma. A Centennial Report*. Poteau: Kerr Center for Sustainable Agriculture.

Mount, Phil. 2012. "Growing local food: scale and local food systems governance." *Agriculture and Human Values* 29 (1): 107–121.

National Agricultural Statistics Service. 2014. "2012 Census of Agriculture—State Data: Oklahoma." Washington, DC: US Department of Agriculture.

Sarmiento, Eric. 2015. The local food movement and urban redevelopment in Oklahoma City: Territory, power, and possibility. Doctoral dissertation, Department of Geography, Rutgers University.

Sarmiento, Eric. 2018. "The affirming affects of entrepreneurial redevelopment: Architecture, sport, and local food in Oklahoma City." *Environment and Planning A* 50 (2): 327–349.

Slocum, Rachel. 2007. "Whiteness, space and alternative food practice." *Geoforum* 38: 520–533.
Smith, Neil. 1986. "Gentrification, the frontier, and the restructuring of urban space." In *Gentrification of the City*, edited by Neil Smith and Peter Williams. Boston: Allen and Unwin.
Tierney, Sean, and Clint Petty. 2015. "Gentrification in the American heartland? Evidence from Oklahoma City." *Urban Geography* 36 (3): 439–456.
Warner, Larkin. 2003. "Impact analysis of MAPs and other significant Central City Investments: executive summary." Report prepared for Central City Development, Greater Oklahoma City Chamber of Commerce.
Watts, David, Brian Ilbery, and Damian Maye. 2005. "Making reconnections in agro-food geography: alternative systems of food provision." *Progress in Human Geography* 29 (1): 22–40.
Wertz, Joe. 2011. "Mapped: An overview of poverty in Oklahoma." *State Impact: A Reporting Project of NPR Member Stations*. http://stateimpact.npr.org.
Whatmore, Sarah, and Catharina Landstrom. 2011. "Flood apprentices: an exercise in making things public." *Economy & Society* 40 (4): 582–610.
Zukin, Sharon. 1981. *Loft Living: Culture and Capital in the Urban Core*. Baltimore, MD: Johns Hopkins University Press.

PART II

Ripe for Growth

Alternative Food Systems

4

The Urban Agriculture Fix

Navigating Development and Displacement in Denver

JOSHUA SBICCA

In 2009, Mayor John Hickenlooper declared May 14 to be Grow Local Colorado Day. Due to community organizing by groups like Denver Urban Gardens, Grow Local Colorado, and Transition Denver, disparate urban agriculture efforts began to cohere. With full recovery from the Great Recession still years away and a national political climate open to urban agriculture, evidenced by the White House vegetable garden planted by First Lady Michelle Obama in 2009, Denver signaled its support for local food. Notably, the city backed an edible public demonstration garden at Civic Center Park, the political heart of Colorado, as well as the city of Denver. Then in 2010, Mayor Hickenlooper formed the Denver Sustainable Food Policy Council. Elected in 2011, Mayor Michael Hancock continued and expanded these efforts. Under his leadership, Denver's 2020 Sustainability Goals proposed to grow and process at least 20 percent of the city's food from the state of Colorado, combat climate change, reduce the rate of obesity, reduce waste, and provide workforce training to support Denver employers.

The increased political support for growing food in the city suggests the influence of practices that achieve city leaders' ideal "triple bottom line" of environmental, economic, and social sustainability. But because urban agriculture in Denver is entangled in a process of "revitalization" that includes the displacement of urban farmers and residents, it is not a "win-win-win" practice (Walker 2016). Instead, it becomes a sustainability goal subordinate to development interests that push for green gentrification. (cf. Checker 2011; Curran and Hamilton 2012; Gould and Lewis 2017). As a Denver reporter for the commercial real estate digital media company *Bisnow* put it in a telling headline, "Way to Grow: Urban Farms Are an Amenity at Many Developments" (Jackson 2018).

Many people in Denver's food movement have felt frustrated by these conditions. Despite urban agriculture being a nimble practice that can use devalued land in the short term for communal benefits, its low-profit mode of production obstructs establishing a long-term claim on land. At the same time, developers build on the green reputation of urban agriculture without honoring the work of the farmers themselves. Moreover, economic and political elites deploy local food to capture the cultural value of the food movement and leverage urban agriculture initiatives to revalorize neighborhoods targeted for economic development after the Great Recession. Urban agriculture was supposed to fix problems, not become a capitalist "fix" used to increase land values and speculative profits.

While the growth imperative of capitalist urbanization compels local governments to pursue green development through sustainability projects in previously disinvested neighborhoods that attract new wealth and displace working-class communities and communities of color (Gould and Lewis 2017), the ways that different land uses contribute to this process remain underspecified (Lees, Slater, and Wyly 2008). The case of urban agriculture as a factor in producing green gentrification is particularly interesting to consider. How does a relatively marginal land use like urban agriculture, which produces little profit, become so linked to gentrification? The answer, which I develop throughout this chapter, suggests that political economy triggers can produce conditions that make it possible for the cultural significance of urban agriculture to revalorize disinvested neighborhoods and induce displacement (Zukin 1987).

The political economy of the Great Recession, developers' hollow green branding, and the experiences of Denver urban farmers navigating gentrification and displacement—especially their role in the process—are important factors to consider in relation to each other. Specifying these details reveals that urban agriculture is a unique land use that can contribute to green gentrification. Urban agriculture can ultimately revalorize a particular place because it is simultaneously economically marginal *and* socially and environmentally praised by an array of competing interests.

Uneven Development and Urban Agriculture Fixes

Urban agriculture exists within a broader neoliberal context where cities respond to increasing environmental pressures and strive to maintain economic growth. But urban agriculture is different than large developer-led projects like New York City's Prospect Park and the Highline. The green gentrification literature tends not to delineate between different types of greening, so it is important to show how a decentralized, economically marginal land use can be coopted to become a force for green gentrification.

Drawing on David Harvey's (2006) notion of the spatial fix, a term used to describe how capitalism tries to spatially manage its crises, While, Jonas and Gibbs (2004) offer the productive notion of an "urban sustainability fix." They define this as the "selective incorporation of environmental goals, determined by the balance of pressures for and against environmental policy within and across the city" (ibid., 552). In other words, growing green to generate investment and profits. What determines the selection is whether the fix will once again stimulate surplus production and reinvestment (Harvey 2010). In order to avoid undermining broader neoliberal agendas, achieving green outcomes co-occurs with green entrepreneurialism. As Nathan McClintock (2018) argues, urban agriculture is part of the process of green gentrification: Urban growth machines draw on its "symbolic *sustainability capital*" to revalorize disinvested parts of cities for redevelopment, which obscures the raced and classed processes that displaced people from a neighborhood and that drew people back in. One of McClintock's main arguments is that this process is necessarily uneven. Yet, one of the unexplored reasons for why there is spatial variation is the role of specific historical moments.

Capitalism never resolves its crises; it merely moves them around (Harvey 2010). Crises, therefore, compel the need for spatial fixes (Smith 2008). So urban sustainability fixes are not just spatial; they are historical and can require a crisis to stimulate the process (see also chapter 5 in this volume). Building on Gould and Lewis's (2017) argument for the significance of "greening events" as triggers for green gentrification (e.g., the building of an elaborate new park; the development of an "agrihood"), I suggest that capitalist crises create the uneven conditions for greening events. A practice like urban agriculture, which has more use value than exchange value, occupies marginal city spaces, which means it chases after land and rarely secures it for long. A massive devaluation of property and job loss that comes with a recession, for example, reduces the barriers to attain land for food production. But unless the devaluation is so extreme as to make that land affordable for poor people, landowners will likely hold on to their property until a large rent gap occurs.

Understanding the uneven post–Great Recession relationship between urban agriculture and green gentrification requires accounting for the emergence of and response to what I call the *urban agriculture fix*. The foreclosure crisis increased the overall ratio of vacant property. To prevent the total collapse of prices due to vacancies and neighborhood flight, developers offered their land to urban farmers to prevent "blight," which "revitalized" the property. This tended to occur in the neighborhoods most at risk of gentrification. Once the economy recovered and housing prices began to increase, developers and investors searched for the next "up and coming" neighborhoods. They looked to those places with the highest post-recession social and ecological investment, which is where the largest exploitable rent gaps can be found. This new round of investment was a spatial fix made possible by an urban agriculture fix. Contradictorily, because urban agriculture faces many profit barriers, especially in Denver where the growing season is five months, both for-profit and non-profit urban agriculture projects are forced to chase "underutilized" land, which they hold until displaced by a more profitable land use. Although there are some differences in how urban agriculture projects can revalorize a place, this general pattern remains. Without long-term leases, regulatory changes to zoning and land use laws, or access to more land, urban agriculture will remain entangled in green gentrification. Ultimately, this chapter tells the story of how, in the wake of the Great Recession, local growth machines were able to use urban agriculture as a tool to build new housing development projects or attract people to neighborhoods while ultimately displacing the farmers themselves.[1]

Recession, Housing Collapse, and Job Loss

In Denver, between 2006 and 2010, 30,741 homes went into foreclosure, compared with only 720 homes in 2016 (Office of the Clerk and Recorder

2017). This stripped many working-class communities and communities of color of a major asset and set them at an economic disadvantage compared to white communities (Rugh and Massey 2010). According to the *Denver Post*, "The bottom one-third of homes in value accounted for 51.7 percent of foreclosures in metro Denver" (Svaldi 2016). Across cities in the Mountain West, Black and Latinx residents experienced the highest foreclosure risks, partially attributable to subprime mortgage predatory lending practices (Hall, Crowder, and Spring 2015). The housing collapse caused financial ruin, but this also rippled throughout the economy.

At its peak in 2010, unemployment in Denver was at 8.4 percent and 18.5 percent of adults lived in poverty (US Census Bureau(a) n.d.). Despite the macroeconomic improvements over the next few years, microeconomic conditions remained unequal. African Americans and Latinx had higher unemployment rates and poverty than whites. Estimates suggest that in 2015, 12 percent of African Americans and 8 percent of Latinx were unemployed, while 30 percent of African Americans and 26 percent of Latinx lived in poverty (US Census Bureau(b), (c) n.d.). Comparing 2000 to the 2010–2014 recovery period, 20 percent *more* poor African Americans and 22 percent *more* poor Latinx lived in neighborhoods with poverty rates of 20 percent or higher. In total, 64 percent of all poor African Americans and 74 percent of all poor Latinx lived in neighborhoods with poverty rates of 20 percent or higher (Kneebone and Holmes 2016).

And yet, years after the official recovery from the Great Recession, the neighborhoods with the highest concentrations of poverty and people of color were vulnerable to or experiencing gentrification (Denver Office of Economic Development 2016). Not only were housing prices increasing, but the class and ethnoracial mix included far wealthier and more white people (Community Facts n.d.). Instead of mobilizing public resources to ameliorate these conditions, the city opted to court young professionals hip to the cultural appeal of local food and urban agriculture.

Urban Agriculture Interventions for "Sustainable" Development

The problem for Denver's food movement is that its political support is entangled in class and racially inequitable neoliberal policy priorities that are at cross-purposes with some of the intended goals of initiatives such as urban agriculture (see also chapters 7 and 8 in this volume). As a mayoral candidate, Michael Hancock laid out an economic development plan that would entice well-educated people to move to Denver. According to his campaign materials, he planned to "re-boot the Denver Office of Economic Development and all of city government to become an efficient, fiscally responsible and strong partner for businesses." As "Marketer-in-Chief" he promised to "aggressively" market Denver to recruit new businesses "to elevate Denver's brand as a business-friendly city with the highest quality of life" (Luning 2010). This is perhaps unsurprising given that Mayor Hancock, along with many local politicians, has come under the increasingly powerful influence of development, business, and corporate interests (Davies 2015; Murray 2016). Until he put forth an affordable housing plan perceived by many residents as weak, Mayor Hancock has avoided making substantive investments or commitments to ensure that Denver is livable for all residents, regardless of income (Carter 2016). When he has made efforts, say, in the plan to tweak a previously failed inclusionary housing ordinance (IHO), these have come after multiple waves of gentrification (Murray 2014). Denver is unaffordable for many working-class people, and most affordable housing developments are integrated into mixed-use developments with more market rate housing. The IHO only requires that 10 percent of units match affordable housing statutes. Gentrification in these neighborhoods is therefore highly likely.

Under this scenario, urban farmers became squeezed between being able to access "underutilized land" after the Great Recession, the popularity of and political support for local food, their precarity once housing prices skyrocketed, and the idea that their work is not considered the "highest and best" use of land. As Jean, a white native Denverite working on a grassroots urban agriculture project, growled,

> I have been watching this for the last few years, and I now finally feel like my city's been invaded. I'm like who the fuck are all these people? Who are you people? You don't respect shit. And that's me, the native in me. Like I'm watching my land disappear has been the story for such a long time, but it's true. So many of the people that I work with—artists, farmers, activists, long-timers—it's like where the hell are we going to? People

are getting kicked out. They're just getting shoved out. . . . it's just a pay-to-play city, a pay-to-play region.

Jean is correct in her assessment that a quick, class-based shift has been occurring in Denver, but while the individual gentrifier might be easy to blame, the economic, cultural, and political forces better help to explain green gentrification, especially the contradictory location of urban agriculture in the revalorization process.

The experience of the Urban Farmers Collaborative is especially illustrative. For five years, beginning in 2010, a group of farmers—one non-profit, Green Leaf Denver, and two for-profits, Granata Farms and Produce Denver—farmed the three-acre Sustainability Park. After their lease expired, they had to find a new location. The farm was located in the historically Latinx and Black working-class neighborhood of Curtis Park. Since 2000, the demographics have flipped from majority people of color to majority white. In 2000, Latinx made up 42.8 percent of the population, African Americans accounted for 26.2 percent, while non-Latinx whites accounted for 27.4 percent. In 2015, non-Latinx whites grew to 64.5 percent of the population, while Latinx shrunk to 20.9 percent, and African Americans to 10.4 percent (Community Facts n.d.). Moreover, the inflation-adjusted average household income was $49,175 in 2000 and almost doubled in 2015 to $81,029 (ibid.). While the Urban Farmers Collaborative held less economic and political power than developers, their social and cultural capital as white and highly educated people engaged in a popular practice allowed them to access land even for a short time. But they held more economic and cultural power than some working-class residents of color facing displacement pressures, which enabled them to become a force for green gentrification in the context of development interests looking for a spatial fix.

The Sustainability Park farm sat on Denver Housing Authority (DHA) land, a historic site of affordable housing dating back to the 1930s. DHA is a quasi-municipal corporation that is subject to local housing laws and city and federal oversight. Its mission is to support affordable housing. However, rather than build affordable housing on the property, it decided to land bank the property until the housing market was strong. DHA could then sell it to a developer for more money. While this speculative strategy may grow the resources necessary for DHA to expand its affordable housing portfolio, it can also lead to gentrification in certain neighborhoods. According to a toolkit provided by the Housing and Urban Development's Neighborhood Stabilization Program, land banks are meant to prevent "the contagious blight that can sweep across urban neighborhoods like a plague, infecting house after house until whole blocks—even neighborhoods—become empty and abandoned shadows of their former selves" (Kildee and Hovey 2010: 2). Land banks set aside property and can be used to create "open green space or a community garden . . . until a new purpose can be determined" (ibid.).

Sustainability Park was *planned* by DHA to revalorize the land (Denver Housing Authority n.d.). As journalist Scott McFetridge (2015) sanguinely commented: "During the Great Recession, downtown landowners and leaders offered up plots for free to get new vitality on empty streets." But with many people clamoring to live in downtown Denver, new housing development is far more profitable than farms. The land was sold to Curtis Park Group, while the exclusive broker is TreeHouse Brokerage and Development, which built S*Park, the condo and townhome project.[2] Seizing the opportunity to co-opt the work of the Urban Farmers Collaborative, S*Park's website claims sustainability is the "ethos for the project" and that the development is "celebrating the spirit of urban community and farming" with a "private park area" and "modern greenhouse." Despite claims that the development creates affordable housing (Rebchook 2016), this project furthers gentrification. Out of the forty-one units in the first phase of development, only five were less than $350,000, and that was for the base model, studios between 500 and 600 square feet (S*Park n.d.). Five to ten years prior to this development, that same money would buy up to four times the square footage across the street.[3] Hoping to attract wealthier millennials and young families to the neighborhood, S*Park's website advertises environmental amenities like parks, public transportation, and walkability, as well as proximity to hip restaurants and breweries. These units sold almost as soon as they were placed on the market.

One of the ironies of the development of S*Park is the simultaneous gentrification of urban agriculture itself. Placing this into a context amenable primarily to local growth machines, Jasper, a white non-profit leader whose urban agriculture organization lost its land, shared, "It's just interesting because there's a lot of political will for redevelopment and bringing in economic development, and grouping our neighborhoods and all that. It's kind of a double-edged sword because that leads into the loss of land for food production. . . . Farmers left and right are losing their land." As the economic climate improved, the notion that a small army of urban farmers could help feed a city facing economic and food insecurity waned. Zane, a white representative working for the City of Denver, explained, "It's become a noisier environment, where food is no longer a top three priority for many people and it's not back in the top ten somewhere, but way back there." This is true politically, and when coupled with the fact that profit-minded enterprises capitalize on the work of equity-minded urban agriculture projects and sideline them in the process, it reveals how urban farmers became economically marginal in a short period of time.

No long-standing for-profit urban farmer or urban agriculture nonprofit is part of S*Park. Instead, the capital flush Altius Farms, Inc. has a large vertical farming greenhouse dedicated to growing greens for local restaurants, with a smaller percentage sold through a CSA to increasingly wealthy local residents.[4] As the CEO Sally Herbert noted before starting operations, "I am inspired by the S*Park sustainable, innovative development. . . . Altius Farms is excited and eager to continue the long history of farming at this neighborhood location" (Armbrister 2017). As a former Reservist in the Air Force, Herbert also merged her work as Board Chair of the non-profit Operation Victory Gardens, which runs its urban agriculture training center out of the Altius Farms greenhouse as part of its work supporting military veterans and "redeploying local food" (Operation Victory Gardens n.d.). While local food and urban farming frames dominate the public materials of these two enterprises, the approach suggests that capital-intensive, patented, high-tech vertical aeroponics farming is the preferred path forward for growing food in cities (Hoppe 2016). As Jeff Olsen, who is a co-founder of Altius Farms and a board member of Operation Victory Gardens, claimed in a radio interview, a farmer growing high-value greens with vertical aeroponics technology could make $250,000 per acre per harvest in a system that can have ten harvests a year (Grant 2014).[5] He then sidestepped the issue of inequity in who can afford this food by claiming that it is necessary to first begin with "early adopters" of local food who are "conscious" and "into this" (ibid.).

Figure 4.1. S*Park townhome and condo development project with Uchi restaurant and Altius Farms, Inc. Photograph by the author.

Figure 4.2. Evidence of gentrification directly across the street from S*Park. Photograph by the author.

The co-option of urban agriculture by S*Park has intensified gentrification in Curtis Park. The wealthier white people who now live here can purchase cortados from places like ink! Coffee, described in the introduction to this volume, which came under fire in 2017 from longtime residents for its sign, "Happily gentrifying the neighborhood since 2014." They can also go to Uchi, the sushi restaurant started by James Beard–award winning Chef Tyson Cole, an Austin, Texas success that branched out to Denver. It is located at S*Park right below Altius Farms. As Cole remarked, "We are always exploring new avenues to expand how we connect with food and the community. Uchi's proximity to the greenhouse space above the restaurant and the community garden at S*Park presents an amazing opportunity" (Zeppelin 2017). Which community? The one that will spend more than $100 a person for a ten-course *omakase* tasting!

Reflections on the Strategic Political Marginalization of Urban Agriculture

There is an acute sense among urban farmers that wealthier residents attracted to the amenity of urban agriculture might displace working-class residents in a post–Great Recession recovery period. Some of the staff at GrowHaus, a multi-ethnoracial food justice non-profit that works with the Latinx community of Elyria-Swansea to increase healthy food access, jobs, and urban agriculture skills, talked about the possibility of their presence as a gentrifying force. Indeed, they are an outsider-founded organization that developed deep local ties and inclusive leadership and have remained in the same location for many years. This work is complicated because they acquired their organizational cornerstone, a large greenhouse, during the trough of the Great Recession through real estate connections, but this space has been pivotal to their positive local reputation. Reflecting on this issue, Gary, a white staff member, offered, "[I]t's like uncovering this neighborhood and are we in some way helping gentrification? Are we making it cool to be here? One of the things that we've talked about is what is the sort of tipping point in which the residents we're trying to serve are being pushed out of this neighborhood and are we a part of that problem?" (see also chapter 13 in this volume for a resident-led alternative).

Given that an economic downturn can create the opportunity for a marginal urban land use like farming to become trendy (and a fix), there is also the question of whether urban agriculture can buck development pressures. In an interview the summer before they closed after seven years of operation, Molly, a white representative of the community development non-profit Feed Denver, explained its precariousness in relationship to local food trends: "[W]e are lucky and take advantage of our environment because we have a huge gentrification issue happening, meaning a lot of money moving in, and people who really don't know these issues, but they like the idea of eating local." Although the organization had maintained collaborative relationships with Sunnyside's working-class and Latinx residents since the Great Recession, their urban agriculture projects became an environmental amenity. Speaking to the role of their farm and market, she added, "What's happening now is this not-valued piece of land that we're on is now valued. We have a very nice market and people will spend money at our market because we have people who have a lot of money who have bought these houses that were going for $60,000 and now are going for $600,000." Ultimately, the skyrocketing housing prices and changing neighborhood demographics eliminated the need for Feed Denver.

Development interests intent on turning urban agriculture into a spatial fix that displaces urban farmers and local residents has led to collective efforts to secure land, but has fallen short of what might be required to prevent green gentrification. Much of the food movement considers these efforts especially urgent because, while there were 307 farms in Denver in 1927, there were nine by 2016. After a multiyear and multi-stakeholder outreach effort to learn what Denver residents think the local food system should be like in 2030, Mayor Hancock adopted the Denver Food Vision in 2017. This strategic policy tool contains many goals that complement the 2020 Sustainability Goals, but more thoroughly articulates how to create an inclusive, healthy, economically vibrant, regionally focused, and environmentally resilient food system (City of Denver 2017). As part of its commitment to support local food production, it pledges to preserve 99.2 acres of land for agricultural production; there were 4,940 acres of land in farms in 1925. This modest goal reinforces the skepticism of many urban farmers that their work is disposable, especially given that this preserved land does not have to be in Denver.

As a point of comparison, a working group of Denver Sustainable Food Policy Council members formed in 2015 to develop a policy to avail more land for urban agriculture (see also chapter 8 in this volume for a different approach). Realizing that accessing private land is expensive or relegates urban agriculture to marginal places, they proposed converting 100 acres of public land to food production by 2020. Based on estimates from Brett et al. (n.d.), which found that farming on 766 acres would provide five common vegetables for all residents for a year, the policy proposal claimed that urban agriculture would greatly benefit Denver. They proposed that this land should be farmed in economically distressed communities with a guaranteed lease of three to five years and should be revenue-neutral for public agencies, with the food producer bearing most infrastructure costs. Although imperfect in that it could encourage further gentrification, privatize costs for an economically marginal occupation, and guarantee land tenure for a very short time, it was better than the land preservation goal of the Denver Food Vision.

Many urban farmers believe that the major planning documents avoid making policy changes that seriously increase the scale of land access and food production *within* Denver. This is especially true for the for-profit farmers. As Sherry, a white for-profit urban farmer with more than a decade of local experience, conveyed,

> The food policy council is a great idea, and I know those people. I like those people. I love those people. I like what they're doing. It doesn't help me. So, it's fine for backyard gardeners. It's fine for homesteaders. It has almost no relevance to me as a production agriculturist, as a producer. There's just no relevance. So, what would I say about the political context? It doesn't encourage me. It doesn't incentivize me. It doesn't in any way help me. In fact, it harms me. The pro-development leanings of the mayor and the city council means all the possible land that could've been in farms is going to be built on.

If the political will existed to maintain a robust commitment to local food production instead of allowing for the unchecked speculative land rush that captures the economic and cultural value of urban agriculture, then perhaps this could begin to reverse the historic farm loss. But these are different times marked by the rapacious need to fix capital in place.

For the foreseeable future, it looks like the only urban farms, at least on private property, will be amenities for green development. Not despite, but because of, urban agriculture's low-profit mode of production, rhetorical support can remain high without adequate material backing, at least until the next recession.

Conclusion: Fixing Urban Agriculture in an Era of Green Gentrification?

Capitalist crises such as the Great Recession can create the uneven conditions for greening events that revalorize neighborhoods. This is one way that urban agriculture becomes a fix for capital. Urban farmers can more easily access land even though growing food is usually not considered the "highest and best use." But because the land tenure is generally short term until property values increase, developers can exploit its cultural appeal to produce a profit. Taken together, the power of capital and culture as mutually constitutive conditions that drive gentrification benefits from placing it in a historical context to explain how particular kinds of alternative food initiatives become entangled in the greening of development.

Practically speaking, the urban agriculture fix and resistance to it in Denver raises several questions. Is setting aside a small amount of public land a release valve for the frustration urban farmers experience with ongoing cycles of displacement? That is, instead of checking the power of developers and boom/bust investment and housing cycles, is providing token support to urban farmers who maintain or increase the exchange value of land during economic downturns meant to dull deeper political action? Given the economic precariousness of urban agriculture, many urban farmers make a Faustian bargain with gentrifying forces to access land. One of the underlying dilemmas urban agriculture faces is the misrecognition of its value to powerful economic interests. While it is important to acknowledge the non-monetary values associated with urban agriculture, this does not eliminate the sociocultural power that prefers maximizing profit by exploiting rent gaps.

Relatedly, there are questions about the capacity of the food movement to resist current trends. Can urban agriculture advocates divorce themselves from neoliberal governance networks and push for economically and racially just political solutions? If they manage to align with political forces that halt gentrification, can they overcome internal differences between non-profit and for-profit urban agriculture? Non-profits fill in the gaps produced by the rollback of social welfare support and the political aversion to mandating living wages and fair housing policies. This is key to why local government often supports social service–oriented urban agriculture. Conversely, for-profit farms must contend in a market dominated by corporate food supply chains and developers who can profit more from building houses than producing food. While a non-profit farm might be able to survive more marginal land tenure arrangements with the subsidies they receive from volunteers and grants, a for-profit farm does not have as many degrees of freedom to work land that will not produce an adequate return on investments of time, labor, and material resources.

Green gentrification is accelerating as cities strategize ways to attract new residents and new capital. Moreover, as environmental crises multiply and combine, residents of cities are looking for ways to stave off their worst effects with practices like urban agriculture that might also generate social and economic development. Yet, their benefits will be for naught if precipitating events like capitalist crises are met with neoliberal policies that do not leverage the power of the state to ensure equitable access to basic needs like housing and food. Urban agriculture can feed people and take care of farmers, or it can be fed to developers to generate profit. It remains to be seen how cities will navigate this tension in the years to come.

NOTES

1 This chapter is based on a project investigating how the Denver food movement works together amid commonly faced pressures that riddle cities, such as poverty and gentrification. My data entail sixty-seven interviews. They represent one or more of a purposive sample of 111 public or private organizations, businesses, or government entities aiming to improve the local food system. Almost all the interviewees are in leadership positions in their organizations and are paid. Of my total sample, 52 percent identifies as female and the rest as male (48 percent). An overwhelming majority of the participants are white (>85 percent), while the rest are roughly split between Asian, Black, and Latinx. More than 80 percent have attained at least a bachelor's degree. These demographics are skewed compared to the general Denver population: white people alone are 53 percent of the population and holders of bachelor's degree or higher are 46 percent of the popula-

tion. I focus here on a subsample of twenty-five interviews whose work includes non-profit and for-profit food production or food system planning on issues of local food and land use policy. I supplement my interviews with reports, meeting minutes, listserv emails, and policy proposals produced by Denver city agencies, the Denver Sustainable Food Policy Council, and Denver Housing Authority. I also rely on local reporting to trace how food system development is understood and interpreted in the context of Denver's rapid economic changes.
2 Curtis Park Group was founded in 2015. Jonathan Alpert and Clem Reinhardt founded TreeHouse together in 2012. The Curtis Park Group includes Jonathan Alpert.
3 I derive this estimate by looking at Zillow's sale history of homes going back to 2005.
4 The organization says that they donate unsold produce to two food rescue non-profits.
5 More than $500,000 was invested in Altius Farms.

REFERENCES

Armbrister, Molly. 2017. "S*Park: Westfield's 99-Unit Rino Project to Offer Diverse Mix of Condos, Townhomes." *Denver Business Journal*, October 16.

Brett, John, Debbi Main, Jessica Cook, Zac Coventry, Amy DePierre, Erin Fiene, Steve Fisher, Debbie Guenther, Kate Oviatt, and Željko Špirić. n.d. "Farming the City: Urban Agriculture Potential in Denver." IGERT Food Systems Research Group. University of Colorado, Denver.

Carter, Eliza. 2016. "Hancock's Affordable Housing Plan Met with Doubts." *Colorado Independent*, August 2. www.coloradoindependent.com.

Checker, Melissa. 2011. "Wiped Out by the 'Greenwave': Environmental Gentrification and the Paradoxical Politics of Urban Sustainability." *City & Society* 23(2): 210–229.

City of Denver. 2017. *Denver Food Vision*. Denver, CO.

Community Facts. n.d. "Neighborhood Data for the 7-County Denver Metro Region. http://denvermetrodata.org/.

Curran, Winifred, and Trina Hamilton. 2012. "Just Green Enough: Contesting Environmental Gentrification in Greenpoint, Brooklyn." *Local Environment* 17(9): 1027–1042.

Davies, Bree. 2015. "Big Money in Denver Elections: 'Developers Run This City.'" *Colorado Independent*. August 7. www.coloradoindependent.com.

Denver Housing Authority. n.d. "DHA Sustainability Park Block H." www.denverhousing.org.

Denver Office of Economic Development. 2016. *Gentrification Study: Mitigating Involuntary Displacement*. Denver, CO. www.denvergov.org.

Gould, Kenneth A., and Tammy L. Lewis. 2017. *Green Gentrification: Urban Sustainability and the Struggle for Environmental Justice*. New York: Routledge.

Grant, Elaine. 2014. "Urban Farms One Solution for Ailing Food System, Colorado Agriculture Activist Says." *Colorado Public Radio*. June 18. www.cpr.org.

Hall, Matthew, Kyle Crowder, and Amy Spring. 2015. "Variations in Housing Foreclosures by Race and Place, 2005–2012." *ANNALS of the American Academy of Political and Social Science* 660(1): 217–237.

Harvey, David. 2006. *The Limits to Capital* (new and fully updated edition). New York: Verso.

Harvey, David. 2010. *The Enigma of Capital and The Crises of Capitalism*. New York: Oxford University Press.

Hoppe, Janice. 2016. "Sky's the Limit." *Food and Drink International*. September 26. www.fooddrink-magazine.com.

Jackson, Margaret. 2018. "Way to Grow: Urban Farms Are an Amenity at Many Developments." *Bisnow*, July 12. www.bisnow.com.

Kildee, Dan, and Amy Hovey. 2010. "What Is a Land Bank?" US Department of Housing and Urban Development Neighborhood Stabilization Program Toolkit. Washington, DC.

Kneebone, Elizabeth, and Natalie Holmes. 2016. *U.S. Concentrated Poverty in the Wake of the Great Recession*. Washington, DC: Brookings Institute.

Lees, Loretta, Tom Slater, and Elvin Wyly. 2008. *Gentrification*. New York: Routledge.

Luning, Ernest. 2010. "Hancock Enters Crowded Mayoral Race." *Colorado Statesman* 111(47), November 19.

McClintock, Nathan. 2018. "Cultivating (a) Sustainability Capital: Urban Agriculture, Ecogentrification, and the Uneven Valorization of Social Reproduction." *Annals of the American Association of Geographers* 108(2): 579–590.

McFetridge, Scott. 2015. "Urban Farmers Find that Success Leads to Eviction." Associated Press, November 25.

Murray, Jon. 2014. "Denver Affordable Housing Efforts Face Uncertainty After Council Vote." *Denver Post*, August 8. www.denverpost.com.

Murray, Jon. 2016. "Denver's Power Set Honors Mayor Michael Hancock with Community Enrichment Award." *Denver Post*, May 26. www.denverpost.com.

Office of the Clerk and Recorder. 2017. "Public Trustee Historical Statistics." City of Denver. www.denvergov.org.

Operation Victory Gardens. n.d. "What We Do." www.operationvictorygardens.org.

Rebchook, John. 2016. "S*Park Condos Under $300,000." *Denver Real Estate Watch*, May 6. www.denverrealestatewatch.com.

Rugh, Jacob S., and Douglas S. Massey. 2010. "Racial Segregation and the American Foreclosure Crisis." *American Sociological Review* 75(5): 629–651.

S*Park. n.d. "Floor Plans." http://liveatspark.com.

Smith, Neil. 2008. *Uneven Development: Nature, Capital, and the Production of Space*. 3rd edition. Athens: University of Georgia Press.

Svaldi, Aldo. 2016. "Foreclosures Continue to Haunt Displaced Homeowners in Metro Denver." *Denver Post*, July 12. www.denverpost.com.

US Census Bureau(a). n.d. "S0201: Selected Population Profile in the United States." *2010 American Community Survey 1-Year Estimates*. Washington, DC: US Census Bureau's American Community Survey Office.

US Census Bureau(b). n.d. "S1701: Poverty Status in the Past 12 Months." *2011–2015 American Community Survey 5-Year Estimates*. Washington, DC: US Census Bureau's American Community Survey Office.

US Census Bureau(c). n.d. "S2301: Employment Status." *2011–2015 American Community Survey 5-Year Estimates*. Washington, DC: US Census Bureau's American Community Survey Office.

Walker, Samuel. 2016. "Urban Agriculture and the Sustainability Fix in Vancouver and Detroit." *Urban Geography* 37(2): 163–182.

While, Aidan, Andrew E. G. Jonas, and David Gibbs. 2004. "The Environment and the Entrepreneurial City: Searching for the Urban 'Sustainability Fix' in Manchester and Leeds." *International Journal of Urban and Regional Research* 28(3): 549–569.

Zeppelin, Andra. 2017. "James Beard Winner Uchi Lands in Denver." *Eater Denver*, March 7. https://denver.eater.com.

Zukin, Sharon. 1987. "Gentrification: Culture and Capital in the Urban Core." *Annual Review of Sociology* 13(1): 129–147.

5

From the Holy Trinity to Microgreens

Gentrification Redefining Local Foodways in Post-Katrina New Orleans

PAMELA ARNETTE BROOM AND YUKI KATO

Pamela's Story

Before I left New Orleans in advance of Hurricane Katrina, I was a gardener. While displaced and living in Durham, North Carolina, and Chicago, Illinois, I continued and deepened my passion for growing as an urban farmer. When I returned to New Orleans eighteen months post-Katrina, I had become an active proponent of urban agriculture as a tool for community revitalization. I returned home in 2008 to a city struggling to realize massive renovation. New Orleans, with its character as a fabled city, was ravaged. In neighborhoods of the city that were among the 80 percent impacted by nearly two weeks of standing flood waters, the landscape begged for healing. Prior to Hurricane Katrina, the vacant and blighted properties count was just under 20,000 and after the storm, 66,845. The world's spotlight was on New Orleans. Thousands converged on the city with mixed agendas, including volunteers, nonprofit organizations, and entrepreneurs. Post-Katrina New Orleans, with its cache of vacant lots, became the frontier for innovative sustainable land use schemes. With the influx of impassioned volunteers came many, primarily young, white adults, who saw vacant lots as the resource to spur a burgeoning urban agriculture movement in New Orleans.

I became one of many global advocates for the cause of transforming vacant, underutilized urban properties into beautiful spaces for growing healthy fresh food. My experience gardening since age eight and the formal training I received from Growing Power in Chicago and

Milwaukee, 2007–2008, inspired me to launch the Women and Agriculture (WandA) Network. In the late summer of 2009, I embarked upon my passion project. My vision was to demonstrate and document an affordable and effective way to install a garden on a vacant city lot that featured the installation of a proper infrastructure: weed abatement plan, secure city water connection with backflow preventer for agricultural use, fencing, and a soil building station. I entered into a no-cost lease agreement with the property's owner for a 65' x 85' square foot corner lot. For three years, from my vantage point in the Central City neighborhood, I was able to experience "the good, the bad, and the ugly" of urban farming.

For two of the three years that I cultivated the Sun Harvest Kitchen Garden, 2009–2012, I experienced the best that farming in the city could offer. The property I grew on was spacious and had full sun exposure. It was located in a highly visible area that was conducive to a feeling of safety. Eighteen months prior to developing the site as a kitchen garden, I participated with a local group, led by a chemistry professor, that conducted a sunflower remediation project to demonstrate how parts of the plants removed lead and other contaminants from the soil. Once the project ended, one of the team members started Sun Harvest but eventually left to pursue another opportunity. I stepped up and, with the help of my daughter, began to transform the space into a beautiful and flourishing example of intensive, sustainable growing. In year three, the garden's location became an unsafe liability. The property was located a block from one of the city's largest homeless shelters. Before that time, the garden drew expressions of admiration from passersby. There was no evidence of vandalism or any sort of intrusion onto the space.

By year three, however, that changed dramatically. When possible, I would arrive at the garden soon after daybreak and often left just before sunset. I began noticing distressing signs of invasion: syringes, beer cans, and wine bottles throughout the garden, and human feces along the rear perimeter. I arrived at the garden early one summer morning and found that a pallet made from a comforter was nestled beneath my large patch of mature okra plants. The scene had a sort of beauty as it showcased the pathological nature of the situation. I took a picture and thought, "This looks like somebody chillin' in the tropics." I also discovered that someone had been, by day, hiding their belongings beneath one of the compost bins. This was around the time when New Orleans' homeless population surged, and my garden's proximity to New Orleans Mission exposed it to these unanticipated uses by the unhoused individuals.[1] After that, I contacted my urban farming friends to let them know that I was closing the garden. This was November 2012. I invited them to come and get fencing, soil, and plants. Despite that unfortunate turn of events, I can see parts of Sun Harvest still flourishing in the patch of echinacea that blankets one of Jeanette Bell's gardens and the black chain link fencing that wraps around one of her other lovely growing spaces. I literally pulled up stakes and continued the gardening aspect of the WandA Network from my backyard and later to another site in the Mid-City neighborhood.

The WandA Network was an after-work and weekend project for me. One of my close gardening friends called me "the tidy gardener," and I accepted that title with pride. I was determined to exemplify the leading models of efficient, sustainable agriculture that could be replicated by anyone who had a desire to garden. Several of the new urban growers who had become aware of my work as Deputy Director of the New Orleans Food and Farm Network contacted me. I invited all interested parties to my garden to witness first-hand the methods I found successful. Most visitors responded with excitement and gratitude. Others, however, exhibited arrogance and a lack of acceptance of local gardening wisdom. All visitors, however, expressed a desire to productively transform a devastated landscape.

Fledgling urban agriculture projects sprung up across the city. Terms like *farmyards, micro-farms, urban farmsteads, city farms*, and *urban agriculture* were used to describe efforts to transform vacant land into sites of fresh food production. These were new terms describing old practices, but the changes were more than semantic. Through my work as a grower, a mentor, and a member of nonprofit organizations, I began taking a closer look at who the new farmers were. I had many questions. What were their missions? How and where were they accessing property to grow on and at what scale? How skilled were they, and what types of resources did they have? My work with the New Orleans Food and Farm Network afforded me the opportunity to use this information to organize training and provide technical assistance to new and seasoned growers. What became apparent to me was that the "programming"

Figure 5.1. Sun Harvest Kitchen Garden under preparation. Photo by Pamela Arnette Broom.

Figure 5.2. Vines gloriously frame one of Pamela's gardens. Photo by Pamela Arnette Broom.

aspect of urban agriculture provided a unique vantage point from which to observe as well as participate in how city farming was taking place in New Orleans.

Often, when I spoke with people about my vision for urban agriculture, I would call attention to the proliferation of post-Katrina vacant and blighted properties, the area's year-round growing season, and the presence of local gardening wisdom as reasons to embrace intensive cultivation in the city as a viable path to revitalization. I cautioned against a romanticized view of city farming. As I sought to engage local young people and adults in gardening, my nostalgic tendencies surfaced. I was advocating for the revival of what I had experienced growing up in New Orleans: a city-wide presence of backyard gardens, a variety of fruit trees on private and public lands, and neighbor-to-neighbor sharing of prized crops. I quickly accepted the fact that we were a couple of generations removed from that reality, and that the "re-education" of locals was needed to take full advantage of those possibilities. I began to ask myself and others the *why* and *who* of whether urban agriculture as a revitalization tool was even possible. A colleague shared an observation that much of what she was witnessing with the *new* urban farmers had very much to do with lifestyle more than community benefit. I supported that observation on some level while experiencing instances where there seemed to be sincere attempts by enthusiastic emergent city farmers to improve their new neighbors' quality of life. Sadly, as I drive throughout the city now, I see the unkempt remains of unrealized urban agriculture projects.

Gentrification of Foodways in the Post-Disaster City

Pamela's experience as a lifelong grower in New Orleans sheds light on the emergence, development, and changes in urban agricultural activities in the decade following Hurricane Katrina. Her close engagement with multiple urban agricultural projects, as a gardener, a mentor, and nonprofit organization staff member since 2005, uniquely positioned her to observe the shifting grounds of the urban agricultural scene. While the expansion of urban gardening and farming activities in the city during these years somewhat actualized her visions of increasing urban cultivation practices, what transpired in the city over time was not a revival of the long-sustained gardening tradition, but *urban agriculture*, a new form of growing in the city that was situated in the new local economy.

In this chapter, we examine the changing notion of *local food* in New Orleans over the decade following Hurricane Katrina, with a particular focus on how it shaped the trajectory of urban agricultural practices in the city. We illustrate how the development of urban gardening and farming activities in post-Katrina New Orleans occurred in the context of the shifting demographic and economic environment of the city, and how the trajectory of the urban agricultural scene became a part of the gentrification of foodways. We begin with a historic overview of local foodways prior to the 2005 storm, then illustrate how the post-disaster urban transition reshaped local foodways. As the economic development of the city expanded the opportunities for growers, the urban agricultural scene that developed in post-Katrina New Orleans distinctly established itself as belonging to the *new* locals, despite the historical precedent of urban cultivation in the city. Throughout the chapter, we emphasize that this occurred despite the heterogeneity of the grower profile, missions, and praxis. We describe this as *gentrification of foodways*, whereby new notions of locality come to compete with, or even replace, the existing folk foodways, while having real consequences on access to resources and opportunities.

The events, experiences, and perspectives described in this chapter come from several sources. First, Pamela Arnette Broom has been growing in New Orleans most of her life. Since 2005, she has mentored dozens of new urban growers and urban agricultural projects in the city, while maintaining her own gardens. She has also worked in partnership with Parkway Partners and New Orleans Redevelopment Authority. Yuki Kato began conducting research on urban agriculture in New Orleans around 2009, examining land access, demographic composition, mission and praxis of urban growers. The illustrative quotes used in this chapter are from the sixty in-depth interviews she conducted from 2014 to 2015 with current and former growers, nonprofit organization staff, as well as local agencies interfacing with the growers. We also rely on historical archives and media reports when discussing relevant events. This chapter was a result of our continued conversations over eight years, during which we shared similar concerns and observations about the unfolding urban agricultural scenes in the city. All names in italics are pseudonyms.

Urban Gardening and Foodways in New Orleans Before 2005

New Orleans' unique foodways are not only a marketed production of authenticity for tourism (Gotham 2007; Thomas 2009) but have also long been an everyday practice among the residents, who associated Mondays with red beans and rice, and waited for the satsuma citrus season in the late fall. Local *folk foodways* were geographically specific (e.g., Creole tomatoes and Gulf shrimp), seasonally specific (e.g., crawfish around the Jazz Fest in the spring), and culinarily specific (e.g., gumbo, étouffée, and po-boys). The Circle Food Store in the Tremé neighborhood, which flooded severely during the storm, was known for its signature sale item: four bell peppers for a dollar. The bell pepper is one of the "holy trinity" of Creole cooking, along with onion and celery, that constitutes the base for many local cuisines. When the supermarket finally reopened in 2014, the longtime owner Dwayne Boudreaux reassured customers that the store would continue the signature sale.

New Orleanians had also been growing and eating *local* long before 2005. There are some archival records that indicate that some of the mansions in the old French Quarter had gardening space for growing vegetables that were separate from their ornamental gardens.[2] Even in the late twentieth century, having a small kitchen garden in a front- or backyard was common practice across the city, as was the growth of fruit and nut orchards around the city. Even if they were not growing in the city themselves, many New Orleanians had familial connections to *the country* or *farming*, with their extended family members owning or operating the farm outside of the city. For example, the following quote from the interview with AumRa Frezel of Algiers neighborhood appears in the poster produced by New Orleans Food and Farm Network (NOFFN) for the Food Talk Project:

> You have to realize that we are basically one or two generations removed from people who pretty much farmed everything that they ate. I grew up in the Lower Ninth Ward in the house that my grandfather built. I came

from a rural family. On my mother's side, they were farmers. On my father's side, they liked to fish and hunt.

The Food Talk Project was piloted by NOFFN as a food system curriculum for youth that fostered relationship-building between students and elders from the community at O. Perry Walker Senior High School in 2007. Beyond gardens and farms, fishing in the bayou or the lake provided local seafood for the family dinner, and the sight of chickens in the neighborhood was not considered unusual, especially in the areas away from the city center such as the Lower and the Upper Ninth Wards.

During the 1980s and through the 1990s, Parkway Partners, a nonprofit organization, initiated a community gardens program in the city. At one point there were more than one hundred gardens registered with Parkway Partners. New Orleans Food and Farm Network had been helping to set up backyard gardens since the early 2000s. Community gardening and backyard gardening were focused on private consumption, and there were few, if any, market activities among urban growers during this time.[3] Booker T. Washington High School's horticultural program had received some local media coverage, where Floyd Jenkins taught cultivation in greenhouses and outdoor planters. The school was severely damaged during the 2005 storm and did not reopen, thus the program was never reinstituted. Across town, Lafitte Housing Project in the Sixth Ward had an active farm on site that was set up by the federally funded Urban Gardening Program in the early 1980s. Started with the guidance of the Orleans Parish office of the Louisiana Cooperative Extension Service, a group of elderly Black men from the area tended the garden and gave away what they grew to their family and friends.

While there were records and accounts indicating the preexisting practices of urban gardening in New Orleans, not everyone was growing or aware of these practices. Most notably, there seemed to be a generational gap in urban gardening knowledge and experiences. By 2005, the number of community gardens dwindled to fewer than thirty, partly due to the aging and relocation of the elderly growers, according to the Parkway Partners staff and other long-term growers. In contrast to the awareness of the culinary traditions, urban gardening had less visible presence in the city prior to 2005. People were eating local food, using locally grown or procured ingredients, but were not calling it *urban agriculture* or *local food* in ways that have come to dominate since the storm.

Post-Katrina and the Emergence of New Foodways and Urban Agriculture

Over the decade following Hurricane Katrina, New Orleans underwent a dramatic transformation. During the early months and years of recovery, the uncertainty about the city's future, the critical examination of the racial injustices that the storm exposed, and the determined reclamation of the city's cultural heritage dominated the media and external narratives about New Orleans. Over time, the tone shifted to a more optimistic and exploratory emphasis on the city's expanding economic opportunities and new reasons to visit the city beyond the historic French Quarter and the Garden District. The expansion of the city's culinary industry and alternative food markets were topics frequently mentioned in this narrative, noting that the city was not only open to business, but also that it was a place for cultural innovation. It was in this context that a new form of local foodways emerged and urban agriculture gained popularity, visibility, and opportunity.

Immediately following the disaster, the traditional foodways in the restaurants were re-established quickly as the city prioritized rebuilding tourism, its primary industry. But as the city showed signs of economic expansion and repopulation, new culinary industry and markets began to shape the new foodways and redefine *local food*. The new fine-dining restaurants that opened in gentrifying neighborhoods outside of the French Quarter were more likely to feature modernized, refined, and reinterpreted Cajun or Creole dishes, appealing to the foodies in search of the new iteration of authenticity and exoticism (Johnston and Baumann 2010). The rapid expansion of food truck businesses in the city capitalized on these trends, marketing the experiences of "hybridized authenticity" to mostly middle-class, younger consumers who followed their businesses using social media or found them as convenient late-night eateries set up outside of the bars (Irvin 2017).

By comparison, the folk foodways struggled to return during the recovery process, with few grocery stores reopening, or else operating on limited hours, offering a sparse selection of food items. As the grocery stores returned to their full business capacity and new food markets opened, the uneven pace of recovery reflected the historical racial and class disparities in the city, with some neighborhoods having more food retail options than ever while others remained scarcely serviced. Furthermore, the new foodscape came to emphasize local food in ways that were distinct from the previous conceptualization of locality, by increasingly framing it as geographic rather than sociocultural quality. It is important to note here that the emergence of the new local foodways occurred in New Orleans as locality became a central organizing concept for branding, marketing, and consuming the city as a part of the symbolic economy of place (Zukin 2010). Construction of locality in the regional commerce during the second half of the decade following the disaster notably shifted the focus away from the long-term residents' grief, resilience, and pride (Otte 2007) to celebrating *anyone* who currently lives in the city to claim their stake in the place. Such transition in the framing of locality was most pronounced in the food industry, from local food markets to urban agriculture.

Five alternative food markets with a focus on local food opened between 2008 and 2015, including a short-lived operation by Good Eggs, a San Francisco-based online market, during 2014–2015.[4] These markets featured locally grown produce, including those grown in the city, and often attracted clientele that were middle-class, educated, and white (Kato 2013). New transplants to the city since Hurricane Katrina were more likely to engage with these alternative markets as customers, volunteers, and suppliers than were long-term residents, though this was not an exclusive place for newcomers, and the planning for two of these markets predated 2005. Urban agricultural activities began to expand and gained prominence in the city during the second half of the decade. There were few growers who continued their gardening even during the earlier months following the Hurricane. A 2006 report in the *New York Times* refers to Jeanette Bell, a long-term African American grower, whose garden in Central City neighborhood was not damaged directly by the flooding. According to the article, she returned to the garden "weeks after the storm, to find the 500 roses she tends in a former vacant lot in full bloom. 'I cut little bouquets and gave them to anybody who came by,' Ms. Bell said" (Raver 2006). By 2015, at least 130 lots were being cultivated as community gardens, urban farms, and school gardens by more than fifty gardeners and growers who were working full- or part-time on these projects.[5]

New *Locals* Growing

The dominant image of the growers operating in New Orleans since 2005 has come to be associated with the demographic characteristics of the YURPs, or Young Urban Rebuilding Professionals (Ehrenfeucht and Nelson 2013; Weil 2008). These were individuals with college educations, in their twenties to early thirties, not originally from the city, with some training in community organizing or with advanced degrees in related fields such as law and public administration who came to assist in the early post-disaster recovery work. In reality, however, individuals engaged in urban agriculture were of more diverse backgrounds in terms of age, experiences in agriculture, and their motives. Some of these *newcomers* included returning New Orleanians, who grew up in the city or have familial roots in the city but had been living elsewhere as adults until Hurricane Katrina. Others were individuals in their forties or older who viewed this as their new career path. The growers were racially diverse, though still predominantly white in the context of a majority Black city, and gender proportion was approximately even.

Few long-term growers continued their practice, as evidenced by the examples of Pamela and Ms. Bell. These growers were mostly over the age of fifty and had been growing in the city in some capacity beyond private home gardening for more than a decade prior to 2005. Some of these long-term growers became mentors to many of the newcomers or new gardening projects. Mentorship took many forms, from volunteering, internship, apprenticeship, to having the long-term growers on the nonprofit project's advisory board. More than a dozen of the thirty-five growers interviewed for Yuki's study who began growing in the city after 2005 mentioned that these long-term growers played an influential role in their starting their career as an urban grower. Some growers, by contrast, especially among those who started after 2012, had little or no direct interactions with these long-term growers. Those growers learned specific techniques and methods from online sources, college courses, workshops, other new growers, or through their own trial and error, and did not express particular interests in the traditional methods of gardening developed by the long-term growers.

Despite the heterogeneity of the growers' biography, the impression that urban gardening is *new* dominated the local narrative of urban agriculture over time. Below, we illustrate three ways in which the practices of urban agriculture have come to be associated with the new form of local foodways that attributes locality to geography, not history, culture or people; media framing of the urban agriculture stories, engagement with the local residents and communities, and the growers' participation in the new local food market. To be clear, our argument is not that these associations between urban agriculture and new foodways were empirically accurate, but that they occurred in the context of shifting urban political economic conditions. As a result, rather than framing the revival of urban gardening as a symbolic and actual validation of the people and their practices of local foodways of the past, it has come to symbolize the arrival and the dominance of the new locality.

Framing the *New* Urban Agriculture Narratives

In 2010, urban agricultural activities taking place in New Orleans began to gain local and national media attention. At first, this coverage highlighted the work and knowledge of long-term residents, but this faded over time. For example, Tracie McMillan's 2010 article in the *Atlantic Monthly* featured five urban farms, all of which were founded after 2008. However, four of the five projects in the article were headed by long-term residents including Pamela, and McMillan situates these projects as a revival of the city's urban gardening tradition. In contrast, the city's Eat Local Challenge organizes an urban farm bike tour as a part of its month-long commitment to "eat local." The tour visits different farms or gardens each year, and typically combines gardens tended by long-term residents and post-Katrina transplants. But the coverage of one of the farms they visited in 2014 exemplifies this trend toward highlighting the contributions of newcomers (Bruno 2014):

> The Magellan Street Garden underwent a major makeover last year after lead gardener Tony Lee's late wife, Linette, reached out to the Tulane

City Center for help. A team of 12 students, led by Doug Harmon and Sam Richards, responded. The newly refurbished garden features a shade structure which not only provides a relaxing place to rest after digging in the dirt but screens a storage area and funnels rainwater off its roof into a small wetland that was constructed on site, along with two ponds.

The article's focus on the recent works by the local private university's architecture center overshadows the work Tony, a long-term African American resident married to a native New Orleanian, had done previously with the community, and undermines the significance of their long-term practice of gardening in the city.

Additionally, when a local public radio show focusing on entrepreneurs called *Out to Lunch* aired an episode on urban agriculture in 2013, two young founders of for-profit and nonprofit organizations were invited as guests. The guests were described on the episode page as "changing the way we grow vegetables in a swampy urban food desert and harvest fruit in an abundant garden of Eden." In the introduction, the host Peter Ricchiuti, a business professor at Tulane University, briefly refers to the city's historical precedent of growing and harvesting food in the city, and both guests, white, post-Katrina transplants in their twenties, acknowledge their awareness of the history. Nevertheless, the rest of the show focuses on the novelty of each of their projects, such as installing hydroponic gardens for private clients and organizing volunteers to pick unwanted fruits from orchards on private properties, leaving the listeners with an impression that the newcomers were leading the way in shaping the new local food movement.

Engaging the *Local* Residents and Communities

As the impression that urban agriculture was for the newcomers began to dominate the local narrative of gardening and farming, some growers also faced challenges in developing informative relationships with long-term residents that lived near their gardening sites. Gardens and farms were located throughout the city, though there was a notable concentration of gardens in areas that had high rates of vacancy, regardless of the levels of flooding in 2005. The relationship between urban agricultural projects and nearby, long-term residents was not necessarily hostile, nor was it always cooperative. The difficulties of establishing positive relationships between the growers and the long-term residents stemmed from a combination of miscommunication about public access to the urban gardens, and the fear of having their residential community being redeveloped as *green* spaces, conjuring the trauma of the green dot controversy, in which a tentative urban shrinkage plan designated heavily flooded neighborhoods to be redeveloped as green spaces rather than residential areas, and fatigue from promises being made and not delivered by nonprofit organizations (Harvey, Kato, and Passidomo 2016).

In some cases, the new growers' framing of urban agriculture as a part of food justice activism did not readily resonate with the long-term residents. During one conversation, a community organizer in the Lower Ninth Ward, a predominantly Black working- and middle-class neighborhood, noted Yuki's use of terms such as "food desert" and "food justice" when discussing the organization's effort to bring in a grocery store to the neighborhood. The organizer, a New Orleans native in her thirties who returned to the city after the storm, noted that she was aware of these terms but would not use them when talking with the community members. When Yuki appeared puzzled, as her work clearly addressed these concepts, the organizer said: "But if I told them, 'Did you know that another neighborhood just got their grocery store?' they get it. They understand what that means." The long-term residents were aware of the historic roots of the residential segregation and the political and economic marginalization of their community. But without effective tools for conveying how urban gardening connects to "food justice," well-intended projects missed an opportunity to build rapport and gain support.

Nearly all growers made their produce or flowers available to nearby residents, either for free or at a discounted rate. Neighborhood children were invited, formally or informally, to come hang out in the garden in the afternoons or on the weekends. Growers also reported sharing gardening tips and loaning tools to the neighbors, who sometimes returned the favor by warning them of some suspicious activities on site while the growers were away. Vandalism, theft, or trespassing occurred sometimes, especially when gardening sites were located in sparsely populated areas or had no fencing. Most growers viewed these as unfortunate but expected costs of growing in the city, especially in a neighborhood with high rates of poverty, vacancy, and crime, rather than as signs of protest against their practices. Except for a few cases, nearby residents did not explicitly express strong objections to these new gardens. But their direct involvement with the projects was limited, when compared to the volume of outside volunteers and visitors that occupied the space on a regular basis.

Urban gardening is physically demanding work, and most projects rely on volunteers to take on tasks from debris removal, weeding, and fencing, to composting. A majority of these volunteers were residents of other neighborhoods, local students, college students on a service trip, or "voluntourists" who reserved a day out of their trip to perform some community service. A few nearby residents volunteered to help in these gardens on a regular basis, but a large number of mostly white, educated outsiders occupying the gardens could have presented these spaces as belonging to *others* (Slocum 2007), not to nearby Black residents.

In other cases, programming on site was more explicitly aimed at the *new* locals. Many gardens and farms organized social events for additional revenue generation. *Dylan*, a white entrepreneurial grower in his twenties who came to the city to attend college after 2005, explained the future plans for the site he runs with his business partner as follows:

> So, we're gonna build about four tables which is where we will be hosting like a weekly pizza night. We'll be opening up for various events. If pop ups want to rent it, or a wedding, or whatever, anything that once we're done we rent it out as a venue. Um, and then we'll be doing an early morning yoga. Garden yoga.

These events more directly aligned with the interests and tastes of the *new* locals, while they also intersected with the emerging economy of food trucks, pop-up restaurants, and microbreweries (Irvin 2017). It hardly matters, then, that this particular grower, a newcomer to the city, originally started his first garden in a vacant lot and worked with local youth in the garden until these young people stopped coming due to incarceration, death, and relocation. In the eyes of the general public, including long-term residents and the newcomers, these farms were part of the new foodways.

Growing *Local* Food

The proliferation of more entrepreneurially oriented urban agricultural projects around 2012 coincided with the development of the new local food markets featuring new local foodways. Establishment of alternative, local food markets and new restaurants that were eager to purchase locally grown food expanded the demand for urban agricultural products. The growers who participated in this new market found a niche demand for specialty produce, especially herbs and microgreens.

When asked how they decide on what to grow, *Christina*, the lead grower for a gardening and community health project, responded as follows:

> First thing is, I mean what grows seasonally. Seasonal planning guides. Number two, what do people want to eat? What does the community want to eat? And that'll be a portion of it. And third of all, as far as being able to have a market garden, what's selling in the market for um, you know. We'll put it this way: you don't want to grow a field of potatoes for market because they're intensive, they take a long time, and they're not going to sell for very much.

Christina came to New Orleans prior to Katrina to pursue a graduate degree, and eventually became involved with urban agriculture. The garden she was leading was developed as part of a community redevelopment project in 2013, and she viewed her role as outreach to the community to foster interests in gardening. Yet she was also highly aware of the market potential of what they grew. When the growers focused on market viability of their products, they found greens and herbs to have a high profit margin, especially for local restaurant sales. As *Theo*, another white, post-Katrina transplant for-profit grower summed up, "It's just a really good avenue, or a good springboard is doing sort of specialty salad and herbs. And (we) can carry into the restaurant economy, you know?" Both of these growers worked closely with the nearby, long-term residents by having them as volunteers, community gardeners, or even as paid staff, and let them grow food that they liked to eat. Yet these growers also grew high profit-margin produce as a way to economically sustain the projects, especially in cases where they did not or could not seek grants.

The most valuable *local* food in the new local food economy became locally grown, specialty crops that were not familiar to many long-term residents or traditional foodways. In other words, locally grown microgreen salads become more local, or at least just as local, as gumbo made with green peppers, onion, and celery grown in California. The popularity of urban agriculture in the context of economic expansion, demographic shifts, and changing tastes therefore contributed to the reshaping of the notion of locality, even as many of the growers aimed to use gardening and farming as a way to empower long-term residents and their communities during the post-disaster recovery and rebuilding process.

Urban Agriculture and Gentrification of Foodways

Previous scholarship on gentrification has noted how symbolic economies drive gentrification by marketing the symbolic and tangible markers of authenticity to the newcomers while displacing the long-term residents who made the place authentic (Hyra 2017; Mele 1996; Zukin 2010). The emergence of new local foodways in New Orleans deviates somewhat from these patterns of gentrification. Valorization of locality occurred while simultaneously redefining its attributes, from sociocultural roots to geographic proximity. In the end, urban agriculture in New Orleans became strongly associated with the thriving new local economy rather than being reclaimed by the long-term residents. That said, urban gardeners were not necessarily themselves gentrifiers in the neighborhood where they grew, since many do not live on site, though they could have been residentially gentrifying other neighborhoods. Those who aimed to use urban gardens as tools of community building may resemble "social preservationist" newcomers, whose intention is to use their privilege for supporting and preserving the local culture and long-term residents (Brown-Saracino 2009). Yet *urban agriculture* was presented to the long-term residents as novel and foreign, rather than connecting the contemporary urban food production and provisioning practices to the history and the memory of the community.

To this effect, the intense, rapid transformation of the city since 2005 prevented food justice–oriented urban agricultural projects from taking root in New Orleans. Urban agriculture in post-Katrina New Orleans developed in the fragile and transitional urban conditions, under which few predicted that the major concern at the ten-year anniversary of the storm would be gentrification. Earlier post-disaster projects that aimed to use gardening as community organizing experienced slow starts due to limited resources, distrust, or lack of interest by the residents, and lack of experience in gardening or community organizing by many of the well-intended newcomers. By the time the conditions for urban agriculture were fertile, some of these projects no longer existed, and the remaining or new projects' participation in the new local food economy validated their status as belonging to the newcomers. We have already noted that the loss of tradition predated the storm, though the disaster accelerated the displacement or the declining health of the elderly former gardeners and the people who remember their gardens. It was not the case that the new growers came into the city with a strong presence of long-term gardeners, but the disconnect between the past and the present growers resulted in the missed opportunity to meld local traditional growing wisdom with the idealistic exuberance of new urban farmers.

Our examination of the development of the urban agricultural scene in post-Katrina New Orleans illustrates how the forces of urban transition could indirectly shape the trajectory of the gardens and farms (Walker 2016). The economic improvement of the city and the demographic changes expanded opportunities for urban agriculture for some, while making it more distant for those whose ancestors engaged in similar practices at one point in recent memory. Alignment of the urban agricultural activities with the new local foodways in New Orleans occurred despite little top-down, explicit cooptation efforts, all the while many garden and farm projects aspired to use the space as a place for building community, providing food security, and creating employment, leisure, and educational opportunities. Nevertheless, it is the expanding economic force that could continue to reconstitute local foodways, with which urban agriculture may not continue to align. In this context, gardens and farms whose practices are consistent with the new foodways or *green gentrification* (Dooling 2009; Gould and Lewis 2017) framework would have the best odds of sustaining for the long term.

Gentrification that strengthened the new local food economy may cast a shadow over long-term sustainability of urban agriculture in the city, as rising property values threaten land tenure and housing security of the long-term residents and the growers. This may become another wave of popularity for urban gardening in the city, but in the wake of current conditions, urban gardening in New Orleans could become disconnected from its history and memory: Why people in the city used to grow and eat the type of food in the way they did. Folk foodways are a tangible embodiment of the history of a place, including ethnic heritage, political economy, and social injustices. Gentrification of foodways is, on one hand, newcomers introducing new ways of procuring, preparing, and consuming food that are not accessible to the long-term residents for economic, social, and cultural reasons. Yet one of the most devastating impacts of gentrification of foodways in places like New Orleans is its effectiveness in depriving the long-term residents and their ancestors from being recognized for their foresights and diligence and their descendants of their opportunity to carry on the tradition that has now revived.

Employing urban agriculture as a quality-of-life tool for equitably securing access to whole, affordable, and enjoyable fresh food has certainly been viewed as a global strategy in an increasingly urban world. As New Orleans revels in the three hundredth anniversary of its founding as a city of international importance, myriad reflections about periods of progress are juxtaposed alongside remembrances of natural and human-made catastrophes that have defined its cultural dynamism and the resilience of its people. Food heritage is central to this story. No matter the race or socioeconomic makeup of New Orleanians, "homegrown" or "transplant," how food is grown, purchased, and consumed will be a cause célèbre.

Pamela remains steadfastly focused and engaged in achieving the success of urban agriculture as a means of supporting environmental vibrancy, healing, and economic benefit for her beloved New Orleans. She is currently working as a project director with NewCorp, Inc., a local community development financial institution that provides non-traditional financial products and services to small, minority, and women-owned businesses. NewCorp is administering the Seventh Ward Revitalization Project (7WRP) in a section of the historic neighborhood that has experienced severe disinvestment post-Hurricane Katrina. In an effort to stave off some of the negative effects of gentrification in this underserved area, Pamela is co-developing the Farmacia Wellness Hub, a signature initiative of the 7WRP that focuses on the intersection between urban agriculture and medicine for community wellness. She and her team are optimistic that this project will provide an improved road map for fostering intergenerational, people-to-people fair engagement regarding the benefits of inclusive and well-managed city farming in New Orleans. The grand vision is that collaborative innovation will be the linchpin that connects local growing wisdom with fresh energy and ideas.

NOTES

1 City of New Orleans compilation of the US Department of Housing and Urban Development Point in Time count data shows that the city's homeless population drastically expanded around 2009–2012, from around 1,600 in 2008 to more than 8,700 in 2009, and remained at 4,903 in 2012 (https://datadriven.nola.gov).
2 "Plan Book for Plans" archive, accessed at New Orleans Notarial Archive.
3 The Crescent City Farmers' Market permitted local gardeners to sell from the "Urban Growers" table, but this did not sustain for the long term (Kato's conversation with Kris Pottharst, 2015).
4 Hollygrove Market and Farm opened in 2008, New Orleans Food Cooperative opened in 2011, the new St. Roch Market and Dryades Public Market both opened in 2015. The new St. Roch Market was established on the site of the original St. Roch Market, which did not reopen after 2005 due to the damage from the storm.
5 Calculation based on the second author's data collection.

REFERENCES

Brown-Saracino, Japonica. 2009. *A Neighborhood That Never Changes: Gentrification, Social Preservation and the Search for Authenticity*. Chicago: University of Chicago Press.

Bruno, R. Stephanie. 2014. "Locavore Bike Tour Pedals Past Urban Gardens." *New Orleans Advocate*, July 11. www.theadvocate.com.

Dooling, Sarah. 2009. "Ecological Gentrification: A Research Agenda Exploring Justice in the City." *International Journal of Urban and Regional Research* 33 (3): 621–39.

Ehrenfeucht, Renia, and Marla Nelson. 2013. "Young Professionals as Ambivalent Change Agents in New Orleans after the 2005 Hurricanes." *Urban Studies* 50 (4): 825–41.

Gotham, Kevin F. 2007. *Authentic New Orleans: Tourism, Culture, and Race in the Big Easy*. New York: New York University Press.

Gould, Kenneth A., and Tammy L. Lewis. 2017. *Green Gentrification: Urban Sustainability and the Struggle for Environmental Justice*. New York: Routledge.

Harvey, Daina Cheyenne, Yuki Kato, and Catarina Passidomo. 2016. "Rebuilding Others' Communities: A Critical Analysis of Race and Nativism in Non-Profits in the Aftermath of Hurricane Katrina." *Local Environment* 21 (8): 1029–46.

Hyra, Derek S. 2017. *Race, Class, and Politics in the Cappuccino City*. Chicago: University of Chicago Press.

Irvin, Cate. 2017. "Constructing Hybridized Authenticities in the Gourmet Food Truck Scene." *Symbolic Interaction* 40 (1): 43–62.

Johnston, Josée, and Shyon Baumann. 2010. *Foodies: Democracy and Distinction in the Gourmet Foodscape*. New York: Routledge.

Kato, Yuki. 2013. "Not Just the Price of Food: Challenges of an Urban Agriculture Organization in Engaging Local Residents." *Sociological Inquiry* 83 (3): 369–91.

Mele, Christopher. 1996. "Globalization, Culture, and Neighborhood Change: Reinventing the Lower East Side of New York." *Urban Affairs Review* 32 (1): 3–22.

Otte, M. 2007. "The Mourning After: Languages of Loss and Grief in Post-Katrina New Orleans." *Journal of American History* 94 (3): 828–36.

Raver, Anne. 2006. "From the Scars of Katrina, Green Shoots and Blossoms." *New York Times*, February 16. https://nyti.ms/2Dakf5J.

Slocum, Rachel. 2007. "Whiteness, Space, and Alternative Food Practice." *Geoforum* 38 (3): 520–33.

Thomas, Lynnell L. 2009. "'Roots Run Deep Here': The Construction of Black New Orleans in Post-Katrina Tourism Narratives." *American Quarterly* 61 (3): 749–68.

Walker, Samuel. 2016. "Urban Agriculture and the Sustainability Fix in Vancouver and Detroit." *Urban Geography* 37 (2): 163–82.

Weil, Frederick D. 2008. "Nola-Yurp Survey—July/August 2008 Preliminary Findings" [Report]. Louisiana State University, August 23. www.lsu.edu.

Zukin, Sharon. 2010. *Naked City: The Death and Life of Authentic Urban Places*. New York: Oxford University Press.

6

The Cost of Low-Hanging Fruit?

An Orchard, a Nonprofit, and Changing Community in Portland

EMILY BECKER AND NATHAN MCCLINTOCK

Tucked between a row of recently constructed single-family, affordable housing and a complex of aging apartments in North Portland is a grid of young fruit trees, some still supported by stakes and twine. A bit farther on, colorful native shrubs—Oregon grape, red-flowering currant, gooseberry—grow beneath a stand of mature trees loaded with ripening figs, Asian pears, apples, plums, pears, nectarines, and hazelnuts. A small group of people move among the trees weeding thistle, hauling wheelbarrows full of mulch, pruning branches, and anticipating the summer harvest to come. A large wooden sign reveals this bustling, verdant place to be the Fruits of Diversity Community Orchard (hereafter, the FOD).

Community orchards are a unique form of urban agriculture that brings together a group of people to design, plant, harvest, and maintain fruit- and nut-producing trees and other woody perennials. Unlike community or allotment gardens, where individuals lease a garden plot to grow and harvest their own produce for personal use, a community orchard is maintained and harvested communally; no one person has any claim to a particular tree or its fruit. While community gardens are often fenced off and accessible only to gardeners, community orchards are usually open to everyone. Participants frequently distribute harvested fruit to the wider public, and passersby may harvest the fruit at any time (Keech et al. 2000). Beyond fruit, however, the goal of orchards such as the FOD is to grow a community of people to care for the orchard. This is particularly important given the long-term commitment required to care for trees that can take several years to bear fruit after planting and that then continue to produce for decades (Ames 2013).

Despite the differences between community orchards and other forms of urban agriculture, scholarship on community gardens sheds important light on community orchards. While many celebrate community gardens as "cultural and social neighborhood centers" (Saldivar-Tanaka and Krasny 2004:404) that bring together a diversity of racial and ethnic backgrounds, critical food scholars challenge the very notion of "community" around which gardens are organized. A garden's intended community is often defined by geography alone, without recognition of the multiple social networks and groups that overlap in a shared space. Participants come to a community garden with different sets of expectations, and there is rarely a common understanding among participants of who the garden belongs to (Bosco and Joassart-Marcelli 2017; Drake 2014; Kurtz 2001). Because "not everyone working to improve communities agrees on what ought to be valorized," the values and desired outcomes of community gardens and orchards are often challenged and in flux (Carolan and Hale 2016:531).

Urban agriculture efforts organized around an idealized community thus frequently fail to cohere; many become exclusionary, and some struggle to attract local residents or—in the case of organizations seeking to improve access to healthy food in low-income areas—their target population. Project leaders, who are typically white staff of nonprofit organizations, are often unaware of the subtle and not-so-subtle ways that their positions, beliefs, class, and white privilege influence the project (Guthman 2008; Kato 2013; Ramírez 2015; Sbicca 2012), or of the ways in which their projects contribute to larger-scale social and structural processes, including gentrification (Pudup 2008; McClintock 2018).

For this reason, critical understanding of community gardens or orchards managed by nonprofits demands close attention to the structural realities that mediate how community is defined and by whom. The neoliberal "turn to community" (DeFilippis, Fisher, and Shragge 2010:26) has elevated the importance of community while diluting the power and meaning of the term; it has become an empty signifier of everything and nothing, an "unequivocal good, an indicator of a high quality life, a life of human understanding, caring, selflessness, belonging" (Joseph 2002:vii). Community-building thus becomes a primary motivation driving the creation of community orchards (Betz, Mills, and Farmer 2017) and of urban agriculture organizations, more broadly, in part because community-building is attractive to funders, and clearly easier—and much less political—than challenging the structural barriers that limit food access (McClintock and Simpson 2018). But while community-building might seem a low-hanging fruit ripe for the picking, it can prove difficult and, as we attempt to illustrate here, can actually come at a cost.

In this chapter, we explore the contested understandings of community in the context of a community orchard in Portland, Oregon. A city once renowned for its quirky, artisanal funkiness—a reputation and model upheld as an ideal around the country (see also chapter 2 in this volume, for example)—Portland also now claims the shameful title of "the fastest gentrifying city in America" (Smith 2015). Drawing on interviews and participant observation, we examine how the involvement of an outside nonprofit organization can transform the very notion—and composition—of community. As an active participant in the process of designing and maintaining the FOD, the chapter's first author observed a marked shift in who was participating, leading us to ask: How did partnering with a nonprofit from outside the neighborhood transform the orchard and the "community" that manages it?[1] In our analysis we call attention to the racial and economic disparity between neighborhood residents and orchard participants, and reflect on the role of outside nonprofits in inadvertently cultivating "white food spaces" (Slocum 2007)—"viscous" agglomerations of white bodies brought together by food production (Ramírez 2015)—within otherwise racially and ethnically diverse neighborhoods. In the context of rampant gentrification, as is the case in Portland, such agglomerations can play an important role in both widening the rent gap that precedes reinvestment and making longtime residents feel out of place (McClintock 2018; Safransky 2014). Our intention with this chapter, however, is not to make the facile claim that community orchards gentrify low-income, diverse neighborhoods. Like many urban agriculture projects, this particular orchard's relationship to gentrification is nuanced, much more distal than proximal, but nevertheless entangled in broader processes of neighborhood change. Instead, our goal is to illustrate how the internal structures and practices of nonprofit organizations can subsume grassroots urban agriculture initiatives and transform them in ways that reinforce dominant power relations and create exclusive white spaces within diverse, low-income neighborhoods. These day-to-day organizational *micro-processes*, we argue, privilege participation by more affluent individuals from outside the neighborhood, most of them white, ultimately resulting in the alienation or exclusion of the very neighborhood residents who helped found the project in the first place.

An Orchard Takes Root in North Portland

The FOD stands adjacent to two ethnically and economically diverse affordable housing developments, on land maintained by Portland's housing authority, an independent public corporation recently rebranded as Home Forward. One of the developments, the 120-unit Tamarack Apartments, is a public housing complex comprised of a dozen or so two-story buildings constructed in 1968. The other, New Columbia, is a dense, 82-acre development of "854 housing units including public housing, affordable rentals, senior housing, and both market rate and affordable homes for sale" (Housing Authority of Portland 2007:1). The housing authority opened New Columbia in 2006, on the former site of a public housing complex called Columbia Villa, which had been built in 1943 to house shipyard workers during World War II. After the war, Columbia Villa became permanent low-income housing managed by the Housing Authority of Portland (HAP), and the largest public housing project in the state. The low-density neighborhood had a distinctly suburban feel, its curvilinear streets and mere handful of entrances isolating it from the surrounding Portsmouth neighborhood. Columbia Villa was originally an entirely white development—HAP did not allow African Americans to live in the neighborhood until 1973—but by 2000, was the most diverse neighborhood in Oregon (Gibson 2007b).

A long history of housing discrimination in Portland created segregated neighborhoods leading to concentrated poverty, income inequality, and crime (Gibson 2007a, 2007b). Through community policing and intensive social services, however, Columbia Villa recovered from a period of violence, drugs, and gang activity in the 1980s and 1990s. Nevertheless, "the Villa" continued to shoulder a racialized stigma as a dangerous place to live, reinforcing the lack of investment in the neighborhood and further concentrating poverty and segregation. In 2001, a confluence of factors—federal divestment from public housing, aging infrastructure, increasing cost of maintenance, and New Urbanist plans to increase density in the city, among others—spurred HAP to apply for $35 million from the federal Housing Opportunities for People Everywhere (HOPE VI) program to redevelop Columbia Villa. HOPE VI emphasized public-private partnerships, allowing private developers to build and manage public housing and build market-rate single-family homes in the neighborhood. Columbia Villa was demolished and rebuilt between 2003 and 2006, displacing 1,300 residents, of whom one-third were Black (Gibson 2007b). To help shed the stigma associated with the former housing project, the new, mixed-income development was rechristened New Columbia.

The transformation of Columbia Villa into New Columbia did more than simply change the housing stock, it also fundamentally changed the socioeconomic makeup of the neighborhood; many of the original residents never returned and many more new people moved in. While the newcomers were still quite diverse in terms of race/ethnicity, they came from a much wider range of economic backgrounds (Gibson 2007b). But as with many other HOPE VI projects (Goetz and Chapple 2010), mixing households from diverse economic strata did not automatically lead to community cohesion and integration in New Columbia. Hopes for "cross-pollination" between income groups faded as residents "rarely mingled" and "kept to themselves" (Parks 2014). Moreover, many older residents had a vested interest in preserving the strong social ties that had existed in the Villa, while newcomers were eager to reinvent the neighborhood in order to overcome its stigmatized reputation.

In 2006, with the goal of building community and bridging some of the differences between New Columbia's new and returning residents, the housing authority invited a community-based organization, Village Gardens, to facilitate a community garden project. As in other cities across North America, interest in urban agriculture in Portland was skyrocketing at the time, fueled in part by support from municipal officials and the nonprofit sector alike. Based in the neighborhood and focused on food access, health, equity, and promoting leadership from within, Village Gardens developed the Seeds of Harmony community garden, a sprawling oasis of garden plots tended by more than seventy families, many of them immigrants and refugees. In hopes of breaking down some of the stigma related to Columbia Villa, the committee

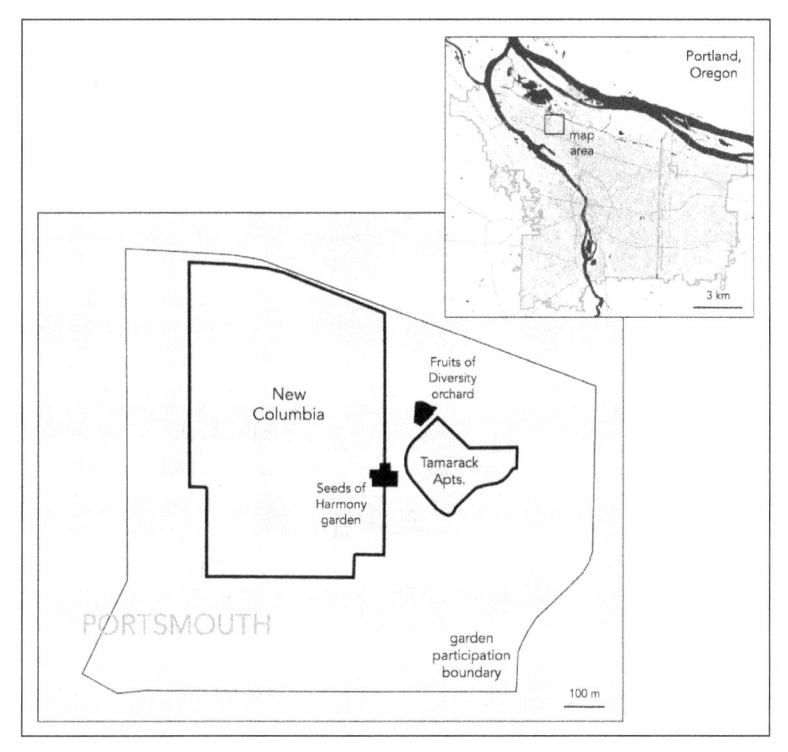

Figure 6.1. Location of the Fruits of Diversity community orchard and Seeds of Harmony community garden in relation to the Tamarack Apartments and New Columbia. The garden's catchment area extends into the surrounding Portsmouth neighborhood.

extended the boundaries of who could participate in the garden to adjacent areas of the surrounding Portsmouth neighborhood (see figure 6.1). For more than a decade now, a garden committee, composed of gardeners from the neighborhood, has managed the garden with staff support from Village Gardens. Committee meetings are translated into multiple languages, and decisions are reached by consensus.

Early on during garden committee discussions, residents brought up the need for fresh fruit. In 2006, garden members planted several fruit trees in a grassy area behind the Tamarack Apartment building. Following a period of neglect, the gardeners recognized that they needed help managing the trees, but also wanted to expand the orchard. In 2012, the

TABLE 6.1. Timeline of key events

1943	Columbia Villa built by Housing Authority of Portland (now called Home Forward) with 462 units to house WWII shipyard workers. Columbia Villa converted to public housing after the war.[a]
1968	Tamarack Apartments built by Housing Authority of Portland with 120 public housing units.[b]
2001	Housing Authority of Portland awarded $35 million grant through US Department of Housing and Urban Development Hope VI program to redevelop Columbia Villa.[a]
2003–2006	Redevelopment of Columbia Villa into New Columbia. New Columbia includes "854 housing units including public housing, affordable rentals, senior housing, and both market rate and affordable homes for sale."[a]
2006	Village Gardens starts Seeds of Harmony Community Garden (SOH) in New Columbia. Decisions are made by a committee of gardeners including the boundaries for participation in the garden and to plant fruit and nut trees behind the Tamarack Apartments.
2012	Seeds of Harmony garden committee invites Portland Fruit Tree Project to partner on orchard expansion.
2013	Groundbreaking and planting of new orchard in February.
2013	Orchard named "Fruits of Diversity Community Orchard" in June by SOH gardeners and non-neighbors who had been participating in the orchard expansion project.
2014	Interviews for this study conducted November 2014–December 2014.
2017	PFTP Board pauses programming in July to "step back, reflect, and reorganize," leaving orchard maintenance to volunteers.[c]

a Housing Authority of Portland, 2007.
b Home Forward, 2011.
c PFTP Board of Directors, 2017.

garden committee decided to partner with an outside organization with expertise in orchards, the Portland Fruit Tree Project (PFTP), a nonprofit whose mission is to "increase equitable access to healthful food and strengthen communities by empowering neighbors to share in the harvest and care of city-grown produce."[2] The new collaboration with PTFP spurred public interest and engagement in the orchard. In April 2013, volunteers from across the city—including Portland's mayor—planted an additional eighteen new fruit trees and more than fifty edible shrubs in the orchard (see table 6.1 for a timeline).

A Fruitful Collaboration?

As we detail in the remainder of this chapter, the collaboration between the garden committee organized by Village Gardens, a community-based organization, and PFTP, an outside nonprofit, in managing the FOD resulted in several marked changes. There was a notable shift in who was participating in the orchard, from a racially diverse group of neighbors to mostly white volunteers from outside the neighborhood. Over time, the orchard morphed from a neighbor-led project with a mission to grow fruit for neighborhood residents, to a project led by outside volunteers to raise fruit for distribution to low-income people, both inside the neighborhood and outside, as well as a place to educate volunteers about fruit trees.[3] In addition to this change in focus, the outside organization brought with it new people and new ideas about how the community orchard should work. While the collaboration also had positive impacts—such as more frequent tree care and healthier trees—several of these changes presented challenges for neighbors and arguably contributed to the shifting composition of participants. Several key micro-processes resulted in these changes: the organization's reliance on electronic communication; a shift away from a consensus-based approach to centralized decision-making; the formalization of volunteer positions; and the introduction of new management practices and orchard features. These internal organizational shifts, we argue, had a significant cumulative impact on who felt comfortable using the space and on the orchard's role in the neighborhood.

Modes of Communication

PTFP's involvement in the orchard's management brought new ways of conducting day-to-day business, including how communication with participants and other neighbors took place. Face-to-face contact between staff and neighborhood participants gave way to communication via email. Village Gardens, with its office actually located in New Columbia, has always been able to knock on doors to promote events in the adjacent Seeds of Harmony garden or recruit participation on the garden committee. During the first year that PFTP and Village Gardens worked together managing the FOD, neighbors and participants from both organizations met nine times outside of work parties to make decisions about the orchard. The year after, however, there was only one meeting, with no neighbor participation. Neighbors felt sidelined. One neighbor, Roy, for example, stated that he felt "like I'm an outside part of it. A branch instead of part of the main tree."

Like many nonprofits, PFTP relies on email to inform volunteers about upcoming events. Given that it requires the least amount of staff time, and because PTFP is based outside of the neighborhood, email was the primary means of communication, both to advertise events and to recruit people to sign up (also done electronically via the organization's website). While perhaps the most efficient and cost-effective way to communicate, this singular mode of communication ultimately privileged participation by people with easy access to the Internet. Since many neighborhood residents access computers only infrequently at the nearby community center if at all, the organization had little success in informing neighbors about FOD work parties. Roy remarked that because he didn't have Internet access at home, he often didn't see emails until after the event had already happened. Debbie, an older adult who does not use email at all, described a feeling of being left out. She complained, stating, "just not being told about things. You know, like when you guys come out to the orchard, I only know it 'cause I see you guys out there."

Exacerbating the situation was that the responsibility for most of the email communication was delegated to an AmeriCorps volunteer. However, the ill-timed staffing of the position meant that at the height of summer, when the orchard requires weekly watering and fruits need monitoring for ripeness and harvest, communications were left in limbo. Furthermore, because AmeriCorps volunteers didn't live in the neighborhood or work in the orchard on a daily basis, there was little opportunity for face-to-face interactions with neighbors to remind them about upcoming events. The AmeriCorps volunteer working with PFTP in 2015 recognized these challenges and tried a variety of tactics to inform neighbors about events, and noted seeing some signs of success in getting neighbors out to events that year. Overall, however, the reduction in face-to-face meeting times, the shift to a predominantly electronic mode of communication, coupled with its management by seasonal AmeriCorps volunteers, created an obstacle to participation by neighbors, while privileging participation by volunteers from throughout Portland who were more used to electronic communication than were many of the neighborhood residents.

Decision-making

Village Garden's partnership with PFTP also resulted in decision-making power changing hands from neighborhood residents to PFTP staff. In the words of a former Village Gardens staff member, PFTP had "become the driving force" leading the project, slowly sidelining the garden committee, which had collectively decided to invite PFTP's participation in the first place. Decision-making became more top-down as staff abandoned the time-consuming but inclusive consensus-based approach used by garden committee members. A PFTP decision to post signs in the orchard is particularly illustrative. The AmeriCorps volunteer sent out a Google document via email to thirteen people, most of them volunteers from outside the neighborhood, asking for feedback on draft language for the signs, which invited people to "taste the fruit" but not to take too much. As discussed above, not all orchard participants have regular access to the Internet, so only those with regular access and who were comfortable with online communication were involved in the decision. Reflecting on the process, the nonprofit's Executive Director at the time explained that the language on the signs had been

> shared with people for their buy-in, but wasn't presented as a robust community conversation. It was more like, "This is what we're thinking. How do you guys feel about it?" essentially. And people were generally on board. We haven't had any objections.

This style of management, where PFTP's ideas were presented for input, seemed to work against the organization's goal of empowering a "core team of volunteers that take on management of the orchard." While PFTP's intention has been to foster the community's sense of responsibility for the orchards, they did not put systems in place to allow for significant community input in decision-making.

Partnering with a nonprofit from outside the neighborhood also resulted in decisions that simply didn't make sense to some neighbors, revealing the disconnect between the dominant culture—in this case, white, nonprofit, foodie culture—within which PFTP operates, and the neighborhood participants. A couple of examples are particularly illustrative. In one case, a neighbor commented on the planting of quince, a fruit that has to be processed before it is eaten: "Quince is only made for jams and stuff. I mean, I don't even have time to make my own dinner! . . . If you've got homemakers in a certain area of the city, go put the quince there. They have more time to work with that." In the eyes of this neighbor, PFTP planted trees that are only useful for people with time to spare, and they failed to understand the needs and realities of the low-income community in which the orchard is located.

In another case, a PFTP staff member remarked, "There's been a lot of people not showing up at the right time," which to the staff meant that the participants were not meeting the organization's expectations. People tended to show up to the FOD after the meeting started, many often left early, and others continued working well beyond the ending time. They simply didn't feel the need to follow PFTP's schedule because they felt like the orchard was their space. While this behavior was actually indicative of the kind of community ownership that PFTP wanted to see in the orchard, it ran up against the prescribed format that the organization used for most of their events: They started each meeting in a circle with introductions and ended by asking participants to fill out a survey. People who left early were unable to fill out the survey. In turn, low participation, as measured by the survey, would look bad for the nonprofit and potentially impact future funding.

These two examples illustrate how PFTP's expectations, coupled with participants' lack of decision-making power, stood as barriers to neighborhood participation and a cohesive community in the orchard. The concern that people wouldn't show up on time or stay through the end of the meeting in order to fill out a survey, as well as the assumption that participants would embrace PFTP's vision of what to plant in the orchard, both point to the staff's lack of awareness of race, class, and cultural differences.

Formalizing Volunteers

A growing sense of exclusion among neighbors went hand in hand with increased participation by those more at ease within the milieu of alternative food nonprofits. Another micro-process that transformed the orchard community was PFTP's creation of formalized volunteer positions, which shifted day-to-day management of the orchard from neighbors to non-neighbors. After the new trees were planted, PFTP began hosting monthly volunteer work parties in the orchard. The next year, PFTP introduced the "Orchard Steward" program, despite lukewarm reception of the idea by orchard participants. A yearlong volunteer position, stewards agreed to attend all monthly work parties, water the orchard at least once in the summer, and help lead a work party. PTFP advertised the positions, which were open to anyone, widely. People who had volunteered previously in the orchard were invited by email to apply, and flyers were distributed to neighbors. In the end, nine people applied, all of whom were invited to become stewards. None of the people who had regularly participated in the orchard before applied to be a steward, however, and only one of the nine was from the immediate neighborhood, while another came from an adjacent part of the Portsmouth neighborhood. The remaining stewards were all from other neighborhoods in Portland and included one person who lived outside of the city. All were white, with one person identifying as white and Hispanic (see table 6.2). PFTP staff's original goal had been to recruit neighbors to fill the steward position but, due to limited time and staff to engage in effective, face-to-face community outreach, moved forward with the cohort of mostly non-neighbor stewards. PFTP and Village Gardens continued to promote work party events to neighbors, and longtime orchard participants continued to attend events, but none took on the steward role.

The introduction of the Orchard Steward program thus shifted the composition of the orchard's volunteer base. Prior to its launch, most of the volunteers at work parties were neighbors, while afterward, most were outsiders. Many of the stewards we interviewed expressed a passionate sense of ownership and dedication to the orchard. They traveled long distances for work parties, brought their family and friends to see it, and talked about it with their neighbors. Their motivations for participating at FOD varied, but many valued the opportunity to learn about fruit tree care, to improve food access in a low-income community, and to help grow an orchard that will provide fruit for decades. However, few of the stewards felt connected to the neighborhood in which the orchard is located. They knew very little about New Columbia or its history, or even of the more recent work of Village Gardens and its role in the development of the garden and orchard.

TABLE 6.2. Race/ethnicity of the neighborhood and orchard participants

Race/ethnicity	Census blocks[a] Pop. (N)	%	Neighborhood[b] Pop. (N)	%	Orchard participants[c] Pop. (N)	%
American Indian	0	0	18	2.0	0	0.0
Asian	14	0.2	12	1.3	0	0.0
Black or African American	1789	30.5	456	50.7	2	6.7
Caucasian or White	3170	54.0	377	41.9	27	90.0
Hawaiian	13	0.2	3	0.3	0	0
Multi-racial	499	8.5	27	3.0	0	0
Other	386	6.6	0	0	0	0
No response / unknown			7	0.8	1	3.3
TOTAL	5871	100.0	900	100.0	30	100.0
Hispanic	1565	26.7	189	21.0	1	3.3
Non-Hispanic	4306	73.3	711	79.0	28	93.3
NR			0	0	1	3.3
TOTAL	5871	100.0	900	100.0	30	100.0

a Two block groups cover most of the neighborhood: Block Group 5, Census Tract 39.01 and Block Group 1, Census Tract 40.01, Multnomah County, Oregon. (US Census Bureau, 2015).
b These data from Portland's housing authority, Home Forward, reflect 100% of Tamarack Apartments residents and 85% of New Columbia residents, those who live in public housing or receive Section 8 assistance. Home Forward does not collect comparable data for the remaining 15% of residents, who live in affordable housing but do not receive Section 8 or public housing, or for the homeowners in the neighborhood (Home Forward Central Database, accessed February 17, 2015).
c Participants who had attended three or more events or were living near the orchard. The race/ethnicity of the orchard participant was assigned by the first author, based on PTFP attendance records and participant observation.

Neighbors welcomed the stewards and appreciated their enthusiasm for the orchard and their willingness to volunteer, but they also considered them to be outsiders. Indeed, only one of the stewards felt they had made strong connections with neighbors. More typical was Colleen, who expressed feeling deeply connected to the orchard space, but that her relationship with orchard participants had not yet developed:

> I almost feel that it's more important that people feel strongly connected to the orchard. Through that, there's a lot of shared connection that would

naturally occur. I think the people that are more connected to the orchard are gonna come out over time and build those strong connections with one another.

Her comments illustrate something we observed frequently: a fundamental difference between how neighbors and outsiders defined the community. Neighbors defined the community as the neighborhood itself, while outsiders included anyone participating in the orchard in their definition. For Colleen, the way to build community is for people to first connect to the orchard space. In her view, making connections to other people comes more easily when working together in the same space than it does by trying to connect through interactions in the surrounding neighborhood. This idea may resonate with outsiders who don't know the other participants or are new to the orchard. But for the many neighbor participants already familiar with one another, they may not feel the need to create a connection to the orchard itself. They are already connected to the surrounding place and their neighbors through their everyday lives.

Rather than connecting to the original orchard community of neighbors, outside participants succeeded in creating a *new* community—albeit a somewhat separate one—within a diverse, low-income neighborhood that would likely have been "off-limits" to them in the not too distant past given its stigmatized reputation. One outsider expressed feeling more affinity with the other outside volunteers who come to the orchard than with neighborhood residents. He said, "I think the people that the PFTP are attracting that have those mutual interests—there might be a little bit more of a stronger connection in terms of certain likeminded things." Building community, in other words, comes with identifying and connecting over similar interests and shared values. Outside volunteers feel a greater sense of connection with other outside volunteers because they are more similar to one another—in terms of race, class, age, shared interests and environmental/foodie values—than to the volunteers from the neighborhood. But in the eyes of neighbors, this new community can appear exclusive. Furthermore, because most outside volunteers who regularly participate are white, their cumulative physical presence—their viscosity—may also have contributed to a perception within the neighborhood of the orchard as a white space, rather than the diverse one enshrined in its name. Ultimately, the formalization of volunteer roles by the PFTP fostered the creation of a separate social network of outside stewards, transforming both the composition of the orchard community and the perception of community itself.

Management Practices and Aesthetics

With new decision-making and a new group of volunteers, the physical orchard itself also changed. Some of these changes created challenges for neighbors, leading to a greater sense of exclusion. Outside volunteers valued and promoted many of these new management techniques—and the resulting aesthetic—as agroecological "best practices." However, these practices challenged the expectations and norms of neighborhood participants. Along with new trees, volunteers planted an understory of edible and native shrubs between the older trees. When flowering, most of these plants attract pollinators to the orchard and many also produce edible berries. Unfortunately, they also make it difficult to mow the grass in the orchard. Volunteers "sheet mulched" the orchard, a common permaculture technique that involves placing cardboard covered by a thick layer of wood chips around the trees and understory plants (see figure 6.2). The practice both smothers the underlying weeds and grass and improves the soil structure.

Both of these management practices—sheet mulching and adding understory plants—became a source of annoyance and frustration for Tamarack residents and for the housing authority's maintenance staff. In Debbie's words:

> They put that cardboard down and then they put the wood chips or whatever the crap that is. But it makes it harder for me with a cane. A couple ladies have walkers and they can't get up in there because you trip over the stupid cardboard. So it's kind of put a hindrance on some of the older people to be able to walk through there.

This particular permaculture practice—widespread in the alternative food movement—made it more difficult for people like Debbie with limited mobility to enter the orchard, and thus impacted the ability of some longtime orchard participants to visit the space and feel part of the community orchard's community.

Figure 6.2. Sheet mulch and native shrubs beneath a fruit tree at the edge of the Fruits of Diversity community orchard. The Tamarack Apartments are in the background.

While the mulching posed a physical barrier to some neighbors, aesthetic changes also led to a growing sense of alienation from the orchard. In addition to the sheet mulching, planting the understory changed the orchard's visual appeal. While appreciative of the flowers and berries, Michelle nevertheless expressed her frustration with the appearance of the orchard:

> What they did to the old orchard by putting the plants there kind of disrupted the whole orchard theme. I mean it just made it difficult to walk through. It made it more difficult to weed it . . . And then it's the point of where the weeds are growing through the dang stuff and—you can't just take a mower and go through it. It needs to be taken care of more frequently. Like keeping the weeds down because for a minute there it was like, eewww. It looked really ugly.

Michelle makes it clear that neighbors felt that they were not consulted about the sheet mulching and understory plants. Her words also point out the difference between PFTP's permaculture orientation and the neighbors' desire to have an aesthetically pleasing and easily accessible pastoral orchard. Permaculture practices such as mulching are ultimately more time- and labor-efficient for the organization, as they are intended to reduce the amount of human disturbance to agroecosystems. But while mulching and planting an understory eventually reduces watering, weeding, and mowing requirements, the space inevitably looks wilder and unmanaged—the very antithesis of the more conventional views held by many residents of what an orchard should look like.

Like the sheet mulching, the planted understory also makes it difficult for the housing authority maintenance staff to mow. One worker pointed out that "it's nice for people to be able to come get fruit," but added that she often cannot tell what is a weed and what was intentionally planted. "It's a mess," she concluded. For newcomers and outside volunteers, on the other hand, these permaculture techniques represented the best agroecological practices, their acceptance as best practice emerging from and reinforcing a shared set of values. But while these practices contributed to building a sense of community among the outside volunteers, they made neighbors less comfortable in the orchard that many of them had helped to establish.

Conclusion

Having a sense of community, a sense of connection to others, is important for many, if not most, people. Wasongolo—an orchard participant, neighborhood resident, and Village Gardens staff member originally from the Democratic Republic of the Congo—explains that a community orchard is an important space of engagement in which to foster such connections. It is

> the place people can meet. If it's [a fruit tree] in your backyard, you pick it and you put on table, you eat it. But as community, you will be there, you will meet somebody, who maybe you will share with. Not only sharing the fruit but also sharing ideas. Sharing culture. Sharing knowledge. Sharing life.

As critical food scholars have demonstrated, urban agricultural sites such as orchards are also spaces where politically and economically marginalized communities can exert some change over their neighborhood and their lives (Ramírez 2015; Sbicca and Myers 2017; White 2011). Indeed, several chapters in this volume describe such spaces of transformation: in Oakland (chapter 10); East New York (chapter 11); Cleveland (chapter 13); and Los Angeles (chapter 14), among others. As our study illustrates, however, an orchard can also be a place where community is negotiated, a site of flux and of contestation over what community means and who takes part. The very conceptual, discursive, and material fluidity of community makes it a space for ongoing change, whether in collaboration or conflict. As we have shown in this chapter, a variety of factors can influence how people define community and who participates, from modes of communication and decision-making to values-based management practices and aesthetic preferences.

Clearly, our findings speak only to this specific orchard site in North Portland. But examining the evolution of even a single urban agriculture project in an affordable housing neighborhood sheds light on how alternative food efforts can become entangled in processes of neighborhood change. While New Columbia and the Tamaracks are buffered somewhat from Portland's skyrocketing housing prices—only 128 of the 854 homes in the development are market rate—the gentrification of the surrounding Portsmouth neighborhood is well under way. As in other previously disinvested areas described in this volume (see chapters 1, 2, 3, and 9, for example), new businesses geared to more affluent consumers—coffee shops, restaurants, and a New Seasons supermarket—have cropped up in the past few years, both a response to a changing consumer base and a signal to developers and homebuyers that the neighborhood is ripe for investment. As gentrification scholars have long argued, displacement doesn't only happen because people are priced out of their neighborhood, but also occurs indirectly when people no longer feel welcome or at home—in short, many older residents leave when they lose a sense of community (Slater 2009).

We are not suggesting here that the FOD orchard is gentrifying New Columbia and the Tamarack Apartments. Rather, we have tried to elucidate the more distal mechanisms through which nonprofit organizations rework urban agricultural spaces and, in turn, are implicated in the transformation of diverse, low-income communities. Confronted with the structural challenges of working with limited staff and precarious funding, urban agriculture nonprofits often go after the proverbial low-hanging fruit; their missions are often guided by what funders and board members see as safe and appealing to the broader, dominant culture (McClintock and Simpson 2018). In the case of the PFTP, reaching for the lowest hanging fruit meant using email and social media to reach a critical mass of willing, mostly white, volunteers, thereby abandoning the time-consuming, consensus-based decision-making and face-to-face outreach that had given rise to the orchard in the first place. They also opted for incorporating labor-saving permaculture best practices that resonated more with the outside participants than with longtime participants from the neighborhood. By both facilitating an influx of mostly white outsiders and alienating longtime participants and neighbors, micro-processes such as these play an important role in subsuming and transforming urban agriculture projects, and ultimately, the sense of community associated with them (see also chapters 5, 10, and 11 in this volume).

In the few years after we conducted this research, PFTP made significant changes in an effort to respond to the challenges discussed here, due in no small part to the findings of this study. In a follow-up interview in 2016, PFTP's then-interim director stated: "We need to redefine the way we work with communities—that's pretty clear. The organization is pretty white—white-led. The lead volunteers are very white. The bench for the board is not very diverse. There's not a lot of cultural competency." But he also noted "a recognition within the organization that it wants to move in an equity direction." The AmeriCorps community orchard coordinator position was turned into a year-round staff position, and the organization began working closely with the Village Gardens staff to ramp up outreach to neighbors. More neighbors began to attend work parties and a grape arbor proposed by a neighbor was planted. The Orchard Steward position was eliminated, leaving neighbors and Village Gardens staff to plan and lead every work party. With these changes, PFTP succeeded in shifting responsibility from the nonprofit back to the neighbors. They want neighbors to feel ownership over the orchard, both for the sustainability of the project and to ensure that the low-income populations the project is meant to serve actually benefit from the orchard.

In July 2017, financial and staffing capacity issues led the organization to pause programming for the remainder of the harvest season. A letter from the Board of Directors explained, "in order to truly fulfill our mission of increasing equitable access to healthful food and strengthening communities by empowering neighbors to share in the harvest and care of city-grown produce, we need to step back, reflect and reorganize" (PFTP Board of Directors 2017). During this restructuring hiatus, the FOD orchard has been maintained by Village Gardens and longtime volunteers from both within the neighborhood *and* outside. The restructuring has thus provided an opportunity to turn the orchard back over to the *multiple* communities that come together beneath its trees: groups of neighbors and outsiders, of Tamarack Apartments residents and New Columbia residents, of new and old volunteers, and of people who want to grow quince and those that do not. Despite the issues outlined in this chapter, neighborhood participants remain hopeful for the future of the project and describe the orchard as "open," "a hopeful space," and "miraculous." As these groups work together in the orchard space, they simultaneously reify the boundaries of their different communities and cross those divides to attain, in the words of one participant, "a genuine experience of human connection." To attain such a goal—to harvest the very Fruits of Diversity for which the orchard is named—has nevertheless required not only a reflexive awareness of the various ways that spaces of urban food production can quickly and easily become gentrified sites of displacement, but also the courage and commitment to make programmatic changes that push back against the momentum generated by nonprofit's funding requirements and the energy of eager outside volunteers.

NOTES

1 The study period spanned from January 2013 to November 2014. The first author began participating in orchard planning in January 2013 and remained an active volunteer over the course of the study, including serving as an Orchard Coordinator when Portland Fruit Tree Project (PFTP) created the position in early 2014. She now serves as the chair of the PFTP Board of Directors. In addition to regularly attending monthly work parties and meetings, watering, and leading a harvest event, she conducted semi-structured interviews with twelve people who had been repeatedly involved in the orchard; a City of Portland staff member who supports community orchards; and the Tamarack Apartments manager. To select interviewees, we compiled a list of thirty potential interviewees based on PFTP records and the first author's observations, sorted the list of potential interviewees into five categories based on role and residence, and invited a purposive sample of

five neighbors, four stewards, five staff, and one orchard coordinator, to participate in an interview.

2 According to the organization's website (www.portlandfruit.org), "Portland Fruit Tree Project is a grassroots 501(c)(3) non-profit *gleaning* organization that provides a community-based solution to a critical and growing need in Portland and beyond: access to healthy food. By empowering neighbors to share in the harvest and care of urban fruit trees, we are preventing waste, building community knowledge and resources, and creating sustainable ways to obtain healthy, locally-grown food."

3 For this study, "neighborhood" refers to New Columbia and the Tamarack Apartments and "neighbor" refers to residents of these two affordable housing communities.

REFERENCES

Ames, Guy K. 2013. "Community Orchards." Butte, MT: ATTRA-National Center for Appropriate Technology. https://attra.ncat.org.

Betz, Megan, Jacob Mills, and James Farmer. 2017. "A Preliminary Overview of Community Orcharding in the United States." *Journal of Agriculture, Food Systems, and Community Development* 7 (2): 13–28.

Bosco, Fernando J., and Pascale Joassart-Marcelli. 2017. "Gardens in the City: Community, Politics, and Place in San Diego, California." In Antoinette WinklerPrins, ed., *Global Urban Agriculture: Convergence of Theory and Practice between North and South* (50–65). Boston: CABI.

Carolan, Michael, and James Hale. 2016. "'Growing' Communities with Urban Agriculture: Generating Value above and below Ground." *Community Development* 47 (4): 530–45.

DeFilippis, James, Robert Fisher, and Eric Shragge. 2010. *Contesting Community: The Limits and Potential of Local Organizing.* New Brunswick, NJ: Rutgers University Press.

Drake, Luke. 2014. "Governmentality in Urban Food Production? Following 'Community' from Intentions to Outcomes." *Urban Geography* 35 (2): 177–96.

Gibson, Karen J. 2007a. "Bleeding Albina: A History of Community Disinvestment, 1940–2000." *Transforming Anthropology* 15 (1): 3–25.

Gibson, Karen J. 2007b. "The Relocation of the Columbia Villa Community: Views from Residents." *Journal of Planning Education and Research* 27 (1): 5–19.

Goetz, Edward G., and Karen Chapple. 2010. "You Gotta Move: Advancing the Debate on the Record of Dispersal." *Housing Policy Debate* 20 (2): 209–36.

Guthman, Julie. 2008. "Bringing Good Food to Others: Investigating the Subjects of Alternative Food Practices." *Cultural Geographies* 15 (4): 431–47.

Home Forward. 2011. "Tamarack Apartments." www.homeforward.org.

Housing Authority of Portland. 2007. "New Columbia: Report on Development Goals." Portland, OR: Housing Authority of Portland. www.homeforward.org.

Joseph, Miranda. 2002. *Against the Romance of Community.* Minneapolis: University of Minnesota Press.

Kato, Yuki. 2013. "Not Just the Price of Food: Challenges of an Urban Agriculture Organization in Engaging Local Residents." *Sociological Inquiry* 83 (3): 369–91.

Keech, Daniel, S. Clifford, J. Kendall, A. King, S. Turner, and G. Vines. 2000. *The Common Ground Book of Orchards*. London: Common Ground.

Kurtz, Hilda E. 2001. "Differentiating Multiple Meanings of Garden and Community." *Urban Geography* 22 (7): 656–70.

McClintock, Nathan. 2018. "Cultivating (a) Sustainability Capital: Urban Agriculture, Eco-Gentrification, and the Uneven Valorization of Social Reproduction." *Annals of the American Association of Geographers* 108 (2): 579–90.

McClintock, Nathan, and Michael Simpson. 2018. "Stacking Functions: Identifying Paradigms of Practice Guiding Urban Agriculture Organizations and Businesses in the United States and Canada." *Agriculture and Human Values* 35 (1): 19–39.

Parks, Casey. 2014. "New Columbia, Neighborhood with State's Largest Public Housing Complex, Sees Decline in Crime, Uptick in Community Spirit." *OregonLive.com*, June 19. www.oregonlive.com.

PFTP Board of Directors. 2017. "Letter from the Board of Directors." July 1. www.portlandfruit.org.

Pudup, Mary Beth. 2008. "It Takes a Garden: Cultivating Citizen-Subjects in Organized Garden Projects." *Geoforum* 39 (3): 1228–40.

Ramírez, Margaret Marietta. 2015. "The Elusive Inclusive: Black Food Geographies and Racialized Food Spaces." *Antipode* 47 (3): 748–69.

Safransky, Sara. 2014. "Greening the Urban Frontier: Race, Property, and Resettlement in Detroit." *Geoforum* 56 (3): 237–48.

Saldivar-Tanaka, Laura, and Marianne E. Krasny. 2004. "Culturing Community Development, Neighborhood Open Space, and Civic Agriculture: The Case of Latino Community Gardens in New York City." *Agriculture and Human Values* 21 (4): 399–412.

Sbicca, Joshua. 2012. "Growing Food Justice by Planting an Anti-Oppression Foundation: Opportunities and Obstacles for a Budding Social Movement." *Agriculture and Human Values* 29 (4): 455–66.

Sbicca, Joshua, and Justin Sean Myers. 2017. "Food Justice Racial Projects: Fighting Racial Neoliberalism from the Bay to the Big Apple." *Environmental Sociology* 3 (1): 30–41.

Slater, Tom. 2009. "Missing Marcuse: On Gentrification and Displacement." *City* 13 (2–3): 292–311.

Slocum, Rachel. 2007. "Whiteness, Space and Alternative Food Practices." *Geoforum* 38: 520–33.

Smith, Darby Minow. 2015. "The 10 U.S. Cities That Are Gentrifying the Fastest." *Grist*, February 6. http://grist.org.

White, Monica M. 2011. "Sisters of the Soil: Urban Gardening as Resistance in Detroit." *Race/Ethnicity: Multidisciplinary Global Contexts* 5 (1): 13–28.

7

Gardens in the Growth Machine

Seattle's P-Patch Program and the Pursuit of Permanent Community Gardens

CHARLOTTE GLENNIE

We've seen it happen over and over. Residents in blighted neighborhoods work to transform vacant lots into community gardens—only to see the fruits of their labors bulldozed when the neighborhood gentrifies and the land is repurposed for something more lucrative. Community gardeners have observed this pattern for gardens on both private and public land (Barraclough 2009; Salvidar-Tanaka and Krasny 2004). Social scientists studying community gardens (Darly and McClintock 2017; Martinez 2010; Rosan and Pearsall 2017) have attributed the pattern to forces of urban political economy, specifically the logic of the *urban growth machine* (Logan and Molotch 1987). The urban growth machine thesis posits that urban land is commodified and that powerful *growth coalitions*, comprised of local business owners, developers, and political leaders, work to increase the *exchange value* of urban land rather than preserving the *use value* that the land holds for residents (Logan and Molotch 1987). The urban growth machine thesis explains both the appearance of community gardens in neighborhoods with low land values and their replacement with more profitable development when the real estate market picks up.

However, gentrification doesn't always doom community gardens. In cities such as New York and Seattle, advocates have managed to preserve at least some gardens despite increasing development pressure. When community gardeners successfully resist development, does that mean they have vanquished the growth machine itself, their interest in use value winning out over the growth coalition's interest in exchange value? It's not that simple—but we can learn a great deal about the relationship between community gardens and urban development by looking at such cases.

To better understand how community gardens articulate with urban development, I conducted an intensive case study of Seattle's P-Patch program, which has achieved a remarkable level of site security for its gardens on public land (a majority of the program's 88 sites). While most studies of community gardens have focused on the social organization of gardens, their meanings for the local community, or garden practices and outcomes, I focus here on the interaction between community garden advocates and city leaders. As an urban land use, community gardens compete with or contribute to other urban institutions such as housing, civic culture, and the local economy, all of which have significant implications for urban residents (Friedersdorf 2014; Hanson and Marty 2012).

In Seattle, community garden advocates perceived the growth machine's threat to their sites but opted not to challenge growth. Instead, as part of their efforts to build good relations with city leaders and garner public support for the P-Patch gardens, they positioned themselves as supporters of growth. Even while campaigning for an initiative to permanently preserve gardens, and thereby impose some limits on development, the advocates promoted the standard growth machine narrative that Seattle would and should continue to grow. They also constructed an implicit argument that gardens attract desirable new residents. Garden advocates thus minimized their conflict with the growth coalition, and they have successfully protected most P-Patch gardens (as well as other Seattle open spaces). However, the P-Patches have become symbols of a particular urban lifestyle that is now connected to gentrification.

Essentially, the gardeners were able to convince city leaders that community gardens benefit both the use and exchange value of neighborhoods, aligning the gardens with growth coalition goals in seeking their preservation. The outcome is mixed: P-Patch advocates were able to win strong protections for the gardens, which do benefit low-income residents and residents of color in direct, tangible ways; however, displacement continues across the city as housing costs increase, with the gardens serving as economically valuable neighborhood assets in a form of *green gentrification* (Gould and Lewis 2017; see also chapter 4 in this volume). Activists may inadvertently contribute to gentrification through efforts to improve quality of life (Alkon and Cadji 2018; Checker 2011), but in the case of Seattle's P-Patches, green gentrification was less an unintended consequence than the outcome of a political strategy. Having positioned themselves as supporters of development, the garden advocates are not equipped to criticize the negative effects of urban growth. My findings suggest that local projects such as community gardens can have different relationships to urban development, and how garden advocates choose to frame their spaces for decision makers will affect their impact on the surrounding community. Understanding more about how community gardens articulate with urban development may help to guide activists and policymakers toward effective, equitable strategies.

The P-Patch Phenomenon

Seattle's P-Patch program is a thriving network of community gardens that has grown to include eighty-eight sites on more than 30 acres of urban land. The City of Seattle has funded the program since 1973, continuously investing in administrative staff and garden infrastructure, and even sometimes purchasing land to create new gardens. From 2013 to 2016, fueled by online retail giant Amazon's expansion and a regional tech boom, Seattle experienced a dramatic, widespread increase in real estate values—yet city leaders never raised the question of replacing any of their P-Patch gardens with other land uses. In fact, the program opened five new garden sites during this period. Clearly, Seattle's community gardens have a different relationship to urban growth than the commonly observed pattern of conflict and displacement.

To understand the strategy by which Seattle's P-Patch advocates secured community gardens as a permanent use of public land, I conducted an intensive case study on the history of the program and efforts to preserve threatened P-Patches. Analyzing thousands of pages of archival documents, media coverage in local newspapers, and interviews with fourteen garden activists and city officials, I developed a model for the pathway to preservation that the P-Patch advocates used in order to protect their gardens. Advocates employed a generally cooperative strategy, emphasizing how community gardens could benefit a growing city rather than focusing on the threats that growth posed. The gardeners appealed to cultural values shared by much of Seattle's elite, such as environmental appreciation and neighborhood planning, and supported growth goals *despite* viewing growth as the source of their gardens' vulnerability.

The unusual security of Seattle's P-Patches today is largely the result of efforts to defend threatened gardens in the 1980s and 1990s. From the mid-1980s onward, a cohort of energetic artists, homemakers, and professionals (mostly white women) came to fill a leadership void at the municipal gardening program and expanded the activity of an all-volunteer nonprofit which serves as the program's counterpart.[1] As far back as 1992, biennial gardener surveys found that a majority of the P-Patch gardeners were renters, a majority were low- or low- to moderate-income, and the program's racial composition included a higher proportion of people of color than the city overall. While the P-Patches host a diversity of gardeners, white middle-class professionals have always constituted the organizational leadership and have used their cultural capital to sway or challenge the elite growth coalition when city leaders sought to redevelop gardens. This is similar to garden advocacy in other cities in the United States: Reynolds (2015) finds that shared cultural capital opens up greater access to public resources. The power of social position will be discussed in more detail below, but we should also keep in mind Reynolds's (2015) caution that urban agriculture will reproduce existing inequalities if not oriented toward challenging unjust power structures.

Organizing through the P-Patch nonprofit, garden advocates lobbied City Hall to continue supporting the program and worked with Seattle's network of neighborhood associations and open space advocates to mobilize the public around preserving green space. Their most impactful victory was the 1997 Protect Our Parks initiative, signed into law by a heavily pressured city council, which prevents the City of Seattle from redirecting any of its land used for parks purposes without first holding a public hearing and furnishing an equal or better replacement lot, for the same purposes, in the same neighborhood. In effect, this initiative prevents the city from selling any of its parks, community gardens, or other recreational open spaces.

That the leading advocates for the gardens had cultural capital and social ties in common with the city's leaders proved important for their strategy to preserve the gardens. Leveraging their social networks, advocates were able to speak informally with current and former city staffers to gain knowledge of the history of city-owned parcels and insight about what mattered to each city councilmember. These understandings helped the advocates shape compelling arguments, and their cultural similarity to elites also helped them present the gardens favorably. For example, gardeners often hold fund-raising events at the P-Patches, including annual concerts, art auctions, and a Harvest Banquet. City officials are invited to these events and are included in photo opportunities. Similarly, through their social ties, gardeners at Interbay P-Patch have had the support of local celebrity chef Tom Douglas, who caters a Chef in the Garden dinner every summer. This event serves as one of the P-Patch nonprofit's primary fund-raisers, and also elevates the gardens' profile citywide.

Endowed with strong organizational networks, cultural capital similar to that of urban elites, and an interest in both use and exchange value of their neighborhoods, the P-Patch advocates somewhat resemble the anti-growth homeowners in Mike Davis's *City of Quartz*. Davis (2006) describes how in the 1970s and 1980s, alarmed by the rate at which growth and densification were changing their communities, wealthy residents in and around Los Angeles mobilized through their homeowners' associations and allied environmental groups to challenge the logic of growth. This no-growth movement won significant policy victories, forcing the mayor and city councilmembers to reverse their positions and alter the city's urban planning framework.

Like the no-growth homeowners in Los Angeles, Seattle's garden advocates first sought to work with the city administration to achieve their goals, and only launched a contentious political fight when they came to believe that city leaders were not acting in good faith. In the first phase, articulating how the P-Patch program benefited elites' wider agenda for growth, garden advocates secured language that legitimized community gardens as part of the city's urban planning framework. Later, when leaders in City Hall sought to sell or relocate specific gardens in favor of attractive development deals, gardeners mobilized the public around a sweeping preservation policy opposed by city elites. In the contentious effort to pass this policy—the Protect Our Parks initiative—garden advocates maintained their explicit support for growth overall. Like Davis's homeowner-led no-growth movement, the P-Patch coalition was able to leverage its resources and networks to win significant policy victories; however, unlike their Los Angeles counterparts, these advocates never ventured into outright opposition to growth, affecting both the character of their movement and its outcomes.

Behind the Scenes: Internal Concerns About Growth

In the 1980s, with perspective gained from their professional and social networks, leaders in the P-Patch program realized that urban development was becoming a threat to their gardens. As Seattle recovered from the Boeing Bust of the 1970s, the urban population began to grow again and local economic conditions were improving. In the mid-1980s, the leaders of the city program attended conferences of the American Community Gardening Association (ACGA) and learned that gardeners in major US cities were losing their leases as local land became more valuable. This information resonated, as a handful of gardens in Seattle had started to experience such development threats: first Eastlake and Pinehurst P-Patches in the mid-1980s, and one to three gardens each year from 1989 to 1995. The P-Patch nonprofit leaders, meanwhile, leveraged connections to city council staff in order to develop a long-range vision for the gardens that would ensure that program funding was not a constant struggle. In this effort, the advocates surveyed available land for gardens. Learning how few vacant lots remained was a watershed moment for their efforts. Development came to be seen as an urgent problem that threatened both existing gardens and the potential for new ones.

The view that urban growth was a threat comes across in the gardeners' newsletter, the P-Patch Post. For example, a 1987 article says that the city's potential new open space policies, which would designate community gardens as a priority use for surplus land, "would be a significant victory as community gardens are now considered an interim use of public land, and *consistently succumb to economic and other pressures*" (P-Patch Post 1987, emphasis added). A 1993 article reporting on activity of the P-Patch nonprofit's newly formed Land Use Committee explains, "The pressures of development to accommodate more people within the city limits makes the few existing greenspaces even more precious" (Moty 1993). The Post also ran a series of gardener testimonials, in which numerous P-Patchers emphasized the vital role that gardens played for them as rare open spaces in an increasingly dense and hectic city.

While the program leaders observed that open space was fast disappearing due to the city's growth, they nevertheless maintained a growth mind-set about how to respond. Post articles mobilizing gardeners around land use and urban planning issues consistently advocated for the program's *own* growth—the growing demand for garden plots, and the need for growth in the number and size of garden sites—not just the preservation of existing sites. In fact, between 1986 and 1995, Post articles about Seattle's urban growth emphasized the need for program expansion twice as often as they depicted urban growth as a threat to existing gardens. For example, one article stated, "In this city, which is growing too fast, more and more people are living in dehumanizing rental units . . . With increased development should come more P-Patches" (P-Patch Post 1991). As the city developed a planning framework for urban growth, the Land Use Committee sought to "get politicians, planners, and private developers to think community garden when they think about open space" (P-Patch Post 1992). In spite of seeing urban growth as a problem, the P-Patch advocates also saw growth as the solution—growth of their own program, through the cultivated support of city elites. They did not seem to consider the logic of growth for exchange as entirely incompatible with growing use value.

From my interviews and review of program documents, it seems that P-Patch gardeners generally perceived growth for exchange value to be inevitable, even if undesirable. There is no evidence that they ever thought to challenge the city's growth goals; rather, they built their own strategy around growing the program and highlighted how gardens could help the city as it grew. Program leaders and other advocates seem to have viewed this as the natural response to population and economic growth, rather than an unwelcome compromise. Perhaps the P-Patch advocates assumed the forces driving growth were beyond the city's control, or that gardeners would not have enough political power to successfully challenge growth. Perhaps the leading P-Patch advocates, because of their socioeconomic positions as homeowners, business owners, and professionals, were actually in favor of urban growth—as long as the gardens remained. Whatever the reason, the P-Patch advocates pursued an advocacy and public relations strategy that affirmed growth—and they were able to win support for growth of the P-Patch program even as real estate demand increased.

Public Participation: Alignment with Growth Coalition Goals

Advocates for the P-Patch program clearly understood the threat that urban growth posed to community gardens, but their strategies for defending the gardens never involved challenging growth. Instead, they constructed an implicit argument about how the gardens would be good for growth and positioned themselves as both defenders of open space and supporters of urban development.

The group of leaders who worked to preserve and expand the P-Patch program starting in the mid-1980s ultimately developed the program's *brand*. Using language that resonated with the city's elites, they characterized the gardens as unique Seattle amenities—attractive to visitors and potential new residents. At a time when the growth coalition was seeking to develop Seattle into a major global city, this argument was particularly effective.

In 1984, the new cohort of P-Patch leaders (described above) had successfully lobbied to save the program from funding cuts and were working to boost the program's visibility in order to shore up its status for future budget negotiations (see figure 7.1). They began streamlining the signage at the various garden sites, seeking more media attention, and networking with the larger urban gardening community through the ACGA. At the same time, the gardeners faced a new set of challenges, as changing economic conditions spurred development that threatened some of the garden sites.

The P-Patch advocates organized their first large-scale preservation campaign for the Pinehurst P-Patch. In 1985 and again in 1986, knowing both years that it might be their last at the site, Pinehurst gardeners applied for the ACGA's annual contest. They won a regional award in 1985, and in 1986 won "best small community garden in the nation." Letters to city councilmembers and Mayor Royer urging the garden's preservation consistently referred to Pinehurst P-Patch as "award winning" or "nationally recognized," emphasizing its prestige as something

Figure 7.1. Signs at the entrances of P-Patch gardens include words for "welcome" in numerous languages, evoking an ethos of openness and the diversity of gardeners served by the P-Patch program. Photo by author.

city officials would value. Interestingly, while more than six hundred Seattleites signed a petition to save Pinehurst P-Patch, the majority of advocacy letters actually came from outside Seattle (via gardeners affiliated with the ACGA) and pressed the point that the garden's national recognition was a benefit to the city. For example, the executive director of the ACGA wrote to Seattle's mayor:

> *Seattle has long been a national model* for its outstanding community gardening program as well as for its humane and livable urban environment. Seattle's gardens consistently receive national attention as outstanding gardens.... What a blow it would be to us if the *showpiece of the best gardening city in the nation* were to be obliterated ... Just as Mayor Koch interceded to save the Clinton Community Garden in New York, you can save the Pinehurst P-Patch. It is inconceivable that the Mayor of Seattle would do otherwise. (Nash 1986, emphasis added)

Similarly, another letter states that Pinehurst was "chosen by the American Community Gardening Association as a *model to other major cities* . . . demonstrating the impact a small neighborhood garden can have" (Thompson 1986, emphasis added). Leaders in the community gardening movement, from San Francisco to Denver, wrote to Seattle's mayor with similar messages, linking the preservation of Pinehurst P-Patch with Seattle's growing national reputation as a green, livable city. When Pinehurst was finally preserved in 1987 (through a deal orchestrated by the city, whereby the developer donated the lot to the P-Patch nonprofit), the ACGA announced it would hold its 1988 annual conference in Seattle—driving home the notion that city officials' support for community gardens would continue to bring national attention (and tourism) to Seattle.[2]

In addition to leveraging their ACGA contacts to frame Pinehurst's preservation in terms of the city's reputation, gardeners advocating for Pinehurst adopted language about the value of community gardens for neighborhood attractiveness—a message that came to characterize the program overall. Urging the mayor to find a way to preserve Pinehurst, Marlene Falkenbury (president of the P-Patch nonprofit) wrote, "This site has been the *focal point of the neighborhood* as well as of the P-Patch Program as it is always *well maintained, beautifully landscaped, and filled yearly with happy gardeners*" (Falkenbury 1984, emphasis added). Internal communications indicate that this reasoning resonated with city officials, who used similar language to justify preservation efforts. Describing a threatened garden as a "focal point," or an "asset" to the community, became a common refrain in letters urging preservation—as did arguments about the maintenance and beautification of public space.

Over the next decade, advocates continued to stress the ways that community gardens benefited neighborhoods overall, sustaining the message that community gardens make Seattle's neighborhoods more attractive places to live. The increasing specificity of these claims suggests that P-Patch advocates were developing a sophisticated argument to convince city leaders that the gardens could help the city meet its wider goals.

For example, in the 1990s Mayor Norm Rice set a broad administrative agenda prioritizing community-building, public safety, accessibility for all, and neighborhood involvement in local planning—goals that the

P-Patch advocates then highlighted in their communications with him. Especially when the mayor supported plans to re-develop two P-Patches (Bradner Gardens, a park slated for market-rate housing, and Interbay P-Patch, on land needed for a golf course),[3] garden advocates framed their appeals in terms of Rice's own goals (see figure 7.2). A leading volunteer in the fight to preserve Bradner Gardens wrote to Mayor Rice:

> Neighbors of all economic levels, ages, languages, and races meet in the gardens to share whatever they have to offer.... What is important is that we know and rely on each other, not on city services. To my mind, this was what you envisioned with the neighborhood planning process. (Friday 1996)

Similarly, regarding the plans to move Interbay P-Patch, a P-Patch gardener wrote the mayor to ask, "Why would the City of Seattle want to destroy such a beautiful community project? Please consider carefully there are special gardens for the disabled and handicapped, vegetables are donated to the Food Bank—it is an amazing community asset—please save this garden!" (Holden and Holden 1996). Through numerous letters and public comments, the P-Patch advocates depicted their gardens as neighborhood amenities that served important public goals—beautifying the city, activating space, facilitating community development, and feeding the needy—all at a relatively low cost to taxpayers.

P-Patch advocates' increasingly sophisticated argument regarding the value of gardens also noted how gardens offer quality of life in an alienating urban landscape. This theme developed internally, through the P-Patch Post's series of gardener testimonials, and was later used to convince city leaders that the gardens were critical to healthy urban growth. Advocates for Interbay P-Patch emphasized its use as a place where apartment dwellers could connect with nature, "a sorely needed, much sought-after source of healing, renewal and productive engagement with Nature in the midst of our urban lives" (Peck 1996). Advocates for Bradner emphasized the role of their park in fighting isolation and forging cross-cultural friendships: "People need projects like this in a large city such as Seattle to help build community and to provide respite from the bustle of urban life" (Kellett and Kuhn 1995). Such statements point to

Figure 7.2. Bradner Gardens Park offers visitors a gorgeous view of the downtown Seattle skyline. When city officials sought to sell the park for market-rate housing, garden advocates speculated that the iconic view made this lot a target for developers. Photo by author.

shared assumptions about the dynamics of urban growth, in line with Logan and Molotch's (1987) growth machine theory. These P-Patch advocates presuppose a general tradeoff between use- and exchange values, predicting that quality of life will become more elusive as the city grows. Despite acknowledging this tradeoff, the advocates take for granted that urban growth will continue, an assumption that Logan and Molotch (1987) identify as essential to the growth agenda. Highlighting the ability of their gardens to buffer against urban alienation, the P-Patch advocates were working with rather than against the growth machine.

In their arguments for garden preservation, the P-Patch advocates conveyed the view that urban growth itself was inevitable. At that time, residents in places like Los Angeles and Colorado had questioned the growth imperative and mobilized *no-growth* movements to oppose development, but the P-Patch advocates avoided this approach. Instead, they made a concerted effort to articulate support for urban growth—particularly when challenging city officials over the fate of Bradner Gardens.

Before Bradner Gardens came up for development, Mayor Rice had succeeded in passing a Comprehensive Plan to manage Seattle's growth—an effort that was met with skepticism or outrage from many corners of the city, as the plan's "Urban Villages" would significantly densify some neighborhoods historically dominated by single-family homes. Resisting the influx of apartment dwellers and added traffic, many neighborhood associations and activists fought bitterly against the plan. In the very public debate about urban growth that accompanied the Comprehensive Plan process, Mayor Rice and city council found themselves with few friends and many critics. The P-Patch advocates, however, were supportive: They had won favorable language in the Comprehensive Plan for adding gardens as the city grew. P-Patch advocates then reminded city officials about their support for densification, as they sought to protect Bradner Gardens.

Though P-Patch advocates were frustrated by Rice's effort to develop Bradner Gardens, they continued to position themselves as supporters of his Comprehensive Plan and allies of growth. An advocate for Bradner Gardens outlined their position in a letter to city council:

> We have tried to work with the city at every opportunity. . . . We have participated in hearings about zoning, about the comp plan [sic], and other things. We have written letters, sat on committees for housing development. . . . We have worked with the Seattle Design Committee to make a draft concept plan for the whole neighborhood. (Heaven 1996a)

In another letter, this advocate affirmed, "We look forward to working together to save Bradner Park and *find appropriate strategies to increase housing density and diversity* in the I-90 communities" (Heaven 1996b, emphasis added). At the behest of P-Patch advocates, state legislators also wrote to Mayor Rice, saying,

> *This is not another NIMBY* [Not In My Back Yard] *protest against new development.* This is the concern on the part of neighbors who are rebounding from years of neglect and hardship and see this small piece of

public land *as a way to accept density* without losing the cultural diversity of this deserving neighborhood. (Peltz, Mason, and Tokuda 1995, emphasis added)

P-Patch advocates thus drew a strong contrast between themselves and any neighborhood movement against densification, highlighting how the gardens were not obstacles to growth—but instead contributed to city elites' vision of a growing, thriving Seattle.

The P-Patch Gardens Today

Since passage of the Protect Our Parks initiative in 1997, Seattle's P-Patch program has doubled in size. Today, the eighty-eight P-Patch gardens are diverse in size, appearance, and constituency, but all are widely seen as assets that contribute to Seattle's quality-of-life and culture of community. As attractive local amenities, with a range of benefits for Seattleites of all socioeconomic levels, the P-Patch gardens serve both the use- and exchange values of Seattle's neighborhoods.

While the growth machine thesis presents use and exchange value as inversely related, more recent urban theory explains how P-Patches could benefit both. Richard Florida's (2003) creative capital theory argues that urban economies in the twenty-first century are built by the *creative class*, dynamic workers and entrepreneurs who are not tied to a particular locality but will attract high-tech jobs and economic growth to the cities where they choose to live. This creative class values urban quality of life, especially places and programs that facilitate *loose community*—social arrangements that foster weak ties among diverse people. Community gardens, then, are exactly the sort of amenity that should attract the creative class, and Florida (2003) indeed named Seattle as one of the leading creative cities. Specifically analyzing the role of urban agriculture, Nathan McClintock (2018) posits that gardens can increase both use and exchange value as a form of *sustainability capital* that signals neighborhood desirability to green consumers (who are typically white, educated, and affluent). Before such ideas were common, the P-Patch advocates seemed to understand instinctively how attractive, open community spaces would make Seattle a more desirable place to live.

We can see more evidence of the P-Patch advocates' success in other Seattle developments. A P-Patch gardener living near Bradner Gardens told me that once the park was preserved, flyers for nearby market-rate housing began to highlight proximity to the garden, demonstrating its value as a neighborhood amenity. Furthermore, the idea of a community garden is considered so attractive to Seattle residents that several new high-end apartments and condominium developments include their own private community gardens. Real estate developers not only choose to feature community gardens, but also describe them in promotional literature as "Pea Patches" to capitalize on the popularity and cachet of the city's program. Similar to S*Park described in chapter 4 of this volume, these developers cash in on the local history of urban agriculture and its appeal to young professionals willing to pay a premium for *green* living. However, whereas developments such as S*Park displace farms and gardens in gentrifying Denver neighborhoods, my Seattle interviewees were unanimous in their belief that the P-Patches would not be removed no matter how much property values rise around them.

The community garden advocates who worked to protect P-Patches from development defined the value of gardens in terms of broader city goals and found an effective way to align residents' interest in preserving use value with growth coalition interest in greater exchange value. Today, the gardens are insulated from development pressure, and they contribute to the overall character of green living and community culture that has helped Seattle attract the creative class, foster a robust high-tech economy—and increase real estate demand citywide. Unfortunately, creative cities have become some of the most expensive and unequal urban landscapes, as Florida (2012) himself has acknowledged.

Seattle was at the vanguard of urban greening to attract the creative class; cities across the United States are now seeking to attract investment and affluent new residents with the appeal of urban sustainability. Recent research into green gentrification suggests this strategy has consequences for the poor. Park restorations, brownfield cleanups, transit improvements, and other top-down environmental initiatives can effectively increase surrounding real estate values, but also displace longtime residents (Anguelovski 2015; Dooling 2009; Gould and Lewis 2017; Wolch, Byrne, and Newell 2014). Similarly, green gentrification can occur following grassroots efforts to improve neighborhood life, such as environmental justice activism (Checker 2011) and local food initiatives (Alkon and Cadji 2018). Whether institutionally organized or driven by neighborhood residents, community gardens can increase surrounding property values by making a neighborhood more visually and symbolically appealing (Voicu and Been 2008; Quastel 2009). Yet these elevated property values can price out longtime tenants, including the gardens and gardeners themselves (McClintock 2018; see also chapter 4 in this volume).

Across Seattle, housing prices have ballooned in recent years, and formerly modest neighborhoods (such as the one containing Bradner Gardens) are undergoing rapid gentrification. While the P-Patch gardens are largely protected from development, many of the gardeners who created these spaces are not as secure. Higher rents have driven many low-income Seattleites out of their neighborhoods. The P-Patch at Bradner Gardens was originally home to many Laotian refugee families, former farmers who valued the chance to continue growing food as they settled in Seattle. According to a longtime gardener who owns a home in the adjacent neighborhood, most of the Laotian families, along with many other low-income residents, have been forced to move farther south as home prices and rents have increased. Modestly priced neighborhoods still exist, but they are increasingly rare.

If displaced low-income gardeners do manage to find affordable housing elsewhere in Seattle, they may continue benefiting from P-Patches. The P-Patch nonprofit has long maintained a "Gardenship Fund" to cover plot fees for low-income gardeners. Also, since at least the early 1990s, the city program has prioritized marginalized groups—directing program expansion toward underserved neighborhoods (including affordable housing developments) to ensure that the P-Patch program is accessible to everyone. Even low-income Seattleites who do not have a garden plot may benefit from the P-Patch program, which encourages its gardeners to grow extra produce for local food banks; donations exceeded 40,000 pounds in 2014.

Organizing volunteer labor to provide important social services, such as food provision and city beautification, the P-Patch program benefits residents of all classes, but may also be serving to advance neoliberalization (Peck and Tickell 2002). A primary critique of urban agriculture holds that some garden programs support institutional efforts to shrink the welfare state and devolve responsibility onto individuals (Alkon and Mares 2012; Pudup 2008; Rosol 2012). Programs aiding this *roll-back neoliberalism* are criticized for smoothing over the impacts of a declining welfare state, focusing on responsibility at the local level, and thereby precluding more radical responses to the pains of neoliberal restructuring (Allen and Guthman 2006; McClintock 2014). In other words, the P-Patch gardens mobilize volunteer labor to grow food for the hungry, develop strong communities, and maintain attractive public spaces—but do not protest against displacement, gentrification, and inequality.

McClintock (2014) and Ernwein (2017) warn against an all-or-nothing approach to critiquing the neoliberal character of urban agriculture initiatives, and indeed it would be unwise to dismiss the P-Patch program on such grounds. The P-Patch advocates can be seen as part of a neoliberal trend whereby community leaders remain relatively apolitical in order to maintain working relationships with city leaders (Pacewicz 2015). Despite limiting the scope of community leaders' work, these strategies can succeed—as they clearly have in this case.

In one sense, P-Patch advocates have effected a stable compromise between growth coalition interests and broad-based residential *quality of life*. The P-Patch program seems to serve both growth-elite and homeowner interests, while also providing tangible benefits for renters, low-income people, and people of color. This inclusive coalition is possible in the context of Seattle's progressive politics and stands in contrast to the no-growth movement in Los Angeles. The P-Patch leaders, sharing cultural capital with the city's elites, found their way into Seattle's *managed growth* coalition—while Los Angeles' no-growth homeowners did not (despite having similar social positions and resources). In Los Angeles, the local growth coalition leveraged racial and class divisions evident in the no-growth rhetoric to stymie these opponents and maintain power (Davis 2006). In Seattle, instead of seeing themselves as under siege from outsiders, P-Patchers viewed their gardens as a bulwark for all residents against the discomforts of growth. Even as population growth threatened P-Patches, the advocates viewed newcomers as potential gardeners, rather than intruders who threatened their way of life—an orientation that underscored the need for more gardens *along with* more residents. Yet with this inclusive view, the leading P-Patch advocates did not seem to consider that well-resourced newcomers *would* threaten ways of life for low-income communities and people of color.

Chapter 6 in this volume describes how an influx of more affluent outsiders can disrupt the sense of community in an urban agriculture site, emphasizing the need for reflexivity on the part of nonprofit leaders overseeing such projects. I do not focus here on the cultural dynamics within the P-Patch gardens; the P-Patch program is structured in such a way that individual garden sites have a great deal of autonomy over their cultural expression and garden maintenance decisions. Yet this case further illustrates how taking the path of least resistance is likely not the best way for urban agriculture nonprofits to serve vulnerable communities. Similar to the Portland Fruit Tree Project in chapter 6, the P-Patch nonprofit relies on volunteer labor that is easiest to draw from gardeners who are economically secure and mostly white. These volunteers have worked hard to win the long-term preservation of P-Patches, but from their social positions the negative impacts of urban growth on low-income residents (and gardeners) may not have been obvious.

Framing their gardens as amenities, the P-Patch advocates have worked successfully with Seattle's growth coalition. When urban elites sought to replace some gardens with new development in the 1990s, the P-Patch advocates pushed back, leveraging enough power to protect and expand the city's garden network, without challenging growth itself. They may never have possessed enough power to fundamentally alter the city's political economy, but in opting to support growth, they have precluded a critique of the city's current wave of gentrification. As much as the P-Patch program works to support and prioritize low-income families, the P-Patch leaders are not able to criticize urban growth for its displacing effects. As the stewards of neighborhood amenities, rather than representatives of the vulnerable communities these spaces are meant to serve, the P-Patch advocates can pursue security for the gardens—but not for their fellow gardeners.

Important questions thus remain about the relationship between community gardens and urban growth. This chapter outlines one strategy for protecting gardens from development pressure, but could such a strategy succeed in less progressive or *green* cities? Can community gardeners who do not hold the same cultural capital as urban elites succeed in convincing the growth coalition to preserve their spaces? What other pathways to garden permanence exist, and do they enable a stronger critique of exchange value–oriented urban development? Can urban community gardens survive as spaces that encourage opposition to growth interests, and if so, how?

Comparative research will help answer these questions, but Seattle's P-Patches alone can contribute to our understanding of green gentrification. Here, grassroots efforts to change both the landscape and the legal status of community gardens have ultimately contributed to gentrification. In the case of the P-Patches, advocates implied to growth elites that thriving, secure gardens might bring desired new residents—though they did not suggest, and may not have anticipated, that the gardens could also contribute to displacement. P-Patch advocates have long expressed support for social justice in the form of garden accessibility, but from the vanguard of green gentrification they did not comprehend or grapple with the possibility of displacement—as garden activists in more recent urban greening movements have (Alkon and Cadji 2018; see also chapters 4 and 8 in this volume). The P-Patches thus demonstrate how displacement and inequality tend to result from urban greening, if equity-oriented policies are not implemented early on (Gould and Lewis 2017). Planners, policymakers, and activists seeking to improve the urban environment should consider how greening and quality-of-life initiatives will distribute benefits, and who may be unintentionally harmed in the process.

NOTES

1 The nonprofit has existed since 1979 but has taken four different names over that time (P-Patch Advisory Council, Friends of P-Patch, P-Patch Trust, and GROW Northwest). For clarity's sake, I refer to this organization simply as "the P-Patch nonprofit."
2 After the Protect Our Parks initiative passed in 1997, ACGA chose to hold its 1998 conference in Seattle. It is unclear if these decisions were deliberate on the part of ACGA, but the timing of both selections suggests a link.
3 While Eastlake, Pinehurst, and Interbay P-Patches are all in historically white neighborhoods, Bradner Gardens is located close to the formerly redlined Central District. After a wave of African American and Asian American in-migrants following desegregation, the Bradner neighborhood was seeing an influx of white residents in the 1990s.

REFERENCES

Alkon, Alison H., and Josh Cadji. 2018. "Sowing Seeds of Displacement: Gentrification and Food Justice in Oakland, CA." *International Journal of Urban and Regional Research.* DOI:10.1111/1468-2427.12684.

Alkon, Alison H., and Teresa Mares. 2012. "Food Sovereignty in US Food Movements: Radical Visions and Neoliberal Constraints." *Agriculture and Human Values* 29 (3): 347-59.

Allen, Patricia, and Julie Guthman. 2006. "From 'Old School' to 'Farm-to-School': Neoliberalization from the Ground Up." *Agriculture and Human Values* 23 (4): 401-15.

Anguelovski, Isabelle. 2015. "Healthy Food Stores, Greenlining and Food Gentrification: Contesting New Forms of Privilege, Displacement and Locally Unwanted Land Uses in Racially Mixed Neighborhoods." *International Journal of Urban and Regional Research* 39 (6): 1209-30.

Barraclough, Laura. 2009. "South Central Farmers and Shadow Hills Homeowners: Land Use Policy and Relational Racialization in Los Angeles." *Professional Geographer* 61 (2): 164-86.

Checker, Melissa. 2011. "Wiped Out by the 'Greenwave': Environmental Gentrification and the Paradoxical Politics of Urban Sustainability." *City & Society* 23 (2): 210-29.

Darly, Ségolène, and Nathan McClintock. 2017. "Introduction to Urban Agriculture in the Neoliberal City: Critical European Perspectives." *ACME: An International Journal for Critical Geographies* 16 (2): 224-31.

Davis, Mike. 2006. *City of Quartz: Excavating the Future in Los Angeles* (new edition). New York: Verso Books.

Dooling, Sarah. 2009. "Ecological Gentrification: A Research Agenda Exploring Justice in the City." *International Journal of Urban and Regional Research* 33 (3): 621-39.

Ernwein, Marion. 2017. "Urban Agriculture and the Neoliberalization of What?" *ACME: An International Journal for Critical Geographies* 16 (2): 249-75.

Falkenbury, Marlene. 1984. "Letter to Mayor Royer," May 17, 1984. Seattle Municipal Archives 5274-01, box 51, folder 33.

Florida, Richard. 2003. "Cities and the Creative Class." *City and Community* 2 (1): 3-19.

Florida, Richard. 2012. "Preface." In *The Rise of the Creative Class, Revisited*. New York: Basic Books.

Friday, Kendra. 1996. Letter to Mayor Rice, October 30,1995. Seattle Municipal Archives 4623-02, box 63, folder 2.

Friedersdorf, Conor. 2014. "How Urban Farming Is Making San Francisco's Housing Crisis Worse." *The Atlantic*, September 3.

Gould, Kenneth A., and Tammy L. Lewis. 2017. *Green Gentrification: Urban Sustainability and the Struggle for Environmental Justice*. New York: Routledge.

Hanson, David, and Edwin Marty. 2012. *Breaking Through Concrete: Building an Urban Farm Revival*. Berkeley: University of California Press.

Heaven, Bonnie. 1996a. Letter to Councilmember Podlodowski, June 18, 1995. Seattle Municipal Archives 4670–02, box 5, folder 8.

Heaven, Bonnie. 1996b. Letter to Councilmember Podlodowski, July 29, 1996. Seattle Municipal Archives 4670–02, box 5, folder 8.

Holden, Paul B., and Dorris L. Holden. 1996. Letter to Mayor Rice, September 16, 1996. Seattle Municipal Archives 5272–01, box 118.

Kellett, Chris, and Jay Kuhn. 1995. Letter to Mayor Rice, October 19, 1995. Seattle Municipal Archives 4623–02, box 63, folder 2.

Logan, John, and Harvey Molotch. 1987. *Urban Fortunes: The Political Economy of Place*. Berkeley: University of California Press.

Martinez, Miranda J. 2010. *Power at the Roots: Gentrification, Community Gardens, and the Puerto Ricans of the Lower East Side*. Boulder, CO: Lexington Books.

McClintock, Nathan. 2014. "Radical, Reformist, and Garden-Variety Neoliberal: Coming to Terms with Urban Agriculture's Contradictions." *Local Environment: The International Journal of Justice and Sustainability* 19 (2): 147–71.

McClintock, Nathan. 2018. "Cultivating (a) Sustainability Capital: Urban Agriculture, Ecogentrification, and the Uneven Valorization of Social Reproduction." *Annals of the American Association of Geographers* 108 (2): 579–90.

Moty, Joyce. 1993. "Greenspaces Policy." *P-Patch Post* 15 (1): 17.

Nash, Beverly. 1986. Letter to Mayor Royer, October 2, 1986. Seattle Municipal Archives 5274–01, box 63, folder 6.

Pacewicz, Josh. 2015. "Playing the Neoliberal Game: Why Community Leaders Left Party Politics to Partisan Activists." *American Journal of Sociology* 121 (3): 826–81.

Peck, Jamie, and Adam Tickell. 2002. "Neoliberalizing Space." *Antipode* 34: 380–404.

Peck, Robert C. 1996. Letter to Mayor Rice, March 10, 1996. Seattle Municipal Archives 4623–02, box 63, folder 2.

Peltz, Dwight, Dawn Mason, and Kip Tokuda. 1995. Letter to Mayor Rice, May 8, 1996. Seattle Municipal Archives 4623–02, box 63, folder 2.

P-Patch Post. 1987. "Office Notes," *P-Patch Post* 9 (2): 7.

P-Patch Post. 1991. "I Like My P-Patch Because . . ." *P-Patch Post* 13 (4): 13.

P-Patch Post. 1992. "Land Use Committee Seeks Volunteers." *P-Patch Post* 14 (2): 4.

Pudup, Mary Beth. 2008. "It Takes a Garden: Cultivating Citizen-Subjects in Organized Garden Projects." *Geoforum* 39 (3): 1228–40.

Quastel, Noah. 2009. "Political Ecologies of Gentrification." *Urban Geography* 30 (7): 694–725.

Reynolds, Kristin. 2015. "Disparity Despite Diversity: Social Injustice in New York City's Urban Agriculture System." *Antipode* 47 (1): 240–59.

Rosan, Christina D., and Hamil Pearsall. 2017. *Growing a Sustainable City?: The Question of Urban Agriculture*. Toronto: University of Toronto Press.

Rosol, Marit. 2012. "Community Volunteering as Neoliberal Strategy? Green Space Production in Berlin." *Antipode* 44 (1): 239–57.

Saldivar-Tanaka, Laura, and Marianne E. Krasny. 2004. "Culturing Community Development, Neighborhood Open Space, and Civic Agriculture: The Case of

Latino Community Gardens in New York City." *Agriculture and Human Values* 21 (4): 399–412.

Thompson, Lynn. 1986. Letter to Mayor Royer, September 30, 1986. Seattle Municipal Archives 5274-01, box 63, folder 6.

Voicu, Ioan, and Vicki Been. 2008. "The Effect of Community Gardens on Neighboring Property Values." *Real Estate Economics* 36 (2): 241–83.

Wolch, Jennifer R., Jason Byrne, and Joshua P. Newell. 2014. "Urban Green Space, Public Health, and Environmental Justice: The Challenge of Making Cities 'Just Green Enough.'" *Landscape and Urban Planning* 125: 234–44.

PART III

Uneven Alliances

Contesting Gentrification from Within and Without

8

Diverse Politics, Difficult Contradictions

Gentrification and the San Francisco Urban Agriculture Alliance

MICHELLE GLOWA AND ANTONIO ROMAN-ALCALÁ

I understand that there are questions about competing priorities for land use given our huge affordability and housing crisis in The City. While housing is a top priority, we also have to balance our housing development in this growing city with some urban agricultural space.
—San Francisco Board of Supervisors member Hillary Ronen (Sabatini 2017)

SF recommits to urban agriculture during housing crisis.
—*San Francisco Examiner*, April 26, 2017 (www.sfexaminer.com)

In April 2017, the San Francisco Board of Supervisors unanimously approved a resolution that recommitted the city government to previously passed legislation that elevated the importance of urban agriculture in city priorities. Urban agriculture (UA) has a long and fruitful history in San Francisco and over the last decade has been codified into city policies in several ways. Much of this work has been brought about by, supported by, and debated by urban gardeners across the city, with gardeners coming to their work from various motivations and positions. Gentrification has frequently been at the center of these debates. In this chapter, we seek to understand how local UA movements have engaged with issues of racial and economic injustice inherent in gentrification, especially considering political-economic changes beyond local community control. How are neoliberal urban processes shaped by, and shaping, UA movement practice? Centrally, we seek to unpack how the institutionalization of such movements into municipal and state policy has reflected the diverse and contradictory politics and interests of urban agriculturists.

Specifically, our case focuses on the work of the San Francisco Urban Agriculture Alliance (SFUAA), a nongovernmental unincorporated organization that "promotes the growing of food within San Francisco and the associated goals of [its] member organizations, through advocacy, education and grassroots action" (www.sfuaa.org). The SFUAA was formed in 2010, during a national surge of interest in UA. The city had already been recognized previously for its innovations in UA practice (e.g., Pudup 2008), but starting in the early 2000s dozens of new UA projects—mostly initiated by grassroots community groups—appeared. One of this chapter's authors (Antonio Roman-Alcalá) was an instigator for multiple such projects, including Alemany Farm, which he co-founded in 2005 and co-managed for years afterward (see figure 8.1). From his experience there, Antonio went on to co-found the SFUAA and co-coordinate it until 2013. Antonio's formative years in San Francisco also included participation in anti-gentrification organizing of the late 1990s. Michelle Glowa has also been involved in UA from 2003 onward working in community gardens, youth UA projects, and at the intersection of social justice and food movements. From 2010 to 2014, she worked with and interviewed dozens of urban agriculturalists across the San Francisco Bay Area as part of her dissertation research. Thus, we bring to this chapter and analysis a praxis-based approach, seeking to theorize on our own work as activists, and to generate insights useful to movements themselves (Bevington and Dixon 2005), of which we consider ourselves part.

San Francisco is certainly not the only city to experience gentrification. But as evidenced by its role in the coining of the term *hypergentrification* (Tiku 2013), the city is an epicenter for the phenomenon. Similarly, while plenty of cities in (so-called) North America have seen surges in UA since the late twentieth century, San Francisco has played an important leadership role in the development of municipal policy to support this surge. Hence, our chapter will address the intersection of UA movements and the development of this policy, in the context of intensifying gentrification. We will begin by outlining the origin and development of the SFUAA, focusing on its internal political diversity. Following this, we briefly present our theoretical understanding of

Figure 8.1. Planting garlic at Alemany Farm, photo by Richard Kay, used with permission.

gentrification and how this relates to the case of San Francisco and its UA. Then we will describe examples from the case of SFUAA and its work to advance UA policy both in San Francisco and at the state (California) level. We conclude with discussion of the dialectical interaction of movements and policy-making institutions, its relation to our central research question, and what these conclusions might say about strategies toward more socially just UA within gentrifying cities.

San Francisco Urban Agriculture, City Government, and the Formation of the SFUAA

Elements of San Francisco city agencies have long been interested in local food, regional food systems, and urban gardening. From the late 1960s to the 1970s, collective urban gardening experienced a revival across the country. In San Francisco, there were seventy-five community gardens managed by the San Francisco Department of Public Works by

TABLE 8.1. Participants in Initial SFUAA Meetings

Orientation	Projects/Entities
Volunteer-/Community-based	Free Farm Free Farm Stand Alemany Farm Hayes Valley Farm
Racial Justice	Northridge COOP Homes Community Garden PODER TNDC's People's Garden
Entrepreneurial	Landscapers incorporating food production (e.g., San Francisco Landscapes, Urban Edibles) Goat rental company (now nonprofit) City Grazing Little City Gardens, the only farm project set up specifically to see if a business model was viable for urban farmers
Nonprofit Organizations	School garden nonprofit Education Outside Garden for the Environment
Governmental Representatives	Paula Jones, Coordinator San Francisco Food Policy Council San Francisco Department of the Environment

1979. However, due to the passage that year of Proposition 13 (which severely limited state property tax revenues) and the end of crucially supportive federal funding, the municipal community gardens program was shuttered by 1980 (Lawson 2005). Some gardeners continued their work under the name of the Urban Agriculture Coalition, which in the early 1980s became the San Francisco League of Urban Gardeners (SLUG; Peirce 1994): Table 8.1 describes participants in initial SFUAA meetings.

From 1981 to 2004, SLUG was a national leader among urban gardening nonprofit organizations. SLUG took over management of the municipal community gardens and by 1986 worked with forty-seven sites on 10 acres (Lawson 2005). In 1986, SLUG contributed significantly to the new city General Plan, which advocated for the expansion of community gardening opportunities throughout the city. Two years later, SLUG and other advocates successfully lobbied for the passage of Proposition E, which continued municipal funding and support for gardens and open space for another 15 years. Unlike in many other US cities, the presence of a consistent and large nonprofit helped maintain the growth of UA through the 1980s and early 1990s, until it became popularized again in the early 2000s. By 2002, SLUG had a yearly budget of $3.5 million and 150–200 employees, with much of this budget generated through grants from and contracts with city and state agencies (Lawson 2005). State funding cuts in the early 2000s left SLUG without crucial funding sources, adding on to reported problems with financial management. The nail in the coffin for SLUG and its programs was political turmoil relating to Gavin Newsom's first mayoral election campaign: SLUG supervisors reportedly told participants in a *jail-to-work* program that they would lose their jobs (and thus return to jail) if they did not campaign and vote for Newsom (Hendrix 2004). Politically well-connected Newsom was never implicated directly in the matter and was elected Mayor in 2003, the year SLUG laid off all employees. Still, this large nonprofit and the many advocates associated with it provided an important foundation upon which a regional movement has flourished.

Starting in the 2000s, a new wave of energy infused the urban agricultural scene in the city, largely coming from communities and non-municipal efforts. Yet, city officials were soon to engage, and in some cases, urban agricultural advocates worked closely with these officials to shape policy changes, including making a prominent place for UA in the San Francisco General Plan; developing a municipal Urban Agriculture Program, updating zoning codes; and developing and advocating for (then becoming the first California city to implement) AB 551, legislation that allows landowners to pay lower property taxes by agreeing to use land for urban farming for at least five years. In 2009, former Mayor Gavin Newsom announced the launch of the *Executive Directive on Healthy and Sustainable Food*, which laid claim to the city's intent to lead on the question of sustainable food. The directive mandated a rethinking of the city's work to support sustainable regional food systems, which included UA. Newsom's administration certainly did not spark the interest in UA, but the Mayor himself seemed to play the classic role of slick-haired politician, sensing which way the wind was blowing and claiming he had provided the wind.

The new round of energy for UA, coming both from the grassroots and city officials, was so noticeable that Antonio, with support from three colleagues,[1] decided in 2010 to convene the at-large UA *community* in a series of three meetings, each attended by roughly fifty people. Suzi Palladino, former staff member at the Garden for the Environment and founding member of the SFUAA, described the genesis of the alliance as "catalyzed by Mayor Gavin Newsom's Executive Directive" (Jones 2010: 53). For others, including Antonio, the alliance arose from the need for collective organization: to avoid competition between projects and groups, to create a stronger sense of cohesion, and to effectively interact with the rise of city government interest in UA. At initial meetings, attendees discussed what the UA community stood for, what it needed and could offer one another, and what its priorities with regard to city government might be.

The very question of the government's role in the emerging alliance, and vice versa, exhibits the SFUAA's founding *political* diversity: While some saw the SFUAA as a definitional *grassroots* alliance, others saw it as a means of influencing city policy. Unsurprisingly, considering the general demographics of the city itself in 2010, and larger trends in the *food movement*, participants in the SFUAA's founding were less diverse *ethnically*, being majority—but not universally—white. Within the SFUAA's founding group were people like Antonio, who were interested in food and farming as political organizing tools to challenge capitalist relations and build community-based power. Though they were not all explicitly radical, anti-capitalist, or focused on community rather than state power (although some were), such participants were less interested (or uninterested) in legal or municipal policy reform efforts. Another set of overlapping UA projects consisted of gardens that were founded to address issues of racial injustice. Projects in neighborhoods of Bayview Hunters Point (BVHP), Mission, Tenderloin, and Chinatown were based in communities of color and built upon ideas of food justice. Other participants included staff from nonprofits and small businesses, and a few city employees. These all constituted strong elements of the SFUAA's constituent projects from the beginning: radical, reformist, racial justice–focused, nonprofit, entrepreneurial, and governmental. Across all these categories, including those motivated by *radical* and racial justice values, many projects received funding from the city or utilized its land.

Because of the way it was founded, the SFUAA's organizational structure was based on a horizontalist ideal of consensus, distributed and rotating (volunteer) leadership, and a commitment to remain autonomous from city government. It did not set itself up as a nonprofit arm of government. However, enough attendees from various political positions held interest in advancing UA goals through government, and so policy became part of the expressed intention of the SFUAA. But this was largely understood as an *outside* orientation, to push the city to adopt better policies in support of the community's stated goals. However, those goals were not necessarily as cohesive as was thought in those initial months, as we will see in the cases discussed below.

Gentrification in the San Francisco Context

The *urbanization of neoliberalism*, while varied across contexts, has meant municipal use of experimental policy to create more favorable opportunities for private investors, such as place marketing, enterprise zones, urban development corporations, and public-private partnerships (Smith 2002: 21). Municipal governments, motivated to bring in jobs and revenues, are subject to an urban political economy driven by the production of space. It is in these processes of urbanization of neoliberalism that we contextualize gentrification in San Francisco. While much of San Francisco has sustained a high level of ground rent over the last half century, neighborhoods such as the Mission and South of Market (SOMA) have followed the patterns of gentrification as described by Neil Smith (2002). For Smith, gentrification was less a process of middle-class families or hipsters moving en masse into a neighborhood and more a question of the coordination of investment of capital into use through urban spatial development. And while we see both factors in gentrification, of consumption-side processes stemming from new Silicon Valley–employed residents desiring to move to San Francisco, and production-side arguments that emphasize the policy and investment dynamics that shape the production of urban space, we feel it is important to emphasize the latter as being key to the processes of urbanization of neoliberalism. Urban scholars have argued that cities have become key sites of economic and social restructuring through the neoliberal period (Brenner and Theodore 2002; Smith 2002). The actions of urban agriculturists indeed may prove relevant in the construction of consumption-side factors in gentrification (e.g., increasing neighborhood appeal through streetscape greening), but our concern pertains more to the *policy* and *politics* side of the equation of neoliberal urbanization.

Many San Francisco neighborhoods are experiencing rapid and massive reinvestment of capital into places that have been inhabited and cultivated by residents over many years. Such neighborhoods have built institutions, identities, and resources through the development of ethnic and cultural communities in place and over time: for example, the Mission's Latinx heritage, the Fillmore and BVHP's long-standing African American communities, or Filipinos South of Market in SOMA. All these communities have in diverse ways manifested economic, cultural, artistic, and political influences on the city at large. What many have called *hyper-gentrification* is causing rapid displacement of San Francisco's lower-income and long-time residents who historically composed these communities. Leland cites Smith calling this a "systematic class-remaking of city neighborhoods" (Leland 2011), though it clearly has a racial dimension as well. Extreme housing prices have contributed to a widening wealth gap, which in San Francisco is growing faster than any other city in the nation (Knight 2014). Today, a regional housing crisis is under way as middle-class San Franciscans and Silicon Valley tech workers spill into surrounding communities.

Much of this change is connected to the rapid growth of the tech industry over the last two decades. The Bay Area region attracts venture capital–backed high-tech industry at a higher rate than any other location in the world (Florida 2013). The Silicon Valley is the national leader in investments bridging tech and real estate development and along with New York represents 36 percent of real estate technology startups worldwide (Ibid.). As the first tech industry expansion was occurring, California passed Proposition 13, causing the state to favor commercial development over residential for its greater potential tax earnings (Chapman 1998). Simultaneously, regional municipalities embraced the economic promise of Silicon Valley, and to attract development they have offered incentives to these industries, including low annual business taxes (Rose 2011). For example, in 2011 San Francisco passed a payroll tax exemption, nicknamed the "Twitter tax break," to entice companies to move into a set of very specific buildings close to downtown. Since moving into the neighborhood, Twitter has opened a gourmet market and private outdoor park called the Twitter Commons. New SOMA residents enjoy access to expensive organic produce, a paleo vegan food vendor, and delicious varieties of fair-trade coffees and chocolates. At the same time, corner stores and bodegas have been closing down, limiting the food options for the neighborhood's large houseless population. San Francisco's popularity for tech development and real estate has contributed to a housing crisis, and to resistance to further development.

Lively protests, direct action, public debate over evictions and tenant rights, the loss of housing to Airbnb, and negative impacts of "Google buses" in San Francisco and the Bay Area have gained national attention. On September 25, 2014, a video went viral of white Dropbox and Airbnb employees repeatedly asking Latinx youth to leave a public soccer field in the Mission because they had reserved the site online (Brooks and Brekke 2014). When the youth and an African American young adult advocate suggested that the field was historically public and open, and that the white men join their game, the men were incredulous, insisting they had paid the $27/hour fee for the reservation and should be able to use the field. The video spread quickly, with vitriol-filled comments

Figure 8.2. Cultivating the soil at Alemany Farm, photo by Richard Kay, used with permission.

about the racism of gentrification in San Francisco, leading to apologies from at least one of the players involved, and more significantly a reversal of the "Pay to Play" reservation system the Recreation and Parks Department (RPD) had instituted. The policy still stands at several other San Francisco fields, highlighting how green spaces, including access to public gardens, are at the center of the city's transformation. Like in Sbicca's description (see chapter 4 in this volume) of the role of gardens in shifting the cultural signification of space and thus investment potentials, fights over green spaces in San Francisco have become more common. Today's debates over urban space have reached electric levels and are reflected in debates about how and where urban gardeners and policies make urban environments available for cultivation.

Case Stories from SFUAA

UA Legislation #1: Zoning Changes, 2011–2012

In 2010, a policy subcommittee, including some members of SFUAA although not a part of the group, was organized to offer suggestions for the San Francisco Food Policy Council's report to the city (Jones 2010) and to review the goals of Newsom's Directive and provide recommendations on goal implementation. In initial SFUAA meetings, a few participants including Paula Jones and a newcomer to the city named Eli Zigas suggested the alliance further develop such policy goals.

In 2010, the SFUAA took up the work to reshape municipal planning code. Working with specific staff members in the San Francisco Planning Department, the SFUAA brainstormed guidelines in its Policy Subcommittee (renamed the Platform Committee internally), conferred with planners on these ideas, and developed legal language to introduce into the code. This effort was sparked in part by challenges faced by SFUAA member Little City Gardens in legally selling their products, as well as their being threatened by neighbors (in a residential district) for not abiding by legal zoning uses—as no regulations since the early twentieth century officially recognized UA as a use. The zoning proposal eliminated the need to apply for an expensive and time-consuming "Conditional Use" permit to be able to sell produce from urban gardens. In addition, it permitted the operation in all zoning districts of community and home gardens—whether food is produced for personal consumption, donation, or commercial purposes—and regulated the sale of urban garden produce (Chandler 2010). On April 20, 2011, the ordinance was signed into law following a unanimous vote from the Board of Supervisors. Surrounded by freshly harvested produce, Mayor Edwin Lee signed the ordinance at Little City Gardens' urban farm and celebrated a victory for gardeners and the city with the SFUAA. The ordinance quickly gained national attention as one of the most comprehensive pieces of recent legislation on UA (Terrazas 2011). Supervisor David Chiu, who co-sponsored the law, stated: "This bill puts San Francisco on the map as a national leader in urban agriculture, and is a tangible example of how government can create more sustainable communities" (Office of the Mayor 2011).

UA Legislation #2: Urban Agriculture Program (2013)

The second policy initiative of the SFUAA emerged from meetings with Supervisor David Chiu, who sought to be seen as a champion for UA. Chiu saw an opportunity to rationalize the city's investments in UA by assessing what money the city already spent on UA-related materials and programs and creating a central coordinating program held in one agency to coordinate these expenditures. The proposed solution was a new "Urban Agriculture Program," including a coordinator staff position. In April 2013, after SFUAA provided guidance to Chiu's office, a City Administrator's Office report recommended housing the Urban Agriculture Program within the Recreation and Park Department (RPD; Miller 2013). This occurred despite RPD being the least favored agency of the SFUAA, due to decades of negative experiences with their bureaucratic management of community gardens and its more recent proclivities for privatization (as noted in the Mission playground case above). RPD was also a main protagonist of the eviction of a community-serving recycling center located on park land, run by the nonprofit Haight-Ashbury Neighborhood Center (HANC). While RPD had hoped to garner UA community support for the eviction by proposing to replace the center with a new garden, SFUAA members opposed the project, viewing it as a political move, made primarily as an attack on HANC. HANC had opposed Newsom's previous anti-poor welfare *reform* legislative effort "Care Not Cash,"[2] and now were opposing the effort to satisfy the newer upper-class residents of the area, who complained about the "homeless" (often, simply low-income) people who utilized the recycling center.

Overall, SFUAA members were appreciative of the efforts Chiu and other city elected officials put into the new legislation, which passed in July 2013. The SFUAA had developed a three-point policy platform shortly after its formation in order to: (1) Expand Organizational Capacity of Urban Agriculture in San Francisco; (2) Increase Access to Land; and (3) Improve Access to Resources. The SFUAA believed that the first goal could be better met by creating an official program paid for by the city to coordinate resources—a "one-stop shop" where, for example, people who find empty lots could find out whether the lot is owned by a city agency, and furthermore learn how (if it is city-owned) they may go about accessing it for UA purposes. The second and third goals would also be advanced through the legislation. Following Newsom's Food Directive, a *land audit* of city property had been conducted to determine potential new spaces for UA. However, this had not resulted in new UA uses, so the advocates hoped this new program would kick start that process. The law also called for setting up garden resource centers to distribute compost and vegetable starts in various locations across the city.

By September 2014, UA had become a popular enough issue that several mayoral candidates, including Chiu, spoke at a forum focused on UA and water issues sponsored by the SFUAA and allied environmental nonprofits. This political engagement has not been uncontroversial within SFUAA. Members have debated the degree to which SFUAA should be making political endorsements or using alliance resources to discuss partisan politics that may advance particular politicians' careers, given their efforts to support the alliance have not required sacrifice, only positive PR.[3] Although Chiu did not win the mayoral election, this and other UA-related press have helped to build his image as a progressive politician. Some have speculated that this likely affected his later election to California State Senate. While Chiu has shown authentic interest in environmental issues (including UA) throughout his political career, he has often appeared on the opposite side of progressive interests with regard to housing and social justice issues (Redmond 2017; Monette-Shaw 2014). One longtime leftist San Francisco activist described Chiu as having "no principles and an abject willingness to prostrate himself before the wealthy and influential," noting Chiu's efforts to legalize Airbnb rentals "without recovering the $25 million in back taxes they just blew off paying" (Carlsson 2014). By validating individual politicians through single-issue advocacy (like that for UA), some members of the SFUAA believed they might inadvertently contribute to politics they do not like.

Returning to the Urban Agriculture Program legislation, though the proposed ordinance was overall supported by the SFUAA, with some adjustments (namely, that it develop job training opportunities and community participation in evaluation), it was more controversial with some UA practitioners. In particular, Bayview Hunters Point organizer Jeffrey Betcher did not agree to support the legislation, as it would put city monies specifically toward UA rather than toward other potential uses that communities may find necessary in a more "holistic" vision of just sustainability (e.g., housing, recreation, education). Betcher worried about whether the San Francisco UA movement shares similar obstacles to the Environmental Movement, namely, its whiteness and focus on particular outcomes. Betcher argued, "if (the urban agriculture movement) were connected to urban community development and social justice movements, it wouldn't look that way . . . People come to me as though of course I agree that if we plop a garden down, we'll build community. And I have to say gardens don't build community, people build community."[4] Ultimately, Betcher did not want to see more advocacy purely for gardens, but instead advocacy that promoted neighborhood-based land use decision-making processes. His concern was also that while UA differs around the city, for the relatively low-income and historically African American neighborhood of BVHP, it could act as a "Trojan horse" for gentrification. For communities like the BVHP, facing a long history of willful neglect from city government, and subject to this day to economic and racialized marginalization, a mostly white group of UA proponents may not have its best interests in mind, nor be attentive to the specific needs of the community. Betcher warned: "I worry that one day people are gonna look at these newly fenced-in, locked spaces with people they don't recognize . . . inside, bickering about weeds in their raised beds and say, 'That's no better than the Google bus that's around. That's just disempowering.'"[5] Betcher, along with others, actively voiced these problems during SFUAA meetings and in written communications.

This raised concern within the SFUAA membership and leadership, some of whom had never considered that UA could have negative effects on the most vulnerable communities in San Francisco, or that the group's activism might have negative impacts on the very communities that UA is ostensibly meant to serve, as is commonly expected in "food justice" discourses. Discussions in this smaller group of the SFUAA led to the suggestion to come up with a formal position on gentrification.

Position on Gentrification (2012)

In reaction to the above intervention—and some members' general concerns for SFUAA not being attuned to the intersection of UA and gentrification—Antonio wrote a proposed "position on gentrification" for approval by the alliance. Some attendees argued that gentrification was "not our issue" and wondered why the group should speak up about it. Opposition to the idea of taking a position on the issue, however, was not fierce. With some toning down of its language (for instance, a mention of the concept of "eco-apartheid" was taken out), the position statement was approved in October 2012. While the statement was mildly controversial, enough of a critical mass of SFUAA members believed that they "can and should link up our struggles with those of others" (SFUAA 2012). "Ultimately," the group proclaimed, echoing Betcher's sentiments, "many of these struggles are about local community control over public resources, and that is a much larger battle" (ibid.).

Thereafter, the SFUAA made greater efforts at outreach and inclusion of UA communities not active in SFUAA. These efforts faced challenges quite typical to *social justice* organizing. People—largely from communities of color—who had not previously been involved in SFUAA expressed hesitation. Factors cited included the travel distance to meetings, the feeling of "another meeting, for what?," and being invited (after the fact) to a group already established as largely white and for the most part composed of people from relatively privileged backgrounds. Of course, SFUAA was not uniform, and did include people of color, people from low-income backgrounds, and people born in San Francisco (like Antonio), but this was not the majority of the group. This no doubt shaped who SFUAA was (politically) and how it was perceived. After about a year of outreach, the membership of SFUAA had not substantially changed in composition, but meeting discussion more regularly addressed social justice issues directly.

The failure of the SFUAA to cultivate relationships with communities being especially impacted by gentrification is not surprising, as both the SFUAA and the leaders it reached out to were also limited by the impacts of gentrification. SFUAA's meeting attendance and participation has, for example, dropped since its first few years, possibly reflecting a general lack of time as higher expenses result in less breathing room for participants, and as fewer *volunteer types* can afford to move to the city. During this period, SFUAA leadership transitioned, as some of the alliance's original organizers (including Antonio and Eli) stepped out of coordination roles, and other members stepped in. Though SFUAA may have experienced reduced membership and participation after its first few years (2010–2013), it has managed to maintain two or three co-coordinators throughout its existence. It could also be argued that the group's members have shifted to reflect the new demographics of a city changing with gentrification. With these demographic changes often come political changes. Entrepreneurial interests in UA were never completely foreign to SFUAA, but arguably became more common within meeting attendees over time—paralleling the tech sector-linked entrepreneurial fervor that was permeating the city. As these changes occur, it becomes harder to imagine an anti-gentrification (much less anti-racist or anti-capitalist) politics gaining much resonance in the SFUAA.

Urban Agriculture Incentives Zone Act—AB 551 (2013)

In January 2013, California State Assembly member Phil Ting's staffers reached out to SFUAA co-coordinator Susan Keuhn, saying Ting wanted to support UA as part of his agenda for sustainable agriculture and healthy diets. Through meetings with SFUAA, Ting became interested in pursuing what became nicknamed the "Williamson Act for Urban Ag." Modeled after an existing policy to keep rural lands in agriculture, the law would incentivize UA across the state by allowing cities to lower certain properties' tax assessment rate based on their *agricultural* rather than *market* value, in exchange for a five-year commitment to use the land for farming or gardening. Inspired by Little City Gardens' high land rent situation and the work of Nicholas Reed and Juan Carlos Cancino, a group of SFUAA advocates, including Zigas and Little City Garden's Caitlyn Galloway, brought this idea (and others) to the first meeting with Ting. Ting gravitated to this idea as he knew tax code well through his previous role as assessor. Working with Ting's office to craft the policy and lobby for its passage, the SFUAA's efforts proved pivotal in ensuring legislative success. In 2013, AB 551, the Urban Agriculture Incentives Zones legislation, became law in California. In August 2014, San Francisco voted to become the first county and city to implement it.

When SFUAA was first brainstorming ideas to bring to the first meeting with Ting's office, Antonio suggested the group take up broader issues that operate beyond (but may intersect) with UA, such as the fiscal austerity fallout from Proposition 13, affordable housing and displacement prevention, or increasing funding for community colleges. He argued that by supporting college funding, the SFUAA could: (a) support UA leaders with jobs as horticulture teachers at the colleges; (b) increase green job training in UA and ecoliteracy, but not in a class-/ race-exclusive context as many permaculture and organic farming courses typically are; and (c) show cross-sector support between UA and other working-class interests via increasing accessible public education. Antonio was told by another Platform Committee member that such ideas were "beyond the scope, expertise, and platform of the SFUAA," and that we need to "balance the effectiveness of focus and the need for broader transformative policy change."[6] The question comes up: Who are UA advocates—particularly the leadership of groups like the SFUAA—accountable to when they conduct political advocacy work? Whose agendas are served, or left out, by this "balancing"?

AB 551 and (Acceptable?) Land Insecurity

AB 551's premise was to encourage temporary access to land for UA. Yet some Bay Area UA organizers have argued that AB 551 might fail to support food justice applications of UA (Havens and Roman-Alcalá 2016). Because of the temporary use of gardens to attract community activity and engagement from more economically advantaged consumer communities, urban gardens have in many cases been linked to rising property values and gentrification (McClintock 2017). The law does not challenge neoliberal urbanization and may even support it by providing an implementable policy model based on tax incentives that benefit landowners. This model is unlikely to support racial justice, except where there is an existing, strong, and racially diverse movement to shape implementation of the policy locally, as has been seen a bit more in Los Angeles and San Jose than San Francisco (Havens and Roman-Alcalá 2016: 11–12). Similar to its model, the Williamson Act, AB 551 has had only limited effects even on its own terms of supporting agricultural land uses: In San Francisco, the only project to have received the incentive was the 18th & Rhode Island Permaculture Garden, in place since 2008.

AB 551 mirrors similar strategies promoted by some gardeners, policy makers, and developers. Through Newsom's Food Directive, two lots in downtown were allocated for temporary garden development as interim-use projects to last between three and eighteen years (Glowa 2017). These became the Hayes Valley Farm and the Growing Home Garden. Both projects lasted less than five years and were terminated when the city sold the properties for housing development. The case of the Hayes Valley Farm ultimately allowed what might have been a more controversial development of market rate housing on once public land, through a *public-private partnership* pursued after creating a short-term *community benefit* of open space. This was only possible through a very large investment of volunteer labor of neighbors and urban garden activists and a small grant of $52,950 from San Francisco's Office of Economic and Workforce Development ("Community Challenge Grants" 2014).

Other examples of gardeners promoting temporary use include projects like NOMAD gardens (Glowa 2017). The San Francisco–based organization, which operated from 2014 to 2017, headed its Indiegogo fund-raising campaign with the statement "Our neighborhood is in flux . . . And we need YOUR help to turn our first vacant lot into an inspiring portable garden & community space!!!" (Stephanie and Kate 2012). Through the creation of portable garden beds which can "roam from vacant lot to vacant lot," the organization aimed to cultivate both food and opportunities for social interaction in what they deemed to be "developing neighborhoods" (Nomad Gardens 2012). The group's founder, Stephanie Goodson, first came to the idea after having problems persuading a local developer to let her use a vacant piece of land for a community garden. In contrast to what she saw as a trend of gardeners becoming too attached to particular parcels and thus discouraging owners who would permit gardening as an interim use, she wanted to develop technologies that would allow developers to "reclaim the land easily" (ibid.). NOMAD gardens used platforms like Airbnb to advertise their community building events, raising additional questions as to which populations the organization intended to attract (Airbnb 2017). Portability facilitates temporary land use and beneficial relationships with owners who are concerned that gardeners may resist displacement, thus in many cases creating concessions to those acting within trajectories of gentrification.

An article published after the passage of AB 551 critiqued gardening in a housing-stressed city and again stirred conversation among gardeners and Bay Area residents (Friedersdorf 2014). San Francisco Housing Development Corporation and others expressed dismay that urban gardens are being promoted in a city with such a shortage of affordable housing and gentrification pressures. Yet Zigas and his employer SPUR (formerly the San Francisco Planning and Urban Renewal Association) do not agree with the dichotomy, arguing AB 551 promotes growing on land that is not likely to be sold for development in the near future (Zigas 2014). SPUR continued to support other cities in the region as they sought to adopt local AB 551 ordinances. As an urban planning organization focused on development and municipal policy, SPUR became an influential San Francisco institution after World War II when the organization, led by business-class leaders, pushed for the city's revitalization through targeted neighborhood demolition of primarily African American communities (Brahinsky 2012). Today SPUR remains an influential organization in the Bay Area, making its position on development and gardening one of importance in the region.

As a policy initiative, AB 551, and other forms of public and private interim-use projects, keep UA in a state of land tenure insecurity. Differing from Glennie's example (see also chapter 7 in this volume) of Seattle gardeners' cooperation with the urban growth machine to protect public gardens, interim-use proponents are implementing a different political strategy. Promoters suggest temporary use as a strategy that provides immediate benefits to gardeners seeking land for short-term projects and benefits for landowners interested in flexibility, yet they acknowledge that lands that could be developed easily are highly unlikely to be accessed via this legislation. The approach, oriented toward win-win, maintains a primary focus on benefiting landowners, not those without land. Gardeners have little to no equity in AB 551's five-year leases. This emphasis on flexibility maintains a material and ideological prioritization of the use of urban land for the purposes of economic development and the accumulation of wealth for landowners. Considering that the zoning changes, the city's UA program, and AB 551 were all built upon the needs established by San Francisco's only commercial urban farm, Little City Gardens, it is unfortunately ironic that the farm was evicted in 2016. Though the majority of neighbors had come to love the farm and led a "Save the Farm" campaign, the farm was still subject to the same old development pressures that continue to face all urban farmers on private land in a capitalist private property regime.

Conclusion

From the beginning, the SFUAA was a space with diverse and sometimes contradictory politics. SFUAA members were pivotal in pushing discussion with policy makers and, in the end, achieving many policy changes with regard to UA. As they sought to institutionalize support for UA in government policy, the SFUAA's diversity was further shaped: by its members' (shifting) cultural and political assumptions and interests; by the changing political economy of the gentrifying city and region; by the underlying economic imperatives that governments respond to. State actors, of course, do not respond mechanistically to the needs of capital. But they are incentivized—ideologically and out of expedience—to promote policies which at the least do not threaten political and economic elites. When this proclivity matches non-state actors (like UA advocates) who are interested and willing to pass such policy, it is more likely to happen. In this case, we see that neoliberal spatial imperatives and UA are a great match, insofar as UA is not construed or presented as a threat to private property or state authority.

Elected officials may be motivated to support UA insofar as they see UA as a constituency to *capture*. UA frequently espouses, represents, or signals a commitment to ecological sustainability, community well-being, and sometimes social justice—even if UA may not significantly advance these goals, or may even serve a counter-justice role in the case of contributing to gentrification. In this case, we see politicians mobilizing and gaining social connections, and thus potential votes, by cultivating political commitments to UA that pose little danger to other interests, for example to local landowners. In promoting legislation, language in city planning documents, and city-sponsored projects that emphasize interim use and the use of non-developable lands for gardens, such city officials and politicians garner support from both urban agriculturalists and developers.

At the same time that San Francisco is in crisis over housing and rapid social dislocation of low-income residents, economic investment and growth are skyrocketing. These crises impact urban agriculturalists both in the ability to continue living in the city and in their communities of practice and advocacy. As gentrification processes developed, we observed a shift in the composition of movement participants in the SFUAA, reflecting at-large changes in the city itself. Along with the shift in UA movement demographics came a shift toward more policy and entrepreneurial efforts. Several organizers and gardeners committed to anti-capitalist and anti-racist work through UA had to leave the city due to rising costs or evictions.

For some UA organizers, the offer of government access and insider status is quite appealing: It appears to validate one's ideas and offers a chance to *influence* government and potentially envision change on a broader scale. Yet this strongly contrasts to key areas where SFUAA's *influence* did not appear to count for much, such as the HANC eviction or RPD's selection as the agency to house the city's UA program. In neither of these cases was the organization authentically able to influence policy: Results had been essentially predetermined by political forces within government. Getting to be on the *inside* may seem appealing to reform-minded UA practitioners, but it is fraught, as it means meeting city officials on their turf and with their imperatives. Even simple constraints of time, format, and *politics of possibility* can shape movement efforts. As we saw with the history of SLUG, tight relationships with city leaders and agencies, while appealing in terms of offering sources of funding, are also tenuous and potentially volatile—whether because of the vicissitudes of government funds, or the dangers of political corruption and compromise.

Tensions over strategies advocating for entrepreneurial urban policies, such as AB 551, have elicited debate among movement actors and city residents. The relatively muted nature of the debate within UA communities, however, emphasizes the entrenched nature of neoliberal ideologies—where policies are construed as a *win-win*, while in reality they sidestep so much of what is actually political about them. These win-win narratives avoid conflicts stemming from competing class interests, institutional and structural racism, or the damages from historical and existing government policies and procedures. In order to cultivate UA movements and projects that can engage with these conflicts and understand the role gardens can play in bolstering or spurring on gentrification, we believe urban gardeners and farmers must be self-critical, while they develop and articulate a strong combination of race and economic class analysis. To think that either UA is simply the Trojan horse of gentrification or that individual UA projects that are justice-oriented can avoid the trappings of urban political economy belies the complexity of the struggles urban agriculturalists must now learn to participate within. To keep their "eyes on the prize," urban agriculturalists committed to food justice must maintain ongoing, critical political engagement in issues beyond UA or food, per se.

NOTES

The authors have contributed equally to this chapter.
1. Elizabeth Martin Craig, Ellen Roggeman, and Susan Coss—all organizers of different sorts.
2. "Care Not Cash" reduced public assistance recipients' monthly checks, on the (classist) premise that too many recipients wasted the money on drugs and alcohol, and that services would be offered in replacement for lost income. It was heavily opposed by San Francisco's nonprofit, anti-hunger, and pro-poor sectors.
3. Personal communication, 2014.
4. Personal communication, 2014.
5. Personal communication, 2014.
6. Personal communication, 2013.

REFERENCES

Airbnb. 2017. "Airbnb for Good-San Francisco: NOMAD Garden." www.airbnb.com.
Bay City News. 2011. "Restrictions on Local Food Growers Lifted, SF Now 'On the Cutting Edge of the Urban Agriculture Movement.'" *San Francisco Appeal*, April 20. http://sfappeal.com.

Bevington, Douglas, and Chris Dixon. 2005. "Movement-Relevant Theory: Rethinking Social Movement Scholarship and Activism." *Social Movement Studies* 4 (3): 185–208.

Brahinsky, Rachel. 2012. *The Making and Unmaking of Southeast San Francisco* (doctoral dissertation). University of California, Berkeley.

Brenner, Niel, and Nik Theodore. 2002. "Cities and the Geographies of 'Actually Existing Neoliberalism.'" *Antipode* 34 (3): 349–379.

Brooks, Jon, and Dan Brekke. 2014. "Mission Soccer Field Incident Prompts Change in Reservation Policy." *KQED News*, October 16. www.kqed.org.

Carlsson, Chris. 2014. "Dog-Whistle Politics in San Francisco" [Blog post]. *Nowtopian*, October 17. www.nowtopians.com.

Chandler, Jeri Lynn. 2010. "Mayor Proposes Code Amendment for Urban Agriculture in San Francisco." *Examiner*. December 15. www.examiner.com.

Chapman, Jeffery. 1998. "Proposition 13: Some Unintended Consequences." In Public Policy Institute of California. www.ppic.org.

Community Challenge Grants. 2014. San Francisco, CA: City of San Francisco. https://data.sfgov.org.

Florida, Richard. 2013. "Why San Francisco May Be the New Silicon Valley." *CityLab*, August 5.

Friedersdorf, Conor. 2014. "How Urban Farming Is Making San Francisco's Housing Crisis Worse." *The Atlantic*, September 3.

Glowa, K. Michelle. 2017. "Urban Agriculture, Food Justice, and Neoliberal Urbanization: Rebuilding the Institution of Property." In Alison Alkon and Julie Guthman, eds., *The New Food Activism: Opposition, Cooperation and Collective Action*. Oakland: University of California Press.

Havens, Erin and Antonio Roman-Alcalá. 2016. *Land for Food Justice? AB 551 and Structural Change* (Land and Sovereignty Policy Brief #8, Summer 2016). Oakland, CA: Food First/Institute for Food and Development Policy.

Hendrix, Anastasia. 2004. "City Workers: We Were Told to Vote, Work for Newsom / S.F. City Attorney Probes Campaign Charge By 9 Street Cleaners." *San Francisco Chronicle*, January 15. www.sfgate.com.

Jones, Paula. 2010. "Executive Directive on Healthy and Sustainable Food: Summary Report." San Francisco, CA. Issued July 9, 2009 by Mayor Gavin Newsom. Prepared by Paula Jones of San Francisco Department of Public Health.

Knight, Heather. 2014. "Income Inequality on Par with Developing Nations." *SFGate*, June 25. www.sfgate.com.

Lawson, Laura J. 2005. *City Bountiful: A Century of Community Gardening in America*. Berkeley: University of California Press.

Leland, John. 2011. "In Williamsburg, Rocked Hard." *New York Times*, May 28. www.nytimes.com.

McClintock, Nathan. 2017. "Cultivating (a) Sustainability Capital: Urban Agriculture, Eco-gentrification, and the Uneven Valorization of Social Reproduction." *Annals of the American Association of Geographers* 108 (2): 579–590.

Miller, Alisa. 2013. "Board of Supervisors Meeting." San Francisco, CA. www.sfbos.org.
Monette-Shaw, Patrick. 2014. "The Three-David Race for Assemblymember." *Fog City Journal*, May 5. www.fogcityjournal.com.
Office of the Mayor. 2011. "Mayor Lee Signs Urban Agriculture Legislation for Greater Local Food Production in SF." April 20.
Nomad Gardens. 2012. "Our Story | NOMADgardens." https://web.archive.org.
Peirce, Pam. 1994. "I Was There . . ." The Trowel, SF's Community Garden newsletter, Spring/Summer 1994 #1. http://foundsf.org.
Pudup, Mary Beth. 2008. "It Takes a Garden: Cultivating Citizen-Subjects in Organized Garden Projects." *Geoforum* 39 (3): 1228–1240.
Redmond, Tim. 2017. "Tenants Call Out Chiu on Key Rent-Control Measure." *48 Hills*, December 5. https://48hills.org.
Rose, Harvey. 2011. "Requested Letter SF Supervisor Farell and Members of the Board of Supervisors from Budget and Legislative Analyst." San Francisco: San Francisco Board of Supervisors.
Sabatini, Joshua. 2017. "SF Recommits to Urban Agriculture During Housing Crisis." *San Francisco Examiner*, April 26. www.sfexaminer.com.
SFUAA. 2012. Position on Gentrification. www.sfuaa.org.
Smith, Neil. 2002. "New Globalism, New Urbanism: Gentrification as Global Urban Strategy." *Antipode* 34 (3): 427–450.
Stephanie and Kate. 2012. "Get NOMAD Gardens Growing." www.indiegogo.com.
Terrazas, Alexis. 2011. "Urban Farming Ready to Take Root with Approval from San Francisco." *San Francisco Examiner*, April 21.
Tiku, Nitasha. 2013. "Twitter Will Cause So Much Gentrification, They Invented a New Word." *Valleywag*, October 17. http://valleywag.gawker.com.
Zigas, Eli. 2014. "Urban Farming Is Not Making the Housing Crisis Worse" [Blog post]. *City Lab*. September 4. www.citylab.com.

9

"Ethical" Gentrification as a Preemptive Strategy

Social Enterprise, Restaurants, and Resistance in Vancouver's Downtown Eastside

ZACHARY HYDE

Between 2005 and 2017, Vancouver's Downtown Eastside neighborhood, often referred to as Canada's poorest postal code, underwent extensive commercial upscaling alongside a spate of both private condominium development and government-subsidized social housing. These changes took place against the backdrop of ongoing anti-gentrification organizing, involving struggles for the preservation of the area's rental housing stock and retail businesses, and against incursion from outside investors. The Downtown Eastside is one of Canada's most politically active neighborhoods; it is historically home to a large white, indigenous and Chinese Canadian working-class population living in social housing and Single Room Occupancy (SRO) hotels, while also being situated on highly valuable land on the southeastern edge of the city's densely developed Downtown peninsula. The area has now also become the setting of Vancouver's most trendy culinary scene and what local restaurant reviewers commonly refer to as a restaurant revolution.

This chapter examines the contestation over restaurant gentrification in the Downtown Eastside and introduces the concept of *ethical* gentrification to resolve several empirical and theoretical discussions within gentrification research. The first goal is to bring the study of social enterprise, a form of business activity that claims to advance a caring and ethical vision of private profit-making, into dialogue with research on resistance to gentrification and reflexive gentrifiers. Resistance to gentrification has remained a lacuna within neighborhood change research (Slater 2006; Brown-Saracino 2016). Early studies of gentrification found a harmful process where newcomers sought to displace existing neighborhood residents, referred to as "urban revanchism" (Smith 1996). However, more recently Brown-Saracino (2009) has discovered that many contemporary gentrifiers are reflexive *social preservationists* who seek to minimize the negative impact of their presence on low-income communities. Thus, while their economic and cultural capital contribute to the process of gentrification in low-income neighborhoods, these newcomers espouse *ethical* intentions and draw strong symbolic boundaries between themselves and less thoughtful *gentrifiers*. This complicates our understanding of how resistance to gentrification plays out, as newcomers proclaim to be "on the same side" as old-timers, even as their presence contributes to rising property values.

While Brown-Saracino's work focuses on residential newcomers, I extend this discussion to the realm of retail gentrification by looking at social enterprise in the context of a low-income neighborhood. My research focuses on a cohort of new restaurant owners in the Downtown Eastside who claim to reject old forms of snobbish exclusivity that characterized Vancouver's high-end dining scene by making gourmet food accessible to a broader clientele. Many of these newcomers also suggest they are community-minded and have devised inclusive business models to *give back* to the neighborhood. These arguments can be understood within the broader context of what Emily Barman (2016) refers to as *caring capitalism*, a discourse of *win-win* between the public and private sectors where "companies can pursue social impact and make a profit in doing so" (Barman 2016:13). This approach reflects neoliberalism's restructuring of the welfare state by making social services the purview of the profit-driven private sector (Kinderman 2012).

Advancing recent discussions on social preservationist newcomers and caring capitalism, this chapter asks: What is the role of social enterprise, particularly restaurants that forward ethical business orientations, in gentrifying neighborhoods? and; How can this phenomenon help us to understand the dynamics of resistance to gentrification? Drawing from original research on restaurant gentrification in the Downtown Eastside, this chapter argues that social enterprise and entrepreneurship work to co-opt dissent and resistance to gentrification through a discourse and set of practices I refer to as *ethical gentrification*.[1] Ethical gentrification shares similarities with the broader trend toward ethical consumption, which sociologists have found is marked by a tension between progressive social values, like environmentalism, and cultural and economic exclusivity (Johnston 2008). Ethical gentrification refers to the practices of newcomers to low-income neighborhoods who seek to redress the problems of gentrification through consumption, which conversely contributes to reproducing and deepening inequality.

Through the practices associated with social enterprise, the solution to problems of inequality is placed in the hands of newcomers, while framing the needs and wants of community organizers and activists as *unreasonable*. I find that ethical gentrification serves as a preemptive strategy on the part of newcomer business owners in the Downtown Eastside to disrupt claims that commercial upscaling is having a negative effect on the low-income community. This version of ethical consumption also works to undermine and delegitimize grassroots attempts at inclusion, food security, and social justice.

The tensions uncovered here can be linked to the broader contradiction within caring capitalism (Davis 2017) between community-mindedness and the goal to pursue private profit. It can also be linked to the tension between the anti-elitism and exclusivity by culturally omnivorous foodies, in what Johnston and Baumann (2010) refer to as "democracy versus distinction." This tension is heightened in the context of gentrification, when newcomers selectively prioritize certain forms of consumable *authenticity*, such as upscaled working-class food and self-consciously kitschy diners, in ways that often fail to align with the food needs, wishes, and tastes of the original community.

Restaurant Reviews and Neighborhood Change

The core of this chapter's arguments come from a critical discourse analysis of 296 newspaper restaurant reviews covering businesses in the Downtown Eastside (DTES) between 2005 and 2017 (for recent studies using similar methodology see Brown-Saracino and Rumpf 2011; Hyde 2014; Zukin, Lindeman, and Hurson 2017).[2] During this period, seventy-eight restaurants opened in the DTES. My analysis focuses on restaurant reviewers as important cultural intermediaries who both reflect and help to shape broader cultural understandings of what constitutes "good food" and is morally appropriate for eating out in a low-income neighborhood. I also collected and analyzed a range of supplementary material, including websites, media interviews with local restaurant owners, the TV series *Gastown Gamble* (2012) which focused on a social enterprise restaurant in the Downtown Eastside and aired on the Oprah Winfrey Network, as well as literature and research reports by community organizers.

To situate the textual material within the broader context of neighborhood change, my analysis also involves ongoing ethnographic observation of controversies over retail gentrification in the area. During a significant portion of this time period, I worked in the Downtown Eastside, volunteered with a community nonprofit, and conducted an academic study of the politics of public-private social housing. I witnessed the opening of numerous restaurants, as well as boycotts and pickets of certain businesses, and attended meetings of community organizers where the discussion of retail gentrification was on the agenda. My time spent in the neighborhood aided my understanding of how restaurants, in particular social enterprise restaurants, were framing themselves and being framed by the media.

The Downtown Eastside: A History of Contentious Politics

The Downtown Eastside is located on the Northeastern edge of Vancouver's downtown core and includes several sub-zoning areas, such as Chinatown, the commercial district of Gastown, and the residential Strathcona. In the early 1900s, the area was known as a premier shopping strip as well as a hub for hotels which housed off-season loggers from camps in the interior of British Columbia (Seager 1986). In the 1960s, amidst the city's deindustrialization, the DTES experienced a decline; the city's commercial district moved west to the downtown peninsula, leaving behind mostly bars, diners, and small family-owned businesses (Ley 1980). The area became known as "skid row," and was associated with substance abuse, crime, and mental health issues.

Alongside problems of poverty and inequality, however, the Downtown Eastside has been a site of intense community organizing (Hasson and Ley 1994). Activism began in the 1960s as residents of Strathcona and Chinatown joined forces with local professionals and intellectuals to contest a plan to construct a freeway through the neighborhood, which would have displaced more than 10,000 residents. In the mid-1980s the community came together again to stop the "Expo evictions," which would have redeveloped the area's Single Room Occupancy (SRO) hotels to house tourists for the 1986 World's Fair Exposition.

In the 1990s and 2000s resistance against gentrification intensified. Alongside struggles for low-income housing, the area became known for activism around drug decriminalization and harm reduction (culminating in North America's first safe intravenous injection site), as well as organizing for greater rights and recognition for Vancouver's indigenous population. One of the key sites of contention during this period was the Woodward's building, a former department store that had closed in 1993 and occupied a block of land in the center of the neighborhood (Blomley 2003; Wyly, Lees, and Slater 2008). After several battles to prevent the conversion of the building into private condominiums in the 1990s, Woodward's became the site of a high-profile housing squat in 2002, leading to the creation of a large public-private social housing redevelopment project.

By the mid-2000s, with the mixed-income Woodward's project introducing more than 1,000 new condo dwellers, and another round of development pressure sparked by Vancouver's agreement to host the 2010 Olympic games, the neighborhood began to show signs of significant gentrification. Average rents between 2008 and 2015 more than doubled, from $444 to $905 CAN per month, due in large part to the renovation and upscaling of SRO units, which had been previously rented out to residents on social assistance and are now being targeted toward more affluent tenants, such as international students who come to Vancouver to attend language school on a fixed-term basis (Swanson, Chan, and Wallstam 2015).

During this same period, several trendy new restaurants began to open in formerly boarded-up storefronts. These were joined by a flood of new retail business, including many coffee shops, nightclubs, and bars, between 2008 and 2015. This can be attributed to the gentrification resulting from internal neighborhood upscaling and condo development as well an increase of nightlife and commercial activity in the area. Historically the Downtown Eastside was a highly stigmatized part of the city that was not considered by middle- and upper-class

Vancouverites to be an ideal locale for shopping, drinking, and dining. This has changed significantly in the past ten years as commercial foot traffic coming from outside of the neighborhood has increased exponentially. While the Downtown Eastside continues to be the city's poorest neighborhood by a large margin (Brethor 2009), where the average median income is $15,000 annually; it is now also home to some of Vancouver's most celebrated restaurants and is a main culinary hub in the city. This has prompted much public discussion and resistance from local community organizers.

Cultural Omnivores in the Downtown Eastside: Constructing the Meaning of *Affordable* Gourmet Dining in a Low-Income Neighborhood

In the sociology of culture, the concept of *omnivorousness* refers to a broad shift in the consumption patterns of high-status elites. Historically, high- and middle-class consumers distinguished themselves by means of exclusion, sticking to high-brow cultural markers such as opera and fine wine, in opposition to parochial markers like rock music and beer (Bourdieu 1984). More recently, however, researchers have noted that high-status consumption is increasingly associated with the ability to consume broadly across the spectrum of high-, middle-, and low-brow culture (Peterson and Kern 1996). In the realm of food, Johnston and Baumann (2010) suggest that cultural omnivorousness has given rise to the phenomenon of *foodies*, who reject old forms of fine dining associated with being a food snob, in favor of a diverse palate of foods deemed to be either "authentic" or "exotic" (see also Zukin 2010).

The restaurant revolution in the Downtown Eastside of Vancouver is tied to a general shift in Vancouver's food scene toward cultural omnivorousness and foodie tastes. Throughout the 2000s, in line with other North American cities, many new restaurants began to feature food they deemed *authentic* and *unpretentious* at a cheaper price point than traditional high-end restaurants. Using the discourse of omnivorousness, restaurateurs and food critics worked to frame restaurant gentrification in the Downtown Eastside as fostering the democratization and accessibility of high-status food for a broader range of consumers. Local celebrity chefs stated they were finally cooking "food for the people," as the lower rents in the Downtown Eastside allowed them to take greater risks and offer lower prices on food. They also suggested the gritty locale of the area helped to inspire dishes that were also more authentic, and hence more delicious.

Newcomer restaurant owners and chefs also maintained the restaurant business need not be only about profit maximization,[3] and many claimed they were happy to make smaller margins if they could cook for a diverse range of consumers, including the middle class and young people who might not be able to afford traditional high-end dining. In a characteristic statement, one chef who left his post at a high-end restaurant to cook pizza in the Downtown Eastside reported, "I realized with Pizzeria Farina and Ask For Luigi you can reach a lot of people who really enjoy food. With fine dining it may be hit or miss and it might not be as appreciated. In fine dining everyone is so serious" (*Vancouver Sun*, December 28, 2013) (see figure 9.1). New casual gourmet restaurants were often framed in terms of a generalized sense of affordability, suggesting that high-end cuisine was becoming accessible to a broad clientele in Vancouver who were coming to the area to dine out.

Even with the claims of inclusivity and democratization, there remains a tension, as the Downtown Eastside's long-term residents cannot afford to eat at many of these new restaurants. The design aesthetics, which often borrow from and reinvent low-brow culture, speak to the tastes of newcomers. For example, hand-painted signs in the tradition of classic diners are a common décor, however, done in the style of self-referential pastiche by art students and graphic designers with post-secondary education. Others adopt a modernist design ethos with concrete, exposed brick, hanging Edison lightbulbs, planter boxes, and light teak or refurbished wood. These elements contrast with the design of long-standing restaurant institutions in the neighborhood, such as brightly lit Chinese bakeries with glass display cases and conventional diners with worn vinyl-covered stools and booths. Zukin (2010) has argued such design cues reflect and reproduce subtle patterns of exclusivity by catering to taste preferences of newcomers for authentic yet refined spaces that can feel unwelcoming to longtime residents. Joassart-Marcelli and Bosco in chapter 1 of this volume also note the

Figure 9.1. Pizzeria Farina located in an SRO Hotel, The Cobalt. Photo by author.

valorization of working-class and racialized authenticity, as they note the over-the-top recreations of Chicano culture in gentrifying restaurants in San Diego's Barrio Logan neighborhood. Thus, new restaurants convey working-class authenticity, however, low-income residents are often conspicuously absent inside the restaurants.

The issue of affordability is not completely lost on restaurant reviewers, who often mentioned "casual gourmet" and street food restaurants are more appropriate for the area than traditional high-end locales, which would be distasteful in the face of poverty. As a reviewer of a casual gourmet Italian restaurant states, "The restaurant is clearly unpretentious and I'm glad, otherwise it's too much tastefulness amid the pain of society's discarded souls, like the woman who approached us in freezing temperatures pleading for a handout" (*Vancouver Sun*, December 24, 2008). Another review makes mention of "a lone prostitute on the corner" of a "desolate stretch of Hastings Street," before going on to praise a local wine bar for its "unassuming yet sophisticated décor" (*Globe and Mail*, April 15, 2009).

Both examples demonstrate a tension between the broader democratization of eating out, "opening up" high-status food to a range of customers, and the exclusionary nature of many of the new restaurants to low-income people. The presence of low-income residents, encountered outside or on the way to the restaurant, is often mentioned alongside the descriptions of the food, and used to convey a sense of *neighborhood authenticity*. By framing certain presentations of high-status food as "unassuming" and "tasteful" in the face of hardship, restaurant reviewers act as important cultural intermediaries, shaping the boundaries around what types of restaurants are *appropriate* for a low-income area of the city. In doing so they also channel the claims of newcomer chefs who suggest that the Downtown Eastside is the ideal location to strip gourmet food of its pretensions. Moreover, the claim that new restaurants are "down to earth" and "sensitive" to the area's poverty in their choice of menu items serves as an important counter-defense to the claims of community organizers, who eventually protested several new restaurants in the Downtown Eastside.

Social Enterprise in the Downtown Eastside: Restaurateurs "Giving Back" to the Community

In addition to the democratization of gourmet cuisine, new restaurateurs in the Downtown Eastside were publicized for their efforts at advancing ethical values through their business practices, known as *social enterprise* or *social entrepreneurship*. By applying these models, newcomers suggested they were advancing values beyond pure profit-making by either "giving back" to society at large or to the local community more directly, to produce what I have described as ethical gentrification. The media bolstered these claims, framing them as a "new breed" of restaurant owners who were younger, savvier, and more socially conscious than traditional entrepreneurs. This type of newcomer shares similarities with Brown-Saracino's (2009) ideal type of social preservationist, who demonstrates reflexivity and self-awareness about their social positions. However, the ethical gentrifier's desire to protect the character of the neighborhood is heightened by their underlying profit motivation as business owners.

Newcomer restaurant owners took up a wide range of initiatives to indicate their socially progressive approach to serving food in a low-income neighborhood. For example, many highlighted the fact that they were offering healthy, organic food in an area that had long been home to greasy spoon diners, small corner stores serving junk food, and Chinese take-out places. They also often stressed being "farm to table," cooking with ingredients from local suppliers and community gardens, or "nose-to-tail," indicating they used the whole animal and eliminated wastefulness in their kitchens. In newspaper restaurant reviews, "nose-to-tail" dining was also linked to the idea that "peasants" and low-income people were historically more environmentally sustainable than the middle and upper classes and knew how to get the most out of foodstuffs. These endeavors are similar to those of the Alternative Food Networks in Oklahoma discussed by Sarmiento in chapter 3 of this volume, in that they emphasize a highly classed version of sustainability that can lead to patterns of neighborhood upscaling and redevelopment.

Beyond this trend, a number of new restaurateurs took measures to "give back" to the local community more directly. This included offering discount menu items to low-income residents in the area, giving out free food around the neighborhood, and engaging with local long-time businesses and community associations. For example, one review of a new coffee shop notes that a "Charitable Gastown Café Has Philanthropy on the Menu," highlighting that "Every Monday, the café matches sales from 9 a.m. to noon with donations to the charities assisting the poor in the Downtown Eastside" (*Vancouver Sun*, January 9, 2014).

During this period, newcomers also took up a number of other initiatives, including volunteering at local community centers, giving away leftovers, and holding fund-raisers. In addition, new business owners made a point of hiring long-term residents, often those struggling with addiction issues, as low-paid dishwashers and handy-persons. Cumulatively, these efforts caught the attention of the local press, and the overwhelmingly positive framing of social enterprise was a persistent finding among restaurant reviews. Heralding these relatively minor gestures points to reviewers' general perspective that newcomers are not fundamentally responsible for the negative impacts of gentrification and that "giving back" is optional and above-and-beyond the call of duty. This ties in with the finding that it is newcomers and the local press who define the parameters of ethical business practices in the Downtown Eastside, rather than the community's long-term residents. For example, the neighborhood has been home to a tradition called "Binner's Dinners," where women from the community cook a pot-luck style meal for salvagers and the low-income-run, subsidized restaurant, the "Potluck Café." However, these forms of food work have not attracted the levels of attention newcomer social entrepreneurs received in the mainstream media.

The most explicit example of social enterprise in the Downtown Eastside came from the efforts of one local business owner to revitalize a long-term butcher shop and cafeteria, Save On Meats, into an inclusive and socially conscious diner (see figure 9.2). This business was the most elaborate effort to engage the local community and was pitched as a model for other area business owners. However, local low-income community organizers eventually rejected both Save On Meats and the paradigm of social enterprise in general.

When the owner of Save On Meats, a long-time butcher shop with a small lunch counter, decided to retire in 2008, the fate of the business was in limbo. After several years, the building that housed the shop was purchased by a local restaurateur, Mark Brand, who owned several casual gourmet restaurants nearby. Brand, one of the first restaurateurs to open shop in the Downtown Eastside, declared his intention to revitalize Save On Meats as an inclusive diner where the area's old-time and newcomer residents could all break bread together.

Brand's efforts to transform Save On Meats into a restaurant with "real social values" attracted significant attention in the local, national, and international press. Brand's work was even chronicled in a reality TV series on the Oprah Winfrey Network titled *Gastown Gamble* in 2012. In the opening credits for the series, Mark Brand's voice narrates over images of Downtown Eastside's back alleyways:

> People feel under attack here, when businesses move in, they get pushed out. But not this time. I've got my own band of misfits and we are going to do business in a way that encompasses real social values. (*Gastown Gamble*, episode 1)

Figure 9.2. Save on Meats, a social enterprise restaurant in the Downtown Eastside. Photo by author.

The new Save On Meats, which reopened in 2011, took a number of measures to ensure the business would be inclusive. While the interior of the restaurant was designed to speak to the young, hip crowd of newcomers, with a jukebox stocked by a famous Canadian DJ and hand-painted signs from a local artist's thesis project, Brand highlighted that his food was both healthy and affordable for low-income residents. Save on Meats offers a $2 breakfast sandwich sold out of a front window counter directly onto the street. Soon after, a program was launched where customers could buy a sandwich token to distribute to the homeless in the neighborhood as form of "alternative currency." This was pitched as a solution for newcomer restaurant goers who might feel uncomfortable giving money to panhandlers, which could be used to buy drugs or alcohol. Brand also hired several low-income residents from the neighborhood as hosts, cooks, and dishwashers to staff the restaurant in its opening months. While Brand's efforts were certainly extensive, they diverged from traditional grassroots forms of community engagement in being largely top-down and by marrying progressive values with profit-making. Brand's business was ultimately labeled by community organizers as a "Trojan Horse" for gentrification. In the next section I discuss challenges to social enterprise, and how those who reject this model of ethical gentrification are framed as "unreasonable" by the local press and outsiders to the Downtown Eastside.

Community Resistance to Social Enterprise: Low-Income Residents Redefine Affordability

While the local low-income community in the Downtown Eastside was initially hopeful about the re-opening of Save On Meats, criticism of Mark Brand's social enterprise quickly mounted. When it was announced that the business would be the subject of *Gastown Gamble*, community organizers advertised a meeting to discuss their critical take on the reality TV show at a local community center. In an attempt to address this critique head-on, Mark Brand attended the meeting, but was asked to leave by local community leaders, including prominent Indigenous Elders, who claimed he was covertly trying to gentrify the neighborhood.

Several months later Brand launched his sandwich token program, which was also covered favorably in the mainstream local press. However, once again his intentions were questioned by community organizers in op-eds in the local online alternative media and at a series of community meetings. One of the persistent critiques of the token program, which has continued to run through 2019, is that it paternalizes low-income people by suggesting they cannot handle "real monies." In addition, organizers have also pointed out that there is no way to account for how many of these tokens are redeemed, meaning that unredeemed tokens could be greatly increasing Brand's private profit margins. Moreover, Brand has since been sued several times for taking money from local community institutions to develop partnership spaces within the Save On Meats building and then failing to meet his obligations.

The critiques of Save On Meats were only the beginning of a larger stand against commercial gentrification that gained momentum in 2012. During this year, several new restaurants opened in blocks of the Downtown Eastside that were symbolically resonant for the low-income community. These included Chuchillo, a Mexican fusion restaurant, which was targeted when a few low-income residents were evicted from the SRO units above the storefront in conjunction with its opening. Protesters also launched a picket line outside of Pidgin, a casual fine dining restaurant, which lasted several months throughout the fall of 2013.

The "Pidgin Protest," as it came to be known, was made up of low-income and homeless residents and organizers of the Downtown Eastside, as well as activists from across the city, who held signs with slogans such as "Feed the Hungry Not the Rich" and "Be Part of the Solution, Don't Go In!" in attempts to converse with and dissuade restaurant goers from dining there. The Vancouver Police Department posted several officers to monitor the scene, as conversations between the patrons, the restaurant staff and owner, and the protesters often became heated. During this period, a general narrative emerged in the media which framed the protesters as unreasonable, while the owners of Pidgin and other local restaurateurs were represented as community-minded social entrepreneurs rather than *bad gentrifiers*. In a characteristic example, one reporter noted that Pidgin was *appropriate* for the neighborhood by avoiding overly ostentatious dishes, and fused coverage of the protest with support for the restaurant's offerings:

> Politics aside, it's interesting that [the protestors] chose Pidgin . . . [it] isn't a fine-dining restaurant . . . You can sit at the bar and snack on chicken wings or reserve the chef's table . . . the bar program really speaks to how traditional dining is being turned on its head. (*National Post*, April 7, 2013)

The suggestion that the new restaurants were being unfairly maligned when they were offering traditional high-end food at "affordable" prices illustrates how the discourse of omnivorousness is used to defend against claims of commercial upscaling. If restaurants had indeed been "too pretentious" in the eyes of reviewers, the protests would have been warranted; however, since they weren't fine dining, they should be "left alone" by community organizers. As described by another restaurant critic, "While demonized as a high-end intruder, with the exception of one dish, nothing is over $20 . . . But make no mistake the food looks haute and tastes divine" (*Vancouver Sun*, February 28, 2013). These remarks, however, overlook the fact that Pidgin's price points are far out of range for those on welfare. While there is one cheap menu item, a pickle for $5, the main dishes at the restaurant range from $17 to $36 Canadian dollars.

An additional discursive tactic used by the local press was to suggest the protesters were in fact outsiders to the Downtown Eastside, namely middle-class graduate students, who did not represent the community sentiment. For example, one reviewer interviewed a local Business Improvement Association (BIA) spokesperson, who stated:

> The protesters are "middle class kids from North Van. It's not like the protesters are actually poor residents" . . . there are better ways to advocate for the poor than "destroying the personal business aspirations of a few entrepreneurs who have hired local people and contributed to the development of the community." (*National Post*, July 12, 2013)

While this may have been true of some of the demonstrators who had joined in as allies, the core of the group of protesters were in fact local low-income residents living on social assistance, several of whom were homeless at the time. The protesters-as-outsiders narrative was most widely broadcast when Rex Murphy, a pundit on Canada's most-watched news program *The National*, weighed in from Toronto. He referred to the group as "social activist bullies" who are "callously trying to ruin one man's business." He concluded his piece by stating, "When angry activists with placards target a single citizen trying to do good in a bad area, using his own money, something is seriously wrong" (*National Post*, January 11, 2014). The protest eventually ended when one of the demonstrators was arrested for entering the restaurant and a local community organization was put under threat of having its funding revoked for supporting the demonstration.

The failures of newcomer restaurateurs to engage directly with low-income community activists in the Downtown Eastside has led to growing skepticism about the potential of social enterprise to redress problems of material inequality. In 2016 I attended a community meeting titled "Social Justice Not Social Entrepreneurs!" that focused on the city's encouragement of social enterprise through a new government grant initiative. The flyer for the event stated, the city's "strategy fails to address the root causes of poverty in the neighborhood, and some of the measures supported by the plan will actually facilitate gentrification and the loss of low-income housing." At the meeting, social enterprise initiatives were framed as a band-aid solution to problems of gentrification, housing affordability, and commercial upscaling.

Subsequent to this meeting, a resident-led research survey was spearheaded to try to measure the extent of commercial gentrification in the area. The project involved collaboration between low-income white, indigenous, and Chinese Canadians affected by commercial upscaling in the Downtown Eastside and the adjacent Chinatown neighborhood. A report from this project, titled "We Are Too Poor to Afford Anything," was released to the public in the Spring of 2017 in both English and Mandarin. The findings detailed the loss of some thirty-one businesses, including drug stores, green grocers, coffee shops, and diners that had served the low-income community. The report also suggested that most new businesses were much less affordable and many functioned as "Zones of Exclusion" (a term coined by low-income community researchers), referring to businesses that are openly hostile to low-income residents and help to facilitate surveillance and policing in the area (see figure 9.3).

However, even as social enterprise is greeted with increasing skepticism by low-income anti-gentrification activists, the practice continues to gain momentum within the business community and mainstream policy circles throughout North America. While receiving significant criticism in the Downtown Eastside, Mark Brand has traveled to numerous cities pitching Save On Meats as an unbridled success story in public lectures and other events such as TED talks. He has a large social media following, and on his website is described as "one of North America's leading social entrepreneurs," offering services such as workshops on

Figure 9.3. We are too poor to afford anything, report on retail gentrification. Image courtesy of Maria Wallstam and the Carnegie Community Action Project.

how to advance progressive business practices. Brand has also stated that he is developing an online "alternative currency" app for smart phones that will allow individuals to transfer meal tokens directly to panhandlers via reclaimed cell phones. Currently, he has undertaken a fellowship at Stanford University's "dSchool" program, which brings together social entrepreneurs from various sectors of the economy. The success of Mark Brand in shaping his social enterprise branding strategy highlights endemic power imbalances in who has the resources to control the narratives over the successes and shortcomings of new forms of ethical profit-making.

The Paradox of Caring Capitalism in Low-Income
Neighborhoods: How Social Enterprise Preempts
Resistance to Gentrification

In this chapter, I argue that newcomer restaurateurs' practices of omnivorousness and social enterprise worked to preempt and co-opt community-based resistance through a discourse of ethical gentrification. New restaurant owners came to the Downtown Eastside with expectations of how they would be viewed, and applied practices that were ostensibly sensitive to the local long-time residents in terms of the food they served and in their efforts to "give back" to the neighborhood. While these initiatives need not be seen in a solely cynical light, and some newcomers may have genuinely good intentions, their consequences for the neighborhood demand a critical analysis.

Most prominently, social enterprise places the solution to problems of inequality in the hands of newcomers, while bypassing the needs and wishes of long-time residents. In contrast with more traditional forms of redistribution, caring capitalism suggests a fusion between progressive social values and profit-making, a phenomenon that scholars have found often produces a high degree of tension (Kinderman 2012; Barman 2016; Davis 2017). This tension is amplified in the context of low-income neighborhoods, where ethical business practices offer benefits that fail to compensate for the overall negative effects of commercial upscaling. What the local media deems "affordable" and "unpretentious" food remains economically and culturally inaccessible to old-time residents. Additionally, newcomers set the priorities and parameters of "giving back" in ways that directly contradict principles of food sovereignty, which define all people, including residents of low-income communities, as having a right to access and determine their subsistence needs.

In addition, social enterprise in the context of gentrification works to co-opt dissent by offering selective incentives to old-timers, such as free foodstuffs and low-wage employment. These initiatives, however, fail to address the underlying basis of material inequality in the area and do not appear to truly empower local residents. For example, while Mark Brand's sandwich token program was heralded by Vancouverites at large, many Downtown Eastside community organizers saw the program as working to disenfranchise low-income people, excluding them from the use and exchange of monetary currency. Moreover, while organizers have worked toward food security in the neighborhood for years, through initiatives like community gardens and nonprofit kitchens, these attempts were rarely publicized in the mainstream media. However, new for-profit gentrifying businesses that "give back" have become media darlings and are able to frame the changes happening in the neighborhood in their favor. In turn, community organizer energy has been diverted from traditional social justice organizing in order to challenge the claims-making of ethical gentrifiers. Cumulatively, restaurant reviewers and the local media have played an important role in framing the efforts of local restaurateurs as morally virtuous, and the critiques of community organizers as overbearing and unproductive.

Conclusion: Ethical Gentrification as a Pathway to Material and Symbolic Dispossession

Previous research on resistance to gentrification has focused on confrontations between pioneer newcomers and long-standing residents under threat of displacement (Smith 1996). Drawing from Brown-Saracino's (2009) conception of social preservationists, I have suggested a more complex picture where many newcomers claim to be "on the same side" as old-timers in their struggles and face challenges to their narrative by the community activists. Food media describe these ethical gentrifiers' businesses as unpretentious establishments that work to "give back" to the local community, legitimizing their presence in the neighborhood while undermining community-based resistance. Researchers should continue to look critically at the discourse and practices of social preservationist newcomers and community organizations to identify the symbolic and material dispossession and appropriation that accompany gentrification. In the case of the Downtown Eastside, this has meant accounting for multiple layers of inequality, including the symbolic appropriation of working-class culture and authenticity by omnivorous chefs and foodies, the loss of material access to groceries and diners that served low-income residents, and finally the co-optation of the language of resistance to gentrification by social enterprise restaurant owners. While the discourse of caring capitalism suggests that progressive social objectives can be achieved through the market, in light of the material imbalances between newcomers and old-timers in cities facing intense development pressure, widespread positive outcomes through ethical gentrification seem increasingly unlikely.

NOTES

1 Thus far I have used italics when referring to the concept of ethical gentrification. This is to connote the contested nature of the phenomenon in question: socially conscious newcomers to low-income neighborhoods frame their business activities as ethical, which is challenged by low-income long-term residents. For the remainder of the chapter I refer to the term without italics for stylistic reasons.
2 Articles were accessed through Lexis Nexus. The textual material on restaurant gentrification was analyzed through the method of critical discourse analysis (CDA) (Fairclough 1992). CDA focuses on the way social reality is mediated and constructed through talk and text, and the role of power and inequality in framings of social phenomena. With the aid of the qualitative software program ATLAS.ti, the material was coded through the iterative process of abductive analysis, for both inductively emerging and deductively applied themes (Tavory and Timmermans 2014). In line with sociologist Pierre Bourdieu's (1990) caution against purely "endogenous" readings of texts, I was careful to situate my analysis of discourse within the larger material struggles over space within the Downtown Eastside.
3 On artists, gentrification and economic disinterestedness, see Ley (2003).

REFERENCES

Barman, Emily. 2016. *Caring Capitalism: The Meaning and Measure of Social Value*. Cambridge, MA: Cambridge University Press.

Blomley, Nicholas. 2003. *Unsettling the City: Urban Land and the Politics of Property*. New York City: Routledge.

Brown-Saracino, Japonica. 2009. *A Neighborhood that Never Changes: Gentrification, Social Social Preservation and the Search for Authenticity*. Chicago: University of Chicago Press.

Brown-Saracino, Japonica. 2016. "An Agenda for the Next Decade of Gentrification Scholarship." *City & Community* 15(3): 220–225.

Brown-Saracino, Japonica and Casraea Rumpf. 2011. "Diverse Imageries of Gentrification: Evidence from Newspaper Coverage in Seven U.S. Cities." 1986–2006. *Journal of Urban Affairs* 33:3: 289–315.

Bourdieu, Pierre. 1984. *Distinction: A Social Critique of the Judgment of Taste*. Cambridge, MA: Harvard University Press.

Bourdieu, Pierre. 1990. *In Other Words: Essays Towards a Reflexive Sociology*. Cambridge, MA: Harvard University Press.

Brethor, Patrick. 2009. "An Exclusive Demographic Picture: Key Statistics in the DTES, Vancouver and Canada." *Globe and Mail*, February 13.

Brown-Saracino, Japonica. 2009. *A Neighborhood that Never Changes: Gentrification, Social Preservation and the Search for Authenticity*. Chicago: University of Chicago Press.
Brown-Saracino, Japonica. 2016. "An Agenda for the Next Decade of Gentrification Scholarship." *City & Community* 15(3): 220–225.
Brown-Saracino, Japonica and Casraea Rumpf. 2011. "Diverse Imageries of Gentrification: Evidence from Newspaper Coverage in Seven U.S. Cities." 1986–2006. *Journal of Urban Affairs* 33(3): 289–315.
Davis, Jonathan C. 2017. *From Head Shops to Whole Foods: The Rise and Fall of Activist Entrepreneurs*. New York: Columbia University Press.
Fairclough, Norman. 1992. *Discourse and Social Change*. Cambridge: Polity.
Hasson, Shalom and David Ley. 1994. *Neighbourhood Organizations and the Welfare State*. Toronto: University of Toronto Press.
Hyde, Zachary. 2014. "Omnivorous Gentrification: Restaurant Reviews and Neighborhood Change in the Downtown Eastside of Vancouver." *City & Community* 13(4): 341–359.
Johnston, Josée. 2008. "The Citizen-Consumer Hybrid: Ideological Tension and the Case of Whole Foods." *Theory and Society* 37(3): 229–270.
Johnston, Josée and Shyon Baumann. 2010. *Foodies: Democracy and Distinction in the Gourmet Foodscape*. New York: Routledge.
Kinderman, David. 2012. "'Free Us Up So We Can Be Responsible!' The Co-evolution of Corporate Social Responsibility and Neo-liberalism in the UK, 1977–2010." *Socio-Economic Review* 10(2): 29–57.
Ley, David. 1980. "Liberal Ideology and the Post-industrial City." *Annals of the Association of American Geographers* 70.2, 238–258.
Ley, David. 2003. "Artists, Aestheticisation and the Field of Gentrification." *Urban Studies* 40(10): 2527–2544.
Peterson, Richard and Roger Kern. 1996. "Changing Highbrow Taste: From Snob to Omnivore." *American Sociological Review* 61(5): 900–907.
Seager, Alan. 1986. *Working Lives: Vancouver 1886–1986*. Vancouver: New Star Books.
Slater, Tom. 2006. "The Eviction of Critical Perspectives from Gentrification Research." *International Journal of Urban and Regional Research* 30(4): 737–775.
Smith, Neil. 1996. *The New Urban Frontier: Gentrification and the Revanchist City*. Oxon: Routledge.
Swanson, Jean, Chan, King-mong and Maria Wallstam. 2015. "Our Homes Can't Wait." *Carnegie Community Action Project Annual Housing Report*. Vancouver: CCAP.
Tavory, Iddo and Stephen Timmermans. 2014. *Abductive Analysis: Theorizing Qualitative Research*. Chicago: University of Chicago Press.
Wyly, Elvin, Loretta Lees, and Tom Slater. 2008. *Gentrification*. New York: Routledge.
Zukin, Sharon. 2010. *Naked City: The Death and Life of Authentic Urban Places*. New York: Oxford University Press.
Zukin, Sharon, Scarlet Lindeman, and Laurie Hurson. 2017. "The Omnivore's Neighborhood? Online Restaurant Reviews, Race and Gentrification." *Journal of Consumer Culture* 17(3): 459–479.

10

"You Can't Evict Community Power"

Food Justice and Eviction Defense in Oakland

ALISON HOPE ALKON, YAHYA JOSH CADJI, AND FRANCES MOORE

On Tuesday afternoons, North Oakland's Driver's Plaza is a lively place. Neighbors gather to listen to music, play chess, hang out, and share a meal. The chef is "Aunti" Frances Moore, a former Black Panther and founder of the Love Mission Self-Help Hunger Program, which has been serving a weekly meal for much of the past decade. Those gathering at Driver's are typical of "the old Oakland," largely but not exclusively African American, and struggling to get by in this rapidly gentrifying city. Many are visibly disabled. Most are elders, though there are also younger adults and children ranging from elementary to high school age. Some rent rooms nearby while others are homeless, crashing with friends or living in vehicles.

While many food justice activists are more privileged, formally educated, and/or white, and have to work to connect to the experiences of those dealing with food insecurity (see chapter 6; Guthman 2008; Moore and Swisher 2015), Aunti Frances shares their traumas. "I have slept on that sidewalk. I've slept on the rooftops. I've slept in the campgrounds and the shelters," she says, "Therefore, I know how to give. I know what you need." What is needed, according to Aunti Frances, is a healthy, well-balanced meal and a place to spend time with your neighbors and friends. This builds a sense that "we're in this together and have to take care of each other." Aunti Frances pays for much of the food with her Social Security check, though there have also been donations from neighbors and even a small grant. More recently, through a partnership with Phat Beets Produce, a local food justice organization that seeks to support farmers of color and increase access to fresh food in marginalized communities, she has also been able to incorporate locally grown produce, and volunteers have planted fruit trees and tree collards in the plaza itself.

For the past eight years, Aunti Frances has rented an apartment a few blocks away. But the triplex where it's located was bought by Natalia Morphy and her parents in 2016, who own several other houses in the city. Oakland's rent control laws limit how much landlords can raise the rent on existing tenants, and follow the tenants even when the building is sold. Median rents have skyrocketed in this gentrifying city and can only be raised to market rates when tenants move out. So even though Aunti Frances pays her rent on time, her new landlords want her out. Rent control also protects tenants from eviction after a building is sold, but a loophole permits new owners of duplexes and triplexes to remove tenants if they move into one of the units. Natalia claims to have done this, though Aunti Frances has never seen her at the building. If the eviction is successful, it is unlikely that Aunti Frances will be able to find affordable housing nearby, as rents in the historically Black and working-class Oakland flatlands have soared. She'll either be forced out of the city, or back onto the streets.

Along with an array of housing rights and anti-racist organizations, Phat Beets has been working to organize an eviction defense campaign. Under the banner "You Can't Evict Community Power," the campaign was launched with a rally in Driver's Plaza that drew more than one hundred supporters, who marched with Aunti Frances to her home to attempt to speak with her new landlord. The campaign's strategies are wide ranging. One organization is representing Aunti Frances in her eviction proceedings, while others attempt to convince the city council to close loopholes in the city's rent control ordinance. A community letter signed by more than fifty nonprofit organizations seeks to persuade the Morphys to withdraw the eviction, as a "powerful act in the face of immense gentrification" and an "act of deep compassion." Phat Beets is supplying food at events and is also working to garner public support.

Phat Beets is in many ways typical of food justice organizations across the country—their work merges support for community-based food systems like urban farms and farmers' markets with a commitment to racial and economic justice. Their founder, Yahya's brother Max, like many food justice activists, is college-educated and class privileged, as were most of the organization's early supporters. Max identifies as mixed race, but passes easily in white-dominated spaces, and most of his early

Figure 10.1. Image from flyers and website for Aunti Frances's Eviction Defense Campaign.

colleagues were also white-identified. In 2014, the organization became radicalized through an encounter with a local realtor, who included their farmers' market and community garden in a video designed to entice new residents to their North Oakland neighborhood, an example of the appropriation of green space by urban boosters described in chapters 4, 5, and 8 of this volume (see Cadji and Alkon 2014; Alkon et al. forthcoming). Phat Beets responded publicly with a caustic video of their own, calling out the processes of divestment and displacement that have long occurred in their neighborhood. Privately they reflected deeply on their own unwitting role in these processes, as well as the ways they benefit from new neighbors already interested in local and organic food.

These reflections have set off major shifts in the organization. They have moved beyond the creation of alternative food systems to engage in community-building and anti-displacement activism more broadly. Food provisioning has become a lens through which to organize on these issues rather than the ultimate goal. This shift in strategy has resulted in changes in Phat Beets's racial composition; it is now made up of predominantly people of color. And while they have fewer customers for their CSA, they have strong alliances with community-based organizations like the Self-Help Hunger Program. Indeed, the two groups are in the process of becoming a single nonprofit organization in order to more easily share resources and expertise. But whether this can help to address the displacement of the Self-Help Hunger Program or Aunti Frances herself remains to be seen.

For more than a decade, research on the ways that food activism can unwittingly reproduce inequalities has concluded by asking activists to become more reflexive about these dynamics in the hopes that doing so will push them toward more radical or transformational approaches (Alkon and Guthman 2017; DuPuis and Goodman 2005; Levkoe 2011). This chapter chronicles the process through which Phat Beets became embroiled in debates about food and gentrification and made concrete organizational changes as a result. After their work was appropriated by a realtor as a sign of North Oakland's "revitalization," they deeply reflected on their role in upscaling the neighborhood. They built alliances with community leaders like Aunti Frances and other long-term residents at risk of displacement. In doing so, they have inspired Self-Help to incorporate permaculture practices, and helped to bridge divides between Self-Help and many of their new, more affluent neighbors. Faced with the prospect of becoming another food-based amenity for new residents, Phat Beets has instead chosen to advocate for resistance rooted in the struggles of those on the front lines of displacement.[1]

Food Activism and the Question of Gentrification

While it is difficult to define a relatively nascent social movement like food justice—the term has only become widely used since the mid-2000s—it can be seen as "the struggle against racism, exploitation, and oppression taking place within the food system that addresses inequality's root causes both within and beyond the food chain" (Hislop 2014). The movement is rooted in efforts to create more environmentally and socially sustainable alternatives to industrial food systems. These alternatives, as many scholars have argued, are too often available only to affluent whites; they are more economically feasible in upscale neighborhoods, the cost of the produce they feature tends to be high and they often invoke language that, while not explicitly racialized, subtly invokes white histories and narratives (Alkon and Guthman 2017). Food justice activists adapt these alternatives to address issues of racial and economic inequality, and to build political power toward food system transformation. In addition to alternative food systems, they cite roots in anti-racist movements, invoking projects such as the Black Panther Party's Free Breakfast for Children Program (chapter 13; Alkon 2012; Broad 2016) and civil rights leader Fannie Lou Hamer's Freedom Farm Cooperative (White 2017). However, despite missions to serve low-income communities of color, the degree to which individual organizations are authentically "of" those communities is often cause for debate (Alkon 2012) and, despite the existence of many well-recognized groups run by people of color, the largest and best-funded organizations are predominantly white-led (Cohen and Reynolds 2016).

Many food justice projects began in marginalized communities like North Oakland that are now rapidly gentrifying (see chapters 4, 8, and 12; Glowa 2017; Meyers forthcoming; Stehlin and Tarr 2016). Although the popular media commonly describes gentrification as a matter of changing tastes—the opening of the hipster coffee shops, restaurants, and bars like those depicted in chapters 1, 2, 3, and 9—scholars largely view gentrification as a fundamentally structural process in which capital expands through the (re)production of urban space (Smith 2008; Harvey 1978; Logan and Molotch 1987). It is also a racialized process predicated on the divestment from the urban core that characterized segregation and redlining, the devastation of segregated neighborhoods through urban renewal, and contemporary predatory lending, over-policing, and racialized violence (A. R. Shaw 2015; Wendy Shaw 2007; Lees, Slater, and Wyly 2007). In short, gentrification capitalizes on racism, lowering property values and providing opportunities for subsequent investment. As Smith writes, gentrification is "rooted in the structure of capitalist society. . . . The economic, demographic, lifestyle and energy factors [of new residents] are relevant only after consideration of this basic explanation (1996: 88; see also Peck 2005).

And yet, because cities compete to attract these new, predominantly white residents, their cultural proclivities, while not the cause of gentrification, remain worthy of study (Zukin 2010; Ocejo 2011). Their tastes cohere around culturally constructed notions of distinctiveness, an association with the so-called creative class (Florida 2002) that is considered apart from the mainstream, even as it increasingly becomes mainstream (Zukin 2010; Johnston and Bauman 2010). Food justice activism, with its community gardens, health food stores, and farmers' markets, fits neatly into this aesthetic, particularly when it brings these amenities to neighborhoods with enough grit to be viewed by gentrifiers as authentic (Hyra 2017). Sociologist Sharon Zukin writes that gentrifiers' "desire for alternative foods, both gourmet and organic, and for 'middle-class' shopping areas, encourages a dynamic of urban redevelopment that displaces working-class and ethnic minority consumers" (2008: 724). In addition, boosters' efforts to re-brand neighborhoods as ripe for capital investment increasingly include urban greening, leading scholars to label this a process of green or eco-gentrification (see chapters 4, 7, and 9; Dooling 2009; Checker 2011; Gould and Lewis 2016; Quastel 2009; Bryson 2013). Food justice activism can provide both green space and destinations for distinctive consumption in neighborhoods where they did not previously exist.

Distinguishing between the role of capital and the actions of middle-class residents is particularly important in cities like Oakland that are experiencing supergentrification, a late stage of the process in which both long-term residents and early gentrifiers are displaced by large-scale capital projects, speculators, and elite workers (Lees 2003). Oakland is the fourth most expensive housing market in the country, and the average rent has doubled since 2010 (Renzulli 2016). As in many other cities, gentrification in Oakland has built upon segregation and under-development, creating a rent gap that investors can take advantage of through the purchase of depreciated properties. As several excellent histories of the city have described, Oakland's long-time status as a low-income, predominantly Black area was produced through a series of real estate and development decisions (Walker 2001; Self 2005; McClintock 2011). Recent demographic shifts have been motivated by developers and city officials whose neighborhood-specific plans have attracted the construction of new housing and businesses. Speculation has made the purchase of existing homes or new condominiums by even middle-class residents nearly impossible, and rising rents have accompanied, and often outpaced, rising property values. Developers have lobbied to lower requirements for affordable housing, and many landlords have subverted and broken rent control regulations in pursuit of windfall profits, creating both displacement and homelessness (Bond-Graham 2017). This process is a racialized one; the city has lost approximately one-fourth of its African American residents, while its white and

Latinx populations are growing. It is also an economic one. Oakland's *supergentrification* is affecting both low-income and middle-class residents, although the latter, of course, have more recourse and options. A recent study by the nonprofit Policy Link (2016) found that the number of Oakland units affordable to both minimum-wage workers and entry-level teachers is the same: zero.

Because alternative food systems are often essential to generating the kind of cityscape that attracts affluent residents and tourists, boosters draw on them to promote gentrification. As we have argued elsewhere (Cadji and Alkon 2014; Alkon et al. forthcoming), activists create spaces that become a part of the "authentic," non-mainstream urban landscape that new residents seek out. Food justice organizations welcome new residents' support for their often struggling farmers' markets, community's agriculture programs, and other initiatives, which depend on these more affluent consumers to create economic value for the farmers and entrepreneurs of color that the organizations seek to support. Boosters can then point to these urban farming projects as evidence of the city's greenness, which can help to attract large-scale development. At the same time, activists like Phat Beets's organizers are increasingly aware of the process of green gentrification and struggle to maintain their commitment to long-term residents.

Saying No to NOBE

Phat Beets's path to becoming radicalized began when they found themselves implicated in the upscaling of their neighborhood. In the spring of 2014, a real estate agent released a video that she hoped would increase interest in what she called NOBE. An acronym for North Oakland, Berkeley, and Emeryville, and encompassing both Aunti Frances's home and most of Phat Beets's projects, the neologism echoes other trendy designations like San Francisco's SOMA (South of Market) or New York's DUMBO (Down Under the Manhattan Bridge Overpass).

Simultaneously, it allows urban boosters to elide the connotations of crime and blackness often associated with Oakland. In the video, the realtor highlighted attributes like walkability, "affordable homes" (at the time, just under a half million dollars, now much more), "new cool bars" and "great restaurants and cafes"—all evidence of what she called a "revitalization." A moment later, she added, "We're super psyched that there's a community garden across the street. That's definitely a bonus to this block!" The camera then panned to one of Phat Beets's gardens, casting it not as a resource for the neighborhood's many low-income, food-insecure residents, but as a selling point for the growing number of affluent buyers who threaten to displace them. This video was not an anomaly. Urban farms and farmers' markets are regularly featured on real estate blogs like Movoto and The Matador Network as reasons, in the words of the latter, that "Everyone Cool and Creative Is Moving to Oakland."

Phat Beets organizers were livid upon seeing their garden used to attract the kind of affluent newcomers whose arrival often signals the racialized dispossession of the land inhabited by low-income communities of color. Describing his opposition to the video, Max said, "Our work wasn't the cause of gentrification, but our programs and our aesthetics were being used to sell land and help displace people" (quoted in Markham 2014). Phat Beets released a scathing counter-video called Neighbors Outing Blatant Exploitation, mocking the real estate company's obvious attempt to remake the neighborhood by, for example, defining NOBE as "a term coined by realtors to destigmatize North Oakland in order to sell the foreclosed homes of long-term black and brown residents to affluent white people." In addition, they demanded their work be removed from the realtor's video, issued a public statement against gentrification, and began to strategize with food justice organizations across the country to combat displacement of the community they seek to serve. Privately, they also reflected on the ways their work contributed to gentrification. Many of Phat Beets organizers were themselves new residents who, while not wealthy prospective homeowners, are generally middle-class and educated. Phat Beets also relies on new residents to sustain their farmers' market and community supported agriculture (CSA) program. In their statement on gentrification, they wrote that "while we are aware and critical of our own role in gentrification through urban greening, we also understand the powerful possibilities that our programming can create when we unite in support of current residents and re-investment in the neighborhood."

That support has led Phat Beets in a number of directions. They continue to work to create community-based food systems through their farmers' market and CSA, which support farmers of color in the region, as well as their Youth Pickle and Catering Company, which hires low-income youth of color for catering gigs and to create value-added products like fermented foods. But despite the focus on supporting producers of color and racial justice education, including, for example, offering workshops on the Prison Industrial Complex and helping to organize a Black Panther Walking Tour of the neighborhood, these programs tend to draw in consumers who are affluent, white, and new residents. Phat Beets has also moved beyond its original mission to create alternative food systems in attempts to more deeply connect with long-term residents. Along with several Black churches, they are a founding member of the North Oakland Restorative Justice Council, which hosts restorative justice circles, community celebrations, and monthly peace and justice walks. In 2015, Max and Yahya began coming to the Self-Help Hunger Program's community meals. After spending a few months getting to know Aunti Frances and others who spend time at Driver's Plaza, Phat Beets and Self-Help began to collaborate.

From Porta Potties to Permaculture

When Yahya and Max first arrived at Driver's Plaza, they found a community group trying to maintain their right to the city amidst rapidly shifting neighborhood dynamics. As Aunti Frances put it, "We are caught up in that vicious whirlpool of redevelopment." There are many new residents, younger, more affluent, and disproportionately white, inhabiting the new condominiums and single-family craftsman homes that surround the plaza. According to Kedar Ellis, a Self-Help regular who was raised in the neighborhood, and whose grandmother was a victim of predatory lending, the new residents and long-standing ones have "different agendas."

> It's a clash now, because the people that have just moved in maybe had a different expectation. The housing prices have gone up and so they were in a certain economic bracket. But still all of the people in the area that have lived here previously aren't gone yet, so now it's like what do we do? They want a quick fix, [a] microwave method of just calling the cops or just getting rid of it like a quick solution. Some of the people here are feeling like they've been displaced.

Figure 10.2. Aunti Frances, surrounded by the food she helped to pack and distribute as part of the 50th Anniversary of the founding of the Black Panther Party. The BPP regularly distributed food as part of their survival programs, which also included schools and medical clinics.

These different agendas have often resulted in problems for the people who spend time in Driver's Plaza. As Kedar elaborated:

> [There have been] complaints on everything. The loudness, the music, the people. My car was parked over there and people were telling me that there's been drug activities. I was like, "Have you seen me deal drugs? I don't deal drugs. Do you suspect it because people hang out and you have a stereotype that it's drugs?" It's been constant. It's just different harassment.

Sandra, a Black woman confined to a wheelchair, offered another example. "Then they had this thing where they were towing all the cars.

Some that they were sleeping in, but they just wanted to get rid of everything." Sandra also felt criminalized just for being in the neighborhood. "There's a lot of stuff that goes on in this world," she continued, "and [the police] are harassing people who ain't doing nothing, but coming up here to sit and eat."

One of the most significant clashes has been over bathroom usage. Kedar elaborates:

> Here's the thing. Their complaints here are that it's too much hanging out and maybe drinking and cussing. One of the top three things are people exposing themselves ... There's some neighbors up the street that have came down with bags of poop and said, "You guys are pooping." "You guys?" You have one bag of poop. There's twenty people out here. I hate the "you guys" term, because who are "you guys"? It could be anybody. Usually if a person is going to take a poop, they're going to do it at nighttime. They probably got a mental problem or in a very desperate situation to have to take a crap.

The Self-Help Hunger Program has tried to resolve this situation by having the city install a porta potty at Driver's Plaza. Kedar continued:

> We had a guy come out ... He works at the Mosswood Engineering right over here. He come out just to see logistically is it possible to get a porta potty? Do we have actually the sewage system and things like? He was like "Yeah, we have this water line." They want to do it. I mean, they have the capability to do it, but do they want to do it?

At one point, there were as many as three porta potties in Driver's Plaza, including one that was ADA accessible. But, according to Sandra, some of the new neighbors complained and wanted them removed. The police came and removed the porta potties, arguing that a city permit was necessary. But the city does not have a permitting process and would not create one. Sandra describes the porta-potty removal as fundamentally dehumanizing. "It's that blatant 'I don't want you here. Keep on pissing on the street. How dare you have a porta potty?' You don't think we deserve to release ourselves, which is a natural function, in a dignified manner."

Today, the lack of bathrooms is not only a nuisance to new residents, but a health risk for the Driver's Plaza Community. As Kedar described:

"Every time the children play around the trees, we have to warn them away from [them]. That's the pee tree. You can get Hepatitis."

Kedar believes that taking away the porta party is part of the city's greater plan.

> The city, they have a 20-year plan of how they want the city to be. They're going to [use] eminent domain. . . . I think this is a part of that agenda that they want to clean this area out and make it look different. I think [the new residents] want to turn [Driver's Plaza] into a dog poop park so they can walk their dogs and come here. Then eventually after they get rid of everybody, then they can make it look nice.

But in the past few years, relationships with new neighbors have improved. Calls to the police are fewer, and several of the Self-Help regulars offer stories of friendly interactions with new residents. Aunti Frances describes this transition:

> There have been some residents that have reached out to us. Last week, the tenants barbecued for us. Instead of just the bad part it's pros and cons. We have come together. It's good progress. We have a monthly thing where we do street maintenance. Two communities. The have-mores and the have-less. Driver's Plaza is very instrumental for neighbors speaking to each other. This is a depo. This is headquarters.

Aunti Frances's warm and inviting nature certainly makes what she calls the "tying of communities together through food" possible. Though she is clearly at the center of Self-Help's work, she describes it as a collaborative effort. "Everybody participates, the neighbors, the merchants, the participants, the community gardens, the community organizations. We are Self-Help." Even during the demonstration profiled in the introduction to this chapter, when she was marching with her supporters to attempt to speak with her new landlord, she insisted that Natalia "be invited in" instead of alienated. While it would be easy to paint newcomers as enemies, Aunti Frances insists on inclusion.

In addition, new residents have become connected to Self-Help through the permaculture efforts spearheaded by Phat Beets. Permaculture is a set of design principles that mimic patterns found in nature (Mollison 1988). Though many of its elements have long been practiced by indigenous people around the world, it became popular among back-to-the-landers in the late 1970s and continue to be employed by many small-scale organic farmers and food justice activists.

The most prominent permaculture element at Driver's Plaza is an orchard in which each fruit tree memorializes, as Aunti Frances puts it, "one of our loved ones that have transitioned on." There are also tree collards (a highly productive perennial leafy green), a living fence made of espaliered (flat pruned) fruit trees, and, for a time, a cobb oven and bench made of a mix of sand, clay, and straw. While the latter was removed by the city, the food production remains. Max explains how this helped to build community:

> The trees, they built that bridge. There used to be a gap between new neighbors and people that come to that plaza. [Now] people come out. We have barbecues together. We have pancake breakfasts together. People are still separated. You have mostly white or older folks and they'll bring out focaccia and whatever. We're making pancakes and eggs. People start intermingling. And then they plant trees when someone dies. We've planted a lot of trees and they've come out. One of the folks there is a really great [new] neighbor. His brother died. We got together and bought a tree for his brother and made a plaque. It was building a bridge. [It's a way of] welcoming people into a space that's not their own. So now they're coming and saying "we're also part of them."

Indeed, the living fence was initiated by a group of new neighbors. They first tried to obtain permission from the city, but after they were denied a permit, they began working with Phat Beets and Self-Help. Max continues:

> The neighborhood group was really interested in doing something [at Driver's Plaza] too. They tried to do the formal process, and then they got denied. Once they went through the experience, then we said, "Okay, we can help you guys do this. We can do it together." Because we had already planted five trees. They wanted to plant a living fence so the kids could play in there. They were just like, "Fuck it. Let's do it."

While some new neighbors remain opposed or indifferent, many have begun to work alongside Self-Help and Phat Beets. Though it does not mention Self-Help per se, the neighborhood association's website contains an article titled "NOBE-We Are Not" that reads "The acronym NOBE is nothing more than a realtor's tool to attract high salaried 'hipsters' and to unreasonably and unconscionably raise sales prices . . . [Our neighborhood] has always been a friendly place to live and our association will continue to build relationships between all neighbors and our community through goodwill and hard work." While we did not conduct formal surveys, we spoke to many supporters at the rally to defend Aunti Frances who were young, white, and new to the neighborhood. With help from Phat Beets, Aunti Frances and Self-Help have turned many of their new neighbors from opposition to allyship.

Oakland Communities United for Equity and Justice

Their experience with the NOBE video, in which a local realtor highlighted their community garden as an amenity for potential homebuyers, prompted Phat Beets to think deeply about the ways that food justice organizations like theirs played unwitting roles in the gentrification of their neighborhoods. While acknowledging that they rely on new residents as customers, this scenario increased their commitment to collaborating with long-term residents and centering their work in the struggles of marginalized communities. Phat Beets's composition has changed over time. Most of the younger, more privileged organizers have moved on, and they have hired more long-term residents and people of color, including Aunti Frances and, for a time, Kedar, into paid positions. In addition to collaborating with Self-Help, Phat Beets is also a founding member of the North Oakland Restorative Justice Council. Of the three organizations, only Phat Beets is a registered nonprofit, and they have used their acumen and privilege to support the other two organizations. For example, Max does much of the administrative work for all three groups and Phat Beets has served as a fiscal sponsor, writing grants that fund the other programs in order to amplify their work.

Figure 10.3. OCUEJ members, including Aunti Frances and Max, distribute food to their unhoused neighbors at a tent encampment under the freeway.

Currently, the three organizations are founding a new nonprofit called Oakland Community United for Equity and Justice (OCUEJ). This, according to Max, will allow some of the work that they do "to be more supported in a way that's not so Phat Beets-centric."

> We're creating this new nonprofit so that Phat Beets is an equal partner on the program we call restorative economics. There's a mixture of economic justice, food justice, and restorative justice, a sense of healing and building economic systems that build power.

But whether this new nonprofit can enable long-term residents to stay in Oakland remains to be seen. For now, by creating supportive relationships with new neighbors, they have ensured that Self-Help's community meals can continue, providing an opportunity for sustenance and gathering to a community dealing with the stresses of displacement and homelessness. They have also amplified the need for Oakland's more privileged progressives to connect with and support the struggles of long-term residents. Though the broad and necessary policy changes have not yet occurred, there are hopeful signs that they are within reach. Community advocates have recently pressured the city council to close two important loopholes in the city's rent control regulations, and a coalition is building to repeal a statewide law that prevents rent control of single-family homes.

Aunti Frances and her supporters have been active in these efforts, but her eviction is so imminent that policy changes cannot be made in time. As a result, supporters have waged a public relations campaign to persuade the Morphys against evicting her. They have sent hundreds of holiday postcards, asking Natalia and her parents to, in the words of one supporter, "stop the eviction of a beloved community member and powerful positive presence in this neighborhood." For her part, Aunti Frances is optimistic that even if she cannot escape eviction, she will find a way to stay in the neighborhood and continue Self-Help's work. She concluded the eviction defense rally with a characteristically positive statement:

> Remember it's not just Aunti Frances. It's us. To let people who have just been displaced out of their home with no voice, [know] that they have a voice. I didn't do this work for nothing. I will not be removed, and even if I'm displaced, I will not give up."

Amidst chants of "Let Aunti stay," supporters marched back to the plaza, ate a lunch provided by Phat Beets, and left to fight another day.

Conclusion

As other chapters in this volume have shown, food activism can foster green gentrification by creating the urban green spaces and modes of consumption that are core elements of the so-called creative city. This is particularly true when the activists are not long-standing members of the community they serve and do not themselves experience food insecurity. When implicated in this process, Phat Beets recognized that, though it depends on new residents as customers, its loyalties lie with the low-income, predominantly Black community that faces displacement. After deep reflection on the ways they could resist gentrification, Phat Beets created new alliances with long-term residents, especially Aunti Frances, who was already engaged in food justice work. Together, they have turned Self-Help's predominantly privileged new neighbors from opponents to supporters, protecting the weekly gatherings from the threats of criminalization and displacement that are inimical to gentrification. And they have created massive support for Aunti Frances herself. Moreover, Phat Beets has provided a model of how a food justice organization, despite not being founded by long-term residents, can root itself in the struggles of marginalized communities and work alongside them to resist displacement.

Postscript

Aunti Frances accepted a settlement from the Morphy family and moved out of her home in the winter of 2018. She was incredibly fortunate to find another apartment nearby.

NOTE

1 This project is based on qualitative research, including participant observation and interviews, conducted over the past five years. It began with Yahya's thesis for his MA in community development. Yahya had been an organizer with Phat Beets before entering graduate school. As the organization became embroiled in conflicts about gentrification, Yahya documented and analyzed these dynamics through one year of intensive participant observation and twenty-one interviews with Phat Beets members and supporters. Although gentrification was an underlying theme in Alison's earlier work on food justice in Oakland (2012), she began to think more critically about its role while serving on Yahya's committee. Since that time, she has expanded their research by interviewing thirty additional activists, city officials, and employees of food businesses with social enterprise missions about the ways that gentrification affects their work. All interviews were audio recorded and transcribed. Alison and Yahya both coded our notes and transcripts by hand, searching for patterns and constructing thematic categories through a grounded theory approach (Glaser and Strauss 1967). One of the most important was resistance, which describes how Phat Beets and other food justice organizations attempt to push back against gentrification. Aunti Frances is not only the subject of

much of our ongoing research, but has also served as an informal advisor, helping to facilitate interviews and critique our ideas and analyses.

REFERENCES

Alkon, Alison. 2012. *Black White and Green: Farmers Markets, Race and the Green Economy*. Athens: University of Georgia Press.

Alkon, Alison, Josh Cadji, and Frances Moore. Forthcoming. "Subverting the New Narrative: Food, Gentrification and Resistance in Oakland, California." *Agriculture and Human Values*.

Alkon, Alison and Julie Guthman. 2017. *The New Food Activism: Opposition, Cooperation and Collective Action*. Berkeley: University of California Press.

Bond-Graham, Darwin. 2017. "Some Oakland Landlords Are Using a Legal Loophole to Exempt Housing from Rent Control." *East Bay Express*. www.eastbayexpress.com.

Broad, Garrett. 2016. *More Than Just Food*. Berkeley: University of California Press.

Bryson Jeremy. 2013. "The Nature of Gentrification." *Geography Compass* 7: 578–587.

Cadji, Josh and Alison Alkon. 2014. "One day, the white people are going to want these houses again": Understanding Gentrification through the North Oakland Farmers Market." In Steve Zavetoski and Julian Agyeman, eds., *Incomplete Streets*. New York: Routledge.

Checker, Melissa. 2011. "Wiped Out By the 'Greenwave': Environmental Gentrification and the Paradoxical Politics of Urban Sustainability." *City & Society* 23(2): 210–229.

Dooling, Sarah. 2009. "Ecological Gentrification: A Research Agenda Exploring Justice in the City." *International Journal of Urban and Regional Research*. 33(3): 621–639.

DuPuis, E. Melanie and David Goodman. 2005. "Should We Go Home to Eat?" *Journal of Rural Studies* 21(3): 359–371.

Florida, Richard. 2002. *The Rise of the Creative Class*. New York: Basic Books.

Glaser, Barry and Anselm Strauss. 1999. *The Discovery of Grounded Theory: Strategies for Qualitative Research*. New York: Routledge.

Glowa, K. Michelle. 2017. "Urban Agriculture, Food Justice and Neoliberal Urbanization: Rebuilding the Institution of Property." In Alison Alkon and Julie Guthman, eds., *The New Food Activism*. Berkeley: University of California Press.

Gould, Kenneth A. and Tammy Lewis. 2016. *Green Gentrification: Urban Sustainability and the Struggle for Environmental Justice*. New York: Routledge.

Guthman, Julie. 2008. "Bringing Good Food to Others." *Cultural Geographies* 15(4): 425–441.

Harvey, David. 1978. "The Urban Process Under Capitalism: A Framework for Analysis." *International Journal of Urban and Regional Research* 2(1–4): 101–131.

Hislop, Rasheed. 2014. "Reaping Equity across the USA: FJ Organizations Observed at the National Scale." Master's thesis, University of California–Davis.

Hyra, Derek. 2017. *The Cappuccino City*. Chicago: University of Chicago Press.

Johnston, Josee and Shyon Baumann. 2010. *Foodies*. New York: Routledge.

Lees, Loretta. 2003. "Super-Gentrification: The Case of Brooklyn Heights, New York City." *Urban Studies* 40(12): 2487–2509.
Lees, Loretta, Tom Slater, and Elvin Wyly. 2007. *Gentrification*. New York: Routledge.
Levkoe, Charles Z. 2011. "Towards a Transformative Food Politics." *Local Environment* 16 (7): 687–705
Logan, Johan and Harvey Molotch. 1987. *Urban Fortunes: The Political Economy of Place*. Berkeley: University of California Press.
Markham, Lauren. 2014. "Gentrification and the Urban Garden." *The New Yorker*. www.newyorker.com.
McClintock, Nathan. 2011. "From Industrial Garden to Food Desert: Demarcated Devaluation in the Flatlands of Oakland, California." In Alison Alkon and Julian Agyeman, eds., 89–120. *Cultivating Food Justice: Race, Class and Sustainability*. Cambridge, MA: MIT Press.
Meyers, Justin. Forthcoming. *Growing Gardens, Building Power: Food Justice and Urban Agriculture in Brooklyn*. New Brunswick, NJ: Rutgers University Press.
Mollison, Bill. 1988. *Permaculture: A Designer's Manual*. New York: Ten Speed Press.
Moore, Kelly and Marilyn Swisher. 2015. "The Food Movement: Growing White Privilege, Diversity, or Empowerment?" *Journal of Ag, Food Systems and Community Development* 5(4): 115–119.
Ocejo, Richard. 2011. "The Early Gentrifier: Weaving a Nostalgia Narrative on the Lower East Side." *City & Community*.
Peck, Jamie. 2005. "Struggling with the Creative Class." *International Journal of Urban and Regional Research* 29(4): 740–770.
Policy Link. 2016. "Oakland's Displacement Crisis: As Told by the Numbers." www.policylink.org.
Quastel, Noah. 2009. "Political Ecologies of Gentrification." *Urban Geography* 30(7): 694–725.
Renzulli, Kerri Anne. 2016. "10 Most Expensive Cities to be a Renter." *Time Magazine*. http://time.com.
Reynolds, Kristin and Nevin Cohen. 2016. *Beyond the Kale*. Athens: University of Georgia Press.
Self, Robert. 2005. *American Babylon: Race and the Struggle for Postwar Oakland*. Princeton, NJ: Princeton University Press.
Shaw, A. R. 2015. "Whites Who Gentrified Oakland Are Calling the Police on Innocent Black Residents. *Rolling Out*. http://rollingout.com.
Shaw, Wendy S. 2007. *Cities of Whiteness*. Malden, MA: Blackwell.
Smith, Neil. 1996. *The New Urban Frontier: Gentrification and the Revanchist City*. New York: Routledge.
Smith, Neil. 2008. *Uneven Development: Nature, Capital and the Production of Space*. Athens: University of Georgia Press.
Stehlin, John G. and Alex Tarr. 2016. "Think Regionally, Act Locally?: Gardening, Cycling and the Horizon of Urban Spatial Politics." *Urban Geography* 38(9): 1329–1351.

Walker, Richard. 2001. "Industry Builds the City: The Suburbanization of Manufacturing in the San Francisco Bay Area, 1850–1940." *Journal of Historical Geography* 27: 36–57.

White, Monica M. 2017. "'A Pig and a Garden': Fannie Lou Hamer and the Freedom Farms Cooperative." *Food and Foodways* 25(1): 20–39.

Zukin, Sharon. 2008. "Consuming Authenticity: From Outposts of Difference to Means of Exclusion." *Cultural Studies* 22(5): 724–748.

Zukin, Sharon. 2010. *Naked City: The Death and Life of Authentic Urban Places*. Oxford, UK: Oxford University Press.

PART IV

Growing Resistance

Community-Based Strategies

11

Community Gardens and Gentrification in New York City

The Uneven Politics of Facilitation, Accommodation, and Resistance

JUSTIN SEAN MYERS, PRITA LAL, AND SOFYA APTEKAR

It is dusk at Highland Park in East New York and a rally against gentrification and for affordable housing appears to be winding down.[1] The event brought together hundreds of residents, community advocates, housing activists, church members, community gardeners, and unionists to speak out against Mayor Bill de Blasio's upzoning of the neighborhood and its detrimental effects on the ability of working-class residents to live in New York City. The night is not over though, as the crowd begins to march down the street toward Arlington Village, a dilapidated and nearly vacant two-story housing complex that was purchased by a private investment firm in 2015 and is under threat of being turned into a series of gigantic buildings ranging up to fourteen stories tall. Led by the Soul Tigers, a marching band from a local elementary school, those in attendance stream down the sidewalk bellowing, "Working families under attack. What do we do? Stand up! Fight back!" Upon arriving at the building originally constructed for returning World War II veterans in 1949, the marchers erupt into a back-and-forth chant: "Whose house? Our house!"

Gentrification has dramatically reshaped the landscape of New York City over the last thirty years (Dávila 2004; Freeman 2006; Mele 2000; Smith 1996). In the Big Apple, many of the communities undergoing this process are also home to food-producing community gardens that emerged in the 1970s, 1980s, and 1990s as a form of resistance to City Hall's efforts to displace working-class residents of color through the withdrawal of public and social services and the bulldozing of infrastructure—processes dubbed *planned shrinkage* by the City

Housing Commissioner (Eizenberg 2016; Greenberg 2008; Martinez 2010; Reynolds and Cohen 2016; Von Hassell 2002). Understanding the history of these food spaces, as a manifestation of residents' right to the city, would appear to cast them into an anti-gentrification role. Yet, urban agriculture has been claimed as a form of *green gentrification*, alongside of parks, greenways, and grocery stores, that makes these communities more desirable for affluent and upwardly mobile individuals (Anguelovski 2015; Checker 2011; Gould and Lewis 2017; McClintock 2014, 2018). This tension raises a question regarding the role of food-producing community gardens in facilitating, accommodating, or resisting gentrification. More specifically, whether and for what reasons do certain food-producing community gardens slow down or resist gentrification while others invite or work with it?

To provide answers to these questions, we compare and contrast gentrification processes as they play out through community gardens in three neighborhoods in the outer boroughs of New York City: (1) Astoria, Queens, (2) Bedford-Stuyvesant (Bed-Stuy), Brooklyn, and (3) East New York, Brooklyn. In Astoria, a community garden has brought together gentrifiers and long-term residents through food, but not without conflicts along race and class lines, as it has helped facilitate gentrification by making the area feel safer to affluent newcomers through resonating with middle-class cultural preferences for visual diversity, green space, and urban agriculture (see also chapters 6 and 7 in this volume). In the Central Brooklyn section of Bed-Stuy, gentrification has led to significant race and class conflicts within gardens between gentrifiers and long-term residents, as well as within the community between long-time gardeners and non-gardening gentrifiers who contest their traditional uses of these community spaces. As a result, long-term gardeners feel under attack and dispossessed by a white wave of gentrifiers who are engaging in cultural, political, and economic processes of exclusion. Unlike Astoria and Bed-Stuy, East New York has largely been removed from processes of gentrification, but akin to Bed-Stuy, the neighborhood is home to a vibrant community gardening network, one that has been empowered through the work of the food justice organization East New York Farms! (ENYF!). However, the community is now facing the prospect of significant redevelopment through a City-led upzoning and affordable housing initiative, a project that ENYF! and a coalition of community organizations mobilized to contest based on fears of displacement (see also chapters 10 and 12 in this volume). Through comparative analysis of these gardens and neighborhoods, we trace the contested and complex relationship between food-producing community gardens and gentrification by situating the similarities and the differences across the three neighborhoods in the history of urban development politics and community activism in each neighborhood, and discuss the implications for food justice in New York City.[2]

Naturalized Cultural Norms and Accommodation in Astoria

Astoria is a neighborhood in the western part of Queens, a short subway ride from midtown Manhattan. Long part of the industrial waterfront and settled by waves of working-class migrants from abroad and the American South, Astoria is now undergoing gentrification. Developers are capitalizing on its proximity to Manhattan and its picturesque East River views, driving up rents and attracting investment. High-rise complexes rub shoulders with Astoria's small industrial spaces, rundown apartment buildings, subdivided family homes, and large public housing developments that are home to immigrants and working-class residents.

Amidst all of this is a half-acre community garden with more than one hundred small individual plots. The garden was started in the mid-2000s by anarchist-leaning organizers and involved a public campaign specifically for a community garden rather than a park on a plot that used to be an abandoned lot. The garden is located on land owned by the Parks Department and administered by the city-affiliated Green-Thumb organization—the same organization that administers many of the gardens in Central Brooklyn and East New York. The 200-plus gardeners reflect the diversity of the neighborhood. There are about forty languages spoken in the garden. Residents of nearby public housing, including African Americans and Puerto Ricans, have plots in the garden. Neighbors with physical and mental disabilities participate in the space. Local artists garden alongside other *bridge gentrifiers* (Zukin 1995, 111), such as actors and writers. There are working-class and middle-class gardeners as well as gardeners who have moved to the neighborhood to live in its luxury housing.

Urban scholars have documented the battles over the aesthetics of community gardens, which parallel struggles over green public space more generally (Eizenberg 2016; Martinez 2010; Zukin 2010). When community gardens encounter the realities of gentrification, their appearance is increasingly scrutinized by newcomers. Cultural preferences of middle-class and upper-class urbanites favor orderly and lush green arrangements of plants over the types of landscape that actually constitute many community gardens: collections of recycled "junk," bent wire fences and locks, stained plastic materials, and markedly un-green spaces where locals might gather and socialize. Often, community gardeners in these neighborhoods are quite invested in growing food, and that dedication itself, when combined with salvaged and recycled agricultural materials, clashes with the aesthetic preferences of new residents.

These tensions and conflicts have played out in the garden in Astoria in ways that do not resist gentrification but in fact accommodate and facilitate it (Aptekar 2015). This does not happen principally because the gardeners are all gentrifiers who are at odds with the surrounding community. Rather, it is driven by a visual aesthetic reproduced by the gentrifier gardeners and the ways in which this aesthetic, coupled with the visible presence of whiteness, makes the neighborhood more desirable for developers and well-off residents. Gardeners with better access to economic, cultural, and political capital, many of whom were gentrifiers, often wanted the community garden to be an orderly lush green space. This green space vision of the garden came into tension with the farm vision, which privileged food production and agricultural experimentation and was often shared by working-class and immigrant gardeners. For instance, plant support structures made from found and recycled materials could be viewed as necessary for the well-being of plants under the farm vision or as eyesores within the green space vision.

In Astoria, tensions over what the garden should look like, and even definitions of green and attractive, were pervasive. Nicos, a younger white gardener active in the local urban agriculture movement, explained:

Figure 11.1. Several garden plots in Astoria garden constructed with found and recycled materials. Photo by Sofya Aptekar.

To some people, a plot that's manicured and it is full of flowers will look wasteful, especially in a neighborhood that does not have a lot of access to fresh produce ... Or maybe one of the Chinese gardeners who use a lot of found objects, a lot of trash. You know, those things might look repulsive and backward. And right, to another person, seeing the image of a manicured plot full of flowers is beautiful because their aesthetic, or what appeals to their aesthetic, is more the Martha Stewart or the Victorian garden ideal ... And I don't think ... the Chinese gardeners are not interested in image, they are not fetishizing that image ... And I think a lot of the people that are responsible for gentrifying Astoria are not necessarily exempt from being affected by image. By fetishizing a certain appearance of something.

When disagreements over the appearance of the garden arose, they were often resolved in favor of those who emphasized a specific version of a green and orderly aesthetic. This meant, for instance, that those whose plots were considered eyesores were forced to dismantle growing structures. Sometimes the dismantling was done by other gardeners in tense confrontations.

One of the factors creating such confrontations was that the future security of the community garden was framed as dependent on conformity to the green space vision. The better the garden looked to outsiders, the less likely the Parks Department and the local politicians would be to revoke its lease and turn it into a traditional park. As Eizenberg (2016) notes, local authorities view community gardeners as akin to park rangers who maintain the green space for free, making community gardens preferable to ordinary neighborhood parks for a cash-poor city. The less open nature of community gardens also helps manage stigmatized behavior. James, an African American gardener who grew up in the neighborhood, compared the community garden to what he called "rinky-dink" parks:

> A community garden, the reason that formula works—they've had parks here before. It don't work. People go in there, and then garbage is in there, and garbage is in there, and then more people in there, and then, you know, it's not maintained and people don't want to go in there because it's dirty. When you start to give people sort of like temporary ownership of a plot, then they go in there and take a bit more pride. And it's really not open to the general community, you see? So, and it doesn't cost Parks anything. Because most people volunteer. Everything in there is maintained by the gardener.

Rather than a poorly maintained park used by public housing residents and working-class immigrants, the community garden is more exclusive and visually conforming to green space norms. As such, it makes the neighborhood more desirable for investment by gentrifiers, City officials, developers, banks, and investment firms.

The dominant aesthetic preference for the green vision did not go uncontested within the community garden. For instance, some gardeners who were more oriented toward growing food on a budget, regardless of how ugly this looked to others, enlisted the support of sympathetic and more resourced gardeners, asking them to speak up in their defense or interpret and respond to official letters. This demonstrated the nascent solidarities that this garden generated. Others spoke vociferously of their long-term roots in the neighborhood, or residence in public housing, or even invoked their rights as disabled people. Some more affluent white gardeners with liberal politics did not want to be cast as violators of rights or displacers, and these discourses could be successful in temporarily subverting dominant hierarchies. In some ways, this community garden went a long way to accommodate difference and raise consciousness of inequities. For instance, much effort was invested in sending mailings to supplement email and Facebook to accommodate the digital divide.

Nevertheless, the gardeners pushing the green space vision were often able to get what they wanted in the community garden. Moreover, what resistance and subversion existed within the garden did not translate to neighborhood-wide resistance to gentrification. As was the case in Central Brooklyn in the next section, this was because many long-term residents had mixed feelings about gentrification, looking forward to improved services and safety, and were unevenly worried about displacement. In addition, some gardeners living in public housing felt they would be protected from displacement. Finally, few connections were made between struggles within the garden and the threat of gentrification because the normative standards of greenness and attractiveness were naturalized, treated as normal, obvious, and objective, rather than a cultural pattern with a specific class signature.

From Resistance to Displacement in Bed-Stuy

The Bedford-Stuyvesant (Bed-Stuy) area of central Brooklyn was especially hard hit by disinvestment and planned shrinkage in the late 1970s, an injustice that residents resisted by creating a significant number of community gardens through their collective sweat equity efforts. Bed-Stuy is a mostly Black, residential neighborhood that is a 30-minute train ride from lower Manhattan and increasingly coveted for its many prewar brownstones on tree-lined streets (Statistical Atlas 2018). As more people are being priced out of other, more expensive neighborhoods in Manhattan and Brooklyn, Bed-Stuy has turned into a rapidly gentrifying area. According to census data, the number of white residents increased from 2.4 to 26.6 percent between 2000 and 2017; subsequently, home prices have been rising, as the median price saw a jump from $380,780 in 2012 to $716,387 in 2016, with median rents increasing from just around $1,650 to $2,300 over the same period (StreetEasy 2018).

Gentrification has had a profound impact on the practices of community gardeners and the culture of community gardens in Bed-Stuy.

Prior to gentrification, community gardens were more socially oriented (with aims such as environmental justice, youth education, cultural connection, and community-building) as opposed to the market-oriented focus of newer urban farms in the area (pounds of produce grown and revenues generated). Moreover, the day-to-day experiences of the community gardeners at the local level have become full of microaggressions that are a microcosm of the institutionalized racism of gentrification occurring at the macro level of Bed-Stuy.

Gardeners of color had a great deal of mistrust of white newcomers, much of which was connected to the history of structural exclusion and neglect from the era of planned shrinkage. One long-time community member revealed: "it was the white man who burned down your building to collect insurance money, the white man will kick you out, the white man will tear down your garden . . . because they have [done it before]." Trepidation of newcomers stemmed not just from the possibility of a loss of gardens to development, but also from the strong possibility of the loss of long-time garden leadership. Interview participants (including GreenThumb administrators) talked about how the new white residents would call GreenThumb to complain about the garden leadership (typically elder people of color). According to interview participants, newcomers complained: "the garden leaders were rude and did not keep the garden open, elder garden leaders were not utilizing the space, and hence they asked GreenThumb to change leaders." Another community gardener, an African American woman and longtime resident of central Brooklyn, recounted the sentiments of the community members when whites entered the garden: "You'll hear it whispered, 'Don't let the white people in,' you know, that's what they say. You find that to be true. I know one gentleman, his garden was in the Park Slope area, and he told me that's what happened over there. They [white people] came and they took over."

This taking over can occur through white gentrifiers occupying the garden space, but it can also occur through imposing their cultural norms on how the gardens are to be used, as occurred in Astoria. Some participants disclosed that white newcomers complained to GreenThumb regarding "noise" when gardeners had community events like block parties. Demetrice Mills, leader of the Brooklyn Queens Land Trust, shared that neighborhood block parties were like family reunions to the African American community in Bed-Stuy, which underscores the importance of the ways in which attacks on these activities by gentrifiers was an attack on the Black community and Black cultural life. In response to gentrifiers saying they have improved Bed-Stuy, Mills said that the neighborhood was always good:

> Everyone up and down the street, we looked out for each other, for each others' houses, for our children, if your child were to start running out of the gate, someone else would bring them back. Now, with a lot of the new faces, that ain't there. They walk by, and don't even say hello. They don't even look at you.

Many community gardeners also commented on the ancestral connection their communities had to working with the earth, even if white society did not recognize that connection or knowledge. Mills recounted: "all of us [founding gardeners] were from the South, so they know how to farm. We had our DNA tracked and we came from Cameroon and Sierra Leone, and we were farmers. And to this day we are farmers. So that's in our blood." Displacement from these spaces for gardeners is therefore a dispossession that disconnects them from their cultural and ethnoracial identities and roots. Additionally, instead of recognizing the importance of ancestral and cultural knowledge, the white newcomers often ignored the older gardeners' experiences, such as assuming that the longtime gardeners did not know to take certain precautions with soil testing (as supported by several interview participants). Beyond denial of the residents' agricultural knowledge and experiences, gentrifiers either did not know of or were dismissive of the political history and significance of the gardens as hard-won spaces against planned shrinkage that manifest people of color's right to the city. Karen Washington, former head of the New York City Community Gardening Coalition, said:

> Urban agriculture is turning into a white hippie movement . . . they [the newer urban farmers] are coming into established gardens and co-opting the work that those gardeners had done in the past . . . these [newer urban farmers] weren't even born at that time . . . [Many of the newcomers] have no idea what the history is about.

Gentrifiers also engaged in microaggressions against long-time gardeners through presuming that white bodies will improve the community while Black bodies are what is holding it back. Deborah Edwards-Anderson, a longtime community member and gardener shared a story of how she was recounting the history of their garden to a group of newer members, one of whom was white. That particular garden was on a piece of property that was previously owned by an African American family who had a successful business in the community. The white newcomer was surprised and said that she thought there was a "crack house" on the lot before the garden. This participant revealed this story as an example of how the white people had a *single story* of the community (Adichie 2009), assuming the longtime community members tolerated and/or promoted violence in their communities while viewing the community through a deficit lens, which ignores the strengths and talents of the longtime community members (Tuck 2009).

According to the longtime community members, the gentrifiers used this *deficit model* as a way to justify the displacement and co-optation of longtime gardeners. Edwards-Anderson articulated this poignantly:

> It reminds me of the ways that settlers characterized indigenous life. That native people weren't really productive with the land. They are wanderers. They are not settled, not making good use of the land, in fact, they are wasting the land. And the parallel that I see is that these community gardeners are puttering a little bit but they are not really growing anything, they are not productive, they can't do this to scale, on and on and on. . . . You see at the core of this, a very kind of class- and race-based discourse that people may not be aware that they are articulating. One question in this discourse deals with the appropriateness and suitability of who is entitled to use the land, about how people use resources and therefore who is best poised to use the resources. I think that's a lot of what this is about.

The conflicts within the gardens between long-term residents of color and white gentrifiers are reflected in and reflective of a broader media landscape that embraces urban agriculture as a legitimate white space while criticizing or stigmatizing the community gardening of people of color (Reynolds and Cohen 2016). These class and race inequities become apparent when examining which resources are considered acceptable to start community gardens and urban agriculture projects. For instance, Karen Washington had this critique:

> Urban agriculture has shifted focus towards efforts like rooftop farms, hydroponics, aquaponics, and all those approaches take lots of lots of money [thousands of dollars in startup costs] that people of color don't have. They [the more recent urban farmers] make it seem like growing on the ground in soil is dangerous because of contaminants, but they don't realize that community gardens build raised beds and create and bring in compost.

Indeed, the *New York Post* ran a few articles defaming community gardens run by people of color during the summers of 2014, which lent credence to Washington's comments (Buiso 2014a, 2014b). The articles had photos of Black gardeners in Brooklyn, such as the Hart to Hart community garden in Bed-Stuy, growing "toxic" food that the *Post* claims was high in lead. One interview participant thought the *Post* was running this story to create the case to destroy more gardens for development by dismissing the contributions of gardeners and even defaming them. The articles did not discuss any white-run urban farms, only people of color–run community gardens. In fact, gardeners affiliated with ENYF!, discussed in the section below, wrote a public response criticizing the *Post* articles as being inaccurate and a misrepresentation of the facts (Vigil 2015). David Vigil, East New York Farms! Project Director, went on to describe the ways in which the gardeners were aware of the lead issue and were actively taking measures to remediate and improve soils through tests and the use of compost. Despite the gardeners' critique, the *Post* article reinforced a common sentiment in the media that frames white urban gardeners as hip and cool (such as from a 2010 *New York* magazine article on the subject) whereas the faces of "contaminated" and "toxic" community gardens were people of color.[3] What is of additional significance here is that the article did not frame the story as an environmental or food justice issue rooted in institutional racism, but used the lead issue as a way to criticize and delegitimize the community-building practices of people of color and their use of and right to this space.

Overall, interview participants repeatedly talked about how gentrification destroyed the strong community bonds that existed in their neighborhoods where community members used to care for each other, relations that the community gardens previously helped to nurture. Instead, they believe that gentrification has made the culture of neighborhoods more individualistic and transient while further marginalizing Black cultural traditions through the urban agriculture practices of gentrifiers as well as the cultural practices of non-gardening gentrifiers.

The Community Gardens of East New York: Against Displacement, For Food Justice

East New York is located in northeast Brooklyn, just south of the rapidly gentrifying neighborhoods of Bed-Stuy and Bushwick. It is a working-class community of color and has a long history of disinvestment tied to redlining, blockbusting, urban renewal, planned shrinkage, and the *war on drugs* (Thabit 2005). It is also home to a vibrant community gardening movement that encompasses more than sixty community gardens and the food justice organization East New York Farms! (ENYF!) (Daftary-Steel and Gervais 2014). The gardens of East New York are similar to those in Bed-Stuy, both emerged through the grassroots sweat equity efforts of residents to convert vacant land and trash-filled lots into functional social spaces. During the 1970s through the 1990s, the community was hit hard by City Hall's strategy of planned shrinkage, which bulldozed blocks and blocks of housing into rubble and enforced austerity on the education, transportation, and public safety institutions in the community (Thabit 2005). Rather than return to the Caribbean or the American South, as City officials desired, residents dug in their heels and worked to improve the community.

There were several reasons that resident activism took the form of community gardens. First, due to a history of disinvestment, East New York has very few parks, public squares, and public gathering places in general. City Hall suggests 2.5 acres of open space per 1,000 residents, but East New York's ratio is only 0.614 acres, less than 25 percent of this recommendation (Savitch-Lew 2015). In such an environment, community gardens became de facto community parks and public spaces. Second, many gardeners grew up on farms or in farming cultures—in the American South, Western Africa, Southern Asia, Latin America, and the Caribbean—and wanted to maintain these traditions in New York City. For instance, while many gardeners grew primarily for themselves, neighbors, and coworkers, and sold to residents at the ENYF! farmers' markets, quite a few gardeners were interested in commercial growing at a much larger scale for the community. One of these gardeners is Andre, a Guyanese immigrant:

> I grew up on a farm the baby of twelve. My dad was a farmer but the town was built around bauxite mining so there was not much farming out there. Yet there was big money at the mine, high wages, engineers, people with education. My dad had acres, acres and acres of pumpkins and corn . . . We all worked the farm. I sell at the table [the gardeners' share table at the ENYF! farmers market], squash, cucumber, you know . . . but I want more land so I can sell and make some money. There's so much land around I want to talk to them [ENYF!] about growing more, commercially.

Another reason for the flourishing of resistance through community gardens is that many East New York residents were unhappy with the quality of produce, and the food in general, that was available in the local grocery stores. Referring to such produce as "second-hand foods," residents turned to growing food in their community gardens to contest the low-quality foods offered by the conventional food system in East New York. Beverly, a longtime gardener from Barbados, speaks to why growing food became so important:

> East New York is one of the lower income sections of New York State with high rates of diabetes, obesity, and high blood pressure, and all those have to do with food. That was one of the reasons for getting involved, helping the community to enhance their health. Look at how many fast food places are in walking distance, McDonalds, Checkers, Burger King, White Castle. Even go to the supermarkets like the Western Beef over there (points down the road) and you see what people put in their shopping carts. They have got six boxes of noodles and eight boxes of doughnuts and you have a bunch of fast food macaroni and cheese, which I love and all that, but there is not an onion, an apple, a garlic or anything in that shopping cart and you will see it ring up and there is nothing there but starch.

Residents' sweat equity initiatives have subsequently been scaled up and strengthened by the food justice organization ENYF! that emerged out of an asset-based participatory planning project (Daftary-Steel and Gervais 2014; Sbicca and Myers 2017). The organization uses food as a conduit to build community-based power through running a social justice–oriented youth program, maintaining several urban farms, networking with more than thirty food-producing gardens, operating two seasonal farmers' markets, and providing workshops, technical expertise, labor, and land to residents to grow and sell food. Notably, the organization is housed within the United Community Centers (UCC), a social justice– and racial justice–oriented community center with roots in the area dating back to the 1950s. ENYF!'s location within UCC has been central to its cultivation of a food justice politics and its attempts to use food to build stronger community bonds (Sbicca and Myers 2017). Former ENYF! Project Director, Sarita Daftary-Steel, underscores how this shapes ENYF!'s youth program:

> We believe it's important for youth to understand that urban agriculture in East New York rose out of a painful history of racial discrimination, disinvestment, and urban decline. With this historical background they can better understand the significance of gardens as a source of pride, and the systemic forces that created segregated, impoverished neighborhoods like East New York. (Daftary-Steel 2015)

East New York, unlike Astoria and Bed-Stuy, has not generally been subject to gentrification or redevelopment pressures and the community is still predominantly working class and people of color, with only 3 percent of the population identifying as white—the vast majority of whom are long-term residents (Myers' calculations, ACS 2012–2016). Consequently, East New Yorkers have been left alone to cultivate a vibrant and strong community gardening network that celebrates people of color, grows food by and for the community, and combats inequitable food access in their community. Nevertheless, this all began to change in 2014, with the unexpected announcement that Mayor de Blasio's affordable housing initiative would include the upzoning of a two-hundred-block section around the Broadway Junction transit hub at the convergence of East New York, Bushwick, and Bed-Stuy. After the announcement,

Figure 11.2. Numerous garden plots growing tomatoes, corn, hot peppers, collards, and callaloo in the Hands and Heart Garden. Photo by Justin Sean Myers.

housing prices increased dramatically, rental prices began to look Bushwick-esque, and real estate speculation became an increasing problem (Center for NYC Neighborhoods 2016; Savitch-Lew 2016, 2017).

Because ENYF! sees their food work as rooted in community economic development, social justice principles, and countering institutional racism, they have become involved in opposing the upzoning through their parent organization, UCC. UCC is a core member of the Coalition for Community Advancement (CCA), an umbrella organization of community groups in East New York that has collaborated with a panoply of community- and borough-based organizations throughout the city to mobilize residents to ensure that any upzoning benefits current residents, not just future ones.[4] Roy Frias, who is a member of the coalition, as well as a former youth intern and current Youth Program Director at ENYF!, underscored that the coalition "came together as a pure reaction to the rezoning. We want to make sure that with this change, there's an investment in the community" (Devlin 2017).

The CCA and its partner organizations mobilized against the upzoning through rallies and marches, community visioning sessions and workshops, attending City-led meetings and workshops, and meeting with borough-wide stakeholders and community organizers (including those who had gone through the Williamsburg rezoning under Mayor Bloomberg). The CCA also threatened acts of civil disobedience, pushed local City Council members to vote against the plan, and put forth their own community-based plan for redevelopment. These actions built on alliances formed through previous battles in the community against Walmart and stop-and-frisk policing and for better funding of child care, public education, public transit, and affordable housing. The coalition-building of CCA, and the knowledge and connections built up by these organizations over decades of existence, was vital to residents' ability to continually put pressure on local politicians, city agencies, and the mayor while demanding an investment in long-term residents, not just gentrifiers. This entailed advocating for broader and deeper affordability when it came to housing and moving beyond a housing-only plan to include the creation of good paying jobs as well as significant reinvestment in community resources to address the decades and decades of disinvestment by municipal and private actors.

East New York was officially rezoned in 2016, but the organizing of community members, including community gardeners, resulted in a number of victories: more than $250 million in funding for new and improved infrastructure, the creation of a community center, a city-run employment center, a public institution of higher education, a fund for distressed working-class homeowners, and deeper affordability targets for new construction. The CCA continues to fight for more units of and deeper levels of affordable housing for residents, the creation of robust anti-displacement policies, and the passage of policies to ensure that new commercial spaces will indeed create good jobs for residents.

Community Gardens and the Politics of Gentrification

While the story of gentrification is often told in a universalizing way, local factors shape how gentrification unfolds in urban neighborhoods. In the case of the community gardens analyzed in this chapter, there are significant similarities and differences that profoundly influence gardeners' relationship to gentrification processes.

Two important factors at play are whether gardens were formed prior to, during, or after gentrification, as well as the reasons for creating the gardens. In Bed-Stuy and East New York, community gardens emerged in response to planned shrinkage and long before gentrification came to these areas. The result is that gardens are rooted in longer histories of community self-determination that resist the racialized and classed politics of the neoliberal city. This was not the case in Astoria, where the garden emerged during gentrification and is instead rooted in an anarchist politics of reclaiming land for the community. Additionally, the severity of planned shrinkage in Bed-Stuy and East New York led to vibrant community gardening movements with little to no competing claims to this land, whereas in Astoria, the garden under study is one of a small number of gardens in an area with little vacant land, and its existence was pitted against the desires of some long-term public housing residents for a park.

These neighborhood and land-use factors also played a large role in whether the gardens in existence embrace or oppose gentrification. In Astoria, the community in the most advanced stage of gentrification, the race and class composition of gardeners has been central to institutionalizing a green space vision that not only devalues and stigmatizes the food-producing practices of working-class, immigrant gardeners, and gardeners of color, but effectively depoliticizes the garden as a space that is connected to broader social struggles. In fact, in Astoria, the cultural, political, and economic capital of gentrifying gardeners increasingly makes the garden not merely a white-dominated space in a community of color but a space that is setting the groundwork for the remaking of the community around white norms and values. This was not the case in Bed-Stuy, where race and class tensions between gentrifiers and long-time residents of color were occurring inside and outside of the gardens, and where gentrifiers symbolically and materially devalued and sought to dispossess gardeners of their right to land and the community. In Bed-Stuy, gardeners of color resisted this attack by gentrifiers on their community practices, their ethnoracial ties to the land, and their sweat equity projects through a variety of practices of resistance. This resistance, however, was largely confined to the micro- or interpersonal level and did not scale up to a broader movement against gentrification during the time of study. A key variable here is that unlike in East New York, City Hall was not as clearly involved in gentrifying Bed-Stuy through a single yet massive upzoning process. It is potentially harder to mobilize people to contest gentrification if it is being done by a variety of smaller real estate companies and developers, as it can make the process feel diffused and disparate and create a situation where it is unclear who residents should mobilize against and how. But if a centralized actor like City Hall is leading the way through zoning changes and if residents have a history of challenging City Hall, then mobilizing against this actor may be less daunting and more effective.

The gentrification experiences of gardeners in Astoria and Bed-Stuy are also quite different from those in East New York due to the geographic distance of East New York from Manhattan and Western Brooklyn, as well as the persistent "unsafe" image attached to this neighborhood compared to the other two, both of which reduced gentrification pressures.[5] Another important factor is that East New York gardeners are particularly well connected to the food justice organization ENYF! and through it UCC and their strong connections to community-based organizations across New York City, which offers the capacity to mobilize and advocate on behalf of gardeners' interests. What emerges from the story in East New York is that for community gardening to be able to slow down or halt gentrification requires it to embrace the values of social justice and equity while grounding itself in the community. This entails community gardens not being stand-alone entities only caring about green spaces or food production, but rather, entities firmly rooted in broader social networks and community organizing spaces and institutions. ENYF! and UCC by themselves would have been able to secure very little from the city and its top-down upzoning process, but with the preexisting networks that UCC has built up over its fifty-plus year history, it was less of an uphill battle to challenge City Hall. The connections and networks that push gardeners beyond food politics is all the more critical because, without such connections and mobilization, gentrification has the potential to turn the gardens for which residents of color fought so long and hard into mere cultural amenities for gentrifiers.

NOTES

1 This event, including the quotes below, is drawn from Whitford (2015).
2 Data for this chapter were generated through three separate ethnographic studies conducted between 2011 and 2015. Aptekar's research was part of a larger project investigating contested uses of public space in Astoria. Lal's focused on urban agriculture movements in Bed-Stuy, while Myers's focused on food justice activism

in East New York. As participant observers, we played a variety of roles, including being plot-sharing gardeners and volunteers with various organizations.
3 "What an Urban Farmer Looks Like" showed seven urban farmers and gardeners in the city and only one was a person of color, although all the urban farms in the article were located in predominantly communities of color (Stein 2010).
4 The CCA consists of Arts East New York, Cypress Hills Local Development Corporation, Local Development Corporation of East New York, Highland Park Community Development Corporation, Muhammad Mosque 7c, North Brooklyn YMCA, Sabaoth Group, St. Peter's Lutheran Church, United Community Centers, COFAITH Church, as well as local houses of worship, residents, and business owners. The CCA has partnered with New York Communities for Change (NYCC), Community Voices Heard (CVH), The Greater East New York Coalition, and The Real Affordability for All (RAFA) coalition, among others.
5 See Thabit (2005) for voyeuristic metaphors describing East New York as "the end of civilization."

REFERENCES

Adichie, Chimamanda. 2009. "The Dangers of a Single Story." July. www.ted.com.

Anguelovski, Isabelle. 2015. "Healthy Food Stores, Greenlining and Food Gentrification: Contesting New Forms of Privilege, Displacement and Locally Unwanted Land Uses in Racially Mixed Neighborhoods." *International Journal of Urban and Regional Research* 39 (6):1209–1230.

Aptekar, Sofya. 2015. "Visions of Public Space: Reproducing and Resisting Social Hierarchies in a Diverse Community Garden." *Sociological Forum* 30 (1):209–227.

Buiso, Gary. 2014a. "Why NYC's Toxic Community Gardens May Give You Cancer." *New York Post*, May 4, https://nypost.com.

Buiso, Gary. 2014b. "Root of All Evil: Vegetables in NYC Gardens Are Toxic," *New York Post*, November 16, http://nypost.com.

Cadji, Josh and Alison Hope Alkon. 2015. "'One Day, the White People Are Going to Want These Houses Again': Understanding Gentrification Through the North Oakland Farmers Market." In *Incomplete Streets: Processes, Practices, and Possibilities*, edited by Stephen Zavestoski and Julian Agyeman, pp. 154–175. New York: Routledge.

Center for NYC Neighborhoods. 2016. *The Impact of Property Flipping on Homeowners and Renters in Small Buildings*. http://cnycn.org.

Checker, Melissa. 2011. "Wiped Out by the 'Greenwave': Environmental Gentrification and the Paradoxical Politics of Urban Sustainability." *City & Society* 23 (2): 210–229.

Daftary-Steel, Sarita. 2015. *Growing Young Leaders in East New York: Lessons from East New York Farms! Youth Internship Program*. East New York: East New York Farms!.

Daftary-Steel, Sarita and Suzanne Gervais. 2014. *East New York Farms! Retrospective Case Study* (1995–2011). East New York: Food Dignity Project.

Dávila, Arlene. 2004. *Barrio Dreams: Puerto Ricans, Latinos, and the Neoliberal City*. Berkeley: University of California Press.

Devlin, Seán. 2017. "East New Yorkers Mull Plan for Affordable Housing, Supermarket on Burned-Out Factory Site." *Brownstoner*, January 26, www.brownstoner.com.

Eizenberg Efrat. 2016. *From the Ground Up: Community Gardens in New York City and the Politics of Spatial Transformation.* New York: Routledge.

Freeman, Lance. 2006. *There Goes the 'Hood: Views of Gentrification from the Ground Up.* Philadelphia: Temple University Press.

Gould, Kenneth A. and Tammy L. Lewis. 2017. *Green Gentrification: Urban Sustainability and the Struggle for Environmental Justice.* New York: Routledge.

Greenberg, Miriam. 2008. *Branding New York: How a City in Crisis Was Sold to the World.* New York: Routledge.

Martinez, Miranda J. 2010. *Power at the Roots: Gentrification, Community Gardens, and the Puerto Ricans of the Lower East Side.* Lanham, MD: Lexington Books.

McClintock, Nathan. 2014. "Radical, Reformist, and Garden-Variety Neoliberal: Coming to Terms with Urban Agriculture's Contradictions." *Local Environment* 19 (2): 147–171.

McClintock, Nathan. 2018. "Cultivating (a) Sustainability Capital: Urban Agriculture, Eco-gentrification, and the Uneven Valorization of Social Reproduction." *Annals of the American Association of Geographers* 108 (2): 579–590.

Mele, Christopher 2000. *Selling the Lower East Side: Culture, Real Estate, and Resistance in New York City.* Minneapolis: University of Minnesota Press.

Reynolds, Kristin and Nevin Cohen. 2016. *Beyond the Kale: Urban Agriculture and Social Justice Activism in New York City.* Athens: University of Georgia Press.

Savitch-Lew, Abigail. 2015. "Fight Over De Blasio Plan for East New York Will Be About More than Housing." *City Limits*, September 22, https://citylimits.org.

Savitch-Lew, Abigail. 2016. "Some Suspect East New York Rezoning Has Triggered Speculation." *City Limits*, March 10, https://citylimits.org.

Savitch-Lew, Abigail. 2017. "Investors Move Quietly in East New York Amid de Blasio's Housing Construction." *City Limits*, July 18, https://citylimits.org.

Sbicca, Joshua and Justin Sean Myers. 2017. "Food Justice Racial Projects: Fighting Racial Neoliberalism from the Bay to the Big Apple." *Environmental Sociology* 3(1): 30–41.

Smith, Neil. 1996. *The New Urban Frontier: Gentrification and the Revanchist City.* New York: Routledge.

Statistical Atlas. 2018. Race and Ethnicity in Bedford Stuyvesant, NY, https://statisticalatlas.com.

Stein, Joshua David. 2010. "What an Urban Farmer Looks Like: A Field Guide to the City's New Breed of Growers." *New York Magazine*, http://nymag.com.

StreetEasy. 2018. Bedford Stuyvesant: Price History, https://streeteasy.com.

Thabit, Walter. 2005. *How East New York Became a Ghetto.* New York: NYU Press.

Tuck, Eve. 2009. "Suspending Damage: A Letter to Communities." *Harvard Educational Review* 79 (3): 409–427.

Vigil, David. 2015. "An Open Letter to the NY Post and the East New York Community." *East New York Farms!*, https://ucceny.org.

Von Hassell, Malve. 2002. *The Struggle for Eden: Community Gardens in New York City.* Westport, CT: Bergin and Garvey.

Whitford, Emma. 2015. "East New York Residents Demand Relief from Gentrification's Tightening Grip." *Gothamist*, http://gothamist.com.

Zukin, Sharon. 1995. *The Culture of Cities*. Cambridge, MA: Blackwell.

Zukin, Sharon. 2010. *Naked City: The Death and Life of Authentic Urban Places.* New York: Oxford University Press.

12

No Se Vende

Resisting Gentrification on Chicago's Paseo Boricua *through Food*

BROOKE HAVLIK

When Hurricane Maria devastated Puerto Rico in September 2017, the island was not only suffering an economic crisis—being more than $70 billion in debt—but in addition, a food security crisis had been in the making for decades. Puerto Rico imports 85 percent of its food from the US mainland but produces only 15 percent of food consumed on the island (USDA 2015). The storm wiped out an estimated 80 percent of local agriculture, leaving a humanitarian disaster and food shortage in its path (USDA 2019).

The gravely insufficient supply of homegrown food for the island's population of three million people was not an accident, but rather a result of colonization and its relationship with the United States. Throughout the nineteenth and early twentieth centuries, Puerto Rico was an agrarian economy that produced most of its consumed foods. Over the last seventy years, a series of economic and agricultural policies largely driven by the United States transformed the island into today's consumer economy dependent on mainland imports (Carro-Figueroa 2002). In the aftermath of Hurricane Maria, therefore, government officials and activists alike see ongoing initiatives to grow Puerto Rico's farming industry and food security as a critical step for self-sufficiency and sovereignty on the island, efforts that have increased in the last two years (USDA 2015; Acevedo 2018).

For the more than 5.5 million members of the Puerto Rican diaspora living on the US mainland (Centro 2018), the island's turbulent colonial relationship is inextricably tied to their current realities, including issues of economic and food insecurity. The links between the island and mainland look different in every context, and this chapter will examine the Puerto Rican diaspora community in Chicago, Illinois, which is home to the fifth largest population of Puerto Ricans in any US city after New York City, Orlando, Philadelphia, and Miami. Around half of Puerto Ricans in Chicago live on the northwest side of the city's central business district in the neighborhoods of Logan Square, Hermosa, Humboldt Park, Belmont Cragin, West Town, Avondale, Portage Park, and Montclare (Puerto Rican Research Agenda 2011).

Today, Humboldt Park is actively experiencing gentrification—the cultural and economic displacement of lower-income residents by an influx of higher socioeconomic residents. In 2014, the real estate website Redfin named Humboldt Park the "10th hottest neighborhood in America" (Unger 2014). From 2017 to 2018, single-family home prices increased by 12.1 percent, making it one of two neighborhoods in Chicago with the largest increase in single-family homes during the year (IHS 2018).

East Humboldt Park's *Paseo Boricua* is the half-mile commercial and cultural capital of the Puerto Rican diaspora in the Midwestern United States. The promenade has more than 114 small businesses, restaurants, and nonprofits, many of them owned and operated by Puerto Ricans (Puerto Rican Research Agenda 2011). Gentrification not only threatens access to affordable housing across the neighborhood, but also wealth-generating opportunities from local businesses, placemaking, and dynamic foodways on or nearby *Paseo Boricua*. Food spaces like restaurants and grocery stores on *Paseo Boricua* preserve and advance cultural identities and membership among Puerto Ricans in the neighborhood. They also connect friends and family to island life in Puerto Rico through both traditional and new foodways.

Popular local restaurants like Papa's Cache Sabroso are serving up *pollo chon* and *jibaritos*, a Chicago-born sandwich that replaces bread with flattened plantains. Yelp (2019) reviewers found the restaurant is "like grandma cooked it 'en el fogon' in Puerto Rico" and "The entire vibe of the restaurant is very authentic and home-y, reminding me of the restaurants back home on the island of Puerto Rico." Café Colao serves popular desserts like *pastelitos de guava* and *flan de queso*, to which one reviewer said, "The smell of the fresh coffee and pastries when you walk in reminds me so much of Puerto Rico." And then there is La Bruquena, which is one of Chicago's oldest Puerto Rican restaurants that often doubles as a community meeting space. On *Paseo Boricua*, food is never just about the body's need to eat, but rather, participation in *foodways* are "manifestations and symbols of cultural histories and proclivities" (Alkon and Agyeman 2011: 10; Douglass 1996).

Traditional Puerto Rican food is a mix of indigenous Taino, Spanish, African, and American food. However, like other diaspora communities worldwide, Puerto Rican foodways in Chicago are not static or a direct transplant from the island. The local food culture has combined with other neighborhood ethnicities to reinvent itself. The Puerto Rican Agenda—a nonpartisan alliance of statewide organizations, elected and community leaders, and volunteers—notes that "Puerto Rican culture, symbols, and language have been invented and reinvented, produced and (re)produced in order to answer the changing needs of a people" (Puerto Rican Research Agenda 2011). The Puerto Rican community's food-based responses to changing demographics and gentrification pressures reflect one of these changing needs.

Sovereignty has been a central organizing force among Puerto Ricans in Chicago since the 1960s, when communities came together to make political demands of local and state institutions (Puerto Rican Research Agenda 2011). Similar to activists on the island, food is an important lever in the political fight for self-sufficiency and survival in Chicago's diaspora community as they experience gentrification.[1] Food sovereignty is "the right of peoples, communities, and countries to define their own agricultural, labor, fishing, and food and land policies so they are ecologically, socially, and economically appropriate to their unique circumstances" (Peña et al. 2017). This chapter examines how some community activists and longtime residents in Humboldt Park are making connections between the colonization of Puerto Rico, foodways, and gentrification through neighborhood-level food security and sovereignty initiatives. The chapter shows the importance of identifying the social contradictions of food gentrification while in the process of developing resistance frameworks that challenge the cooptation of the neighborhood's existing food culture and community.

Humboldt Park, Chicago

Humboldt Park's commercial strip *Paseo Boricua* on Division Street spans from Western Avenue to California Avenue, and two massive

Figure 12.1. *Paseo Boricua*'s welcome flags on Division Street (Personal photographs, 2013).

steel arches in the shape of Puerto Rican flags flank the street (see figure 12.1). In 1995, the City of Chicago and community leaders erected the flags as gateways to both celebrate Puerto Rican culture and demarcate the promenade. Building facades emulate Old San Juan's Spanish colonial architecture, and colorful murals highlight important social and political struggles in Puerto Rican history. Humboldt Park has been self-described by a local non-profit as a "Well-organized, outspoken, sometimes fiery community" that has "mixed reactions to the growing number of higher-income, predominantly white newcomers" (Humboldt Park: Staking Our Claim 2005). For more than two decades, *Paseo Boricua*'s cultural and physical markers, including its restaurants and grocery stores, have drawn a symbolic line in the sand to say: *no se vende*, or not for sale. It is part of a concerted, community-based economic development strategy for self-determination, economic vitality, and cultural preservation.

Paseo Boricua is also a direct response to Puerto Rican history in Chicago. Since the 1950s, Chicago's Puerto Rican community has been displaced from other neighborhoods throughout the city. Like many other US cities, Chicago followed a pattern of "uneven development" in which the "unequal distribution of both public and private resources and capital [followed] racial and class lines" (Fernandez 2012:141). In the 1960s and 1970s, government officials implemented urban renewal projects in the Near North Side and Near West Side, pushing out the majority of Puerto Rican, Mexican, and other Latinx groups (Fernandez 2012). Supported by millions of dollars in city, state, and federal funding, massive demolitions and the use of eminent domain forced many families to move west of the central business district, where Humboldt Park is located. White residents in the western neighborhoods met new Latinx families with verbal assaults and housing discrimination practices, racist actions that police and civil institutions reinforced (Fernandez 2012). The memory of forced displacement is still fresh in many Humboldt Park residents' minds (Personal interviews 2013).

Today, Humboldt Park is a mixed community of approximately 56,274 residents. According to the 2010 US Census, Humboldt Park residents are approximately 51.7 percent Hispanic, 41.5 percent Black, and 5.6 percent white (US Census 2010). While real estate agents, scholars, and community members debate the neighborhood's borders, approximately 26 percent of the population is Puerto Rican under the colloquial or community-defined borders of Western Avenue to the east, Pulaski Road to the west, Armitage Avenue to the north, and Chicago Avenue to the south (Puerto Rican Research Agenda 2011).

Since the 1970s, more than 11,000 jobs have left the surrounding area, and there was a corresponding reduction in retail shops and grocery stores, resulting in reduced access to healthy food (*Humboldt Park: Staking Our Claim* 2005; Margellos-Anast, Shah, and Whitman 2008; *Diabetes in Humboldt Park* 2006). According to the 2011–2015 American Community Survey, 33 percent of Humboldt Park residents live below the poverty line. The median annual household income for Latinx residents was $35,000, compared to $25,900 for African American residents and $57,700 for white residents (Acosta-Córdova 2017). Throughout the city of Chicago, Puerto Ricans have some of the highest poverty rates among Latinx residents. A survey by the Chicago Community Trust found that 49 percent of Humboldt Park households received food stamp benefits and 30 percent accessed emergency food from providers like food pantries or soup kitchens (CCT 2018). More than 20 percent of Puerto Ricans in Humboldt Park are diagnosed with diabetes, compared to 12 percent of mainland Puerto Ricans and 5 percent of Chicagoans overall (Puerto Rican Research Agenda 2011).

Struggles associated with food security and community health, and the consequences of gentrification, came up in my conversations with Puerto Rican residents and community leaders. The Puerto Rican Cultural Center (PRCC) is a leading organization advancing economic and social justice within the community. Julian, a longtime Humboldt Park resident and PRCC representative, spoke about the special relationship between Humboldt Park's food access challenges and US colonization of Puerto Rico:

> Food security is a threat that runs to the heart of colonialism. Since 1898, Puerto Rico turned from a country that grew what it ate, to a country that exported what it ate and imports what it eats. Resulting in some of the worst social indecencies, not only of food, but diabetes, childhood obesity, blood pressure, mental illness, drug addiction, suicide. This means Chicago, becomes much more important. . . . Chicago is actually an example for Puerto Rico. So the townships that we have made relationships with, they come to Fiesta—and they get really into recycling or inner tourism, developing their own tourism for Puerto Ricans from the other side of the island. Food security in that sense is much more of an issue that is transnational. . . . how do we link and develop the education for our community around this stuff.

Julian's comment demonstrates how food insecurity and economic development in Humboldt Park are uniquely transnational issues. Approximately one-third of the island's population emigrated from Puerto Rico to the United States between 1955 and 1970 when there was high demand for manufacturing labor (Perez 2004:10), but there has been circular migration since the 1960s. Today, many Puerto Ricans participate in circular migration and remain intertwined with Puerto Rican politics, events, and people, even if they have never visited the island in person. Any initiatives to improve community health or economic development are not just about Humboldt Park; Humboldt Park is an example for communities in Puerto Rico. Therefore, the loss of community infrastructure due to gentrification would not only be a loss to Puerto Ricans in Humboldt Park but to Puerto Ricans on the island as well.

The Food "Frontier" and Social Preservationists

Despite these long-standing efforts to build economic vitality on *Paseo Boricua*, media sources have credited new Humboldt Park food businesses with breathing life into the neighborhood by infusing it with new cultural attractions, such as artisanal coffee shops serving "boozy steamers" and farm-to-table restaurants. Often this narrative plays out in restaurant reviews and food-related media. A few blocks south of *Paseo Boricua*, a popular food website celebrated, "The burgeoning intersection around Humboldt Park's California and Augusta avenues is slated to get two more interesting, homey, and connected entrants" (Gerzina 2017). A restaurateur and new business owner in Humboldt Park stated the neighborhood is "100 percent the next growth area. It's the next frontier—that's how I feel about it" (Holliday 2014). This reflects the idea of "savior entrepreneurs," who are not only in the business of food, they are also acting as urban developers who use the "nothing there" narrative (see chapter 2 in this volume). Savior entrepreneurs often ignore long-standing communities of immigrants and people of color who have a stake in the neighborhood's development.

Language like "burgeoning intersection" or "next frontier" are gentrification narratives that normalize the racialization of space, an active process in which whiteness becomes the normative power that enjoys social or environmental privileges by controlling both the dominant values and institutions (Kobayshi and Peake 2000). Through food, Humboldt Park restaurateurs and food critics alike are replicating historical images of adventurous spirits and the rugged individualism of white colonizers on the Western frontier (Smith 1996). Colonizers justified their use of space as more rational, desirable, and efficient than indigenous uses of land, which in turn justified forced displacement. And while European colonizers forcefully removed Native people from their traditional grounds, the subtler yet still violent experience of clearing neighborhoods of existing populations block by block is occurring through the daily processes of gentrification, and in this case, specifically through discourse about food and the restaurant industry (Zukin 1991).

However, not all newcomers reproduced such direct colonial narratives or practices. Several of the white residents I interviewed spoke positively of living in a gritty, "up and coming neighborhood." They defined grit as a space that was diverse and authentic, and distinct from white, suburban, and cookie-cutter lifestyles (Brown-Saracino 2010; Hyra 2017). Stephanie, a white, middle-class, twenty-seven-year-old woman who lives in Humboldt Park, noted how dangerous the colonization of space can be when it goes unnoticed or unchecked.

> I talk about this with my partner, and the term "up and coming neighborhood" and how that is such an unfortunate term because there is already so much here. To imply that they're just coming up now is just because more white people are moving in. It's so true and unfortunate that we cannot, I don't even want to say integrate, I don't necessarily think that's true. I think it's really great the way it is. It can just stop on California Avenue; I think it's the perfect distance away from me.

Here, Stephanie demonstrates her concern that the next wave of gentrifiers will clear the neighborhood of existing residents and its culture, what Japonica Brown-Saracino (2010) calls "social preservation." *Social preservationists* are different from gentrifiers who seek high culture and the comfort of fellow "pioneers" to tame the "frontier" (see also chapter 9 in this volume). Instead, they have concern for the people who may be displaced by gentrification, and a desire for "authentic" communities that are colorful, original, and recognize "old-timers'" culture.

Some interviewees spoke directly about food in terms of social preservation. Giaco, a Brazilian Italian middle-class, five-year resident of Humboldt Park, talked about a new diner there, called Grandma J's: "It definitely caters to people who are willing to pay $10 for a breakfast sandwich, the sort of no nitrates kind of people . . . Look, I like wholesome food as well. But keeping in mind the neighborhood and environment you are in, there is something not right about that." Giaco finds the restaurant's prices inappropriate in a neighborhood he assessed as not able to afford or access such products. Although different from the Western frontier language, social preservationists carry their own risks. Not only do they remove their own culpability within the process of gentrification, preservationists may seek to create a narrative about a neighborhood from their own vision or historical memory, and therefore risk homogenizing complex social and political realities of diverse communities.

Resisting and Reimagining Gentrification Through Food

As public spaces, restaurants and other food businesses in any neighborhood hold a distinct and powerful position to create collective community narratives. Narratives are a connected body of stories that hold common meaning, are embedded in culture, and are refined over time to represent central beliefs (Narrative Initiative 2017). In a community setting, narratives operate as a shared form of placemaking and are fundamental to understanding daily life in a neighborhood. A community's narrative can also support economic opportunity and social mobility. The intentional demarcation of *Paseo Boricua* as a Puerto Rican commercial district manifests through Spanish language and symbolic representation of Puerto Rican food, history, and culture. Cultural identification of the *Paseo Boricua* contributes to the collective identity among the long-term Puerto Rican and Latinx residents, while it also contributes to the area's economic vitality.

However, across Chicago and the United States, whiteness remains the normative power and narrative. And just like human bodies that are valued as "normal" or "beautiful" based on their proximity to whiteness, physical spaces are also constructed through their proximity to whiteness and subsequently racialized (Kobayashi and Peake 2000). Long before gentrification, Humboldt Park was defined by outsiders and racialized through stereotypes and its spatial segregation from whiteness in Chicago.

Tensions emerge in gentrifying communities when a strong and well-defined community narrative, like that of *Paseo Boricua*, is juxtaposed against white newcomers who use accounts based on racist stereotypes. In a 2012 video, the owner of Tipsy Cake bakery, Naomi Levine, revealed that her decision to move her business away from Humboldt Park was due to "too many gunshots in the cake" (*Tipsy Cake Local Interview*). Her new bakery location—which has since permanently closed—was moved to Bucktown, a white, middle- to upper-class community that was highly gentrified years prior to her statements. Levine "really wanted Bucktown for a location" because she "could get any type of client in here not feeling nervous." The video concludes as the interviewer takes a bite out of a Tipsy Cake pastry, which Levine jokingly nicknamed, "Humboldt Crack" (*Tipsy Cake Local Interview*).

Similar to the ink! Coffee sign incident in Denver's Five Points (see the introduction in this volume), the video became a flash point for organizing against gentrification. In February 2012, dozens of protesters gathered outside the padlocked bakery, Tipsy Cake. Waving Puerto Rican flags and homemade signs bearing the words "*No Se Vende!*" and "Humboldt Park Is Our Community and We Love It," local leaders spoke out in resistance to remarks made by Levine and called for a boycott of her products. Juanita Garcia, a longtime resident and volunteer at the Puerto Rican Cultural Center (PRCC), spoke at the rally:

> I am a Puerto Rican woman who lives in Humboldt Park, within one block from Tipsy Cake. I have lived in Humboldt Park all my life choosing to also raise my child here, and my perception, like most residents of this community, is completely the opposite of Naomi Levine. How does someone open a business in a community without an interest in learning about it? Clearly, there are lessons to be learned. The business and owner reflect the common occurrence of people coming to this community knowing nothing about its history, people and culture and not wanting to learn about it either. This also serves as an example of how gentrification, which we are consciously struggling against, unfolds within a community. (*Humboldt Park Residents* 2012)

This painful and racist incident within the community reiterates that commercial food spaces are prominent sites in the battle over collective community narratives in gentrifying communities. This bakery may have been a public place, but it was imbued with the ethnoracial and class tensions inherent to the threat of displacement residents faced from a neighborhood long considered Puerto Rican. Here, the use of *no se vende* as a political chant, or even Spanish seen on menus, murals, and cultural spaces throughout the neighborhood, are forms of linguistic or narrative resistance that confront those who do not speak the language or collective narrative. By occupying the bakery space and media coverage of the event, community organizers were disrupting the normalcy of whiteness and its often-unchecked power to occupy space during gentrification (see figure 12.2).

The Tipsy Cake event also demonstrated that there is an existing nexus of organizations and political leaders within the community ready to organize and build solidarity around opposition to gentrification. There are more than seventy-one non-profit organizations in Humboldt Park, and 10 percent have an explicit Puerto Rican identity (Puerto Rican Research Agenda 2011). The most visible organization opposed to contemporary gentrification is the Puerto Rican Cultural Center (PRCC). It is a powerful political organization thanks to its integrative programming and production of cultural festivals. Founded in 1973, the PRCC is a non-profit organization built on "a philosophy of self-determination, a methodology of self-actualization and critical thought, and an ethics of self-reliance best expressed in the motto, 'To live and to help live'" (Puerto Rican Cultural Center 2011). The PRCC recognizes that impending gentrification is one aspect of a long history of colonization and forced displacement of Puerto Rican, Latinx, and Black communities. The organization not only supports advocating for the freedom of Puerto Rican political prisoners, but also has initiated and/or operates Pedro Albizu Campos Puerto Rican High School, a daycare, a youth center called Batay Urbano, yearly festivals, and VIDA/SIDA, an AIDS outreach, prevention, and transition housing for queer youth. The group also works with the National Museum of Puerto Rican Arts and Culture on economic development projects on *Paseo Boricua*.

Additionally, the organization has identified food security as an important contribution to community resiliency and has initiated community-led projects like a farmers' market, community gardening, and urban agriculture. One of the ways the PRCC sought to counter food insecurity, decolonize space, and build a strong community to resist gentrification is through the largely volunteer-run Greater Humboldt Park Urban Agriculture Initiative (GHPUAI). According to its website, the GHPUAI seeks to:

Figure 12.2. A mural, which reads in Spanish, "We resist displacement" located on *Paseo Boricua*, the economic and cultural capital of Puerto Rican culture in the Midwest. Personal photograph 2013.

Develop community self-sufficiency in the production of key aspects of the community's nutritional reserve, where community residents, especially youth, actively engaged in the planning and development of the necessary systems of production, distribution and consumption of nutritious, culturally defined and community-specific produce with the purposeful intent of being self-reliant and food secure in eradicating the prevalence of unnaturally caused illnesses in our community. (Pedro Albizu Campos High School and Puerto Rican Cultural Center 2011)

Julian explains more about the PRCC-led initiative:

The garden is only a part of our plan. There are at least four or five other touch points we talked about—The edible garden, the greenhouse, the community planters, the community gardens, as well as our farmers' market. We wanted to start the "basic basket" which is basically a thing of food and you sign people up for an eight-dollar basic with seasonal vegetables. For twelve dollars it was enough for two. For eight dollars you could have a cruelty-free chicken. There were different levels people could buy in.

The GHPUAI's goal is to make local and organic food accessible *and* inclusive by offering nutritious and culturally appropriate foods grown, processed, and sold by the community for the community. What is interesting to note is that no part of GHPUAI includes inviting large grocery store chains to the neighborhood, which contradicts the desires of other Puerto Rican and white community members I interviewed in 2013. The GHPUAI represents a do-it-yourself community-led model, especially in the face of gentrification.

To increase community power, one of the largest projects the PRCC has taken on is fund-raising and building an educational greenhouse at Pedro Albizu Campos High School to help instructors integrate science, technology, and urban agriculture. Youth are involved in the food projects occurring in Humboldt Park. Students grow food in an 800-square-foot rooftop greenhouse and at several neighborhood gardens and sell the goods at a bodega and local farmers' markets. They sell products both common and uncommon in Puerto Rican cuisine. *Recao*, also known as Mexican coriander, is an essential ingredient for *sofrito* and is sold alongside Swiss chard and kale, which are less common in Puerto Rican recipes.

The goal of the high school urban agriculture programs is to produce leaders for the next generation who can activate change and continue to see the community as a place to invest in. Leaders understand that the cultural shifts of gentrification brought about by new restaurants, bars, vintage stores, and furniture shops risk signaling to young Puerto Ricans that their culture is of lesser value than that of white youth culture. In response, the food-focused work of these high schoolers creates pride in Puerto Rican culture and the community in which they reside. As the high school website explains,

> Since the foundation of our school, Dr. Pedro Albizu Campos Puerto Rican High School has worked to practice critical pedagogy, where the learning in our classrooms is connected to students' developing skills to positively transform the world. This framework of liberatory education,

with roots to the work of Paulo Freire, challenges our teachers, staff and students to imagine a learning experience that helps to arm our students with the ability to control and ultimately transform the conditions in their neighborhoods. (Pedro Albizu Campos Puerto Rican High School 2019)

Clearly, these initiatives represent frontline struggles that link food to resisting gentrification.

There are also signs on *Paseo Boricua* of new business developments that both celebrate Puerto Rican culture and bring new economic opportunities to the neighborhood vis-à-vis the celebration of Latin culture and food. In 2018, the opening of Radio Rhumba, a $10.5 million, Puerto Rican–owned Latin concert hall and supper club, was announced as a space where people "can dine, dance to live music performed by both local and regional musicians and get drinks from the bar." Several respected Puerto Rican community leaders and local politicians approved the development. Radio Rhumba is part of the first phase of a larger project to develop Division Street or *Paseo Boricua* into Chicago's Latin district. The goal is not just to bring Latinx audiences to the promenade but to become a citywide destination for people to enjoy *Paseo Boricua* within the existing community narrative of the neighborhood (Bloom 2018). Unlike the new food businesses that threaten long-term, local businesses as portrayed in chapters 1–3 in this volume, if the financial gains from the business stay within the community and contribute to inclusive economic growth, it could provide an example of commercial development that can help resist displacement pressures, but more research is needed.

In a similar sentiment, Gabriella, a Puerto Rican resident of Humboldt Park, believes there is power in the gentrifiers recognizing where a community has come from and participating as an ally in that space, rather than solely patronizing a separate community of your own:

> Don't get me wrong; I don't think this community can survive just off of being Puerto Rican. It's just not possible. It needs to be mixed income. I am not saying it has to be exclusively Puerto Rican. However, this is a Puerto Rican community and we have struggled for years, more than forty years—there were two riots on the street . . . We have built what we have from ashes. We dealt with slumlords, unbearable living conditions

here. We built this. Humboldt Park has gotten better because we have gotten better. You know, not because people are coming in. It's better because we worked at making it better.

To Gabriella, the memory of the neighborhood's history, including in commercial spaces like restaurants, is critical to understanding and living in the neighborhood. It is also a survival strategy—Puerto Rican–owned business will increasingly need gentrifiers as customers to endure shifting populations and rising rent. By stepping back, questioning assumptions, and fully embracing what Puerto Ricans have established in Humboldt Park, Gabriella suggests that newcomers could take a crucial step toward recalibrating the power dynamics of gentrification.

Conclusion

The Puerto Rican diaspora has reinvented itself throughout the last seven decades in Chicago to reflect the consistently changing needs of its community. In Humboldt Park, food has been a powerful mechanism for strengthening existing community narratives and building new stories around culture, sovereignty, and decolonization. But the threats of urban "revitalization" and "upscaling" businesses and food loom. Although gentrification is now a household word that many can identify when they see it happening, it remains a contentious and unequal process that deepens disparities in many daily aspects of neighborhood life (Brown-Saracino 2010; Jager 1986; Wilson, Wouters, and Grammenos 2004; Munoz 1998). Displacement pressures are exacerbating the long history of marginalization for Chicago's Puerto Ricans.

While much research and activism remain focused on securing affordable housing to resist gentrification, this chapter analyzed threats and opportunities that gentrification places on a collective cultural identity in communities like Humboldt Park. Activism against gentrification in Chicago is framed through the lens of decolonization. This situates the threat of displacement in one neighborhood in the context of the global political economy and history of Puerto Rico. As such, food spaces often play a central role in this fight.

The diasporic legacy of colonization, which is intimately related to land, refracts through the ongoing fights over belonging and place. This chapter demonstrates the significance of how grassroots efforts by those living with memories of that colonial past seek to disrupt the process of gentrification and cooptation of the neighborhood's existing culture and community through community-led food work and commercial food spaces. Non-profit organizations like the PRCC and their efforts to build a youth-led food movement are a direct response to many threats to resiliency facing Humboldt Park's Puerto Rican community, including gentrification. Like the agricultural movements that are growing in Puerto Rico for sovereignty and self-determination, food could be an important lever for Chicago's diaspora community in the fight against gentrification in the years to come.

NOTE

1 I collected data for this research in 2013 while I was living on the border of Humboldt Park and its northern neighbor, Logan Square. My primary data instruments included eighteen qualitative interviews that lasted from 30 minutes to one hour each, with participants who ranged in years of residency (>1–40 years), age (35–70 years), and self-identified racial or ethnic background (Puerto Rican, Latino, Mexican, Black, and White). I contacted participants after meeting them in participant observations through direct emails, phone calls, and snowball sampling. The interviews were semi-structured, and I would often lead off with questions such as, "Tell me the story of your community garden," to understand the lived experiences of each individual participant. I conducted participant observations at three locations: (1) commercial spaces such as grocery stores, farmers' markets, and restaurants; (2) community gardens; and (3) non-profit organizations. I was most active as a gardener in a Humboldt Park community garden with approximately fifteen members. I purchased a raised garden bed and participated in member emails, monthly meetings, casual garden conversations. Together, these data instruments, combined with menu and media research, and a literature review, helped to examine behavior and conversations at these sites and gain an understanding of the context in which those interactions lie.

REFERENCES

Acevedo, Nicole. 2018. "'The Push We Needed': Puerto Rico's Local Farmers Step Up Efforts after Hurricane Maria." NBC News. www.nbcnews.com.

Acosta-Córdova, José Miguel. 2017. "The Latino Neighborhoods Report: Issues and Prospects for Chicago." Institute for Research on Race and Public Policy Great Cities. Chicago: University of Illinois at Chicago.

Alkon, Alison Hope and Julian Agyeman. 2011. *Cultivating Food Justice: Race, Class, and Sustainability*. Cambridge, MA: MIT Press.

Allen, Patricia. 2010. "Realizing Justice in Local Food Systems." *Cambridge Journal of Regions, Economy and Society* 3: 295–308.
Betancur, John. 2011. "Gentrification and Community Fabric in Chicago." *Urban Studies* 48(2): 383–406.
Bloom, Mina. 2018. "Huge New Latin Concert Hall and Supper Club Planned for Humboldt Park." Book Club Chicago. https://blockclubchicago.org.
Bridge, Gary. 2001. "Bourdieu, Rational Action and the Time-Space Strategy of Gentrification." *Transactions of the Institute of British Geographers* 26(2): 205–216.
Brown-Saracino, Japonica. 2010. *The Gentrification Debates*. New York: Routledge.
Carro-Figueroa, Vivian. 2002. "Agricultural Decline and Food Import Dependency in Puerto Rico: A Historical Perspective on the Outcomes of Postwar Farm and Food Policies." *Caribbean Studies*. San Juan: Institute of Caribbean Studies.
Centro (Center for Puerto Rican Studies). 2018. New York: Hunter College. https://centropr.hunter.cuny.edu.
Chicago Community Trust. 2018. "In Humboldt Park, Healthy Food and Health Care Often Out of Reach." https://cct.org.
Diabetes in Humboldt Park: A Call to Action. 2006. Rep. Chicago: Humboldt Park Diabetes Task Force.
Douglass, M. 1996. *Purity and Danger: An Analysis of the Concepts of Purity and Taboo*. New York: Taylor Publishing.
Fernandez, Lilia. 2012. *Brown in the Windy City*. Chicago: University of Chicago Press.
Gerzina, Daniel. 2017. "Humboldt Park to Get a New Bar and Food Stand Courtesy of EZ Inn Owner." *Eater Chicago*. www.chicago.eater.com.
Holliday, Darryl. 2014. "Brendan Sodikoff to Overhaul Clipper, Build Restaurant in Humboldt Park." *DNA Info*. www.dnainfo.com.
Humboldt Park Residents and Businesses Defend Their Community. 2012. YouTube. Puerto Rican Cultural Center. www.youtube.com.
Humboldt Park: Staking Our Claim. 2005. Chicago: Bickerdike Redevelopment Corporation.
Hyra, Derek. 2017. *Race, Class, and Politics in the Cappuccino City*. Chicago: University of Chicago Press.
Institute for Housing Studies (IHS). 2018. "Cook County House Price Index: Second Quarter 2018." Chicago: DePaul University.
Jager, M. 1986. "Class Definition and the Aesthetics of Gentrification: Victoriana in Melbourne." In *Gentrification of the City*, edited by N. Smith and P. Williams, 78–91. London: Unwin Hyman.
Kobayashi, Audrey and Linda Peake. 2000. "Racism Out of Place: Thoughts on Whiteness and an Antiracist Geography in the New Millennium." *Annals of the Association of American Geographers*. 90: 393.
Lefebvre, Henri. 1996. *The Production of Space*. Oxford, UK: Blackwell.
Margellos-Anast, Helen, Ami M. Shah, and Steve Whitman. 2008. "Prevalence of Obesity Among Children in Six Chicago Communities: Findings from a Health Survey." *Public Health Reports*, 123.

Mintz, S. W. and C. M. Du Bois. 2002. "The Anthropology of Food and Eating." *Annual Review of Anthropology* 31.1: 99–119.
Munoz, Vicky. 1998. *Resisting Gentrification and Displacement: Voices of Puerto Rican Women of the Barrio.* New York: Garland.
The Narrative Institute. 2017. "Toward New Gravity: Charting a New Course for the Narrative Initiative." www.narrativeinitiative.org.
"Papa's Cache Sabroso." 2019. *Yelp*, www.yelp.com.
Pedro Albizu Campos Puerto Rican High School. 2019. "Steve Whitman Urban Agriculture." https://pachs-chicago.org.
Pedro Albizu Campos High School and Puerto Rican Cultural Center. 2011. *The Greening of a Food Desert: Building Community through Sustainable, Self-Sufficient Food Production.* www.scribd.com/; originally available at www2.illinois.gov.
Peña, Devon G., Luz Calvo, Panch McFarland, and Gabriel R. Valle. 2017. *Mexican Origin Foods, Foodways, and Social Movements.* Fayetteville: University of Arkansas Press.
Perez, Gina M. 2004. *The Near Northwest Side Story: Migration, Displacement, and Puerto Rican Families.* Berkeley: University of California Press.
Puerto Rican Cultural Center. 2013. *Puerto Rican Cultural Center.* http://prcc-chgo.org.
Puerto Rican Research Agenda. 2011. "60 Years of Migration: Puerto Ricans in Chicagoland." www.puertoricanchicago.org.
Rinaldo, Rachel. 2002. "Space of Resistance: The Puerto Rican Cultural Center and Humboldt Park." *Cultural Critique* 50: 135–174.
Rose, D. 2010. "Rethinking Gentrification: Beyond the Uneven Development of Marxist Urban Theory." In *The Gentrification Debates.* New York: Routledge, 195–210.
Slocum, Rachel. 2010. "Race in the Study of Food." *Progress in Human Geography* 35.3: 303–327.
Smith, Neil. 1996. *The New Urban Frontier: Gentrification and the Revanchist City.* New York: Routledge.
Tipsy Cake Local Interview. 2012. *YouTube.* Performed by Naomi Levine and Scott Starbuck. City Soles TV. www.youtube.com.
Unger, Tommy. 2014. "Hottest Neighborhoods of 2014." Redfin. www.redfin.com.
US Census: Race and Ethnicity in Humboldt Park, Chicago, Illinois. 2010. Statistical Atlas. https://statisticalatlas.com.
USDA. 2015. "Puerto Rico's Secretary of Agriculture Visits NIFA, Addresses Food Security Issues." https://nifa.usda.gov.
USDA. 2019. "Recovery Following Hurricanes Irma & Maria." www.nrcs.usda.gov.
Wilson, David, Jared Wouters, and Dennis Grammenos. 2004. "Successful Protect-Community Discourse: Spatiality and Politics in Chicago's Pilsen Neighborhood." *Environment and Planning* 36: 1173–1190.
Zukin, Sharon. 1991. "Gentrification as Market and Place." *Landscapes of Power: From Detroit to Disney World.* Berkeley: University of California Press, 187–195.

13

Black Urban Growers and the Land Question in Cleveland

Externalities of Gentrification

JUSTINE LINDEMANN

If you have land, you can plant . . . you can put a tent up . . . you can do anything if you've got some land.
—Louise, Cleveland, OH

In this city alone, there are over 3,300 acres of vacant land that is available for us to utilize—not contiguous plots, but sprinkled throughout. A little portion of our 40 acres is right next door.
—Gladys, Cleveland, OH

Most Black growers in Cleveland describe gardening or farming as more than just food production: While they certainly see themselves as producers and stewards of the land they work and live on, they also celebrate and educate younger generations about Black culture and an historical past rooted in a deeply agrarian and even spiritual relationship to that land. The majority of Cleveland's Black population has roots in the American South, with most either migrating directly from southern geographies, or having close relatives who undertook that migration. Producing food and working the land is a part of a specifically Black tradition and is most often described as such by Black farmers and gardeners. While this particular relationship to the land has not always been so predominant—as many of the "second-generation" migrants pushed back against the agrarian lifestyle in favor of grocery stores, already-prepared foods, and more "modern" lifestyle choices—there is a strong resurgence of Black agrarianism among residents of all ages in Cleveland, including the elders, many of whom have taken part in some form of food production for decades if not their entire lives.[1] In Cleveland as well as in other cities across the Rust Belt and beyond, urban agriculture, community gardening, and food production more broadly have become cultural, political, and spatial touchstones within the Black community. And not unlike other American cities, one of the main challenges to overcome in asserting urban food production as a viable strategy for urban resilience—or even subsistence—is in the struggle to establish an alternative way of living in the face of a hegemonic neoliberal valuation of urban space, which includes the land that growers need to access.

This chapter examines the relationship between a large-scale multi-sector transportation project in Cleveland and one of the impacted neighborhoods, Kinsman, that is also home to a 28-acre Urban Agriculture Innovation Zone (UAIZ), as well as several community gardens, agricultural projects, and residents keen on working the land and engaging in food production.[2] The Opportunity Corridor (OC) is a transportation project sponsored, supported, and designed by the Ohio Department of Transportation, the City of Cleveland, as well as several Community Development Corporations (CDCs) across the city. The project will connect a major highway interchange at East 55 Street with the University Circle neighborhood of Cleveland. Its path cuts through several east side neighborhoods and will dramatically change the dynamics of land use and land availability in these neighborhoods. In Cleveland's Ward 5, the Kinsman neighborhood coincides with the intended route of the OC and has already seen many of the impacts of the upcoming construction.

Within Kinsman, there is little risk for gentrification, as it is usually defined: as neighborhood upgrading or change (Hwang and Sampson 2014). Indeed, only the first part of Smith's (1998: 198) definition of gentrification—"the process by which central urban neighborhoods that have undergone disinvestments and economic decline experience a reversal, reinvestment, and the in-migration of a relatively well-off middle- and upper middle-class population"—obtains. Kinsman has not experienced significant in-migration or reinvestment, nor is it likely to in the near future. This area has some of the highest rates of vacant land across the city, as well as incredibly high rates of abandoned and vacant properties, many of which are scheduled for eventual demolition

(WRLC 2015). However, aside from "upgrading," gentrification often signals a series of racialized processes of capital accumulation across space (Perez 2002; see also chapter 10 in this volume). Hence, while the literature tends to limit gentrification to spatial shifts in population income and education level, many of the processes of capital accumulation, relocation of people, and uneven investment across space can—and do—produce externalities that have very real impacts on non-gentrifying communities.

The construction of the OC has ushered in what I am calling *gentrifying forces*, or the ancillary impacts of gentrification, within Kinsman. These mostly accrue benefits and profits to wealthier residents and businesses from other neighborhoods within the Cleveland area, and certainly from outside of Kinsman. The ancillary impacts of this transportation project have not been accompanied by any real indications of neighborhood upgrading, as one might expect to see with gentrification (Hwang and Sampson 2014: 727). The target neighborhood for the OC, University Circle, is the wealthiest neighborhood within the City of Cleveland and home to several anchor institutions, including Case Western Reserve University and the Cleveland Museum of Art. While University Circle has already undergone cycles of gentrification, the impacts of the OC—in facilitating the movement of commuters *through* low-income and marginalized neighborhoods *to* University Circle—engender a gentrifying effect that radiates to non-gentrifying areas. In Kinsman, these ancillary impacts include restricted access to vacant land, loss of property through "right of way acquisition" (OHDOT 2013), and the establishment of businesses that predominantly serve a wealthier population from outside, rather than inside, the neighborhood itself.

In short, this transportation project is in direct tension with the priorities of both Black growers within the community and the goals of the UAIZ: the capacity of residents to access land, to innovate through food production, and to engage in a production of space that values land, people, and community, while also promoting the well-being of an historically marginalized community. This chapter explores the sociospatial impacts of the Opportunity Corridor in particular, through the lens of how development processes affect historically marginalized areas not readily available for gentrification. I am interested in how residents perceive the project as well as the perspective of city planners and development officials.

My research relies mostly on personal interviews and meetings with Black growers, city officials, and community development practitioners, as well as hundreds of hours of participant observation.[3] I examine planning and policy documents concerning vacant land reuse and urban food production in Kinsman, as well as city and state policy relating directly to the OC project, vacant land use, and land management initiatives in Cleveland. While the specter of the OC has been highly influential in community members' understanding of the role of both government and city planners in determining how space is managed, planned, and allocated, only the beginnings of the route itself have been constructed in the easternmost part of the city. The next phase of construction—from the East 55 Street highway interchange through neighborhoods such as Kinsman—began in early May 2019 and is scheduled to last for two years. It remains to be seen how further construction will impact Kinsman residents and the extensive food production ventures within this neighborhood; however, the planning, preparation, and political interventions that occur as a part of the process are indicative of more deeply rooted trends of gentrification, racialization of space, land use politics, and what Smith (2002) has termed the "New Urbanism."

The OC also presents a useful case study to explore an important epistemic tension that exists between Black urban growers and the various arms of the state that they encounter: city planners, community development agencies, and other state officials, such as those working for the two land banks that govern the majority of vacant land within Cleveland. This tension can be described as a contestation over or struggle between value propositions for vacant urban land. This also manifests in competing understandings of development within cities. Community-based growth is often positioned in opposition to the dominant capitalist model of economic development, where traditional determinants of land use and value—the paradigm of "highest and best use"—are prioritized over more abstract use values or social reproduction.

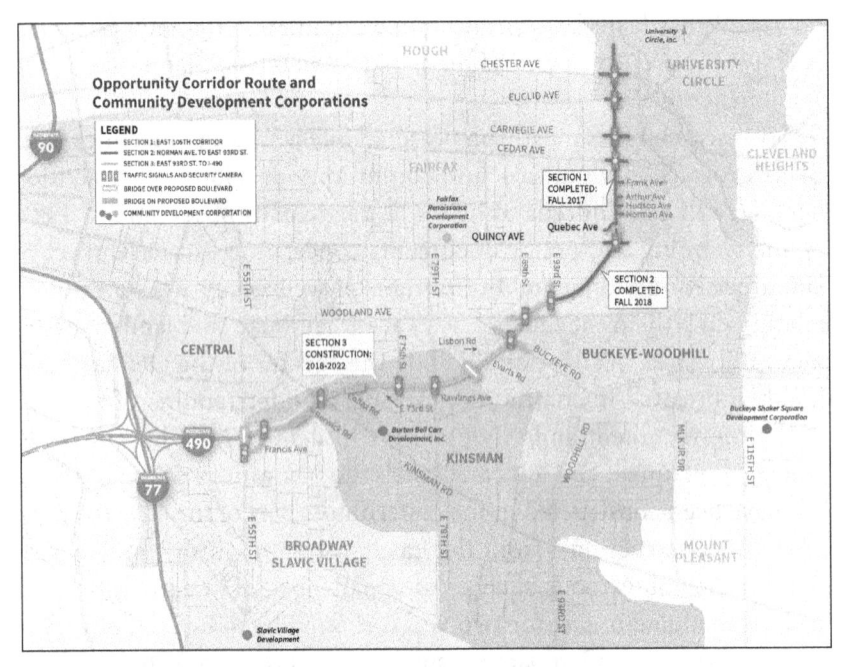

Figure 13.1. Opportunity Corridor Route and Community Development Corporations. Used with permission of the Greater Cleveland Partnership.

Historical Geographical Background

Cleveland—a city of approximately 389,000 people—boasted a population just over 910,000 in 1950. As in other Rust Belt cities like Detroit and Buffalo, the urban population has steadily decreased over the last seventy years, particularly exacerbated by the recent foreclosure crisis which devastated neighborhoods across Cleveland's east side. Such extensive population loss has also catalyzed an abundance of vacant land in the city. More than 3,300 acres of vacant land (almost 28,000 lots) are interspersed throughout Cleveland, with heavy concentrations on the historically Black and formerly redlined east side neighborhoods of Cleveland (WLRC 2015: 37). The east side—including Kinsman—is much more impoverished than the city as a whole and receives little economic investment from the city. In fact, neighborhoods identified by the Western Reserve Land Conservancy's land survey as having the highest percentage of D and F rated properties are all located on the east side of the city, as is most vacant land (WLRC 2015). A small influx of new residents has helped to offset (though not stall) the overall city-wide population loss; however, newcomers mostly reside in more affluent and predominantly white neighborhoods on Cleveland's west side and downtown areas.

Despite its geographical accessibility to both downtown and major highways, Kinsman is in a mostly neglected area on Cleveland's east side. Garden Valley, or lower Kinsman, is also called the Forgotten Triangle; it is one of the poorest areas in Cleveland. The 96 percent Black American neighborhood has an average per capita income of just over $14,000 with almost 30 percent unemployment, and both extremely low education attainment and extremely poor health indicators (US Census Bureau 2012–2016). More than half of Garden Valley receives federal food assistance, and many live in one of the more than 4,000 public housing units in the neighborhood. When a 1976 fire burned down more than sixty homes in Garden Valley, none of the residents had homeowners' insurance (Kerr 2012).[4] What was once a densely populated urban area evolved into a dumping ground for toxic and hazardous materials such as paint cans, old tires and cars, and everything from abandoned refrigerators to dead bodies. "Supermarket redlining" (Eisenhauer 2001), a relic of bank redlining practices, has left this area with no full-service grocery store, but with many businesses that benefit greatly from concentrated poverty, including check cashing stores, corner stores, and alcohol, tobacco, and lotto shops.

Over time, the neighborhood as a whole evolved as well: Families moved to other neighborhoods or out of the city entirely; more houses burned down or were demolished; and what had been a middle-class neighborhood with hundreds of families became the Forgotten Triangle. Garden Valley became overgrown with high shrubs and trees on vacant lots and behind crumbling buildings, tall grasses grew where houses used to sit. Brick streets and sidewalks buckled and crumbled from tree roots pushing their way up and out. This once densely populated neighborhood began to take on an eerily post-urban character with a decidedly rural and agrarian feel (see chapter 14 of this volume for more on abandonment, blight, and "forgotten places").

Despite the abundance of vacant land across the city and within the Kinsman neighborhood, the process of obtaining long-term leases or ownership of plots of land for use other than real estate development remains a challenge. Two separate land banks govern the majority of the vacant land, and the complex bureaucracies that regulate the conversion and sale of land are both understaffed and underfunded. Black growers that I interviewed expressed frustration about these bureaucratic processes and see a direct connection between their capacity to grow and produce food and the opacity and inefficiency of the state (Hilbrandt 2017). Marlisha described her frustration:

> If I come to you, and I want to get a parcel of land . . . the initial steps are just so cumbersome. They want you to sit down and submit a plan, and then they want you to go through all this written stuff as far as what you want (to do). And once we identified a (vacant) spot—it was already a garden, already fenced—guess what they told me when we came to put in our permit? "It's going to take about a year."

The time delay between locating vacant parcels and securing them for use is an oft-cited obstacle to becoming a gardener or obtaining land for other uses. There is little understanding of why it takes so much time either to obtain a lease or to learn that a parcel is unavailable to residents, despite lying vacant. Residents do have a sense, however, that the political aspect of land use and agricultural production is not always transparent, and that there are competing interests at play. Mansfield, a grower who has been involved in politics for quite some time, commented,

> Politics control, well, political decisions decimate the neighborhoods. So, this [farming] is a way of trying to rebuild neighborhoods. From that standpoint, it's highly political. And if you don't have the political clout . . . well, one of the reasons we're as successful as we are is that I know politics and how to play it.

The seeming opacity of, as another grower phrased it, "the politics and procedures" of city government often seems counter to the expressed commitment to urban food production and alternative land use policies. Don, one of the first Black farmers in Cleveland, owns the land he farms. In the context of current and potential development pressures, he explained just how valuable that is. "Everyone is trying to develop around me, and the city keeps trying to buy my land. But when I told them it would cost them $1 million, they laughed in my face."

Growing on Vacant Land: Perspective of the State

In addition to historical reliance on urban food production by city residents, urban agriculture has become an attractive option for vacant land reuse among government officials as well. An "urban garden district" zone was created in the late 2000s, adding a layer of protection against future real estate development for land under agricultural production. Similarly, "chickens and bees" legislation has allowed for the production of small livestock in both residential and commercial areas of the city. The UAIZ in Kinsman consists of the Rid-All Green Partnership Farm (7 acres), the Ohio State University Extension Incubator Farm (6 acres), and Green City Growers, (10 acres of land, 3 acres under greenhouse production), as well as several smaller community gardens and other small agricultural projects. While not zoned as such, agriculture is prioritized in this area, and supported (discursively, politically, and to an extent economically) by both city and development officials. This is in part due to a lack of traditional development prospects.

Urban agriculture and other alternative land uses have been supported by city officials for the last several years, with a variety of organizations and groups developing strategies for vacant land reuse (Cleveland City Planning Commission 2013). The Cleveland Cuyahoga County Food Policy Coalition (CCCFPC) was convened in 2007 as a partnership between The Ohio State University Extension, the City of Cleveland, and several non-profits, CDCs, and other key stakeholders in the city as a facilitated process through which to provide leadership and guidance on food policy–related issues in Cleveland and the surrounding county. The zoning policies creating agricultural districts and regulating the production of chickens and bees resulted from the work of the CCCFPC, although they have not been put into widespread use. In 2012, the City Office of Sustainability focused on local food—including production—as part of their Sustainable 2019 Initiative; the City Council passed a Local and Sustainable Purchasing ordinance (City of Cleveland

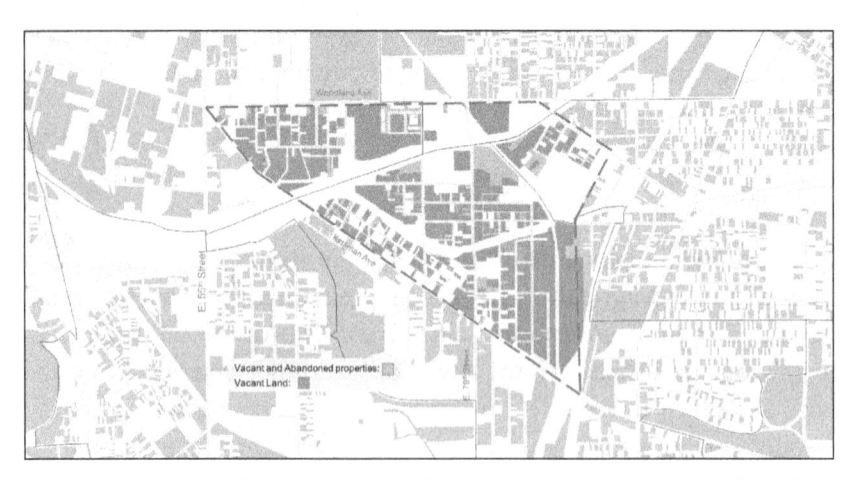

Figure 13.2. Vacant Land and Structures in the Forgotten Triangle. GIS Data from the US Census Bureau and the Western Reserve Land Conservancy, via NEO CANDO, Center on Urban Poverty and Community Development at Case Western Reserve University.

2013). The several planners I interviewed emphasized their support of urban gardening and farming as a definitive asset to the city, including both the current planning director, who described the planning process as producing space that is "reflective of (both) the needs and challenges within the community."

Cleveland reflects the (re)emergence of urban agriculture as politically popular within cities across the country. This is common during times of economic downturn (Salvidar-Tanaka and Krasny 2004), which characterizes not only the recent Great Recession, but also the last several decades of deindustrialization in Rust Belt cities, including Cleveland. Contingent support of alternative land use aligns with the perspective of many of Cleveland's city planners, who are eager to support urban agriculture and food production, but only insofar as there are no other development prospects on the horizon. The Opportunity Corridor, running just north of the UAIZ through Kinsman, presents an interesting example of how the promise of development can impact the value (current or potential) of land, and thus its approved uses, all without necessarily benefiting or "upgrading" impacted areas in any direct or immediate way.

Black Urban Growers in Cleveland: An Epistemic Divide

Black gardeners and farmers conceive of growing food in an epistemically distinct way from city officials and development practitioners. For growers, food production is an integral part of the path to social, economic, political, and spiritual liberation. While community gardens (and most urban farms) do not create significant revenue, they produce urban spaces that draw upon southern rural histories and traditions; they bring marginalized communities together in solidarity; they lead to increased biological and cultural diversity within marginalized urban space (Colding and Barthel 2013); and they contest many of the negative—often racialized—images ascribed to those spaces. The east side of Cleveland is composed of historically Black neighborhoods that, to this day, struggle to overcome the institutionalized marginalization and segregation that materialized during the time of the Great Black Migration. When asked about their background in farming, most research participants draw upon family histories in the American South—Alabama, Mississippi, Georgia—as either a direct influence in their reconnection with the soil, or as a distant memory informing the work that they do.

Louise, an older Black farmer with whom I spent a lot of time, frequently stresses the need for "many hands" to take part in the labor-intensive work of growing, preserving, and cooking food: a commentary on the necessity of community in the Black urban food movement. For the majority of growers that I interviewed, building community constitutes more than just people working the soil together; it includes fostering a spiritual connection to the soil, planting and nurturing the intellectual and ideological inspiration to engage more deeply with socio-natural processes, and to promote a more capacious idea of "development" within urban areas such as the Forgotten Triangle. Gladys, who has been gardening almost her entire life, and considers herself to be an elder within the Black population of growers in Cleveland, expressed it this way: "[W]hen we get our elders out there, and we get our youth out there, I don't even have to worry about them getting healed because Mother Nature's got that." Her perspective is rooted in the power of gardening to heal historical, social, and spatial traumas that the Black community in Cleveland—and elsewhere—have faced, which speaks to "the power of the garden (and) the power of food, period. I want my people to have a better quality of life. I want them to be able to stay here; they have a purpose here."

These more abstract use values cited by Black urban growers contribute to something outside of the traditional capitalist economy and social reproduction that is only intermittently recognized by city planners and officials. Traditional determinants of land use and metrics of success for land use projects typically follow the paradigm of "highest and best use," aligning with a hegemonic neoliberal urbanism and prioritizing real estate and taxable value as a part of a political-economic system governed by profit and growth (Angotti 2015). The city planner for the Kinsman neighborhood explained, "We do encourage (urban gardening), however, we encourage it in specific areas . . . Mainly because of the fact that we are concerned with maintaining our tax base, which is necessary for us to function." According to Amina, an urban farmer just outside of the Kinsman neighborhoods, "[L]ocal politicians, they don't get urban farming. They know how to build bricks and mortar things of that nature. They don't make the connection that urban farming can create jobs, because they haven't seen it happen yet." The economic growth potential of urban farming, according to most Black growers, is embedded in the social relations that uphold the community rather than ever-expanding development ideals. Mansfield commented:

> [W]ealth should stay in the community. Grown in the community, sold in the community, taxed and profit then go towards community corporations to see what benefits (there are), and then decide what you want to do . . . to help your community with the money you're making in your community.

The emphasis is on a hyperlocal community, and communal benefit in a concrete sense. The more abstract neoliberal attempts to achieve the highest possible value for land often occur at the expense of alternative land use projects, and are "a heavy burden for movements concerned with use value" (Purcell 2008: 21).

This epistemic divide between Black growers and city officials represents something of an impasse between the fiscal necessity of increasing the dwindling tax base in Cleveland and the civic responsibility of serving the residents who currently live in neighborhoods across the city. Residents—especially gardeners and farmers—often have deep connections to and a desire for some control over the spaces around them (Weber 2002), including sovereignty over the nutritional, health, and cultural facets of their lives. Notwithstanding, just as city planners recognize the necessity of alternative land use as something that, as Kinsman's city planner said, "needs to be integrated within the community," most Black growers do not eschew capitalist economic relations altogether. The majority of growers want to be paid for their work, want access to resources such as land, seeds, healthy soil, and tools, as well as access to markets (including farmers' markets, grocery stores, and restaurants), and would like to see more philanthropic and government investment in their work. These overlapping interests provide points of engagement between growers and city officials. However, the planning paradigm within the city remains centered around maximizing both tax revenue and profit, limiting the possibilities of long-term alternative land use strategies, while most Black growers engage with community on an ideological and spiritual level that transcends pure economic relations.

Urban Renewal: Revitalization, Gentrification, and the Land Question

In Cleveland, as in many other American cities, large-scale transportation projects such as the Opportunity Corridor began with the Federal-Aid Highway Act of 1956. This Act helped to fund the construction of interstate systems across the United States, including I-90, built across the northern part of Cleveland beginning in the 1950s. In the 1960s, another major freeway project was proposed that would have cut through several eastern suburbs; however, widespread protests among the relatively affluent residents garnered the political will to block these efforts, and those communities remain free of any major highway system. Urban planning "best practices" now question the construction of raised highways through urban areas. Modern transportation projects—like the OC—are often conceived of as street-level projects, with both pedestrian-friendly amenities and commercial opportunities in the impacted neighborhoods. The OC was originally proposed in 2008, but official planning did not begin until 2014, and phase two of construction (which cuts through Kinsman) is expected to be completed by 2020 (Litt 2016; Neff 2008).

Many neighborhood residents are skeptical about the actual benefits and impact of the OC to the neighborhoods through which it will be built. The rhetorical question often posed by research participants in relation to the transportation project is, "Opportunity for *what*?" or "Opportunity for *who*?" There is frustration at the lack of focus on urban blight and green space in favor of commercial development. Growers are critical of patterns of development that coincide with large-scale infrastructure projects, and they desire to see the city work with already-existing structures rather than building something new, which could simultaneously privilege alternative land use and promote increased food production. The following quote from AJ, a Black grower in Kinsman, exemplifies this perspective:

> I think that if the City would be a little bit more open to doing something different instead of doing stuff the same old way, they would find that you have a lot of people that would do a lot more. You know, but it depends on what their agenda is. What their agenda is and our agenda. So, it's hard, we're going to butt heads, because we wanna grow food and you wanna build apartment buildings. Why don't you just rehab fifty houses and we could still grow food. Stuff like that. Something's gotta change.

These voices suggest that growers don't view development projects as beneficial to residents or their neighborhood, but rather see different motivations behind construction, such as the convenience and value to other city inhabitants. The OC mostly serves people from other neighborhoods or commuters from outside the city. The skepticism stems in part from the demolition of houses and the relocation of businesses and residents that is associated with the project. The director of a major food pantry said that in Kinsman alone more than thirty residential units were demolished years before construction was scheduled to begin in that area. While demolishing houses is nothing new to Cleveland, and thousands of vacant and abandoned structures have been razed as part of a federally supported strategy to prevent further housing foreclosures (Rosenman and Walker 2015), the demolition of intact residences and forced relocation of businesses is reminiscent of post-war urban renewal policies, which, in Cleveland, also began and were largely concentrated in the Garden Valley neighborhood of Kinsman (Michney 2011).

Urban renewal and revitalization have long been key parts of Cleveland's development strategy to mobilize increased real estate development within low-income communities and communities of color (Michney 2011; Weber 2002). The historical precedent for urban renewal within the majority Black Kinsman neighborhood dates to the first urban renewal project in Cleveland in 1961 (Kerr 2011; Michney 2011). These projects, while intending to attract middle-class Black families into the neighborhood, in effect produced areas of concentrated Black poverty where renters cycled in and out of over-priced housing that they could not consistently afford. Like the proposed highway projects in Cleveland's eastern suburbs, urban renewal efforts of the early 1960s were met with resident pushback—mostly due to noise and safety issues—which was only ever partially addressed by the city. The tragic death of a child during construction and the violent repression of the mostly peaceful resident protests demonstrate how violence was deployed against Black bodies and in Black spaces during this period of Cleveland's history (Michney 2011).

As one of the most impoverished areas of the city with very low population density relative to the rest of Cleveland, some city and state officials see Kinsman as the most logical location for the construction of the OC. Like urban renewal, this approach to spatial urban management curates the urban aesthetic for the outside (white) gaze, while also working to protect wealthier urban areas from characteristics of impoverished urban space such as vacant, neglected, and abandoned structures and land (Wilson 2007). Not unlike patterns of urban renewal, the OC represents a spatial policy and project that ultimately strives to manage and direct the movement of people and capital though the city. It is not lost on residents who the ultimate beneficiaries of this project are.

Newer food businesses in Kinsman are generally not patronized by Kinsman residents because they are too expensive; however, they are visited by OC construction workers, CDC staff, and other people who work in the neighborhood but do not live there. Another part of the OC construction includes street front improvement projects to beautify specific areas of neighborhoods with a high percentage of dilapidated and abandoned buildings. Beautification and relocation projects rarely consider that which lies beyond the aesthetic or pragmatic aspects of the project. One research participant questioned the decision of the Opportunity Corridor planning team to tear down the building of a business that had been in the neighborhood for decades. She asked, "Was that the intended result of the Opportunity Corridor? To take a business that's been here forever and ever and that's stable, and tear down their building and move them?" In other words, it is not only intense land management and the production of a particular kind of urban space or value, but also managing the public gaze as it moves through "ghetto" areas (Wilson 2007). This tacit aspect of the politics of the OC thus mirrors slum clearance and urban renewal policies of the past.

Skepticism around the project extends beyond the methods and motivation, but there also exists a sense of frustration over the seemingly endless "revitalization" and "development" projects that have been prioritized in some form for decades. Jayla, a Cleveland resident who has worked in Kinsman for several years, points out, "[T]hey just built this huge parking structure. A *huge* parking structure (in University Circle) . . . for all these cars . . . (they) built this road to drive you right here to this parking structure." Residents often see these projects as impediments to other potential initiatives that might create more access to land and other resources in the neighborhood or have a deeper and more holistic impact on neglected communities. Among research participants there is the perception that the city holds onto vacant land, or vacant and abandoned structures, without allowing residents access, as if they are enclosing what could otherwise become a sort of urban commons. A self-described community activist described it this way:

> If you drive around, you see abandoned land, warehouses, and properties across the city. They hold onto the properties so that no one can use them, and wait until the time is right to tear them down. Then they build something there that maybe no one who previously lived there can afford.

In Kinsman, the OC has contributed to this tendency of city officials to hold onto particular parcels, inherently preventing residents from obtaining land for food production. The "Sustainable Development Pattern Map" drawn by the City Planning Commission outlines prioritized development areas: neighborhoods and communities that have been set aside for their potential to accumulate value through future development. Prioritized development areas comprise 32 square miles, or 41 percent of the city's land. Vacant land within or directly adjacent to prioritized areas is no longer accessible to residents. Gladys labeled this process a land grab. She stressed that Black growers—who rarely have the individual or collective resources to acquire significant amounts of land—are left to navigate the often-opaque contours of the two land banks, the Planning Commission, and the CDCs who exert control over much of the city's land. "We have to ask the city to use plots of land. But I also know that certain entities are coming in and buying up land. . . . That's what's going on. There's a land grab going on. . . . It's unfortunate that we—the indigenous people—are not in the position to stave it off."

The Sustainable Development Pattern Map includes a wide radius of prioritized areas alongside the OC, including much of Kinsman and the UAIZ. Despite the lack of development planned for much of the land within Kinsman—and outside of the direct pathway of the OC—parcels remain within the footprint of prioritized development. This approach to urban development is designed to achieve important financial and spatial goals, including increased tax revenue, improved urban density, and growing investment in the city. However, "prioritized development areas" that do not coincide with areas under development or receiving investment remain neglected by the city and inaccessible for alternative use. The coincidence of development priority areas with the UAIZ perfectly highlights the contradictions within the dominant urban planning paradigm: Alternative land use and urban agriculture are valued by city officials, but only insofar as they don't currently—or potentially in the future—overlap with areas of possible real estate development.

In response to resident pushback against the OC, the CDCs and city planners have made efforts to engage directly with residents on this project: to ask questions about the kinds of business and job creation

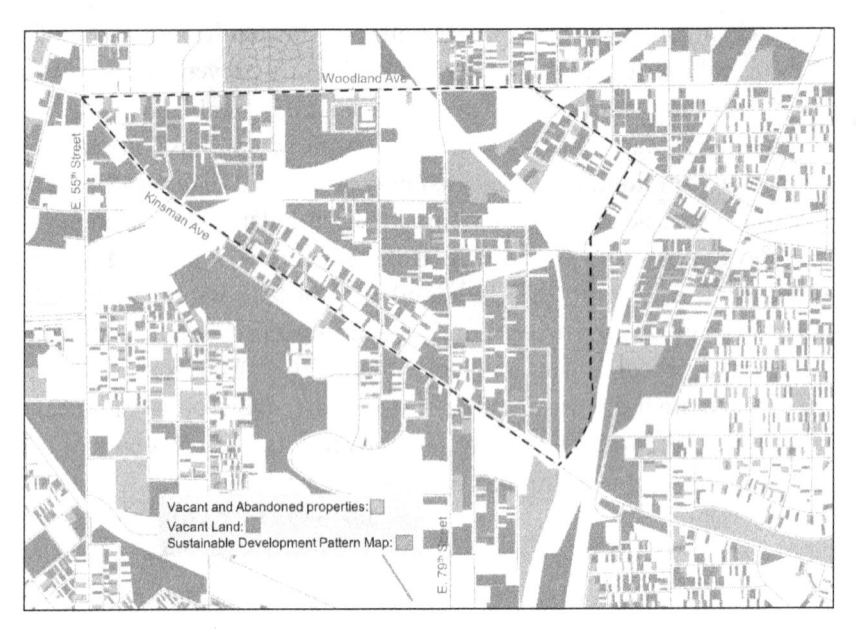

Figure 13.3. Vacant Structures and Land as they coincide with the Sustainable Development Pattern Map. GIS Data from the US Census Bureau and the Western Reserve Land Conservancy, via NEO CANDO, Center on Urban Poverty and Community Development at Case Western Reserve University.

they would like to see, and to create stipulations and community guidelines for the ways in which the OC develops throughout the Kinsman neighborhood (and other impacted neighborhoods). One tangible contribution to the community was evident in improvements to a community recreation center (OHDOT 2013). However, the epistemic divide in land management and valuation remains: The paradigm of "highest and best use" has not been significantly unsettled. Kinsman has some of the highest concentrations of vacant land in Cleveland, and strategic land assembly remains central to development practices within this area. Jason, a CDC employee, reasoned that

> This neighborhood, this particular part of the Opportunity Corridor, *does* have a lot of vacant land. Just blocks and blocks where there's one house, two houses, so I feel like it's the least disruptive because this neighborhood has already been decimated for all sorts of other reasons.

Conclusion

The continued gentrification and persistent development of already-wealthy areas of Cleveland, including University Circle, has important impacts on historically and spatially marginalized neighborhoods within the city. Alternative ways of living and being in the city struggle to take root, and long-standing traditions and practices of Black urban agrarianism are threatened. As long as land is valued and mapped as potential tax revenue and set aside for the future commodification as such, Black urban growers will only have intermittent and contingent access to land, a key resource. Amina, a Black grower close to Kinsman, said, "You can 'hear' gentrification all through this community. [The CDCs] are not worried about sustainability, and they're not worried about urban gardens." Her understanding of these processes goes beyond land access to the larger role the CDCs play within the community:

> The CDCs work with [the gentrifiers], I believe. So we're not getting what we need. But developers are getting what they want, and it's, you know ... they should be helping [us]. If we need soil, and stuff like that, which I do need soil—even if I had to pay a reduced price, that's fine. Just tell me what I gotta do. I don't mind paying a little bit [for soil]. . . . Say the CDC or somebody rents a truck or leases it so we go get all these piles of manure. Goat manure, whatever. That's the kind of stuff they should be doing. But they don't wanna do that. And we don't have dump trucks.

This resident's awareness of the priorities of Community Development Corporations and the City more broadly, and the direct impacts of uneven development on her ability to access necessary resources, are key to understanding the important impacts of gentrifying forces in non-gentrifying areas. The widespread perception of neglect and abandonment that Black subjects feel in light of projects such as the OC is perhaps the most significant externality of gentrification and uneven development in the city.

NOTES

Most names have been changed to protect the privacy of research participants. While there are some names that, at the request of participants, have not been changed, I use only first names throughout.

1   This can be seen in the efforts of different groups of Black growers in Cleveland to organize themselves into cooperative structures; in the emergence of almost one hundred high tunnels (mostly in the predominantly Black east side of Cleveland) funded by the USDA and the Federation of Southern Cooperatives; in the several hundred community gardens supported by The Ohio State University Extension's (OSUe) Summer Sprouts program as well as the proliferation of small grants for community gardens and other agricultural projects through a community-based grants program; and in the interest of Black youth in agriculture programs such as Green Corps (Cleveland Botanical Gardens), whose three urban farms are located in predominantly Black neighborhoods.

2   The UAIZ was established by the local Community Development Corporation, Burten, Bell, Carr, Inc. (BBC), together with the OSUe on 28 acres of mostly vacant land as a way to prioritize urban agricultural innovation and food production. The CDC's purpose in facilitating this zone includes "plann(ing) and prepar(ing) for future development" and "assembl(ing) privately owned land" (Burten, Bell, Carr Inc.). BBC controls and manages access to most of the 28 acres.

3   Over the course of more than two years of field research in Cleveland, I completed just over fifty individual interviews, as well as attended several dozen community and organizational meetings. I am also involved in a resident-led grant project in the Garden Valley neighborhood of Kinsman, which has contributed ethnographic methods to my understanding of the neighborhood's socio-political and spatial dynamics.

4   A "redlining map" sponsored by the Home Owners Loan Corporation from 1934 labeled this particular area as "hazardous." The entirety of the Kinsman neighborhood (as well as most bordering neighborhoods) were redlined, creating areas where banks would not approve loans for home purchases or improvements. Redlining maps were also racialized; predominantly Black neighborhoods were redlined (D), mixed Black and Jewish neighborhoods were either marked in red or yellow (C), while white neighborhoods were given a green (A) or blue (B) rating.

REFERENCES

Angotti, Thomas. 2015. "Urban Agriculture: Long-Term Strategy or Impossible Dream? Lessons from Prospect Farm in Brooklyn, New York." *Public Health* 129(4):336–41.

City of Cleveland. 2013. "Local Foods and Sustainable Business." Office of Sustainability. www.city.cleveland.oh.us.

Cleveland City Planning Commission. 2013. "8 Ideas for Vacant Land Re-Use in Cleveland." Cleveland, Ohio.

Cleveland Cuyahoga County Food Policy Coalition (CCCFPC). 2010. "History and Structure." The Ohio State University Extension. http://cccfoodpolicy.org.

Colding, Johan and Stephan Barthel. 2013. "The Potential of 'Urban Green Commons' in the Resilience Building of Cities." *Ecological Economics* 86:156–66.

Eisenhauer, Elizabeth. 2001. "In Poor Health: Supermarket Redlining and Urban Nutrition." *GeoJournal* 53(2):125–33.

Fiskio, Janet and Vel Scott. 2016. "Cultivating Community: Black Agrarianism in Cleveland, Ohio." *Gastronomica: The Journal of Critical Food Studies* 16(2):18–30.

Hilbrandt, Hanna. 2017. "Everyday Urbanism and the Everyday State: Negotiating Habitat in Allotment Gardens in Berlin." *Urban Studies* 56(2):352–67.

Hwang, Jackelyn and Robert J. Sampson. 2014. "Divergent Pathways of Gentrification: Racial Inequality and the Social Order of Renewal in Chicago Neighborhoods." *American Sociological Review* 79(4):726–51.

Kerr, Daniel R. 2011. *Derelict Paradise: Homelessness and Urban Development in Cleveland, Ohio*. Amherst: University of Massachusetts Press.

Kerr, Daniel R. 2012. "Who Burned Cleveland, Ohio? The Forgotten Fires of the 1970s." In *Flammable Cities: Urban Conflagration and the Making of the Modern World*, edited by Greg Bankoff, Uwe Lübken, and Jordan Sand, 332–52. Madison: University of Wisconsin Press.

Litt, Steven. 2016. "Milwaukee Project Highlights What's Missing in Opportunity Corridor Planning." *Cleveland Plain Dealer*, June 23, www.cleveland.com.

Litt, Steven. 2017. "Cleveland to Roll Out Opportunity Corridor Plans Showing How Neighborhoods Could Benefit." *Cleveland Plain Dealer*, July 3, www.cleveland.com.

Michney, Todd M. 2011. "White Civic Visions Versus Black Suburban Aspirations: Cleveland's Garden Valley Urban Renewal Project." *Journal of Planning History* 10(4):282–309.

Neff, Martha Mueller. 2008. "Cleveland's Opportunity Corridor Project Gets Back on Track." *Cleveland Plain Dealer*, June 27, http://blog.cleveland.com.

Ohio Department of Transportation (OHDOT). 2013. "Cleveland Opportunity Corridor Project Overview." www.dot.state.oh.us.

Perez, Gina M. 2002. "The Other 'Real World': Gentrification and the Social Construction of Place in Chicago." *Urban Anthropology and Studies of Cultural Systems and World Economic Development* 31(1):37–68.

Purcell, Mark. 2008. *Recapturing Democracy: Neoliberalization and the Struggle for Alternative Urban Futures*. New York and London: Routledge.

Rosenman, Emily and Samuel Walker. 2015. "Tearing Down the City to Save It? 'Back-Door Regionalism' and the Demolition Coalition in Cleveland, Ohio." *Environment and Planning A* 48(2):273–91.

Saldivar-Tanaka, Laura and Marianne E. Krasny. 2004. "Culturing Community Development, Neighborhood Open Space, and Civic Agriculture: The Case of Latino Community Gardens in New York City." *Agriculture and Human Values* 21(4):399–412.

Smith, Neil. 1998. "Gentrification." In *The Encyclopedia of Housing*, edited by W. V. Vliet, 198–99. New York: Taylor & Francis.

Smith, Neil. 2002. "New Globalism, New Urbanism: Gentrification as Global Urban Strategy." *Antipode* 34(3):427–50.

US Census Bureau/American FactFinder. 2012–2016. "DP05: ACS Demographic and Housing Estimates." *American Community Survey 5-Year Estimates*. US Census Bureau's American Community Survey Office, 2016. http://factfinder.census.gov.

Weber, Rachel. 2002. "Extracting Value from the City: Neoliberalism and Urban Redevelopment." *Antipode* 34(3):519–40.

Western Reserve Land Conservancy (WRLC). 2015. "Cleveland Neighborhoods by the Numbers: 2015 Cleveland Property Inventory." Cleveland, OH.

Wilson, David. 2007. "City Transformation and the Global Trope: Indianapolis and Cleveland." *Globalizations* 4(1):29–44.

14

Citified Sovereignty

Cultivating Autonomy in South Los Angeles

ANALENA HOPE HASSBERG

Revolution is based on land. Land is the basis of all independence. Land is the basis of freedom, justice and equality.
—Malcolm X

If we don't have land as a group of people, we don't have any power. . . . When we lose our land, we're also losing a part of our history. We're losing a part of our identity in that community.
—John Boyd, National Black Farmers Association Founder

In January 1865, Union General William T. Sherman had an unprecedented meeting with twenty Black Baptist and Methodist ministers in Savannah, Georgia, to ask them what the Negro community most wanted and needed post-emancipation. Their answer, land, became the basis for General Sherman's now infamous Special Field Orders No. 15, which declared that "not more than (40) forty acres of tillable ground" would be "reserved and set apart for the settlement of the negroes now made free by the acts of war and the proclamation of the President of the United States" (Darity 2008).[1] The directive also specified that in this territory, "no white person whatever, unless military officers and soldiers detailed for duty, will be permitted to reside; and *the sole and exclusive management of affairs will be left to the freed people themselves*" (ibid., emphasis added).

To be clear, General Sherman's intent was not to reprieve newly emancipated Africans but rather to punish Confederate planters, and the land redistribution applied specifically to the 400,000 acres along the

Florida, South Carolina, and Georgia coastlines. Still, it was unheard of at the time and downright revolutionary to include Black people in conversations about their own needs and future, and to propose an autonomous, self-governed Black space in a hostile society where Black people were, according to the Supreme Court's 1857 Dred Scott Decision, "so far inferior that they had no rights which the white man was bound to respect" (Taney 1857). After the assassination of Abraham Lincoln in April 1865, incoming President Andrew Johnson swiftly overturned General Sherman's directive and returned the land to Confederate planters, "the very people who had declared war on the United States of America" (Gates 2013). Since then, the phrase *40 acres and a mule* has lived on in the African American lexicon and imagination as a reminder that no reparations—economic or symbolic—have been made to former slaves or their descendants as restitution for the centuries of enslavement and subjugation that built this nation's wealth.

For Black Americans, the transition from *being* property to *owning* property has been fraught with challenges and barriers. Instead of safety nets and social protections to support their transition into American society, the post-emancipation period introduced discriminatory laws and structural policies that would prevent most African Americans from gaining solid economic, political, or social standing in the United States (DuBois 1935; Alexander 2012). Sharecropping and tenant farming arrangements kept newly emancipated Black people indebted to plantation owners through unfair credit arrangements, while Black Codes and later, Jim Crow Laws cemented Black second-class citizenship. Since 1900, the number of Black farmers has plummeted, due in large part to the US Department of Agriculture's inequitable lending practices (Allen and Wilson 2013). Black families were particularly hard hit by the mortgage crisis of the early 2000s, and as a group, Black people are more likely to rent than to own their homes due to decades of systematic discrimination and segregation in the housing market, leaving them with less equity and wealth to pass on to future generations (Rugh and Massey 2010). Although land has long been central to Black life and livelihood (see chapter 13 in this volume), Black Americans have also always had a fraught and precarious relationship to the land and to the spaces we inhabit.

Presently, increasing numbers of Black and other low-income city dwellers are being forced from their homes and communities due to gentrification and redevelopment projects, demonstrating that landownership still translates into political and economic agency, decision-making power, and the opportunity to build and reproduce wealth and equity. People who rent or are housing insecure find that important neighborhood decisions—like the presence or absence of affordable housing and healthful sustainable food—are made without them as they struggle to meet basic needs such as paying bills, feeding their families, and getting to and from (often low-wage) work with limited or unreliable transportation. As evidenced throughout this volume, the foodscape is a major indicator of a neighborhood in flux: Areas once deemed too blighted to host a Trader Joe's or Whole Foods Market become imbued with new value for businesses and investors as new, mostly (but not solely) white bodies enter marginalized spaces. As chapter 8 in this volume demonstrates, gentrification and urban spatial development are largely the result of municipalities offering tax exemptions and other incentives to attract private industry with its accompanying jobs and revenue. In historically underserved neighborhoods, the arrival of cold-pressed juiceries, full-scale supermarkets, and organic restaurants are food-based markers of privilege and capital that signal an impending demographic shift that is often accompanied by the displacement of long-standing residents by way of rising living costs. Ironically, the people most in need of these long-awaited neighborhood amenities can rarely afford to stay and enjoy them once they come about.

For the descendants of enslaved Africans and other persecuted groups, waiting for redress and respite from state or federal governments—the symbolic 40 acres and a mule—has been mostly in vain. Instead, community-based resistance efforts that circumvent traditional political channels can be more effective at improving group health and livelihood. This chapter highlights efforts to create autonomous community landownership as a strategic form of spatial resistance to the rapid and often violent displacement that accompanies gentrification processes and demographic shifts within low-income urban communities of color. Using food as a lens and South Los Angeles as a site of inquiry, I explore the extent to which autonomy and self-governance are possible in what anthropologist Devon Peña (2003) would call "already-made" places: rigidly structured cities with a complex set of geographical, political, and economic conditions like privatized land and resources.

Desert or Deserted? The South Los Angeles Foodscape

Like other urban communities of color, South Los Angeles is grossly underserved by healthy food retail of any kind, from grocery stores to healthy restaurants (see figure 14.1). The food outlets that do exist in South Los Angeles are far less likely to provide options that enable individuals to meet dietary recommendations. There are hundreds of liquor stores and fast food joints, and the few grocery stores in the region are notorious for selling fruits and vegetables that are perpetually on the verge of spoiling. Organic and local ingredients are almost completely absent. In pursuit of healthier food, many South Los Angeles residents regularly leave the neighborhood to shop, incurring the additional costs of transportation and travel time, and increasing the carbon footprint of shoppers and of the food itself, which has likely traveled thousands of miles before landing on a supermarket shelf (Halweil 2002). Shopping in other communities also produces severe retail drainage by funneling money out of the already economically strapped region.[2]

The South Los Angeles foodscape has gained scholarly and popular attention in recent years, particularly with regard to the problem of the American *food desert*: a term that denotes an area where healthy food is scarce. Well-intended outsiders have come to South Los Angeles in droves, intent on saving helpless local residents from their food and health woes. The problem with this brand of altruism (and with the term *food desert* itself) is that it implies scarcity rather than abundance and portrays regions like South Los Angeles as hopeless places, filled with victims in need of rescue rather than agents who can (and regularly do) transform their own food environment. Epidemiologist George Kaplan (2006) points out that the word *desert*, when used as a noun, refers to a place that is barren, unfruitful, and devoid. Like the term *blight*, it qualifies the place rather than the processes that have shaped it. However, when used as a verb, *desert* means to abandon, leave, or turn one's back on. In South Los Angeles and other underserved inner cities, blighted areas become vulnerable to condemnation of homes and businesses, or being uprooted by the construction of freeways or rail lines. In a similar way, using *food desert* as a noun can inadvertently fuel and sustain redevelopment and gentrification processes that displace and uproot long-term residents.

FEAST OR FAMINE
The Glaring Inequality in Healthy Food Access

Healthy eating is not simply a matter of personal choice. Some communities have a bounty of healthy food options while others don't. Where you live can determine your health and quality of life.

SOUTH L.A.
population* 1,009,550

WEST L.A.
population* 637,129

HEALTH STATUS *
South L.A. vs West L.A.

SOUTH L.A. ADULTS ARE **2X** less likely to eat five or more servings of fruits and vegetables a day than adults in West L.A.

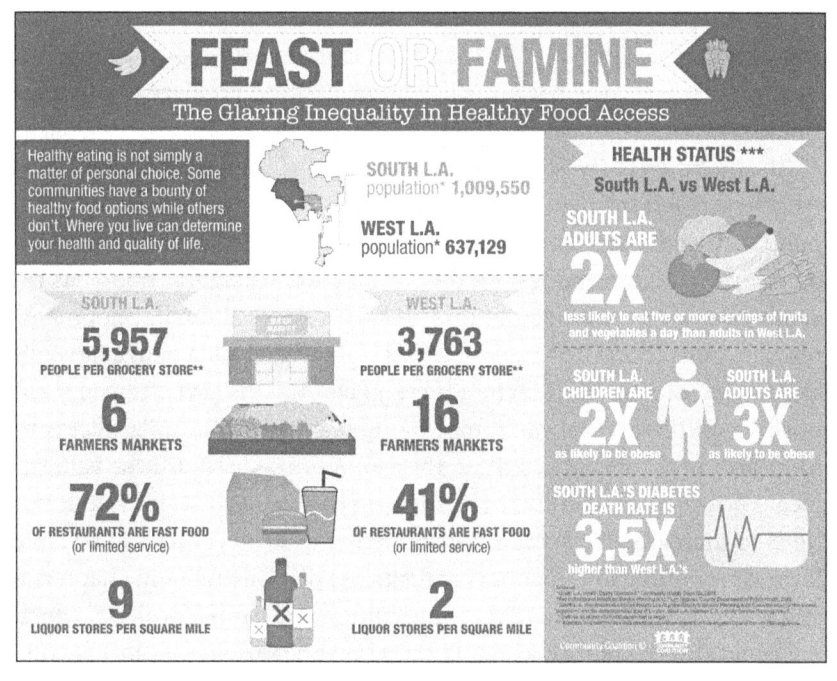

SOUTH L.A.
5,957 PEOPLE PER GROCERY STORE**
6 FARMERS MARKETS
72% OF RESTAURANTS ARE FAST FOOD (or limited service)
9 LIQUOR STORES PER SQUARE MILE

WEST L.A.
3,763 PEOPLE PER GROCERY STORE**
16 FARMERS MARKETS
41% OF RESTAURANTS ARE FAST FOOD (or limited service)
2 LIQUOR STORES PER SQUARE MILE

SOUTH L.A. CHILDREN ARE **2X** as likely to be obese
SOUTH L.A. ADULTS ARE **3X** as likely to be obese

SOUTH L.A.'S DIABETES DEATH RATE IS **3.5X** higher than West L.A.'s

Figure 14.1. Feast or Famine: The Glaring Inequality in Healthy Food Access. Community Coalition. 2013. *Infographic*. Source: Community Coalition.

Using *desertion* as a verb helps to reduce victim-blame and illuminate the structural processes that have produced the uneven foodscape, such as redlining, white outmigration, restrictive covenants, predatory lending, supermarket flight, and privileging corporate and private rather than community ownership (Mascarenhas 1997; Squires 2004; Crowder and South 2008). South Los Angeles is what Gilmore (2008) would call a *forgotten place*: one that has "experienced the abandonment characteristic of contemporary capitalist and neoliberal state reorganization." Indeed, South Los Angeles is a food desert, not because of a cultural or human deficiency, but rather because it has been underdeveloped and deliberately deserted on a number of occasions by industries and policies that make other parts of the city so much more livable. For instance, Lee (1998) posits that during the 1950s, an influx of large supermarkets forced many small South Los Angeles grocery retailers out of business completely, and the ones that remained open shifted from grocery to liquor sales to make a profit. These same supermarkets later fled the area themselves after the Watts and LA Uprisings in 1965 and 1992 respectively, leaving the region with almost no food retailers for decades (ibid.).

The intentional divestment and historical abandonment of South Los Angeles has left the region physically dilapidated and economically and politically weakened. In a cruel and ironic twist, after being flooded with guns, drugs, liquor, and fast food for decades, the neighborhood has recently become a desirable site for private investors and redevelopment/revitalization efforts designed to strategically shape and change the built and social environment. While these place-making projects can yield positive and beneficial outcomes by increasing community access to food, arts, and cultural activities, they sometimes disregard the value of local knowledge and culture (Bedoya 2013). Redevelopment also functions to increase property values and living costs beyond an affordable level for longtime low-income residents. As demonstrated in chapters 8 and 11 of this volume, even urban agriculture and garden projects, which are generally thought of as being social justice–oriented, can inadvertently (or intentionally) gentrify neighborhoods by bringing in newcomers whose presence and capital contribute to higher housing costs, housing shortages, and feelings of alienation among locals.

Citified Sovereignty: Autonomous Urban Food Systems in Los Angeles

Growing your own has become a rallying cry of alternative food movements in opposition to an oppressive corporate food system. However, many city dwellers are precluded from embodying this mantra because they do not own the land on which they live, work, and play. In Los Angeles, the tension between public and private is particularly severe, and even the smallest parcels of land are hotly contested. Community garden projects are constricted by the amount of physical space they have to operate in, and by whether or not the stewards of the land actually own the plots they are cultivating. Apartment dwellers often have limited growing space, and even homeowners might only be able to accommodate potted plants on a front porch, or a few square feet of parkway space between the sidewalk and the street. For instance, in

October 2010, TED Talk sensation and self-proclaimed *gangster gardener* Ron Finley planted a lush edible garden in the parkway space between the sidewalk and the street outside of his South Los Angeles home. The garden beautified the otherwise bleak boulevard and brought fresh (and free) vegetables to a neighborhood characterized by its lack of healthy food. Despite its public use value, Finley was cited and fined by the city of Los Angeles and ordered to remove the garden.[3]

To think through the possibilities of autonomous foodscapes in the urban core, I offer what I call *citified sovereignty*: a theory that attempts to bridge food justice, which is largely a US-based concept applied to urban areas, with food sovereignty—an idea usually applied to rural settings in developing nations. As paraphrased from the Nyéléni Declaration on Food Sovereignty,

> Food sovereignty is the right of peoples to healthy and culturally appropriate food produced through ecologically sound and sustainable methods, and their right to define their own food and agriculture systems. It puts the aspirations and needs of those who produce, distribute, and consume food at the heart of food systems and policies rather than the demands of markets and corporations. (2007)

Food sovereignty centers people over profits and reaffirms food as a basic human right. When communities (rather than corporations) decide what is planted and produced, they become food-secure and self-sufficient. In other words, control of the means of production equates to control of the means of reproduction and long-term survival. Although it is an exciting, generative, and even revolutionary concept, the praxis of food sovereignty demands a different kind of attention in the urban core (see also chapter 13 of this volume). City dwellers have different stakes in the food system depending on factors such as income, free time, skill, and access to land and information. Low-income renters have an especially unstable relationship to rapidly gentrifying city spaces and are often the first to be displaced when property values and prices for goods and services rise. Citified sovereignty composes a multi-scalar narrative to think through equitable urban land use, local ownership, claims to city spaces, and how to change the spatial and ideological composition of the built environment in ways that benefit the people most in need.

My theory of citified sovereignty posits that land ownership and autonomous community control of local foodways counters the potential negative impacts of redevelopment and revitalization efforts by preserving local spaces, identities, practices, and economies. A thriving local food system that addresses the unique needs of the surrounding community contributes to a sense of place and belonging. It ensures that people who cannot easily leave the neighborhood due to lack of transportation, limited mobility, or disability are not stuck with meager options and low-quality food. Additionally, filling the healthy food retail void and increasing the availability of plant-based foods would promote local economic development and help to combat the high rates of preventable food-related illnesses in the region.

Many instances of South Los Angeles–based citified sovereignty precede my coining of the phrase. For instance, in 1992, the Los Angeles Food Bank began growing food on an empty plot of city-owned land adjacent to their building in the industrial Alameda Corridor neighborhood.[4] The city of Los Angeles had granted permission for community members to cultivate the land as part of a citywide effort to rebuild after the civil unrest and uprisings that followed the acquittal of four white police officers caught on videotape brutally beating Black motorist Rodney King (Wolf 2016).[5] Over the next fourteen years, approximately 350 families from countries throughout Latin America would transform the once-empty lot into a lush, thriving paradise with more than 150 different edible and medicinal plant species.

For the farmers, families, and the South Los Angeles community, the South Central Farm provided much more than just food. The plants helped to offset the effects of toxic industrial pollutants from the trains, trucks, and warehouses bordering the farm on all sides. In addition to physical crops, the South Central farmers were cultivating a sense of pride and peace in the heart of the city. Mares and Peña (2011) argue that a space to make one's own is critical to the preservation of indigenous foodways, medicines, and cultural practices. For the South Central farmers—transplanted people whose identities are shaped by the land—the decision to reclaim city soil was a radical survival strategy in the face of hunger, instability, and placelessness created by privatization and violence. The re-territorialization of urban space allowed the diasporic, transnational farmers to maintain their indigenous identities alongside (and through) their indigenous foodways (ibid.). Unlike some community gardens that are planted to beautify and gentrify blighted neighborhoods, the South Central Farm was created and maintained by and for a marginalized community seeking relief from civil unrest, racial persecution, and food insecurity.

Despite its many benefits to public health, the South Central Farm land was reclaimed from the farmers in 2006 and bulldozed to dust. The highly publicized and hotly contested destruction of the farm was perceived by many as an act of violence done in the name of private property, which, in the end, eclipsed the farm's communal land use value (Broad 2013). Still, the very existence of the farm as a self-governed, autonomous site of local food production shifted public consciousness around the uses of urban space on a national and international scale. By transforming the built environment to fit the unique physical and cultural needs of the local community, the farm and its stewards demonstrated that autonomous urban food systems are possible. It enacted a sense of citified sovereignty (albeit temporary) in South Los Angeles, and the contentious struggle with city officials and private property owners has helped to open up new and ongoing conversations about autonomy, place, and the right to city space.[6]

Decades earlier, in the 1960s, the Black Panther Party developed a range of *survival programs* to provide sorely needed social services and free food in poor Black communities. Many Black and poor families could not afford to provide food on a regular basis, and their children were going to school with empty stomachs, which negatively impacted their educational outcomes. In response, the Panthers created free breakfast programs for schoolchildren across the United States, and regularly organized free food giveaways in poor communities.[7] For the Panthers, food was a tool to help oppressed people meet their nutritional needs, and to make an explicit intervention into the effects of American poverty—such as malnutrition, inadequate healthcare, and substandard education. The breakfast programs quickly became the most popular and widespread of the survival programs, and garnered strong community support for the Panthers on a nationwide level (Cleaver 1969; Jones 1998; Alkebulan 2007; Hilliard 2008). By the early 1980s, after more than a decade of government infiltration, politically motivated arrests, and state sanctioned murders, the Party had lost much of its cohesiveness and national influence (Churchill

2014; Churchill and Vander Wall 2002; Conway 2010). Fortunately, the Southern California Chapter of the Black Panther Party had the foresight to found Community Services Unlimited (CSU): a 501(c)(3) non-profit in 1977 to preserve their survival programs and continue to serve the South Los Angeles community for the foreseeable future.

Community Services Unlimited: Serving the People Body and Soul

As the non-profit arm of the Southern California Black Panther Party, Community Services Unlimited has maintained the Party's mantra of *Serving the People, Body and Soul* by promoting self-reliance and sustainability in South Los Angeles through urban farming, low-cost produce, nutrition education, and youth leadership training. Since its founding, CSU has expanded upon the Panther model by adding the extra element of healthy, plant-based food to address the phenomena of preventable diet-related illness and premature death among South Los Angeles residents of color. By bringing fresh, affordable, culturally appropriate food to the region through neighborhood produce stands, a produce bag subscription program, and by sourcing wholesale produce to local stores and restaurants, CSU offers a unique and acutely needed lifeline to the South Los Angeles community.

For the Panthers, food was central to achieving self-determination and working toward autonomy in the inner city. Similarly, CSU uses food to develop a collective place-based identity and to stimulate community economic development in South Los Angeles. For more than forty years, CSU has been at the forefront of a creative, multi-faceted effort to address the most severe issues facing the South Los Angeles community. For example, in 2002, the organization helped to form a youth- and community-driven food assessment of South Los Angeles called "Active Community to Improve Our Nutrition" (A.C.T.I.O.N.), which surveyed more than 750 community members over nine months and found that increased interest in local and organic foods is not limited to middle- and high-income consumers. To the contrary, low-income South Los Angeles residents overwhelmingly indicated that they would regularly purchase more organic, natural, and locally produced foods if they were available and affordable (CSU 2004).

In direct response to the needs expressed by community members in the A.C.T.I.O.N. Food Assessment, CSU launched the Community Food Village Project (CFV), a family of programs working to create a sustainable local food system where food is grown, distributed, and bought within the South Central Los Angeles community. CFV programs educate and train members of the community, create jobs and entrepreneurial opportunities, support the work of local and regional farmers, and teach youth interns real-life application of math and marketing by selling goods at CSU produce stands and through partnering vendors. CSU also developed the Village Market Place (VMP) social enterprise: a wholesale and retail food business that focuses on increasing access to high-quality, locally grown, *Beyond Organic* produce.[8]

In 2004, CSU collaborated with Normandie Avenue Elementary and John Muir Middle Schools to create mini-farms with edible gardens and fruit trees, which CSU maintains and uses for free monthly nutrition and farming workshops. In 2005, CSU joined forces with the EXPO Center in the heart of South Los Angeles to turn an adjacent empty lot into another mini urban farm that is collectively maintained by CSU staff, interns, and thousands of volunteers every year (see figure 14.2). Like the South Central Farm, CSU's mini-farms are a rare patch of green space in the city that provide nutritious food, safe space, and a hands-on intergenerational classroom that offers tangible health and survival tools.[9]

Community Services Unlimited has undergone a series of overhauls and location changes in its nearly four decades of working to create a community-based local food system in South Los Angeles. The organization was housed in Executive Director Neelam Sharma's garage until 2008, when grant funding from the Kellogg Foundation helped finance a move to the original site of the Aquarian Bookshop—a renowned Black-owned bookstore that had caught fire and closed during the 1992 LA Uprisings. In 2012, with the support of a Community Development Grant, CSU was able to expand and create a storefront at the Mercado La Paloma—a bustling South Los Angeles marketplace with vendors and restaurants. The storefront allowed CSU to expand its VMP social enterprise, build a significant customer base, and engage the local community in conversations about health and food justice. Then, in 2013, the VMP relocated to the United University Church (UUC)—an independent

Figure 14.2. "EXPO Center Mini-Farm." csuinc. 2018.

institution on the University of Southern California campus that has historically worked to promote a social justice agenda in line with CSU's mission.

Early in 2015, after decades of renting and changing locations, the organization was finally able to purchase its own parcel of land: the Paul Robeson building at 6569 South Vermont Avenue.[10] The 5,000-square-foot building and 10,000-square-foot lot have since become the Paul Robeson Community Wellness Center (PRCWC)—the region's first organic wellness hub (see figure 14.3). A $3.3 million project, the PRCWC was financed through a combination of construction grants, operating grants, bank loans, and individual and corporate donations. The bottom floor of the building includes an organic market with produce from CSU's mini-farms, a café serving healthy prepared foods, and a commercial kitchen that has allowed the VMP enterprise to operate at a scale that meets the community's urgent healthy food demands. The market also provides items that are virtually nonexistent in South Los Angeles, such as fermented vegetables, dried fruit and nut butters, and herbal salves and tinctures.[11]

The second floor of the building houses CSU's new headquarters, a Cal-Fresh registration site, and two open-plan offices available for lease or short-term rental by community organizations. The PRCWC is LEED-certified by the US Green Building Council and is designed to be a model for sustainable development in the region.[12] Also on-site is the Veggie Bus Classroom Project: a converted school bus once used for produce deliveries that now functions as a stationary seed library, plant nursery, and multipurpose classroom and workspace.

In addition to increasing access to healthy, affordable, locally grown produce and other foods, CSU projects that the PRCWC will support the creation of at least fifteen new living-wage jobs for South Los Angeles

Figure 14.3. Paul Robeson Community Wellness Center Blueprint. Source: Community Services Unlimited.

residents over the next four years.[13] There are frequent opportunities for independent health and wellness practitioners (acupuncturists, massage therapists, clinical therapists, personal trainers, health coaches, yoga instructors, etc.) to offer their services to the community. The market and café provide entry-level work experience, and educators use the garden spaces as hands-on urban farming classrooms for workshops and lessons. Moreover, CSU's expanded purchase of produce and other healthy foods has increased income for urban and rural agricultural producers and local food businesses. Notably, the ownership and revitalization of the Paul Robeson Center has also helped to sustain more than four decades of activism, organizing, and cultural expression in South Los Angeles by providing a physical space for film screenings, speaker series, concerts, and other art productions and community events.

Forgotten and forsaken places like South Los Angeles have become increasingly desirable to investors and developers looking to buy low and sell high. Citified sovereignty projects like the PRCWC attempt to use what Audre Lorde (2007) calls the *master's tools*—in this case, purchasing large brick-and-mortar spaces for profitable enterprise—to spatially resist the physical displacement of gentrification and help local residents maintain a stake in their neighborhoods. As chapter 12 of this volume also demonstrates, the food choices we make—particularly in gentrifying neighborhoods—are inherently political. CSU's holistic food-based programming promotes a healthy urban lifestyle in which it is both desirable and realistic for marginalized people to consume pesticide-free fruits and vegetables that have been locally and sustainably grown. In so doing, they give oppressed groups the political agency to participate in the physical and symbolic spaces of alternative food and wellness movements, which are often exclusionary and coded as white (Guthman 2008).

Mitigating Green Gentrification and the Non-Profit Industrial Complex

Despite all of CSU's good intentions, there is a possibility that the Paul Robeson Community Wellness Center could ironically contribute to green or ecological gentrification in South Los Angeles (see also chapters 4, 5, and 7 of this volume). The region is changing rapidly, with a new rail line well under way, and many long-term residents have already relocated, replaced by an influx of young professionals who have sent property values soaring in formerly undesirable neighborhoods like South Central, Compton, Watts, and Inglewood (Reed 2016). The reality is that the correlation between beautification and gentrification remains, even when a project is primarily meant to engage poor people of color (Gould and Lewis 2016). With its affordable health and wellness offerings, the PRCWC will undoubtedly attract the new gentry and long-term locals alike.

To help mitigate their unintentional impact on community displacement, one of CSU's long-term goals is to help locals lay claim to the landscape through purchasing low-income housing units in the surrounding neighborhoods, and offering workshops on home ownership, buyers' collectives, and renters' rights. CSU is also building partnerships with public and private agencies working on streetscape improvements like installing street trees, bike lanes, sheltered bus stops, and making façade improvements to commercial properties. As Panther Party cofounder Huey P. Newton (1970, 161) has said, "if the people are not here revolution cannot be achieved, for the people and only the people make revolutions." CSU's objective is to ensure that the South Los Angeles residents most in need of a wellness center and all its amenities are able to remain in the region and reap the benefits.

CSU staff and directors work hard to remain ideologically grounded in principles of grassroots resiliency and a tradition of struggle despite their structural positionality as a nonprofit organization. Like other 501(c)(3) groups with staff, overhead, and programming costs, CSU depends heavily on funds from private entities and foundations. This can produce a problematic cycle of continually applying for short-term funding to stay afloat—a phenomenon known as the nonprofit industrial complex (Incite! Women of Color Against Violence 2007). Despite its radical history, CSU has not been exempt from this cycle. The decision to expand the Village Market Place social enterprise was meant to offset this dependency and help the organization to become community sustained. CSU is very selective about accepting financial support from corporate sponsors, and they have forfeited money from funding entities that do not reflect the organization's principles. By fund-raising among community partners to purchase and sustain the PRCWC, CSU invites the people to support and participate directly in the transformation of the local foodscape. CSU goods are not free, but they are affordable, and the proceeds stay in the South Los Angeles community. Put simply, in addition to serving the people, CSU must also pay the bills.

Although the non-profit structure is not inherently revolutionary, Panther Party co-founder Bobby Seale (1991) has argued that "a revolutionary program is one set forth by revolutionaries, by those who want to change the existing system to a better system" (p. 413). Additionally, the Panthers believed that feeding the people was not the revolution itself, but a placeholder to ensure that oppressed people could survive while they organized toward revolution (Newton 2009). Establishing Community Services Unlimited as a nonprofit was an innovative survival strategy put forth by a revolutionary group as a means of self-preservation and community transformation. Similarly, becoming landowners in the increasingly contested city of Los Angeles is a revolutionary act that has safeguarded Community Services Unlimited and their ability to continue making lasting systemic change for the most marginalized groups in the urban core.

Conclusion

The decree of *40 acres and a mule* never materialized, and neither did the promises of industrialization and modernity. As the wealth gap widens and gentrification continues to reshape neighborhoods across the country, it is clear that land is still just as vital to sustainable, self-determined futures as it was when Negro ministers advised General Sherman after the Civil War. It is also clear that, as June Jordan (1980) would say, we are the ones we have been waiting for. The Black Panther Party used food to address state and federal neglect and mobilize Black communities across the country. The South Central farmers used their skill and knowledge to cultivate the land and alleviate food insecurity in a strange and hostile new place. The backlash against these groups demonstrates that cultivating sovereignty for oppressed people within the urban core of a capitalist nation-state is no easy feat. CSU's ownership and control of the Paul Robeson Community Wellness Center models an impressive version of citified sovereignty with exciting and unprecedented possibilities for health, wellness, and autonomy in South Los Angeles. It has never been easy, but it is essential that we continue to organize our efforts, energy, and imaginations in service of what we are for, not simply what we are against. In any garden, the seeds we water are the ones that will grow, and we must nurture the seeds of health, livelihood, and justice if we are to produce sustainable futures for the people most in need.

NOTES

1. On the "mule" in "40 Acres and a Mule": General Sherman's order also included that mules be loaned by the army to newly freed Blacks to help them till their new land.
2. Notably, even shopping locally can produce an economic drain since most businesses in South Los Angeles are not locally owned.
3. Finley and his group, L.A. Green Grounds, garnered community support through online petitions and newspaper articles, and in 2013, the Los Angeles City Council voted to allow Los Angeles residents to plant parkway gardens in the city without expensive permits (Appleton 2013).
4. The land was originally intended to become a solid waste incinerator, but those plans were defeated in the 1980s through grassroots efforts led by the Concerned Citizens of South Central.
5. The Rodney King case is widely considered to be the boiling point (though certainly not the sole source) of rising racial tensions in the city of Los Angeles.
6. The fight for the farm is far from over, as the farmers (now located in Buttonwillow, CA) continue to organize to reclaim the Los Angeles plot of land.
7. Hunger scholars argue that the Panther breakfast programs were the model for contemporary state-funded school food programs (Heynen 2009).
8. *Beyond Organic* refers to fruits and vegetables that are locally and sustainably sourced and grown without chemicals or pesticides. Though not all of the VMP's products are officially certified organic, all products are grown naturally using methods that meet and exceed USDA guidelines. This avoids the expensive certification process and passes the savings on to the people.
9. Monthly workshops are available for South Los Angeles residents to learn how to build raised bed gardens as a means to avoid potential lead contamination, how to plant seedlings, maintain chicken coops, and even build outdoor tandoori ovens.
10. The building was previously a Los Angeles Black Workers Center location. It is named after the legendary actor and activist Paul Robeson. CSU has kept the name and honors Robeson's legacy through murals, art installations, and cultural events.
11. CSU's food comes primarily from their mini-farms and small local farmers in the region. In addition to fruits and vegetables, they also offer a wide range of other "value-added" specialty items such as flours, coffee, dry beans, herbs, jams, sauces, teas, and spices. CSU also offers bulk items to reduce packaging and food waste.

12 LEED (Leadership in Energy and Environmental Design) is a green building certification system developed by the non-profit US Green Building Council (USGBC) for buildings or communities designed to conserve energy and water, reduce CO2 emissions, and improve indoor environmental quality.
13 CSU intentionally prioritizes local South Los Angeles residents in their hiring, staffing, and collaborative practices.

REFERENCES

Alexander, Michelle. 2012. *The New Jim Crow: Mass Incarceration in the Age of Colorblindness*. New York: New Press.

Alkebulan, Paul. 2007. *Survival Pending Revolution: The History of the Black Panther Party*. Tuscaloosa: University of Alabama Press.

Alkon, Alison Hope, and Julian Agyeman. 2011. *Cultivating Food Justice: Race, Class, and Sustainability*. Cambridge, MA: MIT Press.

Allen, Will, and Charles Wilson. 2013. *The Good Food Revolution: Growing Healthy Food, People, and Communities*. New York: Avery.

Appleton, Andrea. 2013. "L.A.'s Ron Finley Wants to Make Gardening Gangsta." *Grist*. August 13. https://grist.org.

Bedoya, R. 2013. "Placemaking and the Politics of Belonging and Dis-Belonging." *GIA Reader* 24(1): 20–21.

Boyd, John. 2015. In Thomas, M. 2015. "What Happened to America's Black Farmers?" https://grist.org.

Broad, G. M. 2013. "Ritual Communication and Use Value: The South Central Farm and the Political Economy of Place." *Communication, Culture & Critique* 6(1): 20–40.

Brown, John, and Radical Education Project. 1969. *An Introduction to the Black Panther Party*. Radical Education Project.

Churchill, W. 2014. "'To Disrupt, Discredit, and Destroy': The FBI's Secret War Against the Black Panther Party." In *Liberation, Imagination, and the Black Panther Party: A New Look at the Panthers and Their Legacy*, edited by K. Cleaver and G. Katsiaficas, 78–117. New York: Routledge.

Churchill, Ward, and Jim Vander Wall. 2002. *Agents of Repression: The FBI's Secret Wars against the Black Panther Party and the American Indian Movement*. Boston: South End Press.

Cleaver, Eldridge. 1969. "On Meeting the Needs of the People." Cited in *The Black Panther*, Saturday August 16, 1969. Reprinted from *Ramparts Magazine*. Southern California Library.

Cleaver, Kathleen, and George Katsiaficas. 2014. *Liberation, Imagination and the Black Panther Party: A New Look at the Black Panthers and Their Legacy*. New York: Routledge.

Community Coalition. 2013. "Feast or Famine: The Glaring Inequality in Healthy Food Access." *Infographic*. http://cocosouthla.org.

Community Services Unlimited (CSU). 2004. "Community Food Assessment." *ACTION: Active Community to Improve Our Nutrition*. https://csuinc.org.

Conway. 2010. *The Greatest Threat: The Black Panther Party and the FBI's CounterIntelligence Program*. Baltimore, MD: I Am We Publications.
Crowder, K., and S. J. South. 2008. "Spatial Dynamics of White Flight: The Effects of Local and Extralocal Racial Conditions on Neighborhood Out-Migration." *American Sociological Review* 73(5): 792–812.
csuinc. 2018. "EXPO Center Mini-Farm" [Instagram post]. Retrieved from www.instagram.com/csuinc/.
Darity, W. 2008. "Forty Acres and a Mule in the 21st Century." *Social Science Quarterly* 89(3): 656–664.
Du Bois, W.E.B. 1935. *Black Reconstruction in America 1860–1880*. New York: Simon & Schuster.
Finley, Ron. 2013. *A Guerilla Gardener in South Central LA*. www.ted.com/.
Gates, Henry Louis. 2013. "The Truth Behind '40 Acres and a Mule.'" *The Root*.
Gilmore, Ruth Wilson. 2008. "Forgotten Places and the Seeds of Grassroots Planning." In Charles R. Hale, *Engaging Contradictions: Theory, Politics, and Methods of Activist Scholarship*. Berkeley: University of California Press.
Gould, Kenneth A., and Tammy L. Lewis. 2016. *Green Gentrification: Urban Sustainability and the Struggle for Environmental Justice*. New York: Routledge.
Guthman, Julie. 2008. "'If They Only Knew': Color Blindness and Universalism in California Alternative Food Institutions." *Professional Geographer* 60(3): 387–397.
Halweil, B. 2002. *Home Grown: The Case for Local Food in a Global Market* (Vol. 163). Washington, DC: Worldwatch Institute.
Heynen, Nik. 2009. "Bending the Bars of Empire from Every Ghetto for Survival: The Black Panther Party's Radical Antihunger Politics of Social Reproduction and Scale." *Annals of the Association of American Geographers* 99(2): 406–422.
Heynen, Nik, Hilda E. Kurtz, and Amy Trauger. 2012. "Food Justice, Hunger and the City." *Geography Compass* 6(5): 304–311.
Hilliard, David. 2008. *The Black Panther*. New York: Simon & Schuster.
Incite! Women of Color Against Violence. 2007. *The Revolution Will Not Be Funded: Beyond the Non-Profit Industrial Complex*. Boston, MA: South End Press.
Jones, Charles Earl. 1998. *The Black Panther Party (reconsidered)*. Baltimore, MD: Black Classic Press.
Jordan, June. 1980. *Passion: New Poems, 1977–1980*. Boston, MA: Beacon Press.
Kaplan, George. 2006. In Mari Gallagher Research & Consulting Group, "Examining the Impact of Food Deserts on Public Health in Chicago." www.marigallagher.com.
Lee, Mary. 1998. *Drowning in Alcohol: Retail Outlet Density, Economic Decline and Revitalization in South L.A.* San Rafael, CA: *Marin Institute*.
Lorde, Audre. 2007. *Sister Outsider: Essays and Speeches*. New York: Random House.
Malcolm X. 1963. "Message to the Grassroots." Public Speech.
Mares, Teresa, and Devon G. Peña. 2010. "Urban Agriculture in the Making of Insurgent Spaces in Los Angeles and Seattle." In Jeffrey Hou, ed. *Insurgent Public Space: Guerrilla Urbanism and the Remaking of Contemporary Cities*. New York, London: Routledge.

Mares, Teresa, and Devon G. Peña. 2011. "Environmental and Food Justice: Toward Local, Slow, and Deep Food Systems." In Alison Hope Alkon and Julian Agyeman, eds. *Cultivating Food Justice: Race, Class, and Sustainability*. Cambridge, MA: MIT Press.

Mascarenhas, Michelle. 1997. "Combating Supermarket Flight in Los Angeles." UEP Faculty & UEPI Staff Scholarship. Occidental College. https://scholar.oxy.edu.

Melcon, Mel. 2013. "Dyane Pascall of Community Services Unlimited Gives Karyn Williams a Bag of Produce Outside St. John's Well Child and Family Center in South L.A." *Los Angeles Times*.

Newton, Huey P. 1970. "Speech Delivered at Boston College: November 18, 1970." In David Hilliard and Donald Weise, eds. *The Huey P. Newton Reader*. New York: Seven Stories Press, 2011.

Newton, Huey P. 2009. *Revolutionary Suicide* (Penguin Classics Deluxe Edition). New York: Penguin.

Nyéléni Declaration on Food Sovereignty. 2007. https://nyeleni.org.

Peña, Devon. 2003. "Autonomy, Equity, and Environmental Justice." *Race, Poverty, and Environmental Justice*. Provost's Lecture Series, Brown University. April 21.

Peña, Devon. 2006. "Farmers Feeding Families: Agroecology in South Central Los Angeles." Keynote Address. *National Association for Chicana and Chicano Studies*. Pullman: Washington State University.

Quigley, John. 2016. "The South Central Farm." Photo. In Jedamiah Wolf, "¡Aquí Estamos! The Movement to Reclaim the South Central Farm." Planet Experts. www.planetexperts.com.

Reed, J. 2016. "Transit Development in Leimert Park, Los Angeles: The Specter of Gentrification and Community Capital as Leverage toward Transforming Redevelopment Projects." Master's thesis for the Environmental Studies Program and Planning, Public Policy, Management Department and the Graduate School of the University of Oregon.

Rugh, Jacob S., and Douglas S. Massey. 2010. "Racial Segregation and the American Foreclosure Crisis." *American Sociological Review* 75(5): 629–651.

Seale, Bobby. 1991. *Seize the Time: The Story of the Black Panther Party and Huey P. Newton*. Baltimore, MD: Black Classic Press.

Squires, Gregory. 2004. "The New Redlining." In Clarence Page, *Why the Poor Pay More: How to Stop Predatory Lending*. Westport, CT: Greenwood.

Taney, R. B. 1857. *Dred Scott v. Sandford* 60 U.S. 19 How. 393 393 (1856).

Thomas, Madeline. 2015. "What Happened to America's Black Farmers?" *Grist*. https://grist.org.

A Conflicted Conclusion

Seeing and Contesting Gentrification through Food

ALISON HOPE ALKON, YUKI KATO, AND JOSHUA SBICCA

In a *New York Times* article describing gentrification in Oakland, an African American lifelong resident, artist, and activist Chinaka Hodge described the changes to her hometown. "We're glad to welcome folks who add value to the city," she said, but "we've struggled to survive here, and the moment that it's cool, not only can we not afford to live here, but our entire history is whitewashed, for lack of a better term." She went on to explain, "I think there are two narratives about Oakland that have existed for my entire life." The first is safety, she said, taking the reporter past former crack houses that have become restored Victorians. "The second narrative has been gaining attention over the last few years... It's the Michelin stars, the cool pop-ups, the Eat Real Festival... Any exposure can be great," she continued, "but I want to be able to afford to live here in 20 years. I want to be able to raise my family in the neighborhood that everyone thought was ugly until [former Oakland Mayor and California Governor] Jerry Brown encouraged 10,000 new people to show up and make Oakland theirs." Hodge is perhaps best known for co-producing a tongue-in-cheek music video with Bay Area rapper George Watsky called "Kill a Hipster" in which long-term residents take on white newbie-zombies in a Walking Dead–style battle. The song is replete with food references––Starbucks, hummus, kombucha, and goat cheese "straight from the fuckin' farm," to name a few.

Food and Gentrification in Theory

Hodge's perspective encompasses many of *A Recipe for Gentrification*'s central themes. First, we have used a food intersections approach to explore the ways that gentrification is enacted and contested. Food and gentrification are certainly linked in the popular imagination; media coverage of gentrification often references food businesses like coffee shops, hip takes on working-class or ethnic cuisines, and farm-to-table restaurants as symbolic of a neighborhood's new upscale or up-and-coming status. And materially, these businesses are typically the first to open in a gentrifying neighborhood, making more visible the presence of wealthier and often white residents who may have begun trickling in, and signaling to other would-be new residents that this space deserves their attention. This dynamic was clearly captured by Durham's savior entrepreneurs, as depicted by Nina Martin in chapter 2, restaurateur-developers who were constantly lauded in the local media for reviving an underdeveloped neighborhood and helping to recast their working-class city as a hip, creative place. We also saw this play out similarly in San Diego (chapter 1) and Vancouver (chapter 9). Alternative food systems are very much a part of this process as well, as realtors and other urban boosters point to community gardens and farmers' markets as evidence of a neighborhood's appeal. Sometimes alternative food activists are blindsided by and work to contest this dynamic, as we saw in Oakland (chapter 10) and Denver (chapter 4), but other times, they see their own best options for future profits and stable land tenure as tied to their city's development. Members of the Oklahoma Food Cooperative chose to orient their business toward the city's new creative class (chapter 3) while Seattle's P-Patch community gardeners worked to convince city officials that gardens were an important amenity for new residents (chapter 7). Taken collectively, these cases demonstrate that food businesses and food activism can foster, or be implicated in, the process of gentrification, particularly when environmental sustainability efforts are (intentionally or unintentionally) cast as green amenities for newcomers (Alkon and Cadji 2018; McClintock 2018; Hyde 2014; Sbicca 2018b).

The message of "Kill a Hipster" and Hodge's broader analysis speaks to one of the key scholarly debates about gentrification. The question of whether it is structural or cultural spans theoretical writing across sociology, geography, and urban studies. Through the lens of food, we can see how gentrification is structurally driven but culturally lived. Hodge rightly refers to planning efforts, such as Jerry Brown's 10K plan, as the major force bringing new housing, and new residents, to her city.

Planning efforts figure prominently in many of the stories told in this volume. For example, Denver Mayor Michael Hancock introduced the city's 2020 Sustainability Goals, which included support for urban agriculture as a capitalist fix for low property values during the Great Recession (chapter 4), while San Francisco's Board of Supervisors elevated the importance of urban agriculture in the city through the development of municipal policy (chapter 8). In both cases, urban policy and planning laid the groundwork for green gentrification, and these chapters remind us that the decreased property values resulting from the Great Recession created the "rent gap" that fostered the current boom (Smith 2008[1982]). Uniquely, urban agriculture was deployed as a stopgap measure to contain "blight" in devalued neighborhoods until property values rose.

And yet, examining gentrification through the lens of food helps us to also appreciate the cultural realities of this process. Individual and community identities and their senses of belonging to long-term or new places are often expressed through food. Seeing one's own or one's cultural food preferences reflected locally can subtly communicate a sense of to whom a neighborhood belongs (or not so subtly, as the ink! Coffee controversy referenced in the introduction makes clear). New residents are attracted to existing "authentic" "ethnic" restaurants in divested communities (Zukin 2010) but also create nouveau, upscale versions of these cuisines. So for example, long-term residents may appreciate the gestures toward their neighborhood culture made by upscale taquerias and "Barrio Doggs" in San Diego, as depicted by Pascale Joassart-Marcelli and Fernando J. Bosco in chapter 1, but more often, these foods signal to long-term residents that their place's deep cultural roots can be commodified for newcomers, and that their neighborhood is no longer for them. This remains true even when a restaurateur is deemed a social entrepreneur, as in Vancouver's Downtown East Side, and makes efforts to include long-term communities through jobs and discounted meals. As Zachary Hyde demonstrates in chapter 9, long-term residents and activists felt marginalized by all the positive press heaped upon these "ethical gentrifiers" and argued instead that they undermined activists' own claims to their neighborhood. Similarly, Emily Becker and Nathan McClintock show that this may not be about the food itself, but about who is growing, maintaining, and distributing it. In chapter 6, they note how the participation of public housing residents in a community orchard in Portland declined when management shifted from a collective of diverse residents to a white-led non-profit organization. Collectively, these chapters reveal that while much has been written about the varying intentions and proclivities of new residents (Brown-Saracino 2009, 2010; Ocejo 2011; Zukin 2010), it is perhaps even more important to study the lived experiences of long-term residents, many of whom have not yet been displaced from, and are struggling to maintain a foothold in, the places they think of as their own.

Examining the experience of gentrification through food also helps us to engage with how this process is (always, already) racialized. While early scholarship on gentrification tended to focus on critiques of capitalism, and to ignore the role of structural racism (Smith 1979; Logan and Molotch 1987), later generations of scholars have demonstrated that this process is predicated on colonial dispossession and exploitation, and racialized policies and practices of segregation, underdevelopment, and urban renewal (Goldberg 1993; Jacobs 1996; Crowder and South 2005; Goetz 2011; Lees 2016). While state-led gentrification is too often regarded as a vestige of institutionally racist history, it is still occurring through transportation projects like Cleveland's Opportunity Corridor (chapter 13). In chapter 4, Joshua Sbicca adds that the Great Recession of the late 2000s, itself a racialized event in that communities of color were often targeted for subprime loans and were disproportionately subject to foreclosure, provided the uneven conditions for the current wave of gentrification, including the green variant highlighted in this volume. And Brooke Havlik shows how the diasporic experience of dispossession and gentrification for Chicago's Puerto Ricans overlaps with their colonial relationship to the United States (chapter 12). These chapters add to our understanding of how colonialism, racism, and capitalism are integral to the production and exploitation of the above-described rent gap (Blomley 2004; Shaw 2007; Hyra 2017).

Scholars in the interdisciplinary field of food studies will be particularly interested in the ways that gentrification demonstrates the malleable, non-deterministic nature of the relationship between food and culture. We've seen examples throughout the chapters herein of how food can be tied to cultural inclusion, as exemplified by the Black urban gardeners and food justice activists in Los Angeles (chapter 14),

Cleveland (chapter 13), and East New York (chapter 11). But the "Kill a Hipster" lyrics associating particular foods with gentrification remind us that food can also lead to cultural exclusion and symbolic violence. Pamela Arnette Broom's experiences, as depicted in chapter 5, nicely weave together these changing dynamics, as she worked alongside new residents in ways that were sometimes positive and respectful. Other times, however, the sheer number of newcomer activists, and their greater access to resources, served to redefine notions of local food as delinked from New Orleans' unique history, culture, and culinary traditions.

Using food to understand gentrification also ties into popular debates about the cultural appropriation and upscaling of ingredients and foodways (Kendall 2014; Ho 2014). Indeed, we intend our volume to extend this conversation beyond discussions of the gentrification of foods themselves to illuminate that foodways intersect with broader processes of urban development and displacement. In some ways, this line of research will bring food studies scholars back to questions of how communities use food and foodways to make place, a question that animated much of the early, celebratory scholarship on alternative food systems (Kloppenberg 1996; Lyson 2004; DeLind 2002). But examining the relationship between food and gentrification complicates these issues by attending to placemaking in the contexts of not only racialization, as much of the work on migrant foodways and food histories does quite beautifully (Hondagneu-Sotelo 2014; Garcia et al. 2017; Peña et al. 2017; Carney 2001), but also urban development.

Food and Gentrification in Praxis

Paulo Freire, the Brazilian educator and philosopher, defines praxis as "reflection and action directed at the structures to be transformed" (1970: 26). The idea is to develop a critical awareness of causes and conditions, and through this understanding, develop strategies for liberation. We hope that *A Recipe for Gentrification* has not only inspired readers to think deeply about the relationship between food and gentrification, but also to devise strategies that stem involuntary displacement and foster broad food justice practices.

Food activism must begin by better anticipating the unintended consequences of alternative food systems and social entrepreneurial endeavors. This insight builds on critical food scholarship that encourages well-meaning food activists, particularly white ones, to be aware of macro-level processes of economic exploitation and racism that imbue them with privileges while constraining the lives of low-income people and people of color (Alkon and Guthman 2017; Kato 2014). Community gardens, farmers' markets, and other food retail, even when grounded firmly in the principles of anti-racism and food justice, can become fodder for urban boosters who cast them as amenities for new residents. Sometimes this becomes a hardship for the activists themselves; community gardeners in Denver (chapter 4) and San Francisco (chapter 8) saw their support from the city wane as property values increased and they were no longer considered the highest and best use for their land. Even more acutely, Black urban gardeners in Cleveland are organizing to resist what they see as an impending contemporary land grab wrought by urban renewal (chapter 13). Other times, long-term residents inhabiting land near alternative food spaces might see the increased popularity of their neighborhoods drive up property values and cause their displacement. This is already the reality in North Oakland (chapter 10), New Orleans (chapter 5), and could soon occur in South Los Angeles (chapter 14). In Oklahoma City (chapter 3), food activists who were not thinking critically about gentrification helped to redefine the meaning of local food from a collective good advancing environmental, economic, and social goals to an elite lifestyle choice. The ensuing establishment of more and larger-scale local food businesses in the city disadvantaged many small producers and detracted from efforts to make local food more economically accessible.

The takeaway for those creating and supporting alternative food systems is to reflect on the potential negative and unintended consequences of the trend toward upscaling both the food itself and the neighborhoods in which it is grown, prepared, and distributed. We argue that those working toward and supporting alternative food systems need to engage in the kind of "reflexive localism" suggested by DuPuis and Goodman (2005) and ask what and who they are really for. The siren song of appeals to the creative class is a seemingly attractive one, particularly for social entrepreneurial businesses that need to generate profits and non-profit organizations seeking to secure their own access to land or to supplement or move away from dependency on grant funding. But in orienting themselves toward new residents, many organizations and businesses abandon or diminish their founding social goals. Missions to expand access to local and organic food and green space, for example, may be at odds with the profit imperative that characterizes even the most socially oriented business model. Moreover, those organizations and businesses that are run by or work directly with long-term residents will see their own employees, as well as those they seek to serve, increasingly pushed out of gentrifying spaces. And even when organizations are state-funded, and not themselves driven by profit, securing their own land by highlighting their attractiveness to wealthy new residents serves to diminish their role as a social good, as we saw in Seattle's P-Patch gardens (chapter 7).

We suspect that greater reflexivity will push food activists and movements toward deeper engagement with low-income communities and communities of color. This is, we believe, important and necessary, particularly when more privileged groups can do the hard work of reflecting on their own advantages and listen to the life experiences of less privileged ones. Such work can be supported by the growing literature on race and food activism, including work by many of the authors in this volume, as well as recent books by Monica White (2018), Ashanté Reese (2019), Devon Peña et al. (2017), Teresa Mares (2019), and Leah Penniman (2018), as well as scholarship on race, intersectionality, and activism more generally (for example, DiAngelo 2018; Taylor 2016). Examining gentrification requires centering the circumstances of those most at risk of displacement *and* hunger, and who have too often been least represented in efforts to create alternative food systems. The experiences of activists in Portland (chapter 6), New York City (chapter 11), San Francisco (chapter 8), and Oakland (chapter 10) show the complexities of whether and how activists embrace this challenge. We hope these chapters will be particularly instructive to food activists who understand the threats of gentrification not only to their own lives and livelihoods but to their broader communities.

Highlighting the importance of comparative analyses like this book, deepening connections between proponents of alternative food systems and those most vulnerable to displacement may involve very different dynamics and outcomes across different cities. Super-gentrifying cities like New York, Vancouver, and San Francisco, for example, have seen the emergence of new alliances between long-term residents, largely low-income and of color, and somewhat newer, middle-class residents who also cannot afford to stay in these places. Middle-class residents in these cities have begun weaponizing their privilege, working with veteran organizations like Anti-Displacement PDX (Portland), the Balanced Development Coalition (Chicago), and the Figueroa Corridor Coalition for Economic Justice (Los Angeles) in order to fight for more affordable housing, inclusionary zoning, and tenant protection laws. But there are challenges. These alliances must navigate affordable housing plans that do not include the lowest income residents, such as New York's recent effort to develop parts of East New York in ways that would be accessible to middle-class teachers and social workers, for example, but not the urban farmers profiled in chapter 11. Even if they can withstand such divide-and-conquer tactics, these alliances face political disadvantages because the planning efforts that drive gentrification in their cities are entrenched. In other words, by the time the consequences of gentrification become applicable to residents with more social capital, adding more resources to the fight against displacement, the political opportunities to engage may have narrowed. In contrast, we hope that progressive food activists and other middle-class residents of cities in earlier stages of the gentrification process—Durham, Oklahoma City, and Cleveland, for example—may see the graffiti on the wall and join struggles against displacement before they are personally affected, and before many political opportunities have closed. In other words, activists and allies in these cities have the potential to highlight the need for social equity in food and green development plans from their earliest stages. One way to achieve this is to strategize how activists and their supporters should work to amplify the existing efforts in these communities, rather than to parachute in as outsider saviors, similar to the well-intended but harmful approaches discussed in chapters 2 and 6.

These new coalitions can also push supporters of alternative food systems and food-based social entrepreneurs to go beyond food activism and engage in broader, progressive struggles that affect both food systems and systems of inequality more generally. Sbicca (2018a) has written about the nexus that food activism shares with campaigns for prison abolition, immigrant rights, and workers' rights, while Alkon and Guthman (2017) trace the roots of newer, more collective forms of food activism to movements for the rights of workers within and beyond the food system, the Occupy movement's attention to growing economic inequalities, and the Black Lives Matter movement's work on the criminal justice system and anti-racism. Given the structural drivers of the many problems social justice movements fight against, let alone their intersections with food, it is important that food activists ally with, and develop support for, a political agenda that combats exclusionary gentrification.

Our reflections on praxis also suggest the need to interrogate leading scholarly approaches to dealing with the entanglements between green amenities like organic food and community gardens and uneven urban development. Chief among these is advocacy for community-led, neighborhood revitalization efforts that are "just green enough" to create "surprising and somewhat hidden greening" without attracting the eye of boosters or hipsters (Curran and Hamilton 2018: 3; see also Wolch et al. 2014; Curran and Hamilton 2012). In their recent edited book on the topic, Curran and Hamilton write that this vision is not about limiting environmental cleanup and amenities in order to protect communities from displacement, but about making central the needs of long-term communities. "It's clean water," they write, "not a waterfront café; equal access to green space, not tourist-oriented parks" (2018: 6). In other words, they argue for environmental health and sustainability without the shallow aesthetic versions of greenness (Gould and Lewis 2017).

The vision put forward in the latter part of our volume builds on this approach. We argue that a commitment to "development without displacement" will allow cities to green equitably by providing protections and opportunities for long-term communities to stay in their homes, express the cultures of their neighborhoods, and thrive alongside new residents. The Paul Robeson Center in Los Angeles (chapter 14) is perhaps the strongest example of this; the facility is beautiful and in line with leading design aesthetics and environmental standards while also fundamentally oriented to community needs. It exemplifies an approach that, instead of attempting to avoid the eye of gentrifiers, explicitly acts to improve communities *and* keep people in places they want to live. After all, low-income residents are as likely as more affluent ones to support well-designed, sustainable, and beautiful green spaces (DuPuis and Greenberg 2019). Provisioning and eating locally is also not a new practice for historically marginalized urban communities (Reese

2019). Visions for greener cities should not simply "incorporate" community input, but rather look to the knowledge and expertise developed in these communities as the starting point to recreate equitable local food systems that socially and economically stabilize neighborhoods. In our final section, we describe various ways that a food intersections approach can contribute to broader efforts for progressive change at a variety of scales.

Ways to Combat Gentrification: A Question of Scales of Food Justice

There is no shortage of think pieces and online conversations on the topic of "how not to be a gentrifier." The writers tend to fall into two categories; articles penned by white newcomers seek to somehow square their liberal political views with the harm they acknowledge causing, while middle-class people of color, some of whom were raised in the neighborhood in question, aim to struggle with the ramifications of their own class and educational privilege while offering advice to newcomers. Most often, these writings revolve around interpersonal relations and individual-level actions like saying hello to new neighbors, including day laborers and homeless people, or learning the history of your new neighborhood. Even film director Spike Lee's now-infamous gentrification "rant" followed this trajectory, focusing on calls to the police and what he referred to as "Christopher Columbus Syndrome," in which new residents believe they've discovered some aspect of a neighborhood or its culture (Coscarelli 2014). More broadly, writers like Dannette Lambert (2014), an Afro-Latina, ask that newcomers "recognize [that] your new home has a very unique and vibrant history and culture and you were attracted to this location because of the energy that is already here. You should be here to add to that history and culture, not erase it."

Food is often integral to these conversations, as writers and community activists ask newcomers to support long-standing restaurants as well as the new and trendy ones that cater to them (see chapter 12). These practices speak to the potential for food to bring communities together, and for eating one another's cultural foods to be a way to develop deeper relationships with new neighbors. As an innovative approach to this, Tunde Wey, the engaging chef-provocateur and racial justice agitator, has been organizing dinners across the United States, where participants engage in candid and challenging conversations about racial injustices. The potential for food to bring communities together can also be realized beyond restaurants; newcomers can patronize other locally owned businesses, including culturally relevant markets common to Latinx and Asian neighborhoods (Anguelovski 2016), food trucks run by immigrant "hucksters" and other people of color (Martin 2014; Agyeman et al. 2017), and farmers' markets dedicated to supporting marginalized producers (chapters 8, 10).

For those who live in gentrifying neighborhoods, and who occupy places of (even relative) privilege, these individual-level solutions feel like an important way to minimize the damage our presence can do. Blogs like Lambert's are asking us to become what Brown-Saracino (2009) has described as social preservationists. These new residents, she argues, are distinct from gentrifiers because they value and seek to engage with existing neighborhood cultures rather than "improve" and commodify them. And certainly, long-standing residents like Pamela Arnette Broom (chapter 5) and Aunti Frances (chapter 10) appreciate being treated with respect and have developed genuine friendships with some newcomers. Social preservationists are also likely to understand the increased police scrutiny that often traumatizes communities of color (Chaney and Robertson 2013). In other words, being nice to one's neighbors, and engaging with a community's history and culture, are certainly good things to do, and can positively affect the lives of long-term residents. But to examine gentrification from a structural perspective reveals that these kinds of actions fail to stem the tide of rising property values and displacement.

At the meso level, newcomers can engage with and support already existing community-based organizations. These may include food organizations like Oakland's Phat Beets (chapter 10) or the San Francisco Urban Agriculture Alliance (chapter 8) who are already grappling with questions of gentrification and building alliances with long-term residents. Other times, activists may encounter organizations rooted in other struggles who are looking to incorporate food into their approaches, such as Chicago's Puerto Rican Cultural Center (chapter 12). However, Portland's Fruits of Diversity Orchard offers an important cautionary tale (chapter 6), as well-intentioned white leadership lessened the participation of people of color, who no longer felt ownership of the space. Early food justice efforts often fell into this trap, as newcomers' desire to "bring good food to others" (Guthman 2008) often blinded them to how local communities perceived their efforts. New residents of gentrifying neighborhoods can mitigate this dynamic by prioritizing involvement in organizations led by long-term residents, and by taking supportive rather than leadership roles. And those who create new organizations can ensure that their staff and board match the surrounding community. In addition, many new residents of gentrifying neighborhoods open small businesses, including food businesses, that cater to other new residents. These businesses can be more inclusive by hiring and training long-term community members, keeping price-points affordable, and being inclusive of, but not commodifying, a neighborhood's culture and cuisine. Business owners can also be wary of the ways that even the most minor efforts in this regard will earn them accolades in the media (chapter 9) and can work to share the spotlight with others whose talents and struggles are too often overlooked.

But this too is inadequate. Gentrification may be culturally experienced, but it is fundamentally a structural process in which urban officials and urban boosters seek to increase the tax base and prestige of their cities through new, fancy development projects, which often include upscale food as a part of their retail strategy. This perspective casts gentrification as a political-economic process that can only be constrained through collective action and policy at more macro levels. Organizations in cities throughout the United States have worked to create new inclusionary housing and zoning campaigns, housing trust funds, and real estate transfer taxes that provide funding for affordable housing and tenant protections such as restrictions on no-cause eviction, rent control, and subsidies for displaced households (NYU Furman Center 2016). East Palo Alto, for example, a predominantly low-income Black and Latinx community juxtaposed to the wealth of Silicon Valley, recently passed a Below Market Rate ordinance requiring that 25 percent of newly constructed units be made available to people who make just 30 percent of the area median income. In another important campaign, New York City's Fifth Avenue Committee is working to create an inclusionary zoning policy requiring developers to include low-income housing within market-rate development, rather than construct segregated low-income housing or pay a penalty, which is often their preferred strategy (Rose 2002). These city-level initiatives have the potential to stem displacement through a combination of penalties and incentives fostering market-based creation of affordable housing and protections and subsidies for renters (NYU Furman Center 2016). None of these policies, however, will be instituted without collective action pressuring governments to work against what they perceive to be their own economic interests (i.e., increased tax bases through wealthy residents). Gentrifiers, who are often college-educated, young, and energetic, may have key roles to play in these campaigns, though we would caution that the voices and experiences of long-term community members must remain at their center.

The most profound effect of gentrification on long-standing communities is their physical displacement, and stemming this requires strong economic policies. This might additionally include robust living wage ordinances that peg wage increases to yearly inflation, especially for food chain workers, often the backbone of a city's economy. Increasing purchasing power is part of the equation, which would be helped by policies that tax major local companies, especially developers, and use the revenue to reinvest in working-class communities, through land trusts and building low-income housing, to lessen economic inequality. Relatedly, cities could rethink the role of development from a strictly economic question to a social question. This might entail drafting and enforcing a renter's bill of rights and a community bill of rights for development, limiting luxury development, and supporting community-owned development enterprises.

All of this brings us ultimately to the land question (Williams and Holt-Giménez 2017). As Analena Hope Hassberg (chapter 14) points out, land is the basis of wealth and building community power. There is no way for gentrification-free food justice and food sovereignty to exist without community control over the most vital of all resources: land. Acting on this point, Tunde Wey floated the idea of buying up every vacant lot in the historically Black North Nashville to prevent future gentrification. His plan: Bring Black and white residents together around the issue of gentrification and the widely appropriated African American–inspired Nashville dish of hot chicken; Black people eat for free while white people pay $100 for one piece of chicken or $1,000 for four pieces (Mock 2019). The provocation of the act is simple. There is a need for wealth redistribution and economic power, not handouts, or tinkering around the edges of policy to slow and ultimately prevent involuntary displacement. One of the original demands of freed Black people was 40 acres and a mule, that is, a means for food sovereignty and a resource that would build up the sociopolitical capacity of former slaves. While a massive demographic shift of people has resulted in more people living in cities, the question of reparations, particularly through the vehicle of land, is more pressing than ever.

Staying true to our contention that food provides a means to understand gentrification through the interconnections of political economy *and* culture, cultural displacement should not be overlooked as a peripheral issue, as this is significant to the experiences of loss and exclusion for long-term residents. The shift in businesses, including food businesses, from familiar restaurants and stores to hipster coffee shops and farm-to-table fare can invoke a pervasive feeling that their neighborhoods now belong to others (chapters 1, 2, and 9). In addition to housing-based efforts to stem displacement, new residents can also fight politically to ensure that their neighborhoods remain culturally accessible to long-standing communities. Efforts to name streets and corridors in ways that reflect their racial and ethnic histories, such as *Paseo Boricua* in Chicago (chapter 12), can commemorate a community's presence and enhance their visibility, though sometimes these can feel like "an artifact" and "commercial rebranding," as Jamal Frederick (2014) wrote of efforts to create a Jazz Preservation District in San Francisco's Fillmore neighborhood. Another way to foster the cultural preservation of a community is through support for community-owned small businesses. This can happen through individual patronage, as described above, but also through policy. For example, food activists such as the Food Chain Workers Alliance have been integral to efforts to legalize and permit street vending in Los Angeles, which the city council did in 2018. Immigrant- and people of color–run food vending businesses have often been targeted by city authorities, even while those run by younger, whiter, and wealthier "trucksters" have been encouraged (Agyeman et al. 2017; Zukin 2010). Policies such as this ensure that the food cultures of long-standing communities at risk of displacement can continue to be a vibrant part of their neighborhoods.

Readers inspired to think deeply about the relationship between food and gentrification can also look to national-level politics to contemplate how these issues fit into broader political platforms. For example, the Movement for Black Lives' (M4BL) policy platform contains a number of demands regarding food and agriculture to "[make] sure our people are safe, healthy, and educated," according to Dara Cooper, a national organizer for the National Black Food and Justice Alliance and a member of the M4BL policy team (quoted in Mantey 2016). These demands include a right to restored land, clean air, clean water, and housing; an end to discriminatory credit policies that prevent access to farmable land; and funding to invest in community-based land trusts, food co-ops, and food hubs. These policies would allow Black communities to access land and capital in order to run food-based businesses in their communities. Though the links to gentrification are not explicit in the platform, the demands for Black agriculture, foodways, and food retail stand in stark opposition to the threats of physical and cultural displacement that many Black communities face. And, as is true of much of the M4BL platform, these proposals are relevant to other poor communities and communities of color. For example, Denver leads the United States in Latinx displacement from gentrification, the second most common ethnoracial community, after Black communities, to experience economic and cultural pressures to leave their neighborhood (Richardson, Mitchell, and Franco 2019). Additionally, Latinx, Native American, and women farmers have, like Black farmers, faced discrimination from the USDA (Minkoff-Zern and Sloat 2016).

Another national policy platform in the United States that will likely be aligned with activism around food and gentrification is the recently revived Green New Deal. At the point of this writing, the details of this policy platform are developing, but its overarching agenda coheres around the goal of addressing economic inequality while transitioning away from fossil fuels. Our food system and cities are critical to this transition (Patel and Goodman 2019; Cohen 2019). No doubt localized and alternative food systems have an important role to play in eliminating greenhouse gas emissions from agricultural industries. At the same time, addressing the economic and racial inequalities at the root of gentrification could broadly stem displacement. The sorts of investments that lie at the heart of the Green New Deal would likely provide jobs and entrepreneurial opportunities to marginalized communities, though they would need to be combined with the above-described housing policies in order to withstand the pressures of escalating real estate markets. This kind of imagination work and organizing to connect food, gentrification, and national-level environmental and economic policies can help to supplement the individual- and consumption-oriented solutions highlighted by popular media.

In sum, *A Recipe for Gentrification* argues that food is intimately bound up with classed and racialized processes of gentrification as they are structurally enacted and culturally experienced. Restaurants and coffee shops are often the first new businesses to be established in neighborhoods as they begin to gentrify, and they continue to be included in the upscale development projects that characterize later stages of the gentrification process. The prestige that a restaurant, farmers' market, or community garden can lend to a neighborhood helps to increase property values, fostering the displacement of long-term residents while shifting local culture to create new inclusions and exclusions. And yet, many activists who oppose this dynamic have found food to be both a powerful symbol and an important tool through which to fight against it at scales ranging from individual consumption to state and national policies. To them, this book can offer a set of strategic considerations, ideas to stew and mull over as well as cautionary tales to peel away. We hope that the stories we have told here will inspire new recipes for our cities that elevate the flavor of environmentally sustainable and culturally and economically inclusive neighborhoods in which a diverse array of communities can thrive.

REFERENCES

Agyeman, Julian, Caitlin Matthews, and Hanah Sobel. 2017. *Food Trucks, Cultural Identity and Social Justice*. Cambridge, MA: MIT Press.

Alkon, Alison Hope and Josh Cadji. 2018. "Sowing Seeds of Displacement: Gentrification and Food Justice in Oakland, CA." *International Journal of Urban and Regional Research*. Published online, https://doi.org/10.1111/1468-2427.

Alkon, Alison Hope and Julie Guthman. 2017. *The New Food Activism*. Berkeley: University of California Press.

Anguelovski, Isabel. 2016. "Healthy Food Stores, Greenlining and Food Gentrification: Contesting New Forms of Privilege, Displacement and Locally Unwanted Land Uses in Racially Mixed Neighborhoods." *International Journal of Urban and Regional Research* 39(6): 1209–1230.

Blomley, Nicholas. 2004. *Unsettling the City: Urban Land and the Politics of Property*. New York: Routledge.
Brown-Saracino, Japonica. 2009. *A Neighborhood that Never Changes*. Chicago: University of Chicago Press.
Brown-Saracino, Japonica. 2010. *The Gentrification Debates*. New York: Routledge.
Carney, Judith. 2001. *Black Rice*. Cambridge, MA: Harvard University Press.
Chaney, Cassandra and Ray V. Robertson. 2013. "Racism and Police Brutality in America." *Journal of African American Studies* 17(4): 480–505.
Cohen, Daniel Aldana. 2019. "A Green New Deal for Housing." *Jacobin*. https://jacobinmag.com.
Coscarelli, Joe. 2014. "Spike Lee's Amazing Rant Against Gentrification: 'We Been Here!'" *NY Magazine*, http://nymag.com.
Crowder, Kyle and Scott J. South. 2005. "Race, Class, and Changing Patterns of Migration Between Poor and Nonpoor Neighborhoods." *American Journal of Sociology* 110(6): 1715–1763.
Curran, Winifred and Trina Hamilton. 2012. "Just Green Enough: Contesting Environmental Gentrification in Greenpoint, Brooklyn." *Local Environment* 17(9): 1027–1042.
Curran, Winifred and Trina Hamilton. 2018. *Just Green Enough: Urban Development and Environmental Gentrification*. New York: Routledge.
DeLind, Laura. 2002. "Place, Work and Civic Agriculture." *Agriculture and Human Values* 19(3): 217–224.
DiAngelo, Robin. 2018. *White Fragility*. Boston, MA: Beacon.
DuPuis, E. Melanie and David Goodman. 2005. "Should We Go Home to Eat." *Journal of Rural Studies* 21(3): 359–371.
DuPuis, E. Melanie and Miriam Greenberg. 2019. "The Right to the Resilient City: Progressive Politics and the Green Growth Machine in New York City." *Journal of Environmental Studies and Sciences* 9(3): 352–363.
Frederick, Jamal. 2014. "What Happened to the Fillmore?" *The Bold Italic*. https://thebolditalic.com.
Freire, Paulo. 2000[1970]. *Pedagogy of the Oppressed*. New York: Bloomsbury.
Garcia, Matt, E. Melanie DuPuis, and Don Mitchell. 2017. *Food Across Borders*. New Brunswick, NJ: Rutgers University Press.
Goetz, Edward. 2011. "Gentrification in Black and White: The Racial Impact of Public Housing Demolition in American Cities." *Urban Studies* 48(8): 1581–1604.
Goldberg, David Theo. 1993. "'Polluting the Body Politic': Racist Discourse and Urban Location." In *Racism, the City and the State*, edited by Malcolm Cross and Michael Keith, 45–60. New York: Routledge.
Gould, Kenneth A. and Tammy L. Lewis. 2017. *Green Gentrification: Urban Sustainability and the Struggle for Environmental Justice*. New York: Routledge.
Guthman, Julie. 2008. "Bringing Good Food to Others." *Cultural Geographies* 15: 431–447.
Haber, Matt. 2014. "Oakland, Brooklyn by the Bay." *New York Times*, www.nytimes.com.

Ho, Soleil. 2014. "#Foodgentrification and Culinary Rebranding of Traditional Foods." *Bitch Magazine*, www.bitchmedia.org.
Hondagneu-Sotelo, Pierette. 2014. *Paradise Transplanted*. Berkeley: University of California Press.
Hyde, Zach. 2014. "Omnivorous Gentrification. *City & Community* 13(4): 341–359.
Hyra, Derek. 2017. *Race, Class, and Politics in the Cappuccino City*. Chicago: University of Chicago Press.
Jacobs, Jane M. 1996. *Edge of Empire: Postcolonialism and the City*. New York: Routledge.
Kato, Yuki. 2014. "Gardeners, Locavores, Hipsters, and Residents: An Alternative Local Food Market's Potential for 'Community' Building." *Journal of Agriculture, Food Systems and Community Development* 5(1): 145–159.
Kendall, Mikki. 2014. "Breaking Black: 1 in 5 Children Face Food Insecurity." *The Grio*, https://thegrio.com.
Kloppenberg, Jack. 1996. "Coming into the Foodshed." *Agriculture and Human Values* 13(3): 33–42.
Lambert, Dannette. 2014. "20 Ways to Not Be a Gentrifier." *Alternet*, www.alternet.org.
Lees, Loretta. 2016. "Gentrification, Race, and Ethnicity: Towards a Global Research Agenda?." *City & Community* 15(3): 208–214.
Logan, John and Harvey Molotch. 1987. *Urban Fortunes*. Berkeley: University of California Press.
Lyson, Tom. 2004. *Civic Agriculture*. Boston, MA: Tufts University Press.
Mantey, J. Ama. 2016. "Beyond Access: What the Movement for Black Lives' Policy Says about Food." https://civileats.com.
Mares, Teresa M. 2019. *Life on the Other Border: Farmworkers and Food Justice in Vermont*. Berkeley: University of California Press.
Martin, Nina. 2014. "Food Fight! Immigrant Street Vendors, Gourmet Food Trucks and the Differential Valuation of Creative Producers in Chicago." *International Journal of Urban and Regional Research* 38(5): 1867–1883.
McClintock, Nathan. 2018. "Cultivating (a) Sustainability Capital: Urban Agriculture, Ecogentrification, and the Uneven Valorization of Social Reproduction." *Annals of the American Association of Geographers* 108(2): 579–590.
Minkoff-Zern, Laura-Anne and Sea Sloat. 2016. "A New Era of Civil Rights: Latino Immigrant Farmers and Exclusion at the USDA." *Agriculture and Human Values*. doi 10.1007/s10460-016-9756-6.
Mock, Brett. 2019. "The Provocations of Chef Tunde Wey." *GQ*, March 6. www.gq.com.
NYU Furman Center. 2016. "Gentrification Response: A Survey of Strategies to Maintain Neighborhood Economic Diversity." http://furmancenter.org.
Ocejo, Rich. 2011. "The Early Gentrifier." *City & Community* 10(3): 285–310.
Patel, Raj and Jim Goodman. 2019. "A Green New Deal for Agriculture." *Jacobin* https://jacobinmag.com.
Peña, Devon, Luz Calvo, Pancho McFarland, and Gabriel R. Valle. 2017. *Mexican-Origin Foods, Foodways and Social Movements*. Little Rock: University of Arkansas Press.

Penniman, Leah. 2018. *Farming While Black*. New York: Chelsea Green.
Ray, Krishnendu. 2016. *The Ethnic Restaurateur*. New York: Bloomsbury.
Reese, Ashanté. 2019. *Black Food Geographies: Race, Self-Reliance and Food Access in Washington DC*. Chapel Hill: University of North Carolina Press.
Richardson, Jason, Bruce Mitchell, and Juan Franco. 2019. "Shifting Neighborhoods: Gentrification and Cultural Displacement in American Cities." *National Community Reinvestment Coalition*, https://ncrc.org.
Rose, Kalima. 2002. "Combating Gentrification through Equitable Development." *Race, Poverty and the Environment* 9(1): 5–8.
Sbicca, Joshua. 2018a. *Food Justice Now!: Deepening the Roots of Social Struggle*. Minneapolis: University of Minnesota Press.
Sbicca, Joshua. 2018b. "Food, Gentrification and the Changing City." *Fuhem Ecosocial* 43: 1–7.
Shaw, W. S. 2007. *Cities of Whiteness*. Malden, MA: Blackwell.
Smith, Neil. 1979. "Toward a Theory of Gentrification: A Back to the City Movement by Capital, Not People." *Journal of the American Planning Association* 45(4): 538–548.
Smith, Neil. 2008[1982]. *Uneven Development*. Athens: University of Georgia Press.
Taylor, Keegana-Yamahtta. 2016. *From #BlackLivesMatter to Black Liberation*. Boston, MA: Haymarket Books.
White, Monica. 2018. *Freedom Farmers: Agricultural Resistance and the Black Freedom Movement*. Chapel Hill: University of North Carolina Press.
Williams, Justine M. and Eric Holt-Giménez, eds. 2017. *Land Justice: Re-Imagining Land, Food, and the Commons*. Oakland, CA: Food First Books.
Wolch, Jennifer, Jason Byrne, and Joshua P. Newell. 2014. "Urban Green Space, Public Health and Environmental Justice: The Challenge of Making Cities 'Just Green Enough.'" *Landscape and Urban Planning* 125: 234–244.
Zukin, Sharon. 2010. *Naked City*. Oxford: Oxford University Press.

ACKNOWLEDGMENTS

Food and gentrification. Seemingly unrelated. Dig a little deeper, though, and it turns out that these two social facts are often planted in the same soil. We quickly learned this as the editors of *A Recipe for Gentrification*. After our own fieldwork taught us about the ways that urban food activists discussed gentrification, and upon hearing from other scholars around North America who were similarly engaged with these issues, we began to wonder what in fact was taking place. This curiosity—and a concern with the inequities connecting what we eat to where we live—drove a series of engagements that ultimately generated the volume you are now reading.

Our individual research projects had been addressing the intersection of food and gentrification, but we collectively began our dialogue after a session on community gardening organized by Sofya Aptekar at the 2016 American Sociological Association's annual meeting in Seattle. It was here that it first became evident that examining food systems in the context of changing urban socio-political landscapes was on many of our minds. Some of us from that session went on to organize two consecutive sessions on Food Justice in the Changing City at the American Association of Geographers conference in 2017 in Boston. We thank the panelists and the audience at these sessions, who motivated us to continue and expand our dialogue at the 2017 Association for the Study of Food and Society/Agriculture, Food, and Human Values Society conference in Los Angeles. There, in a standing-room-only space, we discussed our research, which stimulated a robust conversation including critical questions from the audience. Afterward, the three of us realized the urgent need to pull together a volume analyzing and comparing the relationship between food and gentrification across North America. In addition to the panelists at these sessions, we reached out to our networks and asked around to determine who was writing or could write a chapter—and it turned out many of them were thinking and writing about the topic already. Very quickly we received exciting proposals from the group of authors featured herein, along with strong encouragement and support from the scholars working on similar topics who for various reasons could not contribute.

The next year, we organized a session at the 2018 annual American Association of Geographers Meeting in New Orleans that featured several of the authors in *A Recipe for Gentrification*. Here we had the pleasure of including Tunde Wey, the famed chef and provocateur, as a discussant for the session. Thank you, Tunde, for continuing to push the conversation on food and racial justice forward. As you pointed out, nowhere is this more critical than in how white and wealthy food spaces act as Trojan horses for gentrification. Additional thanks go to all the other food activists, both those chronicled in this volume and those who are not, who are working to create foodscapes that celebrate the vibrancy of low-income communities and communities of color. It is the work of these activists and organic intellectuals that inspires and drives our scholarship, and we hope that our writing can contribute to your efforts.

Additionally, without the passion and dedication of the authors who offer their collective insights to this volume, we would not be able to appreciate the many intersections between food and gentrification. Thank you all for your commitment to this project and especially to the time-sensitive nature of our collaboration. Gentrification vis-à-vis food negatively impacts many communities, and how or whether food activists engage with this reality is critical to the future of both food movements and urban development. These are not easy issues, and each author contributes distinct stories to help students, scholars, practitioners, movements, and policy makers as we navigate the upscaling of our cities through food and the increasing inequalities that follow. But, as some of you show, maybe food offers hope for resistance as well.

We also owe a huge thanks to NYU Press. It has been a pleasure to work with you all. From our initial engagements with Ilene Kalish, we knew we had an advocate for this project. We also appreciate the detail-oriented team of people whose hands touched this manuscript, especially Sonia Tsuruoka and Alexia Traganas, who helped shepherd this manuscript through production and copyediting. Thanks for all the strategic suggestions that improved the manuscript. And of course, this manuscript benefited from the two sets of anonymous reviewer comments. Your encouragement for this volume and concrete suggestions were helpful in fine-tuning the ultimate outcome.

Last, we would each like to thank our families for providing the support, intellectual space, and childcare (!) that makes work like this possible. To our children, two of whom were born during our collaboration on this volume, we hope this text can contribute to the intellectual and social movements that will allow you to enjoy a world in which you can share delicious food and vibrant urban spaces with diverse and overlapping communities.

ABOUT THE EDITORS

ALISON HOPE ALKON is Professor of Sociology at University of the Pacific. She is author of *Black White and Green: Farmers Markets, Race and the Green Economy* and co-editor of *Cultivating Food Justice* and *The New Food Activism*.

YUKI KATO is Assistant Professor of Sociology at Georgetown University. Her research examines the impacts of *green* policies and practices on environmental and food justice causes.

JOSHUA SBICCA is Associate Professor of Sociology at Colorado State University. He is the author of *Food Justice Now! Deepening the Roots of Social Struggle*.

ABOUT THE CONTRIBUTORS

SOFYA APTEKAR is Assistant Professor of Sociology at UMass Boston and Core Faculty in the Transnational, Cultural, and Community Studies program. She writes about public space, gentrification, alternatives to capitalism, and immigration.

EMILY BECKER is President of the Board of Directors of the Portland Fruit Tree Project. A community food systems consultant, she has worked with a range of organizations, including the Oregon Food Bank and Community Food Security Coalition. She received a Master of Urban Studies degree from Portland State University.

FERNANDO J. BOSCO is Professor of Geography and a Director of the doctoral program in Geography at San Diego State University. He received his PhD in geography from The Ohio State University. He works at the intersections of urban, social, and political geography, with interests in social movements, collective action, and the connections between food environments and urban change.

PAMELA ARNETTE BROOM received a Bachelor of General Studies degree in Humanities from Tulane University and completed a master's program in Urban Studies: Applied Anthropology at the University of New Orleans. She is currently directing a New Orleans neighborhood-based revitalization initiative that is designing a wellness hub to focus on the intersection between urban agriculture and medicine for community wellness.

YAHYA JOSH CADJI is a teacher and organizer with Phat Beets Produce, a food justice organization in Oakland, California, and an accomplice to Aunti Frances Moore's Self-Help Hunger Program. He holds an MA in Community and Regional Development from University of California, Davis.

CHARLOTTE GLENNIE is a PhD candidate in Sociology at the University of California, Davis. Broadly interested in social justice, contemporary environmental challenges, and urban change, she researches the intersections of food systems and urban development in US cities.

MICHELLE GLOWA is Assistant Professor of Anthropology and Social Change at the California Institute of Integral Studies in San Francisco. Her research interests include critical political ecology, urban social movements, and agri-food studies. Michelle approaches her research with more than fifteen years of experience working with food justice and urban agriculture organizing in the United States and Mexico.

BROOKE HAVLIK has worked over the past decade in community organizing, public media, and non-profit communications with a focus on environmental justice and human rights. She received an MS from the University of Oregon in Environmental Studies and a BA from DePauw University in Sociology and Anthropology.

ANALENA HOPE HASSBERG is a scholar-activist, educator, and mother committed to the legacy of liberating Black and other oppressed people through food, health, and wellness. With a BA in Africana Studies from San Francisco State University, and an MA and PhD in American Studies and Ethnicity from the University of Southern California, Analena is currently Assistant Professor of Ethnic and Women's Studies at California State Polytechnic University, Pomona, and an active member of several community-based social justice organizations in Los Angeles and the San Francisco Bay Area. Her research investigates food justice, environmental justice, and the role of food in historical freedom struggles and contemporary liberation movements.

ZACHARY HYDE is a PhD candidate in the Department of Sociology at the University of British Columbia. He studies issues of housing, urban development, gentrification, and consumption.

PASCALE JOASSART-MARCELLI is Professor of Geography and Director of the Urban Studies Program at San Diego State University, where she teaches courses such as geography of food, geography of cities, food justice, and community-based geographic research, and conducts research on the relationships between food, ethnicity, and place. She is particularly interested in the role of food in transforming immigrant neighborhoods. Pascale has published more than fifty peer-reviewed articles and book chapters, was the lead editor of a recently released volume entitled *Food and Place* and is currently working on a new book focusing on cosmopolitan foodscapes.

PRITA LAL is a faculty member in Food Justice/Food Policy at The Evergreen State College in Olympia, Washington. Her interests include the intersections of food and environmental justice with social movements, solidarity economics, and community-based learning. She has a PhD in Sociology from the State University of New York at Stony Brook and holds a certificate in Urban Agriculture from Farm School NYC.

JUSTINE LINDEMANN is Assistant Professor in the department of Agricultural Economics, Sociology, and Education at Penn State University. She earned her PhD in Development Sociology from Cornell University. Her work in Cleveland, Ohio focuses on race and the urban food system—particularly vacant land reuse and urban agriculture—as a way to understand how individuals and communities navigate inequities within and across urban space in the struggle for rights to and in the city.

NINA MARTIN is Associate Professor in the Department of Geography at The University of North Carolina at Chapel Hill and the Jordan Family Fellow of Global Studies. Her research areas include economic and community development, immigration and local political conflicts, and the management of nonprofit organizations. She is currently working on a book, *The Pretentious City*, which looks at the transformation of deindustrialized cities in the United States into spaces of affluent consumption, residences, and jobs.

NATHAN MCCLINTOCK is Associate Professor of Urban Studies and Urban Environmental Politics at the Institut National de la Recherche Scientifique in Montreal and is an editor of the journal *Urban Geography*. His work on urban agriculture, food justice, and urban political ecology has appeared in a range of geography, planning, and food studies journals and several edited volumes. He received his PhD in geography from UC Berkeley and MS in agroecology from North Carolina State University and was Associate Professor of Urban Studies and Planning at Portland State University prior to joining the faculty at INRS.

FRANCES MOORE is a community leader in North Oakland, California and founder of the Self-Help Hunger Program, which offers a weekly meal to low-income and homeless neighborhood residents. A former member of the Black Panther Party, her work is rooted in their Free Breakfast for Schoolchildren program, as well as their overall platform.

JUSTIN SEAN MYERS is Assistant Professor of Sociology at Cal State University, Fresno. He received his PhD in Sociology from The Graduate Center, City University of New York, his MA in Sociology from San Diego State University, and his BA in Sociology from Sonoma State University. His research utilizes historical and qualitative methods to examine how marginalized communities are organizing against social, environmental, and food-based inequities.

ANTONIO ROMAN-ALCALÁ has founded urban farms, local alliances, and grassroots policy councils; published in both peer-reviewed and popular outlets; and directed a documentary film on food systems in California. Most recently, he has been working to link academic, grassroots, and advocacy communities to advance agroecology in California and North America while pursuing his PhD at the International Institute of Social Studies (ISS) in The Hague.

ERIC SARMIENTO is Assistant Professor at Texas State University, San Marcos. He researches urban development, culture, and the political ecology of cities.

INDEX

Page numbers in italics indicate figures; page numbers followed by "t" indicate tables.

18th & Rhode Island Permaculture Garden, 195
40 acres and a mule, 305–306, 320

Active Community to Improve Our Nutrition (A.C.T.I.O.N.), 314–315
activism, 19; community gardens as form of, 256–257; in Downtown Eastside, 205–206
activists, alliances between, 15
aesthetics: beautification projects, 297–298; of community gardens, 248–251; of distinctiveness, 227–228; of gentrification, 16–17; of Portland Fruit Tree Project (PFTP), 146–147; restaurants and, 208–209; urban aesthetic for the white gaze, 297
affordability, 219, 297; redefined by low-income residents, 214–218; restaurants and, 207–210, 215–216
African Americans. *See* Black communities
agrarianism, Black, 284–285
Airbnb, 187, 191, 196
Alameda Corridor, 312
Alemany Farm, 180, *181*, 187
Algiers neighborhood, New Orleans, 117
alienation, 310
Alkon, Alison Hope, 239–240n1
Alpert, Jonathan, 108n2
"already-made" places, 307

alternate futures, 86–87
"alternative currency," 213, 219
alternative economies, 16
alternative food systems, 17, 229, 314–318; alternative food movements, 310–314; alternative food networks (AFNs), 71, 86, 87; alternative food spaces, 16; race and, 226–227; unintended consequences of, 18
Altius Farms, Inc., 101–103, 108n5
Amazon, 55, 68n3
American Community Gardening Association (ACGA), 159, 161–163, 172n2
American Tobacco Campus, 57
AmeriCorps, 140–141, 150
anti-elitism, 204
anti-gentrification efforts, 7–8, 14, 18, 20–21, 179–201, 220, 334–340; in Chicago, Illinois, 266–283; in Cleveland, Ohio, 284–304; in Los Angeles, California, 305–324; in New York, New York, 259–262; in Oakland, California, 230; in San Francisco, California, 179–201; in Vancouver, British Columbia, 202–203, 206, 217, 219–220
anti-gentrification organizations, 202
anti-racist movements, 227
appropriation, 220
Aquarian Bookshop, 315
Arlington Village, 245
Arnold, Anita, 85

355

artisanal food, 36
Asian communities, in Durham, North Carolina, 57
assemblage, 87
Astoria, Queens, New York, 246, 247–251, *249*
Atlanta, Georgia, 54
Atlantic Monthly, 122
authenticity, 43–48, 204, 207, 210, 229
autonomy, 171, 314; autonomous community land ownership, 307; autonomous urban food systems, 310–314; cultivating, 21, 305–324. *See also* self-determination

Balboa Park, San Diego, 39
Ball, Bill, 63
Barman, Emily, 203
Barrio Art Crawl (event), 49
Barrio Logan, 31–33, 39, *39t*, 40, 41, 43, 45–50, *48*
Baumann, Shyon, 46, 59, 204, 207
Bayview Hunters Point (BVHP), 184, 186, 191
Becker, Emily, 151n1
Bedford-Stuyvesant (Bed-Stuy), 246, 251–256, 260–262
Bell, Jeanette, 113, 120–121
belonging, 280–281, 312
Betcher, Jeffrey, 191, 192
Better Block OKC, 79
Bhaumik, Sita Kuratomi, 5
"Binner's Dinners," 212
biopolitical connections, 19
Bisnow, 94
Black agrarianism, 284–285
Black Codes, 306
Black communities, 186; in Cleveland, Ohio, 21, 284–304; in cities of Mountain West, 97; demolition of, 196; in Denver, Colorado, 1–2, 97, 99; displacement of, 276, 306–307; in Durham, North Carolina, 57–58; gatherings of, 253; in New York, New York, 247, 251–256; in Oakland, California, 223–242; in Oklahoma City, Oklahoma, 84; in San Francisco, California, 191, 196; second-class citizenship and, 306; urban agriculture and, 253–254
Black cultural traditions, marginalization of, 252–256
Black farmers, 15, 306
Black freedom struggles, 15
Black Panther Party, 223, 227, 231, 232, 314–321; breakfast programs for schoolchildren, 3–4, 313, 321n7; Southern California Chapter of, 314–318; survival programs, 313–318
Black urban agrarianism, 283–304
Black urban food movement, community and, 293–295
Black urban growers/gardeners, 266–283; city governments and, 293–295; in Cleveland, Ohio, 7, 18, 21, 284–304; cooptation of, 254; epistemic divide from city officials and development practitioners, 293–295; food production practices and, 293–295; southern rural histories and traditions and, 293; the state and, 287, 289–292
blight, 96, 100, 111, 112, 115, 154, 289, 296, 307–308, 313, 327
Bloomberg, Michael, rezoning under, 260
Bon Appétit, 54
Booker T. Washington High School, 118
Bosco, Fernando J., 31, 208–209
Boudreaux, Dwayne, 117
Bourdieu, Pierre, 16, 31, 33–35
Boyd, John, 305
Bradner Gardens, 164, *165*, 166, 168, 169, 172n3
Brand, Mark, 212–214, 217–218, 219
branding, 31
breakfast programs for schoolchildren, 313
Brett, John, 105
bridge gentrifiers, 247–248

Brooklyn, New York, 7, 60, 61, 246, 251–256
Brooklyn Queens Land Trust, 252–253
Broom, Pamela Arnette, 111–115, *114*, 116, 121, 129
Brown-Saracino, Japonica, 67, 203, 210, 220, 273
built environment, 19
Bull Durham (1988), 54
Burten, Bell, Carr, Inc. (BBC), 302n2

Cadji, Max, 224–225, 230, 231, 235–236
Cadji, Yahya Josh, 224–225, 231, 239–240n1
cafés, 1–5, 9, 40, 58, 71, 211–212, 267, 316–318, 333
Cajun food, 119
Calderon, Lisa, 1
California, 71; AB 551 in, 183, 193–194, 195, 196–197, 199; Proposition 13, 182, 186, 194
Cancino, Juan Carlos, 194
capitalism, 15–17, 95, 228, 286, 295, 309. See also caring capitalism
"Care Not Cash," 189, 199n2
caring capitalism, 203–204, 219–221
celebrity chefs, 207–208. See also specific chefs
Central City neighborhood, New Orleans, 112, 120
Central Park neighborhood, Durham, 56, 61
Chapel Hill, North Carolina, 58
Charleston, South Carolina, 54
Chesapeake Energy, 71, 78–79
Chicago, Illinois, 111, 266–283; class disparities in, 269–270; development in, 269–270; gentrification in, 10; housing costs in, 267; Latinx communities in, 266–283; Puerto Rican diaspora in, 7, 21, 266–283; Puerto Rican history in, 269–270; racial disparities in, 269–270; responses to gentrification in, 21, 266–283; "uneven development in, 269–270

Chicano culture, 43
Chicano movement, 40, 47, 57
Chicano Park, San Diego, 47
Chinatown (San Francisco), 184
Chinatown (Vancouver), 205–206, 217
Chinese Canadian community, in Vancouver, British Columbia, 202, 217
Chiu, David, 189, 190–191
circular migration, 271
citified sovereignty, 310–314
"Citizen Kale," 2
city farms, 113
City Heights, 47
Civic Center Park, Denver, public demonstration garden in, 93
civic responsibility, 295
class, 246, 254–255, 261
Cleveland, Ohio, 149, 284–304; Black communities in, 21, 284–304; Black urban growers/gardeners in, 7, 18, 21, 284–304; City Office of Sustainability, 291; City Planning Commission, 299, 300; gentrification in, 10; historical geographical background, 288–291; land use in, 284–304; Local and Sustainable Purchasing ordinance, 291; responses to gentrification in, 266–283; revitalization in, 295–300; Sustainable 2019 Initiative, 291; "Sustainable Development Pattern Map," 299, *300*; urban agriculture in, 291–292; urban renewal in, 295–300; vacant land in, 288–292, *292*; withholding of vacant land in, 293–295, 299
Cleveland Cuyahoga County Food Policy Coalition (CCCFPC), 291
Coalition for Community Advancement (CCA), 259–260, 263n4
coffee shops, 1, 5–6, 9, 21, 36, 54, 65, 149, 206, 211, 217, 227, 272, 326, 338, 340. See also cafés
Cole, Tyson, 103
collaboration, 138–139

collective community narratives, 274–275
collective urban gardening, 181–182
colonial narratives, 272–273
colonization, 276; legacy of, 280–281
colonizers, 272–273
Columbia Villa, 135, 136
commercial food spaces, 275–276. *See also specific kinds of spaces*
commercial upscaling, 202–222
communities: benefit of open space for, 195; of color, 15, 252–262; investment in, 259; marginalized, neglect of, 15; power of, 223–242; reclaimed through food and foodways, 14; self-determination and, 261. *See also* marginalized communities; *specific communities*
communities of color, in New York, New York, 252–260
community, 43–48; Black urban food movement and, 293–295; contested understandings of, 134–135; definition of, 133, 145; gentrification and, 132–153; loose community, 167; negotiation of, 149; in Portland, Oregon, 132–153; responses to gentrification, 20–21; sense of, 148
community agriculture programs, 229
community-based food systems, 223–242, 315
community-based growth, 287
community-based urban agriculture projects, 20, 93–110
community-building, 133–134, 136, 163–164, 255
Community Development Corporations (CDCs), 285, 300, 301, 302n2
Community Food Village Project (CFV), 315
community gardeners: of color, 252, 261–262. *See also* Black urban growers/gardeners
community gardens, 13, 15–16, 31, 276–277; as activism, 256–257; aesthetics of, 248–251; critical understanding of, 133; cultural signification of space and, 188; displacement from, 253; of East New York, 256–260; food-producing, 245–246; gentrification and, 260–262; gentrifiers and, 252–253; land use and, 261; in New York, New York, 21, 245–265, 247–251, 249, 251–256; of people of color, 253–255, 261–262; politics of gentrification and, 260–262; in Portland, Oregon, 132–153; resistance through, 154–155, 257–258; restricted space and, 310–311; scholarship on, 133; in Seattle, Washington, 154–175; "toxic," 255; urban development and, 154–175. *See also* community orchards
community health, 271
community movements, 191
community narratives, 274–275
community orchards, 132–153; community building and, 133; low-income neighborhoods and, 134–135
community organizing/organizers, 7, 221–222, 259–260
Community Services Unlimited (CSU), 8, 21, 305–324, 321n11
community supported agriculture (CSA), 101, 225, 230–231
community wellbeing, urban agriculture and, 197–198
Confederacy, 305–306
consensus, horizontalist idea of, 183
consumption: cultural politics of, 17; shifts in, 16
cooperatives, 74–86
cooptation, 80–86, 254
corporate ownership, 309
cosmopolitanism, 34, 38, 43, 48, 50
County of Durham, 57
creative capital theory, 167
creative class, 16, 20, 54–70, 73–74, 76–80, 79, 167, 168, 227
Creole cooking, 117, 119

Crescent City Farmers' Market, 130n3
Cresswell, Tim, 35
critical discourse analysis, 204, 221n2
cultural capital, 8, 60
cultural identities, "authentic," 16
cultural norms, naturalized, 247–251
cultural politics: of consumption, 17; of food consumption, 16, 17; of taste, 20, 31–53
cultural preservation, 269
culture, vs. structure, 16
Currid-Halkett, Elizabeth, 13
Curtis Park, Denver, 99, 103
Curtis Park Group, 100, 108n2

Daftary-Steel, Sarita, 258
Davis, Mike, 158–159
DeBerry, Jarvis, 2
De Blasio, Bill, 245
decolonization, 276, 280
Deep Deuce, in Oklahoma City neighborhood, 85
deficit model, 254
deindustrialization, 292
democracy, 43–48
democratization: claims of, 208, 210; of eating out, 210; of gourmet dining, 210
demographic change, food-based responses to, 268
demographics of research, 107n1
Denver, Colorado, 1–2, 93–110; Black communities in, 97, 99; demographics of, 99; Five Points, 1–2; food movement in, 94, 97–98, 107n1; gentrification in, 1–2, 5, 10, 98; homes in foreclosure, 96; housing collapse in, 96–97; job loss in, 96–97; Latinx community in, 97, 99, 103; *local food*, 93; recession in, 96–97; revitalization, 93; Sustainability Goals, 93, 104; unemployment in, 97; uneven development in, 95–96; urban agriculture in, 20, 93–110
Denver Food Vision, 104, 105

Denver Housing Authority (DHA), 99, 108n1
Denver Office of Economic Development, 98
Denver Post, 97
Denver Sustainable Food Policy Council, 93, 105, 108n1
Denver Urban Gardens, 93
Department of Agriculture, Food and Forestry, 76
desertion, 309
DeSoucey, Michaela, 14
developers, 60–66, 262; "demon developers," 62
development, 1–29, 93–110, 271–272, 299; in Chicago, Illinois, 269–270; community gardens and, 154–175; in Denver, Colorado, 93–110; effects on non-gentrifying communities, 286–304; in Oakland, California, 228; racialization of, 15; resistance to, 22, 154–155, 165–166, 168; "sustainable," 97–103; sustainable, 97–103; uneven, 95–96, 269–270; in Vancouver, British Columbia, 202. *See also* redevelopment
development corporations, 185
Devon Energy, 79
dining, 1–29. *See also* restaurants
displacement, 1–29, 149, 172, 226, 238, 251–256, 308; of Black communities, 276, 306–307; from community gardens, 253; in Denver, Colorado, 93–110; of ethnic minority consumers, 228; green gentrification and, 168–169; housing costs and, 155, 168–169, 311; hyper-gentrification and, 186; of indigenous peoples, 272–273; justification of, 254; of Latinx communities, 276, 280; of low-income residents, 198; in Oakland, California, 228, 231–232; property values and, 311; Puerto Rican communities and, 276, 280; resistance to, 22, 256–260, 279; threat of, 280;

displacement (*cont.*)
    as unintended consequence of CSU, 318–320; of working-class consumers, 228. *See also* eviction
dispossession, 246, 261; ethical gentrification as pathway to, 220–221; of people of color, 261–262. *See also* displacement
distinctiveness, aesthetics of, 227–228
Douglas, Tom, 158
Downtown Eastside (Vancouver, British Columbia), 202–222; activism in, 205–206; community organizing in, 205–206; history of contentious politics in, 205–207; social enterprise in, 210–214
Dred Scott Decision, 306
Driver's Plaza, 223–224, 231–234, 238
Dryades Public Market, 130n4
Duck Pond reality, 69n5
Duke University, 57
Durham, North Carolina, 54–70, 111; Asian communities in, 57; Black communities in, 57–58; City and County database, 69n4; city council of, 69n3; demographics of, 57; featured in New York Times "36 Hours" series, 61; food entrepreneurs in, 60; food industry of, 60–61; food scene in, 58–61; food scene of, 58; gentrification in, 10; Latinx communities in, 57–58; local food movement of, 59; post-industrial decline, 57; residential and business displacement, 62; restaurants in, 59, 68; transformation of downtown, 58; upscale restaurants in, 60
Durham Bulls minor league team, 57
Durham County, 56
The Durham Hotel, 59, 67

East New York, New York, 149, 246, 256–261
East New York Farms! (ENYF!), 246–247, 255, 256, 257, 258, 259, 262

East Village, San Diego, 41
East-West Partners, 63, 69n5
Eater, 40, 50n2, 51n4
eateries, *authentic*, 31
eating out, democratization of, 210
Eat Local Challenge, 122
EBT, 83
eco-gentrification, 228. *See also* green gentrification
economic inequalities, 19, 226–227
Eizenberg, Efrat, 250
elites, 13; consumption patterns of, 207
Ellis, Kedar, 231, 232–234, 236
Elyria-Swansea, Denver, Latinx community in, 103
enterprise zones, 185
entrepreneurial interests, 193, 198–199
entrepreneurs, 19, 60–66, 272
environmental justice activism, 169
Environmental Movement, 191
Ernwein, Marion, 170
ethical gentrification, 220–221, 221n1
"ethical" restaurants, 21, 202–222
ethnic minority consumers, displacement of, 228
ethnoracial inequalities, 19
eviction, 198, 223–242, 238
exchange value, 154, 155, 160, 168
exclusion, 18, 252
Executive Directive on Health and Sustainable Food, 183–184, 188, 195
exploitation, 15, 17
EXPO Center Mini-Farm, 315, *316*
"Expo evictions," 206

Falkenbury, Marlene, 163
Farmacia Wellness Hub, 130
farmers: urban. *See* urban agriculture
farmers' markets, 15–18, 31, 79, 224, 229–231, 276–277
Farmers Public Market (Oklahoma City), 79
farming: harmful practices, 16; tenant, 306; urban. *See also* urban agriculture

farms, 106
farmyards, 113
Federal-Aid Highway Act of 1956, 295–296
Feed Denver, 104
fetishization, 80–86
Filipino communities, 186
Fillmore, 186
Finley, Ron, 311, 321n3
Five Points Intersection, Durham, 58
Florida, Richard, 167, 168
folk foodways, 117, 119–120
food: gentrification and, 9–14, 16; gentrification scholarship and, 9–14; racialized under-development and, 15; resisting and reimagining gentrification through, 274–280; as social construct, 68n1; sustainable, 183; used to reclaim communities, 14
food access, 15, 19, 219, 257, 270–271, 278, 307–310, 309, 312, 314–315
food activism, 12, 14, 18, 226–229, 238–239
food behavior, 68n1
food consumption, cultural politics of, 16
food cooperatives, 74–86
food deserts, 31, 124, 308
food distribution, alternative sites of, 15
food "frontier," social preservationists and, 272–274
food heritage, 129
foodies, 207
food insecurity, 32, 271–272
"food intersections" approach, 14, 15, 16, 17, 19
food justice, 8, 15, 17–18, 184, 223–242, 256–260; economic inequality and, 226–227; food justice activism, 123, 223–242; food justice organizations, 223–242, 239–240n1; food sovereignty and, 310–314; gentrification and, 334–340; racial inequality and, 226–227
food miles, 74
food movements, 17, 107n1, 180, 184

food-producing community gardens, 245–246
food production, 7, 17; Black urban growers and, 293–295; cultural politics of consumption and, 17; organic, 17; political economy of, 16
food provisioning, 225
food research, gentrification and, 14–19
food retail, 12, 15, 17. *See also* grocery stores; restaurants
foods, low-quality, 257
foodscape, 32
food security, 204, 222, 271, 276–277, 311. *See also* food insecurity
food sovereignty, 19, 21, 219, 268, 280, 295, 305–324
food spaces, 275–276
food stamps, 88n7
food sufficiency, 311
food swamps, 31
food systems, 17, 229, 314–318; alternative, 16–18, 71, 86–87, 226–227, 229, 310–314, 314–318; alternative food movements, 310–314; alternative food networks (AFNs), 71, 86, 87; alternative food spaces, 16; community-based, 223–242, 315; inequalities in, 15; local, 312, 314–318; race and, 226–227; regional, 181; sustainable, 183; unintended consequences of, 18
food systems perspective, 19
Food Talk Project, 117–118
food truck businesses, 119
foodways, 8, 117–121, 267–268; folk foodways, 117, 119–120; food retail and, 17; gentrification of, 115–117, 127–130; used to reclaim communities, 14; working-class, 17
Fordism, 71
forgotten places, 309
Forgotten Triangle, 288–292, 292
Foster, Donald, 5
Freedom Farm Cooperative, 227

French Quarter, New Orleans, 117, 119
Frezel, Aumra, 117
Frias, Roy, 259
Fruits of Diversity Community Orchard (FOD), 132–153, *137*, *147*

Galloway, Caitlyn, 194
Garcia, Juanita, 275
Garden District, New Orleans, 119
gardeners, immigrant, 7. *See also* Black urban growers/gardeners; community gardeners
gardens: temporary, 196–197; urban, 7, 12, 13, 22, 117–119. *See also* community gardens
Gardenship Fund, 169
Garden Valley Neighborhood, 297
Gastown Gamble, 205, 212
gastrodiplomacy, 8
"gastropolitics," 14
gentrification, 16, 67, 71, 84, 100, 127, 195, 217, 306–307; aesthetics of, 16–17; alternative food spaces and, 16; Bedford-Stuyvesant (Bed-Stuy), 261–262; boutiquing, 11; in Chicago, Illinois, 10, 21, 266–283; class and, 246; in Cleveland, Ohio, 10, 266–283, 284–304; coffee shops and, 5–6; commercial, 202–222; community and, 132–153; community gardens and, 260–262; community responses to, 20–21, 179–201; consequences of, 10, 168–169, 271; contesting through food, 325–344; definition of, 285–286; in Denver, Colorado, 1–2, 5, 10; in Durham, North Carolina, 10; as dynamic process, 10–11; eco-gentrification, 228; "ethical," 202–222; externalities of, 284–304; food activism and, 226–229; food-based responses to, 268; food justice and, 334–340; food research and, 14–19; of foodways, 115–117, 127–130; green, 13, 93, 95–96, 106–107, 128, 154–175, 228–229, 238–239, 246, 310, 318–320; hypergentrification, 180–181; "institutional scaffolding" for, 11; land use and, 261; local factors in, 260–261; in Los Angeles, California, 10, 305–324; narratives of, 272–273; in New Orleans, Louisiana, 2–3, 6–7, 10, 111–131; in New York, New York, 10, 21, 245–265; in Oakland, California, 3–5, *4*, 21, 223–242; in Oklahoma City, Oklahoma, 10, 71–90; politics of, 260–262; in Portland, Oregon, 132–153; public sentiments toward, 13; race and, 16–17, 188, 227, 228–229, 246; reimagining through food, 274–280; resistance to. *See* anti-gentrification efforts; resisting through food, 274–280; responses to, 14; restaurants and, 202–222; retail, 202–222, *218*; in San Diego, California, 31–53; in San Francisco, California, 179–201; seeing through food, 325–344; spread of, 10; supergentrification, 229; taste of, 33, 36–39; "Trojan Horses" for, 191, 199, 214, 346; urban geographies of, 39–42; in Vancouver, British Columbia, 21, 202–222. *See also* green gentrification
gentrification scholarship, food and, 9–14
Gentrification Trends and Locations of Highly Rated Restaurants in Central San Diego, *42*
gentrifiers, 67, 202–203, 246; as allies, 279–280; community gardens and, 252–253; cultural norms imposed by, 252–253; desire for alternative foods and, 228; microaggressions by, 254; reflexive, 202
gentrifying forces, 286–304
Gibson-Graham, JK, 16
Gilligan, Johanna, 2
Gilmore, Ruth Wilson, 309
"giving back" to the community, 210–214, 219, 222
GlaxoSmithKline, 56
Glennie, Charlotte, 196

Glowa, Michelle, 180
Goodson, Stephanie, 195–196
Google, 187
Gould, Kenneth, 95
gourmet dining: democratization of, 210; in low-income neighborhoods, 207–210
Granata Farms, 99
grassroots resiliency, 319
Great Black Migration, 293
Greater Humboldt Park Urban Agriculture Initiative (GHPUAI), 276–278
Great Recession, 93–94, 96, 103, 106, 292
Green City Growers, 291
Green Corps, 302n1
green distinction, 13
Greenfire Development, 63
green gentrification, 13, 128, 310; in Denver, Colorado, 93, 95–96, 106–107; displacement and, 168–169; food activism and, 238–239; mitigating, 318–320; in New York, New York, 246; in Oakland, California, 228, 229; in Seattle, Washington, 154–175; urban agriculture and, 106–107
Green Leaf Denver, 99
green living, 168
green spaces, 123; green space vision, 250–251, 261
green supermarkets, 82
GreenThumb 247, 252
grocery stores, 15, 278, 309–310. *See also* food access; supermarkets
Grow Dat Youth Farm, 2
GrowHaus, 103
Growing Home Garden, 195
Growing Power, 111
Grow Local Colorado, 93
growth, 198; community-based, 287; managed, 170
growth coalitions, 154, 170, 171
growth machine theory, 165, 167
Guthman, Julie, 71

Haight-Ashbury Neighborhood Center (HANC), 189
Hamer, Fannie Lou, 227
Hamnett, Chris, 37
HANC eviction, 198
Hancock, Mayor Michael, 93, 98, 104
Hands and Heart Garden, 259
Hansman, Heather, 2
Harmon, Doug, 123
Hart to Hart community garden, 255
Harvey, David, 95
Hayes Valley Farm, 195
health, 19
health food stores, 16
healthy food, 15, 31, 312. *See also* food access
Heldke, Lisa, 45
Herbert, Sally, 101
Hickenlooper, Mayor John, 93
Highland Park, 245
Highline, New York City, 95
Hillcrest, San Diego, 42
Hollygrove Market and Farm, 130n4
Home Forward, 135
homelessness, 112, 228, 238
Home Owners Loan Corporation, 302n4
"homesteaders," 67
housing: affordable, 217, 228, 267, 280, 307, 310, 319. *See also* housing costs
Housing and Urban Development, Neighborhood Stabilization Program, 100
Housing Authority of Portland (HAP), 135, 136
housing costs, 280, 310; in Chicago, Illinois, 267; displacement and, 155, 168–169, 311; gentrification and, 168–169; in Oakland, California, 224, 228; in Portland, Oregon, 149; in Vancouver, British Columbia, 206
housing crisis, in San Francisco, California, 186–188, 198
housing discrimination, 135–136
Housing Opportunities for People Everywhere (HOPE VI) program, 136

housing shortages, 310
Humboldt Park, Chicago, 266–283
Humphries, Stan, 5–6
hunger, 84, 312
Hurricane Katrina, 111, 115, 120–121
Hurricane Maria, 266
hypergentrification, 180–181, 186

IBM, 56
identities, 14, 16; indigenous, 312–313; taste and, 31
immigrant communities, as stakeholders, 272
immigrant gardeners, 7
immigrant rights, 15, 19
inclusion, 204, 208, 234
inclusionary housing ordinance (IHO), 98
"inconspicuous consumption," 13
Indigenous Elders, 214
indigenous food sovereignty, 19
indigenous foodways, 312–313
indigenous peoples, displacement of, 272–273
IndyWeek, 66
inequalities, 19, 172, 217, 219; economic, 19, 226–227; in food system, 15; racial, 19, 226–227; structural, 11–12
instability, 312
Interbay P-Patch, 164
interim-use projects, 196
investment, 11; in communities, 259; in San Francisco, California, 198; structural, 12

Jackson, Jocelyn, 5
jail-to-work programs, 183
Jameson, Fredric, 47
Jarosz, Lucy, 71
Jazz Fest, New Orleans, 117
Jenkins, Floyd, 118
Jim Crow Laws, 306
Joassart-Marcelli, Pascale, 31, 208–209
John Muir Middle School, 315

Johnson, Andrew, 306
Johnston, Josée, 46, 59, 204, 207
Jonas, Andrew E. G., 95
Jordan, June, 320
junk food, 31
justice, 184; food justice, 8, 15, 17–18, 123, 184, 223–242, 239–240n1, 256–260, 310–314, 334–340; racial justice, 17, 184, 195, 258; radical justice, 184; social justice, 17, 84, 180, 191, 192, 197–198, 204, 217, 222, 258

kale, 6–7
kalegate, 2–3, 6–7
Kaplan, George, 308
Kato, Yuki, 116, 121, 124
Kellogg Foundation, 315
Kendall, Mikki, 7
Keuhn, Susan, 193
King, Rodney, 312, 321n5
Kinsman neighborhood, Cleveland, Ohio, 285–304

labor conditions, activism focused on, 15
Lafitte Housing Project, 118
land insecurity, 194–197
land tenure insecurity, 196
land use, 18, 183, 193–194, 287, 294, 299, 300; alternative, 289–292, 299; community gardens and, 261; equitable, 311; gentrification and, 261; politics of possibility, 287; temporary, 196–197; transportation projects and, 285–304
land use value, 313
land value, 287
Laotian refugees, 169
Las Cuatro Milpas (restaurant), 43
Latin American immigrants, 312
Latinx communities, 103; in Chicago, Illinois, 266–283; in cities of Mountain West, 97; in Denver, Colorado, 97, 99, 103; displacement of, 276; in Oakland, California, 229; in Oklahoma

City, Oklahoma, 84; in San Francisco, California, 186, 187
Lee, Edwin, 189, 309
Lee, Tony, 122
Lefebre, Bobby, 5
Leland, 186
Lenovo, 57
Levine, Naomi, 274–276
Lewis, Tammy, 95
Liberty Warehouse complex, 56, 62, 64, 64, 66, 66
Lincoln, Abraham, 306
lines of flight, 87
Little City Gardens, 188, 189, 194, 197
Little Italy, San Diego, 41
living costs, rising, 307, 310
Lloyd, Richard D., 11
local culture, 310
local distribution, 17
local food, 73, 80–82, 86, 87n3, 88n6, 101, 116, 118–119, 127, 181; emergence of, 74–76; local food economy, 127; local food initiatives, 169; local food movement, 20, 54–70, 71–90, 87n1; local food retailers, 17; local food systems, 312, 314–318
local foodways, 15, 21, 111–131, 305–324; autonomous community control of, 312; racialization of, 16–17
local knowledge, 310
Logan, John, 165
loose community, 167
Lorde, Audre, 318
Los Angeles, California, 8, 149, 195; autonomous urban food systems in, 310–314; cultivating autonomy in, 305–324; foodscape of, 308–310; gentrification in, 10; local growth coalition in, 170; responses to gentrification in, 305–324; Watts and LA Uprisings in, 310
Los Angeles Food Bank, 312
Louisiana Cooperative Extension Service, 118

Love Mission Self-Help Hunger Program, 223–242
Lower Ninth Ward, New Orleans, 118, 124
low-income neighborhoods: community orchards and, 134–135; gourmet dining in, 207–210; paradox of caring capitalism in, 219–220; restaurants in, 207–210; social enterprise and, 202–222; urban agriculture spaces and, 149–150
low-income residents, displacement of, 198

Magellan Street Garden, 122
Malcolm X, 305
managed growth coalition, 170
Mares, Teresa, 312
marginalized communities, 293–295; empowerment of, 148–149. *See also specific communities*
Marxism, 16
the *master's tools*, 318
The Matador Network, 230
McClintock, Nathan, 167, 170
McFetridge, Scott, 100
McMillan, Tracie, 122
media, 17–18, 123, 272. *See also* social media
Metropolitan Area Projects Plan (MAPs), 73
Mexican Americans, 47
microaggressions, by gentrifiers, 254
microbreweries, 31
microfarms, 113
micro-processes, 135, 139, 150
Mid-City neighborhood, 113
middle-class residents, 228
Mills, Demetrice, 252–253
Mission, San Francisco, 184, 185, 186
Mission Hills, San Diego, 42
Molotch, Harvey, 165
Moore, "Aunti" Frances, 21, 223–224, 226, 228, 230, 232, 233, 234–235, 236, 238; eviction defense campaign of, 224, 225, 238

Morphy, Natalia, 224, 238, 239
Mountain West, cities in, 97
Movement for Black Lives, 19
Movoto, 230
Murphy, Rex, 216
Murrah Federal Building, 1993 bombing of, 73

narratives, 274–275
National Black Farmers Association, 305
National Register of Historic Places, 47
Native Roots Market, 79
neighborhood authenticity, 210
neighborhood change, 204–205; neighborhood change research, 202–203; restaurant reviews and, 204–205
Neighbors Outing Blatant Exploitation, 230
"neo-bohemia," 11
neoliberalism, 133, 169–170, 199, 261, 294, 309; roll-back, 170; urbanization of, 15, 185, 195; welfare state and, 203
New Columbia housing complex, 135, *137*, 143, 149, 151
newcomers, 2, 7, 11–14, 17–18, 21, 32, 38, 66, 170–171, 219–221, 230, 234, 289; in Chicago, Illinois, 269, 273–274, 280; in Los Angeles, California, 310, 326–327; media and, 123; in New Orleans, Louisiana, 120–123, 125, 127–129, 136, 148; in New York, New York, 246, 248, 252–254; socially conscious, 221n1, 334–336; in Vancouver, British Columbia, 202–204, 208, 210–213; volunteering by, 211–212; "well-intended," 14. *See also* gentrification; gentrifiers
newcomers, 121
NewCorp, Inc., 129
New Orleans, Louisiana, 54, 95, 111–131; engaging local residents and communities in, 123–125; foodways in, 117–121; gentrification in, 2–3, 6–7, 10, 127–130; growing local food in, 126–127; homeless population of, 113; kalegate in, 2–3, 6–7; local food in, 116, 117, 126; as a majority Black city, 121; new local foodways in, 127, 128; new locals growing in, 121–122; new urban agriculture narratives in, 122–123; post-Katrina, 111, 115–116, 119, 128, 130; sixth Ward, 118; urban agriculture and, 20, 111–131
New Orleans Food and Farm Network (NOFFN), 113, 117–118
New Orleans Food Cooperative, 130n4
New Orleans Mission, 113
New Orleans Redevelopment Authority, 116
New Season supermarket, 149
Newsom, Gavin, 183–184, 188; anti-poor welfare reform legislative effort "Care Not Cash," 189, 199n2; Executive Directive on Health and Sustainable Food, 183–184, 188, 190, 195
Newton, Huey P., 319
new urban agriculture narratives, 122–123
New Urbanism, 136, 287
New York, New York, 40, 245–265; Black communities in, 247, 251–256; communities of color in, 252–260; community gardens in, 21, 245–265; gentrification in, 10, 260–262; green gentrification in, 246; Parks Department, 247, 250; Puerto Rican communities in, 247; resistance in, 251–256; responses to gentrification in, 21, 245–265; upzoning in, 245
New York City Community Gardening Coalition, 253–254
New York Post, 255
New York Times, 54, 61, 120
no-growth movements, 165–166, 170
NOMAD gardens, 195–196
non-gentrifying communities, 285–304
non-profit industrial complex, 318–320
non-profit organizations, 21, 318–320. *See also specific organizations*

Normandie Avenue Elementary School, 315
North Oakland, Berkeley, and Emeryville (NOBE), 229–231, 231–236
North Oakland, California, 223–242
North Oakland Restorative Justice Council, 231, 236
North Park, San Diego, 31–33, 39, 39t, 41, 45, 48
North Portland, 130n4, 149
NVivo software, 51n4
Nyéléni Declaration on Food Sovereignty, 311

Oakland, California, 3–5, 4, 7–8, 149, 223–242; Black communities in, 223–242; development in, 228; displacement in, 228, 231–232; gentrification in, 3–5, 4; green gentrification in, 229; housing costs in, 224, 228; Latinx communities in, 229; rent control in, 224; responses to gentrification in, 21, 223–242; revitalization in, 229–230
Oakland Communities United for Equity and Justice (OCUEJ), 236–238, 237
Obama, Michelle, 93
Ohio, land use in, 291–292
Ohio Department of Transportation, 285–286, 300
The Ohio State University Extension, 291; Ohio State University Extension Incubator Farm, 291; Summer Sprouts program, 302n1, 302n2
Oklahoma, farming in, 88n4
Oklahoma City, Oklahoma, 71–90, 87n1; banking collapse in, 73; Black communities in, 84; central business district (CBD), 73; creative class in, 73, 76–80; gentrification in, 10; homeless individuals in, 73; hunger and, 83; Latinx communities in, 84; local food movement in, 20, 54–70, 71–90; local food retailers in, 17; oil bust in, 73; revitalization, 86; before revitalization and local food, 73–74; revitalization of, 76–80; urban revitalization in, 71; Whole Foods Market and, 78
Oklahoma Food Cooperative (OFC), 74–76, 78–79, 81–83, 86, 87n3, 88n3, 88n8
Olsen, Jeff, 101
omnivorousness, concept of, 207–208, 215–216
open space, community benefit of, 195
Operation Victory Gardens, 101
O. Perry Walker Senior High School, 117–118
Opportunity Corridor (OC), 285–304, 288
oppression, 15, 17
Oprah Winfrey Network, 205, 212
Orchard Steward program, 143, 150
Orleans Parish, 118
Out to Lunch, episode on urban agriculture, 123

Palladino, Suzi, 183–184
Parkway Partners, 116, 118
Paseo Boricua, 7, 266, 267–270, 269, 272, 274, 276, 277, 279
Paul Robeson Community Wellness Center (PRCWC), 316–321, 317, 321n10
Pedro Albizu Campos High School, 276–278
Peña, Devon, 307, 312
people of color: community-building by, 255; community gardens of, 253–255, 261–262; dispossession of, 261–262; as stakeholders, 272. See also specific communities
People's Kitchen Collective (PKC), 3–5, 4, 7
permaculture, 148, 226, 234–235; Portland Fruit Tree Project (PFTP) and, 150; as set of design principles, 234–235
Phat Beets Produce, 7–8, 21, 223–226, 229–231, 234–239, 239–240n1
"Pidgin Protest," 215–216

Pinehurst P-Patch, 161–163
Pizzeria Farina, 209
place, 280–281, 312; place-based identity, 314; placelessness, 312; placemaking, 274, 310; place marketing, 185; taste and, 32–36
"Plan Book for Plans" Archive, 130n2
planned shrinkage, 245–246, 252, 256, 261
plantation owners, 306
policing, 217
Policy Link, 229
policymaking, 11
political economy: of food production, 16; urban, 154
politics, 261
politics of possibility, 198; land use, 287
portability, 196
Portland, Oregon, 60, 61, 132–153, 151n1; community gardens in, 132–153; community in, 132–153; gentrification in, 132–153; history of housing discrimination in, 135; housing authority of, 135; housing discrimination in, 135–136; housing prices in, 149; urban agriculture, 136
Portland Fruit Tree Project (PFTP), 132–153, 137, 151–152n1, 152n2; aesthetics of, 146–147; collaboration and, 138–139; decision-making and, 141–142; formalization of volunteer roles and, 142–146; management practices and, 146–147; modes of communication and, 139–140; permaculture and, 148, 150; race/ethnicity of neighborhood and orchard participants, 144; timeline of key events, 138t; volunteers and, 150
Portland urban gardens, timeline of key events, 138t
Portsmouth neighborhood, Portland, 137
Por Vida, 47
post-Katrina newcomers, 123
post-structuralism, 16
"Potluck Café," 212

poverty, 217
power relations, 16, 134–135
P-Patch program, 162, 172n1; alignment with growth coalition goals, 161–167; internal concerns about growth in, 159–161; P-Patch gardens today, 167–172; public participation in, 161–167; in Seattle, Washington, 156–159
praxis, 329–334
predatory lending, 309
Preservation Durham, 63
prison abolition, 15, 19
privatization, 312
Produce Denver, 99
profit motivation, 210
property, ownership of, 306
property taxes, 183, 193–194
property values, 195, 227, 228, 310, 311
Proposition 13, 182, 186, 194
Proposition E, 182
Prospect Park, New York City, 95
Protect Our Parks initiative, 157, 158–159, 167, 172n2
public gaze, 298
public housing, 135–136, 202
public-private partnerships, 185, 195, 319
Puerto Rican Cultural Center (PRCC), 271, 275, 276–278, 281
Puerto Rican diaspora, 7, 21, 266–283; circular migration of, 271; displacement and, 276, 280; in New York, New York, 247
Puerto Rican foodways, 267–268
Puerto Rican–owned businesses, 279–280
Puerto Rico, 266

race, 8, 19, 144t, 226–227; alternative food systems and, 226–227; gentrification and, 246; racial inequality, 254–255, 261
racialization, 274; of everyday life, 15; of gentrification, 16–17, 228–229; of local foodways, 16–17; racialized underdevelopment, 15; of space, 272–273, 287

racial justice, 17, 184, 195, 258
racism, 15, 188, 227, 274–276
radical justice, 184
Radio Rhumba, 279
Raleigh, North Carolina, 58, 68n2, 69n5
Ray at Night (event), 49
real estate companies, 229–230, 236, 262
real estate development, 299
real estate speculation, 228
redevelopment, 21–22, 54–70, 228, 246–247, 306–307, 310, 312
redlining, 302n4, 309
Reed, Nicholas, 194
reflexivity, 202, 210
regional culinary traditions, 16
regional food systems, 181
rent control, 224, 228
rent gap, 228
Research Triangle Park, Durham, 56
restaurateurs, 20, 207, 215, 217, 220, 272, 326–327; branding of businesses as "of the community," 11–12; "giving back" to the community, 210–214; savior, 60–61
restaurant reviews, 267–268; neighborhood change and, 204–205
restaurants, 31; access to, 219; affordability and, 209, 215–216; design aesthetics of, 208–209; "ethical," 21, 202–222; gentrification and, 202–222; in low-income neighborhoods, 207–210; in New Orleans, Louisiana, 78; reviews of, 204–205; in Vancouver, British Columbia, 202–222, 209
restrictive covenants, 309
revalorization, 99
revitalization, 21, 76–80, 79, 84, 226, 229–230, 280, 295–300, 312
Reynolds, Kristen, 157
Ricchiuti, Peter, 123
Rice, Norm, 163–164, 166–167
Richards, Sam, 123
Rid-All Green Partnership Farm, 291
The Rise and Fall of Liberty, 65

Robeson, Paul, 321n10
Rolando's Taco Shop, 46–47
roll-back neoliberalism, 170
Roman-Alcalá, Antonio, 180, 183–184, 192, 193, 194
Ronen, Hillary, 179
Royer, Charles, 161–162
rural economies, 88n4

San Diego, California, 11, 31–53; Barrio Logan, 7; clusters of 'good taste' in, 40; food landscape of, 40; gentrification in, 10; kernel density of highly rated restaurants in, 41
San Diego Brewer's Guild, 50n2
San Diego Magazine, 50, 50n2, 51n4
San Francisco, California, 40, 179–201; Black communities in, 191, 196; city government of, 181–185; entrepreneurial interests in, 193, 199; gentrification in, 185–188; growth in, 198; housing crisis in, 186–188, 198; investment in, 198; land audit of city property in, 190; Latinx communities in, 186, 187; Office of Economic and Workforce Development, 195; payroll tax exemption in, 186; "Pay to Play" reservation system in, 188; Proposition E, 182; Recreation and Park Department (RPD), 188, 189; responses to gentrification in, 179–201; tech industry in, 186; "Twitter tax break" in, 186; urban agriculture in, 179–201
San Francisco Board of Supervisors, 179, 189
San Francisco Department of Public Works, 181–182
San Francisco Food Policy Council, 188
San Francisco General Plan, 183
San Francisco Housing Development corporation, 196
San Francisco League of Urban Gardeners (SLUG), 182–183, 198

San Francisco Planning Department, 188
San Francisco Urban Agriculture Alliance (SFUAA), 21, 179–201; case stories from, 188–197; diversity of, 184, 197; ethnic composition of, 184; formation of, 181–185; as grassroots alliance, 184; influence of, 198; organizational structure of, 184; participants in, 182*t*; political diversity of, 184; political engagement and, 190; position on gentrification, 192–193; UA legislation #1, 188–189; UA legislation #2, 189–192; Urban Agriculture Incentives Zone Act—AB 551, 183, 193–194, 195, 196–197, 199; urban agriculture program, 189–192; volunteers and, 184, 193; zoning changes, 188–189
San Jose, California, 195
Savannah, Georgia, 305
"Save the Farm" campaign, 197
"savior entrepreneurs," 54–70, 272
Sbicca, Joshua, 15, 188
Schewel, Steve, 57
Seale, Bobby, 320
Seattle, Washington, 55; green gentrification in, 154–175; P-Patch program in, 156–159
"second-hand foods," 257
Seeds of Harmony community garden, 136–137, *137*, 138, 146
segregation, 228, 274. *See also* Jim Crow Laws
self-determination, 269, 276, 314–315
Self-Help Hunger Program, 21, 225–226, 231, 233–239
self-reliance, 314
self-valorization, 62
Seventh Ward Revitalization Project (7WRP), 129
sharecropping, 306
Sharma, Neelam, 315
sheet mulch, 146–148, *147*
Sherman, William T., 305–306, 320

Sherry, 105
Silicon Valley, 185, 186, 336
Single Room Occupancy (SRO) hotels, 202, 206, *209*, 215
Smith, Neil, 185, 186, 227, 285, 287
social differentiation, 13
social enterprise, 202, 210–214; community resistance to, 214–218; in Downtown Eastside, 210–214; low-income neighborhoods and, 202–222; resistance to gentrification and, 219–220
social entrepreneurs, 202–222
social justice, 17, 84, 180, 192, 197–198, 204, 217, 222, 258
social justice movements, 191
social media, 31, 32, 40, 46, 49, 50n1, 50n2, 51n4, 186, 267
social positioning, 16
social preservationists, 13, 21, 67, 203–204, 210, 220, 272–274
social reproduction, 287
Soul Tigers, 245
South Central Farm, 312–313
Southern Living Magazine, 54
southern rural histories and traditions, Black urban growers and, 293
South Los Angeles, 305–324; abandonment of and divestment from, 310; foodscape of, 308–310
South of Market (SOMA), 185, 186–187
sovereignty, 268, 280, 295, 310–314
space: claims to, 311; cultural signification of, 188; decolonization of, 276; marginalized, 307; private vs. public, 310–311; racialization of, 272–273, 287; spatial resistance, 307; urban space, 8, 72, 73, 85, 188, 293–295, 307, 312–313. *See also* land use
spatial policy, 297
spatial urban management, 297
SPUR (San Francisco Planning and Urban Renewal Association), 196
stasis, 80–86

the state, Black urban growers and, 287, 289–292
stereotypes, racial, 274–276. *See also* racism
Strathcona, 205
STREETS! 4
St. Roch Market, 130n4
structural exclusion, 252
structural inequalities, replication of, 11–12
structure, vs. culture, 16
Sunflower Farmers Market, 81, 82
Sun Harvest Kitchen Garden, 112, 113, *114*
Sunnyside, Denver, Latinx residents, 104
supergentrification, 229
supermarket flight, 309
supermarkets, 309–310
surveillance, 217
survival programs, 313–318
sustainability, 97–103, 197–198, 291–292, 314
sustainability capital, 95, 167
Sustainability Park (S*Park), 13, 99, 100–101, *102*, 103, 168
sweat equity initiatives, 258, 261
symbolic boundaries, 38, 49, 203

Tamarack Apartments, 135, 137, *137*, 138*t*, 144*t*, 146, 146–147, *147*, 149, 151, 151n1
taste, 8, 31, 32; Bourdieu's notion of, 16; cultural politics of, 20, 31–53; of gentrification, 33, 36–39; identities and, 31; place and, 32–36; production of, 16–17
Taste of North Park (event), 49
tax base, 295
tax incentives, 195
tech industry, 186, 193
tenant farming, 306
Tenderloin (San Francisco), 184
territorialization, 73
theory, 325–329
Thrillist, 40, 50n2, 51n4
Ting, Phil, 193, 194
Tipsy Cake event, 274–276

Transition Denver, 93
transportation projects, 285–304
TreeHouse Brokerage and Development, 100
Tulane University, 123
Tulsa, Oklahoma, 76, 79, 83
"turn to community," 133
Twitter, 186

underdevelopment, 15, 228
understory plants, 146, 148
"uneven alliances," 20–21
United Community Centers (UCC), 258, 259, 262
University Circle, 285, 286, 301
Upper Ninth Ward, New Orleans, 118
upscaling, 202–222, 280
upzoning, 245, 259–260, 261, 262
Urban Agrarian, 76
urban agriculture, 8, 12–13, 22, 94, 111, 113, 133, 136, 224, 230, 258, 276–277; Black communities and, 253–254; city government and, 181–185; in Cleveland, Ohio, 291–292; community wellbeing and, 197–198; as constituency to capture, 197; in Denver, Colorado, 20, 93–110; ecological sustainability and, 197–198; food justice and, 194; green gentrification and, 106–107; interventions for "sustainable" development, 97–103; media and, 17–18, 123; new narratives of, 122–123; in New Orleans, Louisiana, 20, 111–131; popularity of, 292; programs aimed at new locals, 125; in San Francisco, California, 179–201; social justice and, 197–198; strategic political marginalization of, 103–106; underdevelopment and, 15; uneven development and, 95–96; as white space, 254–255
Urban Agriculture Coalition, 182
Urban Agriculture Incentives Zone Act—AB 551, 183, 193–197, 199

Urban Agriculture Innovation Zone (UAIZ), 285–304, 302n2
urban agriculture nonprofits, 132–153
urban agriculture programs, 183, 189, 191, 278–279. *See also specific programs*
urban agriculture spaces, 149–150
urban boosters, 17–18, 19, 22, 229–230
urban development. *See* development
Urban Farmers Collaborative, 99, 100
urban farms, 224, 230. *See also* urban agriculture
urban gardening: collective, 181–182. *See also* community gardens
Urban Gardening Program, 118
urban gardens, 7, 12, 13, 22, 117–119. *See also* community gardens
urban geographies, of food gentrification, 39–42
urban greening, 168–169, 172, 228, 238–239
urban growth, concerns about, 159–160
urban growth machine, 154, 196. *See also* growth machine theory
urbanization: neoliberal, 195; of neoliberalism, 185
urban planning, 196, 295–296
urban policies, entrepreneurial interests and, 198–199
urban political economy, 154
urban renewal, 31, 297–298
"urban revanchism," 203
urban space, 293–295; debates over, 188; development of, 307; production of, 8; resignifying, 72, 73, 85; reterritorialization of, 312–313; uses of, 313. *See also* land use
urban theory, 167
Urry, John, 35
USDA (U.S. Department of Agriculture), 76, 80
U.S. Department of Housing and Urban Development, 130n1
use value, 154, 155, 168, 287, 294
U.S. Supreme Court, 306

valorization, 99, 127, 209. *See also* revalorization; self-valorization
Vancouver, British Columbia, 202–222; 2010 Olympic games in, 206; anti-gentrification organizations in, 202; Business Improvement Association (BIA), 216; Chinese Canadian community in, 202, 217; commercial upscaling in, 202–222; development in, 202; drug decriminalization and harm reduction in, 206; "ethical" restaurants in, 21, 202–222; housing affordability in, 217; housing costs in, 206; neighborhood change in, 204–205; Police Department of, 215; politics in, 205–207; public housing in, 202; responses to gentrification in, 21, 202–222; restaurants in, 202–222, *209*; social entrepreneurs in, 210–214
Veggie Bus Classroom Project, 317
Vigil, David, 255
Village Gardens, 132–152, *137*, 138t
Village Market Place (VMP), 315–317, 321n8
violence, 312
Vogue, 54
volunteering, 211–212
volunteers, 169–170, 171, 193, 195

Waldrop, Bob, 75, 80, 82, 88n3, 88n5
Washington, Karen, 253, 255
water rights, 19
"Way to Grow: Urban Farms Are an Amenity at Many Developments," 94
wealth gap, widening, 320
welfare state, 170, 203
Western Reserve Land Conservancy, 288–289
White, Monica, 15

white colonizers, 272–273
white flight, 73
white gaze, aesthetics and, 297
"white guilt," 14
White House vegetable garden, 93
whiteness, 49, 191, 248, 272, 274, 276; normativity of, 272–273, 274
white outmigration, 309
white space, urban agriculture as, 254–255
white spaces, 134–135
Whole Foods Market, 5, 77–78, 80–81, 84
Williamson Act, 193, 195
win-win, discourse of, 197, 199, 203
Women and Agriculture (WandA) Network, 112–113
Word clouds of Common terms used in Reviews of popular restaurants in North Park and Barrio Logan, *44*
workers' rights, 19
working-class consumers, displacement of, 228
working-class culture, appropriation of, 220
World's Fair Exposition, 1986, 206
World War II, 135

Yelp, 31, 32, 40, 46, 49, 50n1, 50n2, 51n4, 267
Young Urban Rebuilding Professionals (YURPS), 121
Youth Pickle and Catering Company, 231
youth programs, 258, 278–279, 313. *See also specific programs*
youth UA projects, 180

Zagat, 40, 50n2, 51n4
Zane, 101
Zigas, Eli, 193, 194, 196
Zillow, 108n3
Zones of Exclusion, 217
zoning: codes, 183; policies, 291
Zukin, Sharon, 50n2, 64, 228